BONDS OF AFFECTION

BONDS OF AFFECTION

AMERICANS DEFINE THEIR PATRIOTISM

EDITED BY JOHN BODNAR

PRINCETON UNIVERSITY PRESS

PRINCETON, NEW JERSEY

Library of Congress Cataloging-in-Publication Data

Bonds of affection : Americans define their patriotism / edited by
John Bodnar.
p.   cm.
Includes bibliographical references and index.
ISBN 0-691-04397-3 (alk. paper). — ISBN 0-691-04396-5 (pbk. :
alk. paper)
1. Patriotism—United States—History.   I. Bodnar John E., 1944–
E169.1.B695   1996
973—dc20   95-26683   CIP

This book has been composed in Linotron Bembo

Princeton University Press books are printed on acid-free paper
and meet the guidelines for permanence and durability of the
Committee on Production Guidelines for Book Longevity of the
Council on Library Resources

Printed in the United States of America by Princeton Academic Press

10 9 8 7 6 5 4 3 2 1

10 9 8 7 6 5 4 3 2 1
(Pbk.)

We are not enemies, but friends. We must not be enemies. Though passion may have strained, it must not break our bonds of affection.

—ABRAHAM LINCOLN, *first inaugural address, March 4, 1861*

CONTENTS

BONDS OF AFFECTION

Introduction

THE ATTRACTIONS OF PATRIOTISM

JOHN BODNAR

WALT WHITMAN knew why Americans were patriotic. He saw it in the devotion they exhibited during the Civil War. As he stood by the beds of dying soldiers in Washington, he marveled at the way they faced death and their refusal to show "cowardly qualms." Their gallantry, in the opinion of the noted poet, was rooted in their dreams of democracy.

> The movements of the late secession war and their results, to any sense that studies well and comprehends them, show that popular democracy, whatever its faults and dangers, practically justifies itself beyond the proudest claims and wildest hopes of its enthusiasts. Probably no future age can know, but I well know, how the gist of this fiercest and most resolute of the world's war-like contentions resided exclusively in the named, unknown rank and file; and how the brunt of its labour of death was, to all essential purposes, volunteered. The People of their own choice, fighting, dying for their own idea, . . . not for gain or even glory, nor to repel invasion—but for an emblem, a mere abstraction, for the life, for the safety of the flag.[1]

How accurate was Whitman? Was patriotism in America largely grounded in the aspirations of its people for democracy and equal rights for all? At plenty of moments in American history this certainly appeared to be the case. Abraham Lincoln told his audience at the Gettysburg battlefield in 1863 that the sacrifices made at the site were justified only if living Americans continued to foster the creation of a nation of equals devoted to the principles of government of the people, by the people, and for the people. A century later Martin Luther King, Jr., in a speech to demonstrators for civil rights insisted that the nation must deliver on its promise of equality for all citizens. Both Lincoln and King were patriots: they saw their fates interconnected with the

This introduction has benefited from the valuable criticisms of Casey N. Blake. The entire collection benefited from the assistance of Barb Truesdell and Beth Glenn.

[1] Walt Whitman, "Democratic Vistas," in *Leaves of Grass and Other Selected Prose*, ed. Ellman Grasnow (London: Everyman, 1993), 616–19.

destiny of other citizens in a common project to build a democratic and egalitarian society.[2]

But there were other rationales for serving flag and country. In 1782, George Washington rebuked an officer of the Revolutionary Army for suggesting that he accept the crown of a king as a reward for the role he played in serving the new nation. Washington felt that virtuous men manifested loyalty by serving the common good with no expectations of return. The first president said nothing about creating a nation of equals, but he did aspire to the values of eighteenth-century republicanism and its promise of a society where prominent men would serve and govern the public rather than tyrannical despots or the "unknown rank and file." And what are we to make of the loyalty of either Boston protestors in 1976 who carried an American flag to denounce "antiwar hippies and radical blacks" and defend their working-class neighborhood against government plans for school integration or Ku Klux Klan organizations in the 1920s that sought to purify their nation of certain religious, ethnic, and racial groups? They did not appear to be calling for either more virtue or democracy. But how do these citizens relate to the views of Lincoln or Whitman?

This collection of essays on the manner in which Americans defined their patriotism describes a people with a complex understanding of the nature of loyalty and affiliation. The beliefs of Lincoln and Whitman were widely shared and central to American political thought over time. But patriotic thought could be a maze within both the minds of individuals and the nation as a whole. In the eighteenth and nineteenth centuries, citizens were influenced powerfully by the ideas of republicanism and classical liberalism. They often blended ideals of service to the common good of all with hopes for a nation that would insure individual freedom from any form of tyranny. Frequently, their veneration of universal ideals such as virtue masked more particular goals of male domination. In the twentieth century, the articulation of specific goals in patriotic language became more pronounced. Workers invoked the traditional symbols of freedom and democracy to call for the right to unionize, and women asked for fairness from their government in the quest to meet family and career responsibilities. But Americans also debated more extensively the issue of national power. Some patriots attacked the state for wielding excessive influence over their private lives. Others applauded the dominance of the nation over other nations. Throughout this collec-

[2] Roy Basler, ed., *Abraham Lincoln: His Speeches and Writings* (Cleveland: World Publishing, 1976), 577, 579–91, 734; Joyce Appleby, *Liberalism and Republicanism in the Historical Imagination* (Cambridge: Harvard University Press, 1992), 1–3, 20–24; James Melvin Washington, *A Testament of Hope: The Essential Writings of Martin Luther King, Jr.* (San Francisco: Harper Collins, 1991), 217–20.

tion of essays we must keep in mind an important point made by Merle Curti, a pioneer in the study of American patriotism: loyalty in the United States derived its strength from its ability to accommodate several interests at once.[3]

In the late twentieth century, the need to understand the tangled history of this patriotism is compelling. Some Americans feel that their fellow citizens have lost many ties they formerly had to their country. This anxiety over loyalty has revolved to a great extent around the issues of multiculturalism and individualism. Lewis Lapham, editor of *Harper's Magazine*, wrote in 1992 that he felt himself to be just a "plain American" because he could not place an adjective before his nationality. He lamented that citizens now only "acquire a presence as an old American, a female American, a white American, a rich American, a black American, a gay American, a poor American, a native American, or a dead American." When Lapham argued that the subordination of the noun to the adjectives mocked the "democratic spirit," he meant to affirm the universalist character of the liberal view of patriotism and critique the more insular expressions of various groups. Inferentially, he also rejected the twentieth-century pattern of expecting rights and benefits from the liberal state as a grounds for loyalty, although such expectations may explain the proliferation of narrow identities he abhors.[4]

Authors like Arthur Schlesinger and Allan Bloom crafted best-selling books that discussed the threat of multiculturalism to the existence of the American nation. Both writers felt that the increased veneration of racial, gendered, and even individual identities poses a distinct threat to the common project of nation building. Schlesinger scolded extremists who distorted the teaching of United States history for the sake of engendering pride in minority groups. The prominent historian feared that minorities were forgetting that, in the absence of common ethnic and racial origins, the United States was held together by adherence to "ideals of democracy and human rights." For Schlesinger a "cult of ethnicity" had emerged among minorities that challenged the dream of creating "one people."[5]

[3] Washington's letter of rebuke, along with other "republican" expressions of patriotism, is reprinted in William J. Bennett, *The Book of Virtues: A Treasury of Great Moral Stories* (New York: Simon and Schuster, 1993), 671–72, 717–18. Ronald P. Formisano, *Boston against Busing: Race, Class, and Ethnicity in the 1960s and 1970s* (Chapel Hill: University of North Carolina Press, 1991), 151. Merle Curti, *The Roots of American Loyalty* (New York: Athenaeum, 1968), viii.

[4] "Who and What Is American: The Things We Continue to Hold in Common," *Harper's Magazine* (January 1992), 43–49. See John Schaar, "The Case for Patriotism," *The American Review* 17 (May 1973): 59–99.

[5] Arthur M. Schlesinger, Jr., *The Disuniting of America* (New York: W. W. Norton, 1992), 102–26.

Allan Bloom's *The Closing of the American Mind* located the threat to national unity and loyalty in the selfishness of individuals rather than in the group-based interests of minorities. In place of Schlesinger's "multicultural zealots," Bloom saw the nation threatened by egocentric citizens who appear to have few group attachments of any kind. Thus, he saw the sexual revolution, rising divorce rates, and an overall transformation in private life as destructive of social stability. Like Schlesinger, he also detested the fragmentation of the educational curriculum and the failure to teach a common core of subjects that offer instruction in human values and civic responsibility. Both authors, to an extent, longed for a return of past ideals: Schlesinger for Whitman's and Bloom for Washington's.[6]

The persistent critique of narrow interests and group loyalties and the quest for a common ground originated, moreover, in more than just the fear of social fragmentation. It also represented a deeply held belief in American exceptionalism. The political culture of the United States was thought exemplary in its ability to moderate group differences through its faith in the notion of equality and democracy. And to a great extent this was a true, if at times myopic, point of view. Modern studies of nationalism, in fact, demonstrate just how unique the idea of a nation totally committed to "democratic vistas" has been. For instance, after visiting modern battlefields of nationalism in Croatia, Serbia, and the Ukraine, Michael Ignatieff distinguished civic nationalism from ethnic nationalism. The former affirms that a nation is composed of citizens, equal regardless of their special identities; such a political community is held together by a patriotic attachment to the ideals of equal rights and democracy. To the contrary, ethnic nationalism (or any particularistic form) fosters the idea that a community of racial, ethnic, or religious groups defines the individual and the nation. The fundamental appeal to loyalty is usually made as part of an effort either to defend the political community against external threats or to purify it of unwanted elements within the community. Equality, reciprocity, and fairness do not count for much in this conception.[7]

Scholars now acknowledge, perhaps more than they once did, that nationalism is greater than a dream of equality and that narrower interests

[6] Allan Bloom, *The Closing of the American Mind* (New York: Simon and Schuster, 1987).

[7] Michael Ignatieff, *Blood and Belonging: Journeys into the New Nationalism* (New York: Farrar, Straus, Giroux, 1993), 7–11. For a discussion on the appeal of equality and fair treatment for all citizens as a basis for nationalism and patriotism, see Benedict Anderson, *Imagined Communities: Reflections on the Origins and Spread of Nationalism* (London: Verso, 1991), 141–54. For an incisive and fresh discussion of the idea of America's unique political culture, see Michael Kammen, "The Problem of American Exceptionalism: A Reconsideration," *American Quarterly* 45 (March 1993): 1–43.

were never far removed from the politics of nationhood. As Tony Judt has incisively suggested, the "optimistic universalism" of the liberal vision may have been confined only to a "few fortunate people and places during the past two centuries." Most nationalisms, in fact, have emerged from encounters with external forms of power and fears of further domination by others, often generated in the breakup of old empires. This was certainly the case for Greece as it emerged out of the old Ottoman Empire or Croatia as it grew from what was Yugoslavia.

Liah Greenfeld has underscored the point that nationalism almost always promises self-respect and relief from domination by others. Thus, she argues that ethnic forms of nationalism make people feel better (and more secure) than civic nationalism with its unspecified pledge of equality. I would add that they are also potentially more attractive than simple but earnest calls to moral action and selflessness. Put another way, it may be easier for people to feel self-respect in belonging to a group of heroic soldiers, proud blacks, or chosen Protestants than to a larger, unspecified community of equals. Greenfeld argues correctly that the United States went further in achieving civic nationalism and liberal patriotism than nearly every other country, and in this sense it is unique. She attributes this to its rich legacy of English liberalism and to the New World's absence of entrenched hierarchies that usually counter such liberal impulses. But this collection also suggests that the attachments to particularistic loyalties—gendered, ethnic, racial and religious—were not only pervasive (which most people know), but also fundamental to popular understandings of patriotism. As much as most of us want Lincoln to be our hero, his vision was modified throughout American history.[8] This is the import of a recent essay by political scientist Rogers M. Smith. Directly confronting the myth that American politics has been largely dominated by the adherence of its people to free and egalitarian ideas, Smith advances a more nuanced view. He prefers to talk of "multiple traditions" when describing American political culture.[9]

From the beginning of the American nation, political culture was variegated. The republican attempt to create a society in which public affairs were conducted by men in a disinterested fashion and animated by virtue rather than self-interest was never a true reflection of what most citizens thought and felt. Republican patriotism was fixed on the notion of self-sacrifice for the good of all, but it was extended by liberal aspirations for a more democratic and equal society. The problem with republicanism

---

[8] Liah Greenfeld, *Nationalism: Five Roads to Modernity* (Cambridge: Harvard University Press, 1992), 400–484; see also Tony Judt, "The New Old Nationalism," *The New York Review of Books* 42, no. 10 (26 May 1994): 44–51.

[9] Rogers M. Smith, "Beyond Tocqueville, Myrdal, and Hartz: The Multiple Traditions in America," *American Political Science Review* 87 (September 1993): 549–66.

was its failure to address the democratic and special aspirations of the masses. As Gordon Wood has so brilliantly explained, the egalitarian impulses inherent in the republican dream of replacing a monarchy with a society of virtuous citizens gave way to the stronger attraction of equality and democracy. Most leaders of the American Revolution would not have been comfortable with fostering such a pervasive leveling of American society, but the issue moved beyond their control. By the era of the Civil War, as James M. McPherson discovered in reading letters and diaries, soldiers in both the North and the South were moved to fight because of a genuine belief in the ideas of freedom and liberty. The Union men saw their ideal threatened in the attempt to destroy national solidarity; rebels viewed the federal government as a danger to their states' rights version of political aspirations.

But equality was not just an end in itself. Even in the eighteenth century, Wood is quick to note that both republicanism and liberalism had limits. While people eagerly pursued democracy, they also attempted to use their membership in the new nation and their "equality" to secure private interests. "Everywhere," Wood writes, "the 'tender connections among men' that the Revolution was supposed to foster were being 'reduced to nothing' by 'the infinite diversities of family, tribe, and nation.'" In both the American past and present the pursuit of equality involved the quest for advantage as well.[10]

The expression of narrow interest became so widespread by the middle of the nineteenth century that some political leaders sought to defend and expand the power of the central government more forcefully over its constituent parts. At this point in the nation's history Lincoln purposefully transformed the notion of liberalism that had inspired so much patriotism and national sentiment. In the crisis of the Civil War, Lincoln concluded that it was no longer sufficient to venerate the ideals of popular government and equal rights alone. As J. David Greenstone has so effectively argued, the sixteenth president realized that political institutions now had to intervene in society and resolve moral issues such as slavery. Unlike many abolitionists who felt that moral problems could be settled by attempts at transforming the ethical outlook of individuals, Lincoln, retaining his faith in democracy and equality, now added the ideal of an activist state to the ideology of American liberalism. He could not, of course, foresee the vast expansion of state power in response to industrial capitalism in the twentieth century. Lincoln raised the expectations of citizens by inferring that the state could not simply represent

[10] Gordon Wood, *The Radicalism of the American Revolution* (New York: Knopf, 1992), 249–52; James M. McPherson, *What They Fought For, 1861–1865* (Baton Rouge: Louisiana State University Press, 1994), 6, 9, 35–36.

ideals but had an obligation to engage in practices that would correct injustices in the real world. He would not ask citizens simply to have faith in American ideals as Schlesinger did. Rather, he offered the possibility that American political institutions could not expect support if they did not actively pursue a just society.[11]

Following the war and Lincoln's death, the powers of the central government and the state steadily increased, although not always in pursuit of equal rights for all. Curti demonstrated how the conception of the nation as an organic whole that subordinated the interests of its various parts—states, classes, ethnicities—emerged more forcefully in the late nineteenth century. This movement, however, was not some falsehood foisted by powerful industrial leaders to facilitate the growth of a national, capitalistic economy; rather, it was a joint effort of managerial, professional, labor, agricultural, and cultural ranks to create a new form of state-managed liberalism, often called corporate liberalism. Unfairness was not eradicated, and equality remained an unfulfilled dream. New immigrants, African Americans, and women certainly held marginal voices in this political world. But the direction was toward some form of accommodation between many constituent parts of society under the aegis of a strong state. Leading political figures like Theodore Roosevelt staunchly defended the concept and combined a belief in state power over private interests, a love of country transcending devotion to any section or class, and the need for reciprocity. Roosevelt could not see how allegiance to the country could exist if the country did not make life worth living for its diverse citizens.[12]

The activist role of the liberal state became so great by the 1930s that economic justice and industrial democracy became its stated political goals. In the twentieth century equality was pursued through organized groups who used the state to advance their interests and return their loyalty in the form of influence or benefits. They did this not because they had abandoned hope in popular government and equal rights but because they now believed, as Lincoln did, that state intervention was necessary for attaining a liberal society. The New Deal favored working men and class interests over matters more defined by race and gender, but the administration of Franklin Roosevelt did attempt to redistribute political power to workers and farmers so that they could compete effectively against business and acquire the wages needed to sustain a consumerist

[11] J. David Greenstone, *The Lincoln Persuasion: Remaking American Liberalism* (Princeton: Princeton University Press, 1993), xx–xxxii, 244–54, 284–85.

[12] Curti, *The Roots of American Loyalty*, 92–93, 174–79, 196–97; John Bodnar, *Remaking America: Public Memory, Commemoration, and Patriotism in the Twentieth Century* (Princeton: Princeton University Press, 1992), 28; Martin J. Sklar, *The Corporate Reconstruction of American Capitalism, 1890–1916* (Cambridge: Cambridge University Press, 1988), 35–36.

economy. As Gary Gerstle has shown, the New Deal was able to tap a "reservoir of patriotism" from the American public because it was perceived to be in part a "moral crusade" for economic justice. Working-class leaders now joined the traditional liberal language of equal rights and democracy with the mechanism of an activist state.[13]

Not until the 1960s, when the liberal state was attacked by various groups for its policies regarding race and South Vietnam, did Lincoln's idea of a state that resolved moral issues and Roosevelt's notion of one that settled economic issues fall into disfavor. Certainly some patriots felt Roosevelt's path toward state management of social life was contrary to older traditions and, therefore, unpatriotic. During the 1940s the government relied on both traditional liberal promises of egalitarianism and modern ones of rewarding loyal citizens to generate support for its war policies. But in the 1960s an erosion of faith in an activist liberal state opened up public space for celebrations of power and particularistic loyalties in ways that resembled the 1920s. Thus, lower middle-class whites used patriotic symbols and language to resist court-ordered (and state-sponsored) integration of their schools and neighborhoods because they no longer felt the state supported their moral views. Various religious groups fervently opposed the state sanction of a woman's right to an abortion and the plan to pass an equal rights amendment to the constitution. Black power advocates and radical feminists expressed reservations toward any form of veneration of the liberal state, an institution they saw as merely a bastion of white male domination. The demise of the liberal state continued into the 1980s and 1990s with victories by conservatives who sought to dismantle or alter much of the liberal agenda. Indeed, precisely at the moment when the activist state lost much of its hold over the popular imagination did public anxiety over patriotism and national cohesion emerge so forcefully. Today, what Raphael Samuel has written of postwar Great Britain can be applied to the United States: "these years have seen a decline in the majesty of the state . . . and a valorization of the private at the expense of the public sphere."[14]

---

[13] See Steven Fraser, *Labor Will Rule: Sidney Hillman and the Rise of American Labor* (New York: Free Press, 1991), 330; Gary Gerstle, *Working-Class Americanism: The Politics of Labor in a Textile City, 1914–1960* (Cambridge: Cambridge University Press, 1989). Gerstle, "The Protean Character of American Liberalism," *American Historical Review* 99 (October 1994): 1043. The illiberal patriotism of the 1920s, especially nativism, is incisively discussed by John Higham, *Strangers in the Land: Patterns of American Nativism* (New Brunswick, N.J.: Rutgers University Press, 1955), 264–99.

[14] See Leo Ribuffo, "Why Is There So Much Conservatism in the United States and Why Do So Few Historians Know Anything about It?" *American Historical Review* 99 (April 1994): 438–99; Alan Brinkley, "The Problem of American Conservatism," *American Historical Review* 99 (April 1994): 409–29; Anthony D. Smith, "Nationalism and the Historians," *International Journal of Comparative Sociology* 33, nos. 1–2 (1992): 58–80. Marian Wright

This collection intends to demonstrate that, indeed, the nature of patriotism in the United States is controversial. The appeal of egalitarianism and the promise of democracy is powerful but limited. Throughout U.S. history desires for a more equal society have clashed with sectarian aspirations of purity and dominance. The attempt to encase patriotism within the dream of equality or the call to virtue was contested by many who sought rewards for their loyalty in more explicit forms or wanted to realize desires for power and mastery. The liberal version of patriotism was an agreement between not only citizens and the nation but also citizens themselves. Each person had to respect both the nation-state for its ability to protect the ideal of equality and the right of fellow citizens to fair treatment. The attempt to direct loyalty to the nation-state alone, an effort that consumed much time in the past, was never a guarantee that citizen rights would be protected. And citizens saw this flaw. As this collection of essays shows, the call to obligation toward the nation and exhortations toward virtuous behavior, which punctuate the culture today, were continually refashioned by popular expressions of equality, justice, self-interest, and power.

By taking Washington, Whitman, Lincoln, and King further than they wanted to go, these essays suggest that the meaning of patriotism in America was molded by competing understandings of what the nation should be. Lincoln's terms of loyalty were sustained and expanded to an exceptional extent; alternative versions abounded. Contemporary disputes over whether patriotism is disappearing in the United States, as a matter of course, almost never raise the issue of how its citizens have defined their allegiance.

Our bonds of affection have always been subjected to complex interpretations. The earliest view of a virtuous nation of equals gave way by the late nineteenth century to a dream of a powerful nation rooted in the desires of powerful men and women who supported it for order and moral certainty at home and in the world. This position, often presenting patriotism as a virtue, was heavily influenced by the more aggressive sentiments of nationalism and the quest for domination of others, both inside and outside the United States. In this version true patriots were often represented as male warriors. Alternatively a liberal version of patriotism was grounded in the hope of fair treatment for all citizens. In the

Edelman, *The Measure of Our Success: A Letter to My Children and Yours* (New York: Harper Perennial, 1993), 19, 43, 54–55. On the relationship between feminism and state power, see Catharine A. MacKinnon, *Toward a Feminist Theory of the State* (Cambridge: Harvard University Press, 1989), 157–60. Also see Anne McClintock, "Family Feuds: Gender, Nationalism and the Family," *Feminist Review* 44 (Summer 1993): 61–80. Raphael Samuel, "Introduction: Exciting to Be English," in *Patriotism: The Making and Unmaking of British National Identity*, ed. Samuel, 3 vols. (London: Routledge, 1989), 1:xxix.

nineteenth century this view, restricted to general appeals for equality and democracy, received its strongest manifestations in the eradication of slavery. In the twentieth century this outlook involved a more explicit call for reciprocity from the nation in the form of state intervention in both private and public life and in the form of benefits. Because all people and groups are susceptible to the attractions of power and justice, and because both coexisted in the language of patriotism, its appeal frequently crossed class, ethnic, regional, and gender borders and took unexpected turns. Citizens used patriotism for good and for malice. Thus, this history of patriotism cannot be confused with our society's endless calls for patriotism by voices that are often more partisan than they appear.

In the early nineteenth century, as Cynthia Koch shows, the public discussion over patriotism was dominated by the tenets of republicanism and the standpoints of powerful men. George Washington stood as an emblem: a citizen who served his country to promote the common good, and a male who protected women. Asking for nothing in return, he acquired power but did not want to keep it. His philosophy of republicanism certainly sought to create a society more just than the one it replaced. But it also moderated drives toward democracy and equality, not by venerating national power, but by celebrating virtue.

After the Civil War the opinions of males, especially veterans and businessmen, continued to dominate the discourse over patriotism. But the essays of Cecilia O'Leary, Stuart McConnell, Gaines Foster, and Andrew Neather demonstrate that agreement over the meaning of loyalty in the late nineteenth century was not easily achieved. Despite a strong tradition of republicanism and the pleas of Lincoln at Gettysburg to link loyalty and democracy, the doctrines of virtue and equality were widely challenged. This collection explains that the period from the Civil War to World War I presented American citizens with new problems that forced them to redefine their notion of faithfulness. The emasculation of southern manhood, the need for political reconciliation, the intensification of class conflict, and the acquisition of economic and world power all combined to encourage a greater idealization of male warrior heroism and aggressive nationalism at the expense of older republican and democratic dreams. O'Leary's work shows that the drive for reunification resulted in the valorization of battlefield deeds and the creation of heroic warriors by veterans in both the North and the South. The veteran construction of patriotism not only replaced the focus on virtue with valor but also eradicated the patriotic struggle for black rights from the public memory of the war.

A militaristic, masculine sense of nationalism alone could not hope to attract the interest of men and women in a society as diverse as the

United States, however. Stuart McConnell explains that a determined effort emerged in the 1890s to create an even more abstract form of national unity that could appeal to various regions and groups. As American society simultaneously became more integrated economically and more diverse culturally, an attempt was made to fashion patriotic symbols that would appeal to the broadest possible segment of the nation. McConnell's study of the "patriotic boom" of the 1890s suggests that the ideals of republicanism or liberalism were insufficient to sustain loyalty by themselves in the face of growing class and ethnic conflict and inequality. Thus, to reduce the attachments people had to vernacular symbols, the veneration of patriotic symbols like the national flag was intensified.

Andrew Neather offers a unique contribution: he demonstrates that the forces celebrating greater national unity and power met resistance from the old attachment some Americans had to the ideals of equality. Neather shows that the late-nineteenth-century working class made a determined bid to use patriotic messages and symbols to sustain the notion of equality, but a spirit of empire and commerce cut the proletarians short. Responding to the longing of many males for domination over others, workers and businessmen rallied to a vision of empire and loyalty that was determined more by nationalist than by democratic aspirations. The idea of a powerful nation-state became so pervasive by 1900 that, as Gaines Foster implies, it could successfully compete with older religious loyalties that had been deeply held for years. Although many Americans continued to believe that the nation was part of God's overall plan, reason enough to elicit their loyalty, the grounds for patriotism were becoming more secular than sacred and implicated in the lust for power to a greater extent than the dream of fairness.

The triumph of state liberalism was pivotal to the history of patriotism in the twentieth century. Although based partially in an attempt to insure justice for workers, farmers, professionals, and businessmen, state liberalism also led more directly to the glorification of state power and a more robust form of nationalism. This fact ultimately had two crucial implications for our times. First, a powerful state was inevitably a masculine state—a reflection of male longings for dominance at home and abroad. The gendered aspect of loyalty was fortified by the tumultuous experience of warfare in this century and the opportunity it created to venerate the sacrifices of male warriors for the nation. Second, the awesome power of the state turned it into a battleground. Conservatives who feared the authority of the state but not the concept of authority mounted efforts to protect local interests from a centralized government. This idea was manifested by the marchers in Boston in 1976 as well as by the Ku Klux Klan in the 1920s or the Moral Majority in the 1980s. Liberals, however, retained a faith in the state to both promote fairness and reward loyalty in just and beneficial ways. Thus, modern feminists who worked for more government money for child care also thought of themselves as patriotic. They proved the assertion that Kimberly Jensen makes in her essay: the more the state demanded of its citizens, the more they were able to ask in return.

Dreams of power and dreams of fairness continued to collide to an exceptional extent even in wartime. The essays of Kimberly Jensen, David Glassberg and J. Michael Moore, Lawrence Samuel, and Robert Westbrook reveal how crucial war is to the modern definition of patriotism and how much it forces the state to concede the basic point that citizens earn credit for their loyalty. Consequently, Jensen demonstrates how during World War I some women in different sectors of American society exhibited their devotion in the hope of gaining a greater voice in public affairs. She complements O'Leary and Neather by revealing that despite the rise of a masculine, business-centered patriotism and its ability to undermine the public view of women and minorities, the dream of equality did not vanish. In a few instances, voices of women completely opposed to the very concept of a warrior nation were heard. David Glassberg and J. Michael Moore make this point in their study of how one town in Massachusetts finally decided to commemorate World War I.

In a similar manner, Lawrence Samuel and Robert Westbrook find American citizens expressing hope that their service to the nation and national institutions will be rewarded in the 1940s. Samuel's examination of how war bonds were sold to African Americans during World War II presents the case that racial minorities still clung to ideals of justice, reciprocity, and solidarity despite the reality of injustice and subordination. The wartime administration of Franklin Roosevelt, obviously sensitive to these desires, in return for support of the war effort determined to promise more rewards to not only blacks but all American citizens. Westbrook further acknowledges that popular patriotism during the war was strongly based both in private interests and the dream of reciprocity. Astutely investigating the reaction Americans had to Japanese political culture during World War II, Westbrook shows that Americans were attached to a sense of individualism and particularistic goals. They certainly found the culture and loyalty of the Japanese that called for unquestioned devotion to state authority and unlimited sacrifice unappealing. Thus, Westbrook's work effectively raises the issue of how a liberal society, committed to a vision of free and equal individuals, can nurture strong bonds of affection to other citizens and to the nation itself. He suggests that in the war with Japan the American state maintained loyalty only by extending the vision of Lincoln with promises to reward and protect the particular ties Americans had to families and local, ethnic, and racial communities. But much of the collection suggests that this was a central theme of American patriotic meaning throughout the twentieth century.

In the flush of postwar victory American patriotism became more tangled than ever. The last half of this century has witnessed a decided struggle over whether illiberalism with its devotion to individualism and abstract symbols of national strength will gain supremacy over explicit calls for justice and democracy through state action. In the aftermath of the "Good War," it was difficult to deny the attractive symbols of a strong nation and the men who defended it. Thus, John Wayne was a patriotic box office hero by 1950. The reality of the Cold War further reinforced the power of illiberal patriotism and its need to venerate national strength. In this climate masculine versions of nationalism pervaded the culture at large. The fruits of victory were delivered more directly to the warriors in the form of jobs and educational supports. Women were generally expected to vacate their wartime occupations and return to serving men in the home. The quintessential patriotic symbol of the wartime experience, the Iwo Jima Memorial, conveyed the supremacy of masculine power and the authority of a triumphant and united nation. Thus, it comes as no surprise to learn that when Wendy Kozol investigated the manner in which *Life* magazine represented and discussed the nation in the 1950s it stressed the value of the nuclear family. Kozol notes that the wartime version of patriotism was now reconceptualized into images of female domesticity and consumerism, a formula that left the public life of the nation largely in the hands of men.

Unlike World War II, the conflict in Vietnam did not result in promises that loyalty to the nation-state would be rewarded in victory. Government officials were busy attempting to defend their policies from many who came close to fitting John Schaar's description of citizens who no longer thought patriotic thoughts.[15] The loudest proclamations of patriotism in the 1960s emanated from groups who associated it with the desire to win the conflict in Asia. Studies by George Lipsitz and Barbara Truesdell also prove that efforts to define loyalty in terms of masculine heroes and a strong nation continued even after the war was lost.

Lipsitz's inquiry into the version of patriotism that dominated American discourse in the 1980s makes clear that masculine dreams and warrior heroes were not erased from public memory or political discourse during the 1960s. Lipsitz describes how the "new patriotism" of the 1980s differed from the old patriotism of the 1940s. In the recent era government leaders like Ronald Reagan rarely addressed aspects of our national identity like the four freedoms defined by Franklin Roosevelt. In place of

[15] Schaar, "The Case for Patriotism."

what the state could do "for the people," especially those dislocated by plant closings and corporate restructuring, patriotism in the 1980s offered spectacles of power and the veneration of elite groups of warriors. The "new patriotism" even attempted to revise the memory of Vietnam: the war was recalled not as a loss or a mistake but as a valiant effort to preserve the free world. Women who supported this masculine version of the nation and national loyalty are ably described by Barbara Truesdell who visited a national meeting of the Daughters of the American Revolution. She found these patriotic women celebrating not only male warriors but patriot missiles as well.

As America entered the 1990s, however, the meaning of patriotism was unresolved. Public opinion polls suggested some ambiguity. A 1994 Gallup survey found that while 64 percent of Americans felt they were "extremely" or "very" patriotic, 35 percent described themselves as "somewhat" or "not especially" loyal. Visions of the nation grounded in unity, virtue, democracy, reciprocity, and group interest were all expressed with regularity. Commentators like Schlesinger and Bloom blamed multiculturalists and egoists for abandoning "liberal creeds" and moral traditions; these authors refused to confront the intricate history of American patriotism. In our times virile patriotism was strongly opposed by many defenders of state liberalism. In the eyes of Robin Wagner-Pacifici, the masculine and militarized renditions of national loyalty are actually under severe stress, perhaps more than the nation itself. President Bill Clinton, in his support for homosexuals and failure to accept the role of a warrior-patriot in his youth, evoked open hostility from the guardians of traditions of a strong nation. Wagner-Pacifici's study of encounters between the new president and the military revealed that the promotion of a feminized and more democratic vision of the nation was strong but not unopposed. In an examination of how a working-class community recalled the experience of loyalty in the past, my essay on an industrial town reveals a complex story that, despite its local base, approximates the mixed nature of patriotism on the national level. Informants exhibit both an attachment to the ideal of reciprocity as a basis for devotion, a fundamental ingredient in twentieth-century liberal thought, and a dream of national unity and solidarity. Despite particularistic communal attachments, much of their narrative about the past is told in the present out of a genuine concern that the nation remain a viable community of citizens with some concern for each other.[16]

This book does not cover all aspects of the history of American patriotism or the career that it has enjoyed over two centuries. But the volume

---

[16] The Gallup poll was conducted 17–19 June 1994. I would like to thank Kim Elaine Neighbor of The Gallup Organization for sending me the results.

does indicate that Americans drew upon certain fundamental ideals time and again when thinking about how they would pledge allegiance. Universal and parochial aspirations intermingled; elements of liberalism in both classic and modern forms were remarkably powerful. The concluding essay on Europe by William Cohen infers that the intermingling of traditions within the idea of a nation was not unique to the United States. But Cohen's essay also suggests that Europe may have been more consumed with a fear of foreign domination throughout the nineteenth and twentieth centuries than the United States. Thus, European nationalisms and patriotisms were more focused on national unity and power at the expense of a powerful tradition of liberalism. This collection suggests also that current debate over loyalties is not new. Past and present Americans took the idea of nationhood seriously and extensively debated its character. What else can explain all the arguments over the bonds of affection?

Chapter 1

TEACHING PATRIOTISM:

PRIVATE VIRTUE FOR THE PUBLIC GOOD

IN THE EARLY REPUBLIC

CYNTHIA M. KOCH

> We have changed our forms of government, . . . but it
> remains yet to effect a revolution in our principles,
> opinions, and manners, so as to accommodate them to the
> forms of government we have adopted.
> (*Benjamin Rush*)[1]

A S THE ARMIES withdrew in 1783, Americans began the task of self-definition—a revolutionary process that continues to this day. As modern students of the Revolution have shown, from the beginning the United States was a nation of competing interests, variegated in its cultural composition. Those who held political power shared but perhaps a single commonality—the need to assure the survival through peacetime government for the ideology their military victories had at least momentarily secured.

Somehow the high emotions of the revolutionary period had to be perpetuated into a constructive national sensibility. Political leaders turned to those they had constituted as the *polis*—largely property-owning white males—and began to shape a national consciousness. Those new Americans, born as British colonists, needed to *feel* themselves Americans. In the face of continuing threats to national survival—externally from a British government that had hardly conceded defeat and internally from a populace that still carried cultural ties to mother England—a patriotic canon began to emerge in the first decades following the Revolution.

Emotional attachment to a cause is at its highest as individuals in a society embark on cultural transformation, such as a revolutionary war,

---

[1] Quoted in Lawrence Cremin, *American Education: The National Experience 1783–1876* (New York: Harper & Row, Torchbooks, 1980), 1.

and success depends on the routinization of such enthusiasm until ultimately the new culture is maintained through the preservation of doctrine and the performance of ritual.[2] The political leaders of the American revolutionary generation faced this task as the war drew to a close and they turned from the high excitement of the *rage militaire* to the more sober task of nation building. Inheritors of the British distrust of the military and a traditional Protestant worldview, these men were also Enlightenment intellectuals who believed in the value of decentralized power and the use of reason to improve human affairs. Most important to this discussion of early patriotism, they also held a common faith in the value of education as a means of perpetuating the Revolution's goals.

Jefferson wrote to Madison from Paris in 1787, "Educate and inform the whole mass of the people. . . . They are the only sure reliance for the preservation of our liberty." Washington's *Farewell Address* stressed a fundamental relationship between education and good government: "In proportion as the structure of government gives force to public opinion, it is essential that public opinion should be enlightened." Madison found a system of primary education a "vital desideratum" and endorsed the recommendations of Monroe, Hamilton, and Washington for the establishment of a national university. John Jay considered knowledge the "soul of a Republic," and John Adams argued that the states' revenues could be put to better use providing public education than in "maintaining the poor." In the language of the 1787 Northwest Ordinance, their commitment to education was first affirmed in law: "Religion, morality, and knowledge, being necessary to good government and the happiness of mankind, schools and the means of education shall forever be encouraged."[3]

Among these voices were those who expressed the opinion that not just education, but rather *patriotic* education, was the surest foundation for a lasting republic. These leaders intuitively grasped the importance of emotional attachment to one's country. Perhaps because there was no long history and few national traditions, perhaps because they perceived a continuing threat to national independence despite the absence of armed conflict, and perhaps because they were appealing to an unsophisticated male audience, the authors of this patriotic canon employed the story of America's war for independence to organize a logical and emotionally

[2] Anthony F. C. Wallace, "Revitalization Movements," *American Anthropologist* 58 (1956): 275.

[3] Washington, Jay, Adams, and Madison are quoted in Merle M. Odgers, "Education and the American Philosophical Society," *Proceedings of the American Philosophical Society* 87 (1944): 19; Thomas Jefferson to James Madison, 20 December 1787, in *The Life and Selected Writings of Thomas Jefferson*, ed. Adrienne Koch and William Peden (New York: Random House, 1944), 440; the Northwest Ordinance is quoted from Monica Kiefer, *American Children through Their Books* (Philadelphia: University of Pennsylvania Press, 1948), 132.

gripping patriotic story that would perpetuate their republican vision. Expressed with particular clarity in the popular schoolbooks of the era, its elements are recognizable today as icons of American patriotism.

Such an education had to be established quickly because the success of the fledgling nation depended on the rapid dissemination of the values, attitudes, and ideology of a new culture.[4] It needed to be powerful, dramatic, and true. It needed to be *mythic*. Noah Webster was one of the most articulate spokesmen for patriotic education:

> Our constitutions of civil government are not yet firmly established; our national character is not yet formed; and it is an object of vast magnitude that systems of education should be adopted and pursued which may not only diffuse a knowledge of the sciences but may implant in the minds of the American youth the principles of virtue and liberty and inspire them with just and liberal ideas of government and with an inviolable attachment to their own country.[5]

Modern political theorist George Fletcher describes patriotism as an "attitude of sentiment and devotion" toward a state or nation into which we are born. Like learning a first language or religion, exposure to a political culture and learning a national history normally occur as part of a socialization process. It involves few independent choices and is integral to an individual's identity. Inherent in personal character, patriotism is an active emotional attachment born of early training and affinities. A similar definition of patriotism is advanced by Charles Taylor who emphasizes the concept of emotional attachment by describing patriotism as based on an "identification with others in a particular common enterprise" that involves binding commitments "somewhere between friendship, or family feeling, on one side, and altruistic dedication on the other." Altruism requires a commitment to all people everywhere, while friendship or family attachments are highly specific. Patriotism entails ties to a broad group of people, most of whom are strangers but who share emotional allegiances based on a "common political entity." He describes patriotic ties in a republic as particularly strong because people are bound together by their "common history," much as in a family or friendship where shared experiences intensify the emotional bonds.[6]

But in the early American republic precious few bonds of history were

---

[4] Wallace, "Revitalization Movements," 270, explicates this process and terms it "mazeway reformulation."

[5] Noah Webster, "On the Education of Youth in America," in *Essays on Education in the Early Republic*, ed. Frederick Rudolph (Cambridge: Harvard University Press, 1965), 45.

[6] George P. Fletcher, *Loyalty: An Essay on the Morality of Relationships* (New York: Oxford University Press, 1993), 17, 140; Charles Taylor, "Cross-Purposes: The Liberal Communitarian Debate," in *Liberalism and the Moral Life*, ed. Nancy L. Rosenblum (Cambridge: Harvard University Press, 1989), see esp. 166.

shared, and the new nation lacked all the traditional cultural affinities—a national literature, a common religion, or the authority of a monarchy. No child living in 1790 had developed patriotic attachment to the United States in the normal process of socialization: all such sentiments among the populace were the products of the extraordinary upheavals of war. Worse yet, in the usual expressions of culture based on language, literature, religion, and even political tradition, America's ties were strongest to England, the nation against which the United States most needed to assert its cultural independence. And many Americans and Britons continued to see this relationship in familial terms—the mother country and the newly independent offspring—and held varying opinions on the wisdom and long-term success of the United States of America as a nation.

Just how did the leaders of the new republic go about the business of promoting patriotism in such a country? Most Americans are familiar with the political history of the federal years: how, after recognizing the inadequacies of the Articles of Confederation, the disparate interests of the former colonies were forged together under the new Constitution and Bill of Rights. We have learned about the founding of such basic institutions as the U.S. Mint and the postal service, the election of George Washington as first president, and the building of a "Federal City." National symbols—the eagle and the flag—were adopted, and the states reluctantly submitted to taxation to secure common economic goals and national defense; at the same time the new government struggled with questions of the degree to which political power is vested in the central government. But this familiar story does not tell us much about the cultural values that made this political history possible. What was the ideology behind the nation building of the federal years? How did some Americans set themselves to the task not just of forming a government, but of fostering emotional attachment to this new government?

INVENTING AMERICAN PATRIOTISM

American Revolutionary leaders were not entirely without cultural traditions. With their republican counterparts in Europe, they shared a deep intellectual faith in the value of education in shaping the political sensibilities of a populace. Like the French Physiocrats of the 1790s, who demanded secular schooling supervised by the state including the basics of morality as well as reading, writing, and arithmetic, they saw education as essential to political reform. For the French it was to be a useful education in the rules of public morality, divorced from the church and suitable for the unlettered masses, not the higher learning that involved sophisticated social and political theory. These political reformers, according to social historian Harvey Graff, envisioned a nation of "minimally educated, virtuous, and peaceful farmers and workers. That would be a major step toward the new society of a population capable of being well-governed. A properly educated people would understand and accept its place in life and society."[7] The development of republican education in America was not very different, and the inculcation of patriotism was at its core.

Virtue was most important among the moral concepts the republican educators sought to instil, and it carried highly specialized meaning in this period. Drawn largely from Enlightenment philosophy, especially deism, virtue applied equally to public and private life by moderating individual morality as well as the integrity of nations. This conflation of individual and national character formed the basis for the popular identification of either Washington's morality with American national policy or the American struggle for independence with God's will. As a regulator, virtue was not unlike the system of checks and balances so carefully built into the frame of government. But unlike the Constitution, which was the product of human reason, virtue was the expression of divine will. Without virtue, as James Madison put it, even the the most elegantly crafted republican government was doomed to failure: "No theoretical checks, no form of government can render us secure. To suppose that any form of government will secure liberty or happiness without any virtue in a people is a chemerical [*sic*] idea."[8]

Just how social harmony was linked to virtue was explicated in a highly popular schoolbook lesson of the period. "Virtue our Highest Interest," by the little-remembered essayist James Harris (1709–1780), appeared in four different texts—three of them compiled in England, but highly popular in the United States, and one by the American compiler James Staniford.[9] The essay described humankind's common interdependence as the strongest argument for the practice of virtue: "I find myself existing upon a little spot, surrounded every way by an immense, unknown expansion.—Where am I? What sort of place do I inhabit? Is it exactly accommodated in every instance to my convenience? . . . Is every thing subservient to me, as though I had ordered all myself? No—

---

[7] Harvey J. Graff, *The Legacies of Literacy* (Bloomington: Indiana University Press, 1991), 179; see also 341 for similar educational philosophy in America.

[8] Quoted from Barry Schwartz, *George Washington: The Making of an American Symbol* (New York: Free Press, 1987), 115.

[9] The schoolbooks discussed in this essay were the subject of my dissertation, "The Virtuous Curriculum: American Schoolbooks, 1785–1830" (Ph.D. diss., University of Pennsylvania, 1991). See 108–9 for sources on the following extracts from James Harris and Richard Price.

nothing like it—the farthest from it possible." Harris, describing the ways in which each individual thrives on mutual support, equated humanity's "social interest" as akin to that of the "bee, the beaver, and tribes of herding animals." But he described humanity's ties to one another as even greater and included the general intercourse of "arts and letters" and an interest in "honor and justice . . . [and] the whole train of moral virtues . . . and all I owe to this great polity, and its great Governor, our common Parent." In Harris's popular formulation, virtue was moral action in human society that is controlled by the individual's effort to behave in accordance with—and glorify—divine intention. The English nonconformist minister and philosopher Richard Price (1723–1791), also excerpted frequently in the schoolbooks, described virtue not as the "creature of [human] will," "not local and temporary, but of equal extent and antiquity with the Divine mind." Virtue was in fact nothing short of "everlasting truth . . . the guide of all power." Most important, Price described the social value of virtue as "the foundation of honour and esteem, . . . the source of all beauty, order, and happiness." Without it a reasonable being suffers "hideous deformities." Virtue alone is "honour, glory, wealth and happiness. . . . Secure this, and you secure every thing. Lose this, and all is lost."

Republican America was a place very much in transition. As Gordon Wood demonstrated in his recent history, it had strong roots in the monarchical and hierarchical world of the eighteenth century, but by the early nineteenth century, Americans proudly proclaimed themselves a nation of the "middling sort," even as they ignored the plight of millions of enslaved African Americans.[10] To our eyes America was a highly stratified society, and we see distinctly the differences in status between whites and nonwhites, free and enslaved, men and women. The majority of the population—slaves, women, Native Americans, and landless white men—were not only excluded from the political process, but they were also to a greater or lesser extent dependent on those who were more affluent, better educated, and situated because of their class, race, or sex in a more powerful social position. This dependency was a condition of life, and the smooth functioning of society was seen, not only by the ruling classes, as one of its proper results.[11]

White republican America grew from approximately four to close to thirteen million between 1790 and 1830, while African Americans, 90 percent of them slaves, numbered about three million by 1840. The white population was ethnically and economically homogeneous: almost

[10] Gordon S. Wood, *The Radicalism of the American Revolution* (New York: Alfred A. Knopf, 1992), discusses the monarchical and hierarchical state of colonial American society on 11–42 and the new middle-class consciousness on 347–49.

[11] See Wood, *Radicalism*, 51, 56, 89–92.

two-thirds was of English descent, and more than 90 percent resided in small towns and rural areas.[12] People such as these saw themselves, and they in the eyes of their contemporaries were seen, as members of a virtually classless society by the early nineteenth century. Such a vision was revolutionary in a society where inherited class difference, buttressed by religious and civil ideology, had always inveighed against the leveling of society.

A growing literacy was one measure of this transition. Wealthy men, and those engaged in business, had been literate since colonial times, but in the early republic, often in response to republican ideology, many more people began to be educated. By the late eighteenth century, American society could boast a white male literacy that was nearly universal in New England and approached two-thirds in other regions of the country. Beginning in the 1790s opportunities for women increased, a few more schools were opened (in the North) for African Americans and Indians, and education for white males extended to more Americans. By 1840 it seems that only the lowliest white men could not at least sign their names, although other groups continued to lag behind.[13]

This literacy was achieved through educational activities that took place in a patchwork of homes, private schools, common schools, libraries, and voluntary societies supported by local governments and charitable agencies. But this was traditionally a moral education and not directly related to the way most people earned their living. Reading and writing were unnecessary except for those whose daily occupations involved government, trade, or religion. Members of the elites read the newspapers, delivered the sermons, wrote the books, and taught in the schools. And as republican government admitted new members to the *polis*, it became increasingly important that moral education include large doses of patriotic training as well.

Yet most people's contact with the written word continued to be through oral communication. Reading aloud, memorization, and recitation, in both schools and families, were important, essentially oral, activities. Printed sources were increasingly important, but as Harvey Graff has shown, America continued to be a "semi-literate society." As they had since colonial times, printed sources were important because they validated social discourse conducted conversationally. Newspapers

12 U. S. Bureau of the Census, "Bicentennial Statistics," reprinted from *Pocket Data Book, USA, 1976* (Washington, D.C.: 1976), 79, figure 41; 372, table 580; 373, tables 581, 582. The population figure for 1830 is taken from *Information Please Almanac* (1977), 703.

13 Kenneth A. Lockridge, *Literacy in Colonial New England* (New York: W. W. Norton, 1974), 72–74; Linda K. Kerber, *Women of the Republic: Intellect and Ideology in Revolutionary America* (Chapel Hill: University of North Carolina Press, 1980), esp. 199–231; Graff, *Legacies*, 248–52, 340–43.

in the colonial period serve as an example. With their "fine print, long reports from European courts, and polemics in a learned style" they were hardly readable by a mass audience whose literacy, where it existed at all, was rudimentary. Instead, "persons of rank were expected to receive the more important messages contained in the fine print through reading aloud and through conversations at courthouses, ordinaries, and other places of assembly as news became part of the common stock of knowledge, opinion and feeling." Even in the law, "it was not in printed opinions of authors, but in ritual actions, in face-to-face familiar meetings in the courthouse, that the reality of law unfolded in a formal setting modulated by routine and repetition." Much the same took place through popular schoolbooks, which were often advertised for use in *homes and families* as well as schools. Contemporary educational methods, in which a number of students shared a single textbook and which emphasized reading aloud, repetition, memorization, and recitation, meant that much of the texts' educational value was transmitted orally.[14]

Through such means people exchanged information, values, beliefs, and attitudes. A changing world such as Americans were experiencing made sense in terms of its resemblance to familiar things and familiar ideas—Bible stories, legends, parable, heroes, and demons. Stories, orally communicated, were the real transmitters of culture, but only shadows of these oral stories remain today. The patriotic story told through the popular schoolbooks is one way of hearing those stories. And the persistence of traditional ways of life—and a limited functional literacy in a newly enfranchised republic—helps us make sense of the limited worldview they projected.

Because they were successful in their day, the most widely used schoolbooks are valuable today as expressions of popular patriotic sentiment. More editions were printed because more parents and educators found them to be reliable vehicles for inculcating cultural values. As compilations of textual material from a variety of printed sources, the stories they carried as lessons became, quite literally, the earliest elements in America's patriotic canon. In important ways they helped shape a mythology, a series of important stories conveying the political and moral values of a culture, that motivates patriotism to this day.[15]

---

[14] Graff, *Legacies*, 252–55, 342; Charles Carpenter, *History of American Schoolbooks* (Philadelphia: University of Pennsylvania Press, 1963), 15–17.

[15] Koch, "The Virtuous Curriculum," 28–29. William G. Doty, *Mythography: The Study of Myths and Rituals* (University: University of Alabama Press, 1986), 11, 17. Michael Kammen's *Mystic Chords of Memory: The Transformation of Tradition in American Culture* (New York: Alfred A. Knopf, 1991) applies myth theory to later periods of American history; his discussion of myth is set forth on 18–19.

The origins of American patriotism, unlike that of most nations, are not obscured in preliterary traditions. In fact, those who set about to craft this story told us exactly what they were doing. "Americans, unshackle your minds and act like independent beings. . . . You have been children long enough, subject to the control and subservient to the interest of a haughty parent. You now have an interest of your own to augment and defend: you have an empire to raise and support by your exertions and a national character to establish and extend by your wisdom and virtues."[16] In the language of a religious zealot or conquering general, Noah Webster sounded the alarm in his first reader, published in 1785. He urged his countrymen to reject specifically European values associated with governments now viewed by Americans as not only the enemy but also as corrupted models for national well-being. A corollary to this thinking sought to diminish the amount of British cultural material contained in the textbooks used by American students.

The stories we see in the schoolbooks were disseminated by a group of cultural leaders who were broadly engaged in education, they were expected to shape society and provide its leadership, particularly its moral leadership. They were clergymen, elected officials, medical doctors, teachers, and authors of books on diverse subjects. Only one of them was female. As so often stated in the prescriptive literature of the period, they were responsible for preparing the people of the new nation for self-government. Of particular concern were the new white male voters of the new middle class. The schoolbook compilers shared the republican belief in the value of education to advance civic goals.[17]

The American press was already quite active during this period; more than 113 different titles of school readers were issued between 1785 and 1830. Like most American imprints, identical (or nearly identical) schoolbooks were issued in "new" editions by different printers in different parts of the country, sometimes over a period of twenty years or more. Many of these were originally British texts; their mere printing in this country made them (by some accounts) "American" editions. In all, some 882 editions of school readers were printed in the United States between 1785 and 1830.[18]

[16] Quoted in Cremin, *American Education*, 265.

[17] Schoolbook compilers were among the active opinion makers in early national America. See Koch, "The Virtuous Curriculum," 59–75. On educational imperatives in the new nation, see Graff, *Legacies*, 341, which summarizes the substantial literature on this subject.

[18] Among these, only eighteen titles, issued in 658 editions, were used in my study because they were the most popular of their type; they represented 57 percent of the textbooks used in schools and private education during the 1785–1830 period. These figures and a methodology for assessing popularity were developed in Koch, "The Virtuous Curriculum."

But the concerns of American political and educational leaders become more understandable when we realize that half of the readers' titles, two-thirds of the editions, and nearly three-quarters of the content of those readers were of British origin. Shakespeare, Blair, Pope, Milton, and Addison headed the list of the most popular sources for lesson material. The only American author used with any frequency at all was Benjamin Franklin.[19] Continental European writers were used far less often, but English-language stories based in France, Germany, Italy, Spain, and the Middle East likewise provided some exposure to other cultures. All this contributed to the endurance of the old ways, the monarchical way of life deemed by republicans so antithetical to the new vision for the new nation.[20]

This reliance on European culture led to an insecurity in matters of arts and letters that was hotly debated in American schoolbooks and had broader implications for the development of strong attachments to the new nation. To be fully a nation, and by extension to be worthy of patriotic loyalty, patriotic educators knew that the United States needed focal points for national pride. In the schoolbooks they focused on accomplishments in learning and the arts. For example, in "A Forensic Dispute, On the Question, Are the Anglo-Americans Endowed with a Capacity and Genius Equal to Europeans," the theory was advanced (somewhat defensively) that it was only a matter of time before Americans became intellectual leaders; as a "natural cause" conducive to advanced development, America's temperate climate, great rivers, and vast mountains produced an environment equal or even superior to that of Europe. Even more optimistically, one schoolbook argument dismissed the significance of natural causes that were conceded as promoting European advancement in the arts. Instead, America's "state of society" presaged a more important future in the democratization of learning. Just as "republican government and habits . . . cherish equal rights and tend to an equal distribution of property," it has the "same tendency to promote an equal distribution of knowledge and to make us emphatically a 'republic of letters'" with a strong "propensity to useful employments."[21]

This argument is but one of many that sought to link the necessity for an educated citizenry to republican patriotism. The emphasis on "useful employments" is important because Americans were proud that not only

[19] There were twenty-one British authors more popular than Benjamin Franklin, who was the source for only seven lessons. The typical popular British author was far more frequently cited: Shakespeare 89 citations; Blair 40; Pope 35; Milton 31; *The Spectator* 29; Thomson 27; Sterne 24; and Addison 24.

[20] Wood in *Radicalism* describes the prevalence of this social structure in his opening chapter, "Monarchy."

[21] Caleb Bingham, *The Columbian Orator* (Philadelphia: Isaac Pierce, 1819), 296–99.

were many citizens educated but that education was necessary in the defense of republican government: "In a government where the people fill all the branches of the sovereignty, *intelligence* is the life of liberty. An American would resent his being denied the use of his musket; but he would deprive himself of a stronger safeguard, if he should want that *learning* which is necessary to a knowledge of his constitution."[22] Fourth of July orations, such as this one from Boston in 1787 reprinted in seven successive editions of Caleb Bingham's popular *American Preceptor*, early on linked the national interest and patriotic education. The widespread use of tracts such as this also perpetuated a "siege mentality," which helped to lend the urgency of the Revolution to the task of republican education and the development of patriotic emotional ties. Sharing this ideology, popular American schoolbook compilers—along with their peers in politics and law, the press, pulpit, and classroom—entered the war for cultural independence.

Lacking literary traditions and dedicated to "useful learning," the compilers turned to American history and put it to pragmatic use. In so doing they altered a tradition of historical education long employed by their British counterparts where historical knowledge, along with a familiarity with literature, ancient languages, and the arts, was accepted as an important attribute of the educated man's intellectual and moral training. In an approach not much changed from the days of Shakespeare's great tragedies, the British valued history because "it amuses the fancy as it improves the understanding, and as it strengthens virtue" by illuminating generalized instances of human courage, heroism, and moral dilemma.[23] The American educators, by contrast, besides employing Fourth of July speeches and political oratory from the Revolution or Congress, also consistently adapted the history of the Roman Republic and ancient Greece or drew upon the history of Britain, Europe, and South America to amplify American patriotic themes.[24]

That the selection of American patriotic material for the schoolbooks was self-conscious political activity is amply evident in the frontmatter of a number of texts. Webster's 1789 *American Selection of Lessons in Reading and Speaking* set forth the most avowedly nationalistic agenda: "In the choice of pieces [for the text], I have been attentive to the political interest

---

[22] Caleb Bingham, "Extract from the Oration of Thomas Dawes, Esq. Delivered at Boston, July 4, 1787," *The American Preceptor* (Boston: Manning and Loring, 1805), 107.

[23] Quoted from William Scott, *Lessons in Elocution*, "Advantages of History" (Hume), 116.

[24] Thirty-nine of seventy lessons on British history recorded in the schoolbooks were found in American texts and illuminated issues relating to Anglo-American relations. Britons, by contrast, often employed British history only in character studies of the monarchs tempered by religious issues. Koch, "The Virtuous Curriculum," chap. 4.

of America. I consider it as a capital fault in all our schools, that the books generally used contain subjects wholly uninteresting to our youth; while the writings that marked the revolution, which are not inferior in any respect to the orations of Cicero and Demosthenes, . . . lie neglected and forgotten."[25] But if Webster was the most ardent, all American compilers were sensitive to the issue. Content analysis of schoolbook lessons shows that fully 97 percent of the American historical material was found in American-compiled texts; the remainder was found in so-called American editions of British texts.[26] Timothy Dwight's endorsement of Albert Picket's 1818 *Juvenile Mentor* repeated what had by then become a standard recommendation of American texts for American youth: "The American people are zealous in the right education of their offspring; knowing that on it rests the perpetuity of the national independence, and the propagation of our blessed religion. Good schools, proper school books, and well qualified instructors, add much to a nation's blessings. . . . We are not much excelled by any nation on the globe, in the means of useful instruction."[27] In the preface to an American text that would achieve immediate popularity upon its publication in 1823, James Pierpont indicated something of the discord that persisted as American educators continued to press for popular acceptance of American texts:

> [This book] is the result of an attempt to supply the want . . . of a book of Exercises in Reading and Speaking better adapted, than any English compilation that has yet appeared, to the state of society in this country; and less obnoxious to complaint, on the ground of its national or political character, than it is reasonable to expect that any English compilation would be, among a people whose manners, opinions, literary institutions, and civil government, are so strictly republican as our own.[28]

Pierpont's *American First Class Book* was remarkable among the popular schoolbooks for its inclusion, as early as 1823, of some of the most contemporary American authors. His stated reason for using American materials looked toward a future where American literature was read for its own merits, rather than to satisfy the demands of American chauvinists.[29] Among the American authors he selected for his reader were those destined to become American classics—William Cullen Bryant, Ben-

---

[25] Noah Webster, *An American Selection of Lessons in Reading and Speaking* (Philadelphia: Young and McCulloch, 1789), preface.

[26] Koch, "The Virtuous Curriculum," 133, table 4.1.

[27] Albert Picket, *The Juvenile Mentor* (New York: Daniel D. Smith, 1818), "recommendations" (in frontmatter).

[28] James Pierpont, *The American First Class Book* (Boston: William B. Fowle, 1823), 3.

[29] Ibid, 5.

jamin Franklin, Washington Irving, Daniel Webster, and William Ellery Channing. "American Sages," which was published in Bingham's earlier *Columbian Orator* (1797), addressed the nation's budding scientific culture in a paean to the research of Benjamin Franklin, David Rittenhouse, and Thomas Godfrey.[30]

But all such efforts to celebrate American accomplishment paled in comparison to the richness of European cultures. Moreover, reading textbooks, by long-standing tradition,[31] were compilations; beyond Franklin and his circle, compilers seeking to develop an American cultural tradition had scant material on which to draw. American cultural independence required a novel approach, a break with the past in terms of content, if not form. American compilers, apparently unwilling to experiment with established pedagogy and depart from the reader-as-compilation format, instead set themselves to the task of creating a culture based on the story of that which was unique in America—the new republican political order. Chiefly using extracts from speeches and historical documents, but also writing much of their own material (itself a revolutionary departure from established practice), they seized upon the story of the founding of the United States as the motivating element in a great saga that advanced their twin goals of patriotic and moral education.

DOMINANT STORIES IN THE NEW PATRIOTISM

The story of America's "discovery," the hardships of the colonial period, the struggle for independence, and the political genesis of the new nation under the leadership of Washington as savior-patriarch became an epic told and retold with liturgical regularity. In its simplest form, the story took on a biblical symbolism, translating the newness of America into a familiar cultural language that carried the weight of history and spiritual authority. The result was the beginning of a uniquely American patriotic canon, which married political history to moral philosophy and religious symbolism. An examination of the elements in the mythic American story follows.

[30] Bingham, "American Sages," *Columbian Orator*, 261. Thomas Godfrey was the inventor of the quadrant.

[31] On the history of schoolbooks, see James Bowen, *A History of Western Education*, 2 vols. (New York: St. Martin's Press, 1972); Carpenter, *History of American Schoolbooks*; Ruth Miller Elson, *Guardians of Tradition: American Schoolbooks of the Nineteenth Century* (Lincoln: University of Nebraska Press, 1964); John A. Nietz, *Evolution of American Secondary School Textbooks* (Rutland, Vt.: Charles E. Tuttle Co., 1966); John A. Nietz, *Old Text Books* (Pittsburgh: University of Pennsylvania Press, 1961).

The Story of Columbus

Americans in the new United States looked to Columbus as the prophet, even amidst the corruption and ignorance of the Old World, of their national independence. His voyages of discovery marked the beginning of the inevitable break with the Old World that culminated in the American Revolution. This vision is perhaps most plainly seen in a schoolbook lesson in which "Columbus . . . saw, once more, bright Del'ware's silver stream/And Penn's throng'd city cast a cheerful gleam." The explorer is imagined as a heavenly figure sitting in benevolent judgment as Randolph, Washington, Franklin, Lee, and the whole founding panoply gather in sanctified political assembly leading a wronged people to reluctant Revolution:

> Nash, Rutledge, Jefferson, in council great,
> And Jay and Laurens op'd the rolls of fate.
> The Livingston's, fair freedom's gen'rous band,
> The Lees, the Houstons, fathers of the land.
> . . . .
>
> Adams, enrag'd, a broken charter bore,
> And lawless acts of ministerial pow'r;
> Some injur'd right in each loose leaf appears,
> A king in terrors and a land in tears.[32]

Ever virtuous, Americans are pictured as instruments of fate and reluctant warriors driven by British perfidy to a war of self-defense. Washington, most directly symbolic of the nation, "on Britain still . . . cast a filial eye / But sovereign fortitude his visage bore, / To meet their legions on th' invaded shore."

The history of Columbus in the New World was interpreted through a lens focused solely on the birth of the North American republic. While Columbus's voyages most directly opened the West Indies and South America to European colonization, people in the United States, with the benefit of considerable hindsight, saw as inexorable the "progress of civilization" leading directly from Columbus to Washington.

Such sentiments found expression in popular verse such as "Columbia," a paean to the United States in iambic pentameter that appeared in Bingham's *American Preceptor.* Here Columbus was feminized into the allegorical Columbia, representing the new land, the exotic wilderness of North America. She became the symbolic counterpart to George Washington, who was seen as imposing order and reason upon the land

---

[32] Bingham, "Description of the First American Congress from the Vision of Columbus," *Columbian Orator,* 133–35.

through republican government. Both were memorialized in countless ways during the federal period, from naming the nation's capital to illustrating chapbooks.

But in the schoolbooks, which relied on biography for much of their instruction, and elsewhere, the male Columbus also retained historical identity, albeit heavily overlaid with moral and patriotic interpretation. In this guise he often became an Old Testament patriarch struggling to achieve his mission against the forces of ignorance and reaction; Columbus as the new nation's Moses unfolded in tales of the struggles entailed in the voyages of discovery.[33] They recount how over an eighteen-year period the explorer sought patronage for his first voyage; Columbus was portrayed as loyally applying first to his native Genoa and next to his adopted Portugal before seeking support from Ferdinand and Isabella. American compilers went to great lengths to recite various acts of chicanery to which Columbus was subjected in an obvious effort to dissociate him from a leadership role in the course of Spanish colonial development, which was uniformly criticized as corrupted by Old World vices.[34] America's cultural founders clearly sought to claim Columbus for the (in their eyes) more virtuous cause of American nation building.

Much of the injustice that Columbus suffered, according to lengthy discussion in the texts, derived from dishonorable opportunists whose venality only embellished Columbus's virtue: the king of Portugal secretly mounted an unsuccessful voyage of exploration based on Columbus's plan even as the explorer awaited word from him on his request for support. Later, following Columbus's third successful voyage, the schoolbooks tell us that Ferdinand and Isabella were incited to jealousy by Columbus's enemies. They removed him as viceroy of the colony that he founded and empowered the evil Francis de Bovadilla, under whose rule the natives were subjected to "a most miserable servitude" and who introduced "disorder and licentiousness" throughout the colony. Columbus was carried off in fetters to Spain. On the death of Queen Isabella, "his last and greatest friend," Columbus appealed unsuccessfully to Ferdinand that the terms of his original contract be fulfilled and sought support for a fifth voyage, only to be rewarded with a final round of royal treachery:

[33] Bingham, "Account of Columbus," *American Preceptor*, 39–43; Webster, "History of Columbus," *American Selection*, 70–80; Bingham, "Description of the First American Congress from the Vision of Columbus," *Columbian Orator*, 133–35; Webster, "Columbus to Ferdinand," *American Selection*.

[34] The Spanish were portrayed in the schoolbooks as greedy and cruel aggressors against their South American colonists. Typically these lessons emphasized the virtues of national self-determination and soundly criticized Spanish imperialism. See Koch, "Virtuous Curriculum," 201–2.

Ferdinand, cold, ungrateful, and timid, dared not to comply with a single proposal. . . . He therefore delayed and avoided any decision . . . in hopes that the declining health of Columbus would soon rid the court of the remonstrances of a man, whose extraordinary merit was, in their opinion, a sufficient occasion of destroying him. . . . Columbus languished a short time, and gladly resigned a life, which had been worn out in the most essential services perhaps that were ever rendered, by any human character, to an ungrateful world.[35]

The schoolbooks described a selfless hero subjected to unbearable obstacles and indignities in his single-minded pursuit of an inner vision. This portrayal placed Columbus with regard to the Spanish court in much the same position as the American colonies vis-à-vis the British: long-suffering and reluctant instruments of inevitable change directed by the "unseen hand."

Columbus was thus the one who triumphed over unenlightened opposition and succeeded in planting "civilization," albeit corrupt, in the New World. Columbus's forbearance in the face of difficulty, his failure to secure personal fortune from his ventures, and his pitiful death all signify important elements of the schoolbook formula for the virtuous personality.

The American Wilderness

As in any great epic, the passage of time in the schoolbooks' rendering of America's beginnings was more symbolic than chronological. The almost three centuries that passed between the Columbian voyages and the American Revolution were important to the patriotic story for their value as exposition of the American colonial experience.

That experience was most often and most graphically conveyed to American students through lessons involving Native Americans. Stories involving Indians functioned in a number of ways: Native Americans were used as examples in lessons on Christian morality; their involvement in colonial warfare added dramatic impact to colonial history; and Indians were the object of social instruction that urged toleration of native culture. Significantly for our discussion of early patriotism, Indians also played an important symbolic role as the personification of the American landscape. At once threatening yet benevolent, honorable yet primitive, hospitable yet brutal, American Indians were portrayed in the schoolbooks with all the ambivalence that white Americans have historically reserved for their love-hate relationship with the land as both wil-

---

[35] Quoted here and above from Webster, "History of Columbus," *American Selection*, 80, 79, 78, respectively.

derness and paradise. From the seventeenth through the nineteenth centuries, the wilderness carried for Americans connotations of danger, hardship, and immorality—the latter because it was not bound by the so-called civilizing strictures of Christianity. For Europeans far removed from the reality of life in the New World, America as paradise was a well-tended garden, its wildness controlled by human cultivation. Beginning in the late eighteenth and early nineteenth centuries, wilderness took on a new appeal with the growth of deism, which found religious meaning in nature, and the Romantic movement, which celebrated mystery, solitude, and the untamed. In cities in Europe and America—far from the frontier—literary gentlemen thus found a new fascination with the wild even as their contemporaries on the frontier continued to fear and "civilize" it.[36]

Schoolbooks most frequently portrayed Indians as "noble savages" and used their interactions with white settlers as opportunities for moral education based on the Indians' close connection with the natural state. They were seen as embodiments of divine intention unencumbered by the weaknesses inherent in "civilized" people who were plagued by the wrong application of advanced human reason. Columbia herself was often portrayed as an Indian princess nobly garbed in Roman dress. A number of early nineteenth-century lessons touted Indians' cultural separateness as morally correct and their culture, in terms of fidelity to principle, as superior to that of whites. But all treatments of Indian culture were hardly so sympathetic. Some lessons described Indian massacres of white settlers, while others quoted William Pitt's plea to Parliament to resist the use of Indians (considered a "malicious weapon" in eighteenth-century terms) against England's cultural kin, the American revolutionaries.

Indians were at once a powerful example in the educators' storehouse of homilies teaching the universal value of the gentle virtues of hospitality, civility, and familial affection, and they were the object of a schoolbook campaign for tolerance that contradicted prevailing negative attitudes toward Native Americans.[37] But these were not the lessons in

---

[36] Roderick Nash in *Wilderness and the American Mind* (New Haven: Yale University Press, 1967) discusses how biblical and medieval notions of the wilderness as a fearsome unknown were transplanted to America by settlers living on the frontiers; see esp. chaps. 2, 3.

[37] The number of duplicate lessons employed is a good indicator of cultural unanimity concerning the place of Indians within the dominant culture. A remarkable 70 percent of the twenty-four American Indian lessons were duplicated in one or more popular texts. This contrasts sharply with other American cultural material, which, excluding the Indian lessons, demonstrates only a 38-percent duplication rate overall. Most of these lessons used the "noble savage" as a moral example for Christian education. Twenty-seven of thirty lessons on Indians were in American-compiled texts; see Koch, "The Virtuous Curriculum," pp. 151–63.

which Indians played a role in patriotic education; here the message was more mixed, and tales of Indian "massacres" and wartime atrocities belied the positive image in a small but significant group of lessons, all of them in American-compiled texts.[38]

In some patriotic stories, extraordinary Indians were praised for helping Americans survive in the wilderness, or, better yet from the whites' perspective, they were portrayed as directly assisting white Americans' political interests. Although the story of the First Thanksgiving had not yet been popularized, the symbolic model it represents had begun to take shape in the promulgation of the Pocahontas story, which was already a staple, appearing in Bingham's *American Preceptor* and Picket's *Juvenile Mentor*.[39] Another popular lesson celebrated Indians as American allies during the American Revolution: "Brothers! . . . We are ready to do any thing for your relief, and shall be guided by your counsel. Brothers! . . . if you send me to the fight, . . . let me fight in my own Indian way. . . . Only point out to me where your enemies keep, and that is all I want to know."[40] This lesson, which records a speech of the chief of the "Stockbridge Tribe," was identified as delivered to the General Court of Massachusetts in 1775. While in actuality Indians most frequently allied themselves with the British during the Revolution, the schoolbooks' educational purpose of advancing peaceful coexistence was better served by popularizing this extraordinary instance of allegiance to the American cause.[41]

William Penn's treaty with the Indians is perhaps the most enduring of the popular stories involving Indians in the colonial period, and it too reveals the ambiguous relationship as perceived by Anglo-Americans: "Wm. Penn, who was distinguished as a good as well as a great man, took care to acquire the best of titles to his lands, by legal purchases from the natives, the sole proprietors of the soil. He introduced into his settlement a most liberal plan of civil and religious policy—he tolerated all religious sects, and thus invited not only his own sect, the friends, to remove from England, but also vast numbers of all denominations from

[38] Descriptions of Indian hostilities toward whites were limited to six lessons out of thirty-two (20 percent) on relations between the races; see Koch, "Virtuous Curriculum," 150, 152–54. Lessons on Africans, Jews, and Roman Catholics stigmatized these groups, which were the only other population subgroups identifiable through content analysis.

[39] Bingham, "History of Pocahontas" (Chastellux), *American Preceptor*, 14; Picket, "History of Pocahantas," *Juvenile Mentor*, 109–12.

[40] Bingham, "Speech of an Indian Chief, of the Stockbridge Tribe, to the Massachusetts Congress, in the Year 1775," *Columbian Orator*, 54–55; John Hubbard, *The American Reader* (Troy, N.Y.: Wright, Goodenow, and Stockwell, 1808), "Speech of an Indian Chief, of the Stockbridge Tribe, to the General Court of Massachusetts, 1775," 116–17; quoted from p. 117.

[41] This lesson was sufficiently popular to have been published in three texts.

Ireland and Germany."[42] Penn, like Washington and the revolutionaries, brought the perceived benefits of civilization—in this case rule by English law and land-holding customs—to the wilderness even as he invited into this wilderness those who would evade the law when it conflicted with their belief systems. In his insistence on Europeans' rights to express dissent through a life-style and legal system founded in differing belief systems, Penn was seen as a precursor to the American revolutionaries whose Enlightenment credo was similarly ideological. Obviously, neither Penn's nor the revolutionaries' worldview could give full legitimacy to the culture of the Native Americans; nevertheless, in celebrating the Penn Treaty story, white Americans found their strongest model for an amiable relationship with Native Americans. This relationship, wholly founded in English religious and legal systems, was idealized in the schoolbooks for its tolerance of racial and cultural difference. Americans were proud of themselves in the treaty story because the rights of Englishmen were extended to people whom the prevailing attitudes perceived as subhuman. The story illustrated the most liberal worldview possible in early national America—tolerance rather than annihilation.

Pierpont, for example, dwelt at length on Penn's Treaty; he betrayed its egalitarian spirit in the course of a lesson extracted from the *Edinburgh Review* that described Native Americans in pejorative and potentially threatening terms: in contrast to the "moderate attendance of friends," an "innumerable multitude of the Indians assembled in that neighborhood . . . with their dark visages and . . . arms, moving, in vast swarms, in the depth of the woods which then overshaded the whole of that now different region." The lesson reported Penn's words in detail, as well as the conditions of the agreement. Of the "Sachems'" response, "no more seems to have been remembered, but that 'they pledged themselves to live in love with William Penn and his children, as long as the sun and moon should endure.'"[43] When offered a fair deal by "good" colonists, "good" Indians were expected to accept it and live in peace.

The Penn Treaty story—and other colonial history anecdotes—in the schoolbooks fostered a sense of inherent American moral superiority, which was to find full expression in the American frame of government that institutionalized toleration through the separation of church and state and the Bill of Rights. Another example in support of this worldview took the form of an imaginary dialogue between William Penn and Fernando Cortez, in which Penn castigated Cortez for cruelty and greed in

---

[42] Webster, "Discovery and Settlement of North America," *American Selection*, 80–90; quoted from 86–87.

[43] Pierpont, "Interesting Account of William Penn's Treaty with the Indians Previous to his Settling in Pennsylvania," *American First Class Book*, 60–63; quoted from 60–61.

his dealings with American Indians: "The prince of darkness may, per-haps, place thee as high upon his black list of heroes as Alexander or Cesar. . . . What *right* hadst thou, or had the king of Spain himself to the Mexican empire? [emphasis added]." Cortez, the antithesis of the "good" colonist, responded in a remark meant to reveal the authoritarian source of his Old World inspiration and his essential irrationality: "The pope gave it to my master."[44] Penn, by contrast, operated from a basis in English law (accentuated by the reference to "rights") not blind obe-dience to the will of another mortal being.

Although shocking today for its anti-Catholicism, in the federal period such a comment was a useful instructional vehicle because it supported prevailing notions about legitimate government. Conquests undertaken by kings in the name of the Pope (with God unnamed) were demonized, while the North American venture was pictured as a legalistic undertak-ing conducted by individuals who respected the rights of other individ-uals (the Indians) regardless of the latter's cultural norms. Of course, the American colonists, as products of the Protestant Reformation and En-gland's legal system and limited monarchy, were seen as virtuously car-rying forth God's word, in contrast to the unenlightened Roman Catho-lics who were pictured as enslaved to a religion whose leaders and adherents were corrupted by superstition, avarice, and the lust for power. In respecting the "rights" of Native Americans, Penn had peacefully ne-gotiated a contract; Cortez, personifying old ideas of absolute monarchy and Roman Catholic orthodoxy, used violence in his colonial conquests. This lesson, seen through the lens of Enlightenment political philosophy and later constitutional guarantees, was intended to demonstrate the rightness of Americans' separation of church and state and legal guaran-tees of individual rights. It pointed also to the North Americans' sense of themselves as divinely appointed leaders chosen to tame the wilderness in the name of enlightened Protestant Christianity. Unfortunately for the inhabitants of the wilderness, the American Indians embodied both suc-cess and tragedy for these New World Israelites.

Nowhere was the tragedy more profoundly expressed than in a lesson reprinted in a popular schoolbook, "Letters from a British Spy." It was an extract from a work of the same title by American author William Wirt. Highly condemnatory of the popular images of Penn's Treaty and the Pocahontas story, the narrative presented the purported musings of a British nobleman visiting the abandoned site of the once flourishing "In-dian town, Powhatan." With the benefit of hindsight, the "British Spy" clearly saw how payment for the land, in the manner of William Penn,

---

[44] Bingham, "Dialogue between Fernando Cortez and William Penn," *American Precep-tor*, 52–55; quoted from 52.

was poor recompense for the depredations of the whites: "The people here may say what they please; but on the principles of eternal truth and justice they have no right to this country. They say that they have bought it; bought it! yes: of whom? of the poor trembling natives, who knew that a refusal would be vain, and who strove to make a virtue of necessity, by seeming to yield, with grace, what they had not power to retain." In light of this history, Wirt found Indian resistance completely justifiable: "Poor wretches! No wonder that they are so implacably vindictive against white people; no wonder that they refuse to associate and mix permanently with their unjust and cruel invaders and exterminators; no wonder that, in the unabating spite and phrenzy [sic] of conscious impotence, they wage an eternal war as well as they are able."[45] Wirt presented his fellow Americans with a powerful corrective to their romanticization of the "noble savage." Where most Americans used euphemism and idealizations of Indian character to mitigate the harsh realities of the cultural warfare taking place, Wirt voiced powerful social criticism. Speaking as a "British Spy," his observations must have been most painful to Americans who congratulated themselves on their new nation as a triumph of virtue over the corruption and injustice of Europe. Wirt and the compilers who carried this lesson saw the Pocahontas and William Penn stories and the countless other depictions of the "noble savage" for what they were: comfortable ideology for the whites, and genocidal for the Indians.

Politically active in social reform, Wirt (and the schoolbooks that carried his essay) expressed through their interpretation of the unjust treatment of Native Americans perhaps the most important patriotic tradition in the schoolbooks—the power of free speech and political protest: "Driven from river to river, from forest to forest, and through a period of two hundred years, rolled back, nation upon nation, [the Indians] find themselves fugitives, vagrants, and strangers in their own country." Sadly their voices did not prevail. But they could and did indicate for thousands of American school students the hypocrisy being seamlessly woven into the new nation's cultural fabric: "Go, administer the cup of oblivion to recollections and anticipations like these, and you will then cease to complain that the Indian refuses to be civilized." Nevertheless, much as they viewed the wilderness itself as a place to be tamed even as it was celebrated, most Americans clung to popular romantic representations of the "noble savage" even as they pursued a politics of conquest.

Inextricably bound into this patriotic story, the tradition that roman-

---

[45] Quoted here and above from Hubbard, "Observations on the Indians of Virginia," *American Reader*, 212–15. The lessons were also reprinted in Pierpont, "Part of a Letter of the British Spy," *American First Class Book*, 324–29.

ticized the American Indian treated the land in much the same manner. Seen as wilderness to be conquered and civilized—at the center of which were very real memories of war with the Indians—the hardships of the colonial period were used to justify political ends as the colonial period drew to a close. Joseph Warren, in a popular speech commemorating the Boston Massacre, cited struggles in the American wilderness by earlier generations of British settlers as a sort of rite of passage, the hard-won privileges of which were violated by Britain's colonial policies of the 1760s: "Certainly it never entered the hearts of our ancestors, that after so many dangers in this then desolate wilderness, their hard earned property should be at the disposal of British parliament; and as it was soon found that this taxation could not be supported by reason and argument."[46] Again a thoroughly legalistic worldview prevailed, securely founded in rights and privileges of English law and custom. Recalling the colonial period as a time of hardship and suffering, the lesson cited the final burden borne by American colonists: oppression from the "mother" country whose troops, instead of offering protection, turned against her loyal children "contrary to our just rights as possessing all the liberties and immunities of British subjects." At the conclusion of this important chapter to the American patriotic story, the very ideology of law and toleration that the Americans so paternalistically extended to the Native Americans was denied them by their own patrons, the English.

The American Revolution

The ambiguous ideological wilderness of the colonial period, which left open the possibility of advocating the cultural rights of Native Americans, came to an abrupt and decisive close with the onset of the American Revolution. None of the lingering doubts about American morality inhered in lessons that presented national independence—and eventually the nation itself—in terms sanctified by divine law. Again, quoting Warren, Americans saw their virtuous stance in stark contrast to the injustices inflicted upon them in the name of a corrupt British colonial policy:

If you . . . oppose the torrent of oppression; if you feel the true fire of patriotism burning in your breasts; if you . . . despise the most gaudy dress that slavery can wear; if you really prefer the lonely cottage (whilst blest with liberty) to gilded palaces, surrounded with the ensigns of slavery, you may have the fullest assurance that tyranny, with her whole accursed train, will hide their

[46] Bingham, "Extract from Dr. Warren's Oration, Delivered at Boston, March 5, 1772," *American Preceptor*, 96–97; Webster, "Oration, Delivered at Boston March 5, 1772, by Dr. Joseph Warren," *American Selection*, 123–29; quoted here and below from Webster, 126.

hideous heads, in confusion, shame and despair—if you perform your part, you must have the strongest confidence, that *the same Almighty Being* who protected your pious and venerable forefathers—who enabled them to turn a barren wilderness into a fruitful field . . . will still be mindful of you their offspring. [emphasis original]

All the now-familiar elements of the popular history of the American Revolution are represented in this schoolbook lesson. Charges were hurled of political oppression and cultural dissonance as British policy, carried out in "gilded palaces," was characterized as "slavery" in "gaudy dress." A virtuous and humble America became a "land of liberty," benevolently governed in the name of the "Almighty Being." Above all, American martyrdom became a virtue in the national saga as colonists, although "blest with liberty," endured economic and physical isolation in their "lonely cottage." Ultimately America's pain gave birth to a millennial vision linking America's national destiny and world freedom: "May our land be a land of liberty, the seat of virtue, the asylum of the oppressed, a name and a praise in the whole earth, until the last shock of time shall bury the empires of the world in undistinguished ruin!"[47] This lesson, typical in its exaggerated tone and virulent anti-British sentiment, posited American patriotism as equivalent to virtue. And like all schoolbook treatments of the Revolution, it offered no detailed political or military history; even victories went uncelebrated. The Revolution was portrayed as a moral war, an ideological contest. The explication of political principles linked to divine intention—an emotional declaration of Americans' common rights violated by English injustice—received attention in the schoolbooks.

From the American perspective, the most effective critics of British policy were the British opposition leaders whose pro-American parliamentary addresses were the subject of numerous popular oratory lessons. Among these, William Pitt the Elder was a particular favorite: nine lessons in five popular texts, overwhelmingly by American compilers, represented Pitt as an impassioned voice in an otherwise venal British Parliament unsympathetic to the American cause.[48] In extracts from a number of speeches, Pitt was portrayed as arguing forcefully the merits of American grievances during the Stamp Act Crisis; urging the removal of troops from Boston in 1775; and in three speeches from 1777, pleading for mercy for the American rebels, describing the conquest of America as "impossible" and opposing Lord Suffolk's advocacy of the use of Indians against the Americans. Similarly Caleb Bingham carried "Colonel

---

[47] Quoted here and above from Webster, "Oration . . . by Dr. Joseph Warren," *American Selection*, 128–29.
[48] Koch, "The Virtuous Curriculum," 150.

Barre's Speech in the British Parliament, 1765," which defended American liberties in the face of British oppression, and the "Speech of Mr. Fox, in the British Parliament, on American Affairs, 1778," which argued cynically against continuing the fight in America in preference for a direct conflict with France. On the literary side, Pierpont carried Lord Byron's "American Republick," adding to the litany of English voices supporting American independence, while Bingham published "Epilogue to Addison's Cato," which maligned Great Britain for forcing the Americans to revolt.[49]

Other compilers used the voices of American patriots to demonstrate the rightness of the American cause. Webster, in his 1789 *American Selection of Lessons in Reading and Speaking*, was the earliest compiler to begin to tell the story of the Revolution. Besides his own "History of the Late War" printed in that schoolbook, he included "The First Petition of Congress to the King, in 1774"; this article, listing three pages of grievances against Parliament, was followed by "A Declaration by the Representatives of the United Colonies of North–America, Setting forth the Causes and Necessity of their Taking up Arms, July 6, 1775."[50] In both lessons the colonists were represented as moderate, peaceable, and respectful of British law, men who sought only to protect their liberties as Englishmen.

Significantly for our modern patriotic canon, Webster did *not* include the Declaration of Independence among his important documents of the Revolution. Rather, he introduced the principles of just government by reprinting Governor William Livingston's hortatory speech to the New Jersey legislature following America's first victories at Trenton and Princeton. This powerful patriotic paean for generations of American students characterized the Revolution as "a war on our side founded on the immutable obligation of self-defense, and in support of freedom, of virtue, and every thing tending to ennoble our nature, and render our people happy." The British, however, were described as "prompted by boundless avarice, and a thirst for absolute sway." But even more damning, British acquisitiveness was "built on a claim repugnant to every principle of reason and equity" and violated the social compact between government and the governed. The refusal by Parliament and George III to address American grievances through lawful means recalled absolute

[49] Bingham, "Colonel Barre's Speech in the British Parliament, on the Stamp-Act Bill," *Columbian Orator*, 252–54; ibid., "Epilogue to Addison's Cato," 69–70; ibid., "Speech of Mr. Fox, on American Affairs, 1778," 172–75; Pierpont, "The American Republick," *American First Class Book*, 164–65.

[50] Webster, "The First Petition of Congress to the King, in 1774," *American Selection*, 129–34; "A Declaration by the Representatives of the United Colonies of North-America," 135–41; "A Sketch of the History of the Late War in America," 111–22.

monarchy and authoritarian rule, which was in turn *"subversive of all liberty, natural, civil, moral, and religious; incompatible with human happiness, and usurping the attributes of Deity, degrading man and blaspheming God"* [emphasis original].[51]

Lessons that incorporated descriptions of tarring and feathering or that condemned Benedict Arnold helped set the parameters of sanctioned political behavior, thereby imposing external standards on the sentimental emotions of patriotic fervor. In 1789 Noah Webster's schoolbook singled out Benedict Arnold as an example of the man who rejected virtue and allowed his passions to get the better of him. Described as a man who resented the actions of others who had "given him offence" and sought revenge, Arnold turned against his country and, generations of schoolchildren were told, was "despised by all mankind" and his "conduct has stamped him with infamy."[52] Arnold was the supreme example of the man who violated duty: as an officer in the Continental Army, he let personal interest overcome virtue and abandoned his responsibilities to the nation.

In other schoolbook stories, Americans who remained loyal to the Crown were reviled in anecdotal accounts whose humorous tone concealed the underlying message of social ostracism.[53] In one tale for his sympathies to the king loyalist McFingal is tarred and feathered by a raucous mob of fellow townsfolk. That night "the tory Pandemonium muster" of McFingal and his friends gathered in McFingal's cellar (humbled in status as they sat on kegs amid stored turnips) to plot their revenge and reminisce over earlier days when the loyalists—as members of the town's ruling gentry—controlled the votes by "guiding hand" and "new commissions" rolled into their coffers. This lesson described mob violence in a satiric style evocative of the periodic rioting documented by Gordon Wood as controlled means by which the lower classes expressed their frustration without threatening the hegemony of the elites in colonial America.[54] By the early nineteenth century, with a new political order anxious to establish its legitimate authority, the old elite—now safely banished to England and Canada—was the subject of ridicule and demonization. As reminders of the force of revolutionary zeal, the fate of loyalists and the treasonous were firm warnings of the harsh treatment

[51] Webster, "Speech of His Excellency, William Livingston, Esq.," *American Selection*, 146.

[52] Webster, "A Sketch of the History of the Late War in America," *An American Selection*, 120.

[53] Hubbard, "A Humorous Scene, Describing the Method of Tarring and Feathering, Practised in the Late American Revolution," *American Reader*, 181–84; ibid., "The Meeting of McFingal and His Friends," 184–86.

[54] Wood, *Radicalism*, 77–92, discusses political power and social standing in his section on patronage.

reserved for those whose behavior was at odds with the nationalistic and philosophical goals of the new nation.

George Washington Symbolizes the Nation

In defining patriotism cultural leaders needed to describe clearly not only those actions to be seen as treasonous but also positive values and attitudes, often characterized as virtuous, that would enhance their vision for the republic. Such essentially educational activity was crucial to building a national consciousness, among not only youth but also adults, in a nation whose cultural and political independence seemed so dangerously insecure. As the country moved into the 1790s, the task of governing the new United States added complexity to the relatively simple, friend-or-foe characterizations that marked the early nationalists' conceptualizations of the colonial and revolutionary periods.

One approach was to attempt to infuse new generations with the moral certainty and patriotic emotional attachments of the wartime generation. Patriotic speeches were commonly reprinted in newspapers and pamphlets as well as in schoolbooks where long after their original delivery such speeches provided fodder for students' rote recital and memorization. A 1793 Fourth of July speech by the young John Quincy Adams, who paid homage to the revolutionary generation, was reprinted between 1794 and 1818 in at least sixty-four editions of Bingham's *American Preceptor*. In it Adams exhorted young people to recapture the "rapturous glow of patriotism" that characterized 1776 in order to preserve the hard-won liberties of that era, despite the "calm and settled moderation of the mind" that then prevailed.[55] But this moderate view was hardly universal. While many Independence Day orations in the schoolbooks looked back on the Revolution as a glorious time of national unity and urged a rekindling of that spirit, these and other patriotic lessons began to reflect new political realities as the Constitution was put to work. Sectionalism, states' rights, and international disputes all made their way into the schoolbooks prior to 1810.[56]

A patriotic education that included the discussion of political controversy was, then as now, a double-edged sword, and the schoolbook authors and other cultural leaders knew it. Like good storytellers (and mythmakers) everywhere, they turned instead to simple, familiar, and powerful imagery. For people accustomed to seeking a monarchical fa-

[55] Bingham, "Extract from Mr. John Q. Adams' Oration, Delivered at Boston, July 4, 1793," *American Preceptor*, 143–45; this text was reprinted in identical form through at least 1818.

[56] Koch, "The Virtuous Curriculum," 143–46.

ther figure, this meant most often that the story of the nation's founding was personified through George Washington who became a paternalistic savior, an icon for patriotic cultural values. As republican Americans uniformly reviled Great Britain, and the king in particular as its head, a sanctified George Washington—infused with political and moral virtue— became an important focal point for social stability in the face of change.[57]

The association between Washington and divine favor was particularly important for establishing patriotic attachment. "Thanks to the mercy of Almighty Heaven/For Washington to fair Columbia given!" He became an exemplar for American virtue—and by extension for the national character itself: "WASHINGTON . . . bequeathed to his beloved fellow citizens a *glorious legacy in his example, his character, and his virtues*, which ought to render them *pure and virtuous* in their morals, *devout* in their *religion, fervent* in their *patriotism, just in the cabinet, and invincible* in the field."[58] As Washington's personal character became iconographic for national character, his successes signified heavenly approval for the national enterprise he came to symbolize. Male, powerful, and benevolent, it was easy to come to know Washington as a father figure or a god or even a king (for those who still believed in monarchy as the right order of things). Through such familiar associations, he became the central figure in America's patriotic story for these early educational and cultural leaders seeking to instill an emotional attachment to the new nation, even as they shaped that nation's definition. "WASHINGTON, is the strict narration of the truth, and the loftiest character which we can assign to him, *is the very display of himself*" [emphasis original].[59]

The American schoolbooks presented their favored elements of Washington's character in a standard set of lessons that followed a remarkably uniform interpretation. Many were drawn from popular eulogies that circulated in the press immediately following Washington's death in 1799; others were extracts from his own speeches or celebratory verse. With twenty-three lessons devoted to him, Washington was by far the single most popular figure, supplanting even Christ, in the school readers. He was a particular favorite of Daniel Staniford who used ten

[57] Schwartz in *George Washington*, chap. 1, argues convincingly that Washington functioned as an important symbol of the revolutionary cause by serving as the focal point for public veneration in the place of George III. Later Washington personified what Schwartz calls public virtue; he served as a model of popular republican values involving the renunciation of self-interest for the public good. This gave him enormous symbolic importance in nation building (chaps. 2 and 5).

[58] Staniford, "Extract From a Poem Entitled, 'Agriculture,' or 'Happy American Farmer,'" *Art of Reading*, 226–27; and ibid., "Extract from the Answer of the Senate to the Speech of the Lieutenant Governor of Massachusetts," 83.

[59] Staniford, "Extract from Judge Minot's Eulogy on General Washington," *Art of Reading*, 83.

Washington lessons in his *Art of Reading*. Albert Picket, who otherwise borrowed most of his *Juvenile Expositor* and *Juvenile Mentor* from English texts, used Americans Staniford and Bingham as his source this time. Adams and Hubbard also carried lessons on Washington. He was the subject of one-quarter of the total number of American history lessons in the popular readers, while the general topics of the American Revolution and lessons involving American Indians each involved one-third of the lessons; a miscellaneous group encompassed other patriotic topics.[60]

This use of Washington as *the* patriotic symbol occurred during a relatively short period, roughly 1790 to 1820.[61] Through the outpourings of the popular press and pulpit at this time the nation came to terms with the loss of its living symbol of a divine national mission. This canonization endured as the texts compiled during this period were memorized and recited by succeeding generations of students and made their way into the popular vocabulary of patriotism.

In both war and peace, Washington was celebrated for two principal character traits that educators sought to associate with America's national character: devotion to duty and the renunciation of celebrity and ambition. For patriotic educators he was an ideal role model in an era when the moral education of the individual was understood as the firmest foundation for family, community, and national well-being; all were securely and hierarchically linked by a belief in a divinely ordered universe of human affairs. Washington the individual was important because he was seen to have literally embodied *virtue*, both personally and metaphorically for the nation.

Washington's resignation of command of the Continental Army in 1783, *First Address to Congress* as president, decision not to seek a third presidential term, and reluctant return to public life in resuming command of the Army in 1798 were the popular schoolbook lessons that formed the substance of the original Washington legend; his victories in battle or illustrations of perseverance and integrity did not contribute

---

[60] Although Washington did not appear in any popular British schoolbooks used in the United States, he was still by far the most popular biographical figure to appear in contemporary schoolbooks, either American or British. Fifteen of the twenty-three Washington lessons, a stunning 65 percent, were drawn from eulogies and two-thirds were duplicated in more than one text. See Koch, "The Virtuous Curriculum," 138, 150, 167–68, 179, 186–88, 317 for comparisons with other popular figures—Christ, St. Paul, Franklin, Caesar, Alexander the Great, King Alfred, William Pitt, and Franklin.

[61] No lessons on Washington appeared in Webster's 1789 *An American Selection*, the earliest of the American readers; he was only mentioned in the course of Webster's treatment of the Revolution, "A Sketch of the Late War," 114. Lessons on Washington were similarly absent from Pierpont, whose text *The American First Class Book* first appeared in 1823. It relied not on Washington as the singular American icon, but instead sought to advance American patriotism by popularizing a native literary tradition.

substantially to Washington's canonization. The modern Washington persona, remembered as an extraordinary individual endowed with heroic capacities of perseverance, honesty, and military cunning, had not yet appeared. Crossing the Delaware and defeating the Hessians at Trenton, felling the cherry tree, surviving the winter at Valley Forge, offering the prayer at Valley Forge, throwing the silver dollar across the Potomac, commissioning the flag from Betsy Ross became the mythic measures of Washington's moral character as later nineteenth-century popularizers focused more on individual accomplishment and less on fidelity to ideology.[62] Even the few early national period lessons that acknowledged his military accomplishments (Washington as Cincinnatus) cited his joy in domestic and agricultural life and emphasized a diffidence for the role of warrior. "Agriculture, Or the Happy American Farmer" celebrated Washington the farmer and his ties to the hardy yeomen of the new republic.[63]

The importance ascribed to *Washington's character*, even more than his exploits, in the American founding story points to the importance of virtuous education as a primary element in patriotic development during the early national years. At the same time that cultural leaders of the post-revolutionary generation looked for emotional vehicles to transmit the political and military fervor of the 1770s to subsequent generations, they also began to link the success of the new republic to a number of specific social values—not incidentally, the very values they so energetically celebrated as Washington's crowning glories. As a direct corollary to Enlightenment philosophy and contemporary moral education, emulation of Washington not only honored the man, but it also offered endurance through divine favor for the nation that he symbolized.

OTHER AMERICANS, OTHER STORIES

Alternative voices to this patriotic story were heard in those few educators who called attention to the lives of those left out of this new middle-class America. The plight of Native Americans, characterized at once as "noble savages" and embittered enemies engaged in a war of cultural

---

[62] See Kammen, *Mystic Chords*, and Karal Ann Marling, *George Washington Slept Here: Colonial Revivals and American Culture* (Cambridge: Harvard University Press, 1988) for discussions of the popularization of Washington in the nineteenth and twentieth centuries.

[63] Although Washington's devotion to his rural domestic life was woven through most eulogies and speeches, two lessons focused on this theme alone: Daniel Adams, "Description of Mount Vernon," *Understanding Reader* (Dedham, Mass.: H. Mann and Co., 1816), 47–48, and Staniford, "Extract from a Poem, Entitled, 'Agriculture,' or, "Happy American Farmer," *Art of Reading*, 226–27.

annihilation, was one of the most obvious contradictions to popular patriotism's promise of freedom and liberty. A few other schoolbook lessons expressed toleration for Roman Catholics and Jews; at least in word, if not in practice, they made true the Constitution's promise of religious freedom. Yet all such counsel held fast to conceptions of the superiority of the Protestant faith and argued only for toleration as a tenet of a dominant Christianity.[64] Commentary on the status of women was even more restrictive. The schoolbooks uniformly decried as frivolous the activities of republican women who were depicted as wearing themselves out with card playing, novel reading, and other entertainments at the expense of their families and their own health. Conservative schoolbook authors warned the young ladies to return to the domestic circles of their grandmothers. A virtuous republican woman had but two life options: devotion to family, where her interest lay in securing the virtue of her husband, or dissipation, where the promised reward was future misery.[65]

Beside Native Americans, African-American slaves were the only cultural group acknowledged in the schoolbooks as holding a status contradictory to the prevailing patriotic vision. In popular lessons that appeared in two-thirds of the schoolbooks, educators registered a strong abolitionist voice.[66] For example, in a popular extract from William Cowper's *The Task* slavery was condemned for its violation of basic human, but not political, rights: "There is no flesh in man's obdurate heart/It does not feel for man." Racism was similarly denounced: "He finds his fellow guilty of a skin/Not colour'd like his own."[67]

Other antislavery lessons evoked the schoolbooks' romanticized treatment of Native Americans and sought to counter prejudice by depicting blacks as virtuous, productive members of society. One of the most popular of this genre, "The Generous Negro," told the "true story" of Joseph Rachel, a West Indian merchant who was a pillar of his community. Rachel's high moral character was demonstrated when he released a fellow (white) merchant from debt and offered him money to rebuild following a hurricane.[68] "A Family Conversation on the Slavery of the Negroes," recounted the inhumane conditions of the capture, transport,

[64] See Koch, "The Virtuous Curriculum," 355–59.

[65] Ibid., 454.

[66] Ibid., 405–12.

[67] Cowper's *The Task* was excerpted in Hubbard, "On Slavery," *American Reader*, 200–201; Murray, "Indignant Sentiments on National Prejudices, Slavery, Etc." *English Reader*, 200–201; Pierpont, "Slavery," *American First Class Book*, 181–83 [two lessons]; and Staniford, "Peace and Benevolence," *Art of Reading*, 234–35; quoted from Murray.

[68] Lindley Murray, "The Generous Negro," *Introduction to the English Reader* (New York: Collins and Co., 1826), 34–35; Picket, "The Generous Negro," *Juvenile Mentor*, 89–90.

sale, and labor of the Africans. Personal responsibility for the continuation of the practice was also introduced when children in the family pledged to forego the material comforts of their way of life now recognized as products of slave labor.[69] But the children's activism was discouraged by their father who explained the political and economic realities of slavery's persistence:

> Many persons of great talents and virtue, have made several fruitless attempts to obtain an act for the abolition of this trade. Men interested in its continuance have hitherto frustrated these generous designs; but we may rely upon the goodness of that Divine Providence, who cares for all creatures, that the day will come when their rights will be considered: and there is great reason to hope, . . . that the rising generation will prefer justice and mercy, to interest and policy.

It is left to Providence, not the workings of democratic government, to incite the "rising generation" to recognize the rights of African Americans. Perhaps most tellingly, the children were advised how to best cope with the status quo: use the "same principle of benevolence" that led to their "just indignation at the oppression of the negroes [sic]," to be "gentle towards your inferiors, kind and obliging to your equals, and in a particular manner condescending and considerate towards your domestics." Only the merest glimmer of a consciousness of equality emerges: "Requir[e] no more of [your domestics], than you would be willing to perform in their situation; instruct . . . them when you have the opportunity; sympathiz[e] in their afflictions; and promot[e] their best interests when you have the opportunity." Such a view virtually assured that the progress toward equal rights for African Americans was not connected to American patriotic will. The problem, like the fate of the nation, was left to divine dispensation: "Negro woman, who sittest pining in captivity, and weepest over thy sick child, though no one sees thee, God sees thee; though no one pities thee, God pities thee. Raise thy voice, forlorn and abandoned one; call upon him from amidst thy bonds, for assuredly he will hear thee."[70] As they had with Native Americans, the schoolbooks registered social protest on behalf of the rights of an oppressed minority, but their words evoked Christian mercy and romantic sentiment rather than the language of equal rights and individual freedom. They clearly prescribed a lowly socioeconomic status for blacks and others who were

[69] Murray, "A Family Conversation on the Slavery of the Negroes," *Introduction to the English Reader*, 71–74; Picket, "A Family Conversation on the Slavery of the Negroes," *Juvenile Mentor*, 206–8.

[70] All quotations from Murray, "A Family Conversation," *Introduction to the English Reader*, 71–74 passim.

assumed to be the social inferiors of educated Christian whites and left it to the will of God to change the situation.

Only a tiny minority of American educators addressed issues of political freedom without reference to conservative religious teaching. Milcah Moore, a Philadelphia Quaker (and the sole woman among the popular schoolbook compilers), published "A Dream," which envisioned humility and equality for all.[71] Two others, Daniel Staniford and John Hubbard, published "On the Liberty of the Press," which debated the line between "the liberty and licentiousness of the press" and proclaimed an unflagging egalitarianism in protecting the "good name" of a "virtuous man" even if it meant exposing an author "sanctified by high birth or exalted station" to "publick view, . . . to receive his sentence from a discerning publick."[72] This lesson, a rarity in the schoolbooks, directly addressed individual rights—that is, the absolute right of anyone (presumably white male) to equal protection under the laws of the new republic.

Issues of toleration and social reform were topics in only about seventy lessons among the more than two thousand in popular readers of the period, and the weight of the education these texts promoted was focused on the moral conduct of the individual, not political or patriotic issues. Prescriptions for specific moral action were not collective concerns; rather, they were seen as the rational outcome of individual behavior based on a thorough grounding in conservative Protestant ideology.

To modern Americans this patriotic story may seem both familiar and incomplete. If this was truly the symbolic legend that motivated a popular revolution and ensured the stability of the resulting republican government, why was so little said about citizens' rights? Where is the patriotism of Lincoln or Whitman grounded in equality and popular democracy? With African Americans, Native Americans, most white women, and landless white males excluded from the franchise and living in various states of dependency, this story, which supports the status quo yet speaks of liberty and freedom, reads as empty rhetoric today and surely must have seemed so to most Americans then.

But such was apparently not the case. With its stress on conformity to religious and civic values, its strong biblical overtones, messianic imagery, and paternalistic heroes such as Columbus and Washington, this was a patriotism for a different time and place. Although it rings hollow

[71] Milcah Martha [Hill] Moore, "A Dream," *Miscellanies Moral and Instructive* (Burlington [N.J.]: Neale and Kammerer, June 1796), 68–69.

[72] Hubbard, "On the Liberty of the Press," *American Reader*, 59–60; Staniford, "Liberty of the Press," *Art of Reading*, 143–44; quoted from Hubbard, p. 60.

today, this myth engendered patriotic feelings in a nation quite different from ours. Another patriotic vision—one that encompassed political rights for all, or respect for the culture of Native Americans, freedom for slaves, or greater toleration for political dissent or religious differences— would have been rooted in notions of individual rights among a populace of social and political equals. Instead, contemporary patriotism strictly limited individual rights to those land-holding white males who enjoyed the political participation guaranteed by the Revolution. They, in turn, as heads of households represented the extension of the *polis* to their social and economic dependents.

Patriotism in this society valued individual rights much less than like-mindedness. In the period that saw enactment of the Alien and Sedition Acts and suppression of Shay's Rebellion, the demonization of Tories and Benedict Arnold, schoolbook lessons condemned the ideas and irreligion of Thomas Paine and Voltaire.[73] With the remarkable exception of instances of divine intervention to the contrary, such as the American Revolution, individuals and nations alike were to find happiness in contentedly accepting the status quo because both self-interest and the common good were served through virtue and achieved in a hierarchically ordered universe through unity with the Almighty's great plan.

Where the French republicans had focused on the overthrow of the Church as the enemy of liberty, American political reformers as patriots took aim at only the English crown, leaving most social relationships and Protestant religious traditions intact. And for them patriotism, to the extent that it sustained the status quo, was an appropriate arena for their moral leadership. Like educational reformers of the Protestant Reformation or the Enlightenment, the patriots' aims for mass education were hegemonic and conservative: they looked to education to foster piety, civility, orderliness, patriarchy, and military preparedness.[74] Revolutionary as their mythic tale of American freedom sounded and, in fact, truly was, America's patriotism made sense to people in the early republic because they, like the republic itself, had deep roots in the ways of the much-reviled Old World.

In such a world, perpetuation of the nation seemed wholly dependent on a continuing application of the lessons of traditional Protestant morality infused with patriotic fervor:

[73] Voltaire was condemned, largely for deism, in Hubbard, "Singular Character of Voltaire, 1694–1778," *American Reader*, 61. Thomas Paine was the subject of a series of lessons against atheism in Abner Alden, "God's Justice in Punishing Sin" (Watson to Paine), *The Reader*, 3d ed. (Boston: J. T. Buckingham for Thomas and Andrews, 1805), 81; "Letter from Watson to Paine," 56; "The Redeemer" (Watson to Paine), 96; "Weight of Evidence" (Watson to Paine), 87–88.

[74] Graff, *Legacies*, 12–13, 178.

Let this sacred maxim receive the deepest impression upon our minds, that if avarice, if extortion, if luxury, and political corruption, are suffered to become popular among us, civil discord, and the ruin of our country will be the speedy consequence of such fatal vices. But while patriotism is the leading principle, and our laws are contrived with wisdom, and executed with vigor; while industry, frugality, and temperance, are held in estimation, and we depend upon public spirit and the love of virtue for our social happiness, peace and affluence will throw their smiles upon the brow of individuals; and our commonwealth will flourish; our land will become a land of liberty, and AMERICA an asylum for the oppressed.[75]

By using as a foundation a dramatic story of divine direction—their own ancestors' discovery and settling of the continent and their fight for political independence and social stability—the new nation's cultural leaders crafted a definition of American patriotism that involved moral and religious, as well as republican, principles. In this process the story of America took on mythic proportions that promised more—America as asylum for the world's oppressed—than it was prepared to deliver.

[75] Quoted from Bingham, "Extract from an Oration, Delivered àt Boston, March 5th, 1780, by Jonathan Mason, Jun., Esq.," *Columbian Orator*, 300. This was the final lesson in the *Orator*.

Chapter 2

"BLOOD BROTHERHOOD": THE RACIALIZATION

OF PATRIOTISM, 1865–1918

CECILIA ELIZABETH O'LEARY

A T THE END of the Civil War, the struggle to establish the primacy of one nation-state moved from the battlefield into the arena of political, economic, and cultural life. However, despite the Union triumph, national unity remained tenuous and fragmented. In this chapter I explore how organizations of self-conscious patriots sought sufficient cultural authority to define the language, symbols, and rituals of loyal Americanism. The two former enemies—the Grand Army of the Republic (GAR) in the North and the United Confederate Veterans (UCV) in the South—engaged in a process of cultural negotiation over four different but interrelated questions: First, will the "valor" of Confederate soldiers be memorialized by patriots? Second, whose interpretation of the Civil War and Reconstruction would be recognized as the official history? Third, will the broadening of democracy and racial equality articulated during the struggle to end slavery prevail against the resurgent white supremacy? And fourth, what role will Confederate symbols and rituals play within national life? Although patriotic culture might appear timeless and consensual, it requires an on-going negotiation of competing points of view and interests. Nations are held together not by their essential unity but through the articulation, always partial, of different forces. Rather than being "natural" or "God-given," nations are "imagined," patriotic traditions are "invented," and social forces struggle over which historical memories, symbols, and rituals will dominate national discourse.[1]

An earlier version of this article was delivered as a paper at the annual meeting of the Organization of American Historians, Anaheim, California, April 1993. For their helpful criticisms and suggestions, the author wishes to thank John Bodnar, Lydia Chavez, John Coski, Pete Daniel, Gaines Foster, David Glassberg, Michael Kammen, Michael Kazin, Harold Langley, Lawrence Levine, Waldo Martin, Stuart McConnell, Charles McGovern, Tony Platt, Mary Ryan, and the reviewers for this collection.

[1] For a fuller discussion of culture as a contested terrain, see Stuart Hall, "The Question of Cultural Identity," in *Modernity and Its Futures*, ed. Stuart Hall, David Held, and Tony

Less than fifty years after the bloodiest civil war of the nineteenth century, white Union and Confederate veterans declared themselves "brothers" once again. Their new unity came at the cost of abandoning Reconstruction and severing the link between the memory of the Civil War and the struggle for racial equality. Organized veterans moved away from the early republic's definition of patriotism, with its emphasis on citizen virtue and moral behavior, and toward the celebration of male warrior heroism. Although the language of patriotism continued to speak of democracy and equality, the glorification of battlefield deeds facilitated the reincorporation of Confederate heroism. By the 1913 anniversary of the Battle of Gettysburg and the Emancipation Proclamation, the racist terms of reconciliation were complete. When Woodrow Wilson arrived on July 4th to give the keynote speech, a Confederate veteran carrying the Stars and Bars and a Union veteran carrying the Stars and Stripes formed his honor guard. In his Gettysburg address, President Wilson congratulated "the Blue and the Gray" on having "found one another again as brothers and comrades, in arms, enemies no longer." Without any mention of the Emancipation Proclamation, Wilson praised the "blood and sacrifice of multitudes of unknown men" in their battle "to make a nation."[2] The inclusion of Confederate veterans as patriots in the "national brotherhood," however, had not been a foregone conclusion. As long as Reconstruction held, freedmen and women formed the backbone of patriotic celebrations in the South. For a brief historical moment, white and black supporters of racial justice had secured a significant voice in debates over the values of postwar America.

"SWEET LAND OF LIBERTY": RECONSTRUCTION AND THE BATTLE FOR AMERICA'S CONSCIENCE

At the end of the Civil War, black southerners emerged as the region's patriots. In the nineteenth century, black leaders and spokesmen represented a range of positions, but the majority was not ambiguous about identity and allegiance; they were both black and American. During the

McGraw (Cambridge: Polity, 1992); and "Notes on Deconstructing 'The Popular,'" in *People's History and Socialist Theory*, ed. Raphael Samuel (London: Routledge, 1981). See Benedict Anderson, *Imagined Communities: Reflections on the Origin and Spread of Nationalism*, rev. ed. (London: Verso, 1991). See Eric Hobsbawm, "Mass-Producing Traditions: Europe, 1870–1914," in *The Invention of Tradition*, ed. Eric Hobsbawm and Terence Ranger (Cambridge: Cambridge University Press, 1983). See Raymond Williams, *Keywords*, rev. ed. (London: Fontana Press, 1990), 87–93.

[2] Report of the Pennsylvania Commission, *Fiftieth Anniversary of the Battle of Gettysburg* (Harrisburg, Pa.: Wm. Stanley Ray, State Printer, 1913), 174–76.

Civil War, black abolitionists seized the ideological initiative and claimed the language and symbols of the American Revolution in the cause of their freedom. They believed that their liberation struggle would not only affect the future of slaves but would also purify American ideals and redeem America's destiny.[3] Patriotism carried a distinctive meaning for black and white defenders of Radical Reconstruction. The language of patriotism expanded traditional conceptions of willingness to die for one's country with more radical notions of social, political, and racial equality. Black leaders held America's republican values up to the nation as a mirror and warned that as long as slavery and inequality endured America would never be able to "raise her flag of liberty and spread it out unstained and uncontaminated for the world to look upon and admire."[4] Following emancipation, most black people refused to abandon their claim to an American nationality. "We are Americans," declared the citizens of Norfolk, Virginia. Recovering their history in the Revolutionary War, the black Virginians pointed out that a "colored man, Crispus Attucks," shed the "first blood."[5]

Probably at no other time during the nineteenth century would blacks consider themselves so fully American as they did during the early years of Reconstruction. Newly freed slaves created local holidays to celebrate President Lincoln's issuance of the Emancipation Proclamation. July 4th was important because it marked the political birth of the nation, but, to Frederick Douglass, emancipation promised to "put peace forever between the conscience and the patriotism of the people." Douglass predicted that January 1st, 1863, would become the "most memorable day in American Annals."[6] Local communities developed their own distinctive rituals by combining cultural elements from slave holidays, religious observances, and patriotic rituals for Freedom Day ceremonies. Their rituals reflected the myriad emotions slaves experienced upon hearing of their freedom—ranging from religious thanksgivings to exuberant social gatherings reminiscent of slaves' Christmas season holidays. Some communities borrowed the singing of a freedom anthem and the reading of a freedom document from ceremonies created by West Indians after their

[3] Leonard I. Sweet, *Black Images of America, 1784–1870* (New York: W. W. Norton & Co., 1976), 1–5.

[4] Nathaniel Paul to William Lloyd Garrison, *Liberator*, 12 April 1834, in Carter G. Woodson, ed., *The Mind of the Negro as Reflected in Letters During the Crisis, 1800–1860* (Washington, D.C.: Association of the Study of Negro Life and History, Inc., 1926), 170.

[5] "Equal Suffrage: Address from the Colored Citizens of Norfolk, Va., to the People of the United States," in *A Historic Publication*, ed. Maxwell Whiteman, no. 216 (Philadelphia, Pa, n.d.), 2, 8.

[6] Frederick Douglass, "January First, 1863," *Douglass' Monthly* (Rochester, N.Y.), January 1863, 769–70.

emancipation in 1834. Abolitionist songs such as "John Brown" and anthems such as "America" could be heard.[7]

Thomas Wentworth Higginson, a white Union commander of a black Civil War regiment, attended a freedom celebration on 1 January 1863. Higginson recalled:

> Just as I took and waved the flag, which now for the first time meant anything to these poor people, there suddenly arose, close beside the platform, a strong male voice (but rather cracked and elderly), into which two women's voices instantly blended, singing, as if by impulse that could no more be repressed than the morning note of the song-sparrow—
>
> > "My Country, 'tis of thee,
> > Sweet land of liberty
> > Of thee I sing!"[8]

Henry McNeal Turner, a leading black minister, shared the initial sense of optimism and anticipation. Speaking before a large gathering of freed slaves on Emancipation Day in 1866, Turner proclaimed that while in the past "every star was against us; every stripe against us, we can claim that protection of the stars and stripes. The glories of this faded escutcheon will ever bid us go free."[9] The assertion of citizenship rights and equal participation in the national culture, however, would not go unchallenged. Prophetic of future unrest, the Hamburg Massacre of South Carolina erupted in 1876 during the celebration of the July 4th centennial by the town's black militia. By the end of the rampage, Hamburg—once a stronghold of black Reconstruction power—lay ransacked with seven black Americans dead. The *Sumter True Southron* triumphantly announced: "We may not be able to carry the State at the ballot box, but when it comes to a trial of the cartridge box we do not entertain any doubt of the result."[10] Despite the governor's request for additional federal troops to restore public order, President Grant refused to comply and insisted that the state take sole responsibility for executing its laws.[11]

The language of patriotism continued to speak in universal terms of

[7] William H. Wiggins, Jr., *O Freedom! Afro-American Emancipation Celebrations* (Knoxville: University of Tennessee Press, 1987), xi, xix–xx, 34–35.

[8] Thomas Wentworth Higginson, *Army Life in a Black Regiment* (Boston: Fields, Osgood, & Co., 1870), 40.

[9] Henry McNeal Turner quoted in John Dittmer, "The Education of Henry McNeal Turner," in *Black Leaders of the Nineteenth Century*, ed. Leon Litwack and August Meier (Urbana: University of Illinois Press, 1988), 254–55.

[10] *Sumter True Southron*, July 1876, in *The Negro in Our History*, ed. Carter G. Woodson, (Washington, D.C.: Associated Publishers, 1922), 415–16.

[11] *The Daily Critic* (Washington, D.C.) 19 July 1876, 20 July 1876.

equality and democracy, but conflicts and divisions deepened along racial lines. The next year Reconstruction irrevocably ended with the inauguration of Rutherford B. Hayes and the subsequent withdrawal of Republican support for biracial government. Black Americans, forced out of the South's political life, largely commemorated patriotic holidays in their own communities. In 1883 the Supreme Court, by ruling the Civil Rights Act of 1875 unconstitutional, allowed white southerners to triumphantly claim that the "people of the United States have, by their suffrages, remitted to the Southern people, temporarily at least, control of the race question."[12] The Supreme Court also ruled that the equal protection clause of the Fourteenth Amendment applied only to states, thus denying federal protection to anyone who suffered racial discrimination. Once the obstacle of Reconstruction was removed, political and cultural space opened for building a New South that did not challenge the reassertion of white supremacy.

"THE REBELS ARE OUR COUNTRYMEN AGAIN": THE ARMY'S ROLE IN NATIONAL RECONCILIATION

The first signs of national reconciliation emerged during the Indian wars as the Army pursued a strategy of annihilation toward Plains Indians who refused to be forced onto reservations. Immediately on the heels of the Civil War, the U.S. government implemented a new policy of abolishing the Indian Country in order to clear the way for western expansion.[13] Within a month of General Custer's defeat in 1876 at the battle of Little Bighorn, some Confederate veterans volunteered to fight the new common enemy. "As this is the Centennial year of American independence," wrote a former Confederate commander from Kentucky, "I desire to let the world see that we who were once soldiers of the 'lost cause' are not deficient in patriotism." He went on to request that his congressional representative from Kentucky intervene on his behalf and offer President Grant the "services of a full regiment, composed exclusively of ex-Confederates to avenge Custer's death."[14] Other Confederates linked their demand for the removal of federal troops from the South with the need to fight Indian Wars more effectively in the West. Without the enthusiasm of a popular imperialism generated first by the Indian Wars and

[12] "In Black and White: A Reply to Mr. Cable," *The Century* 29, no. 6 (April 1885): 911.

[13] Russell F. Weigley, *The American Way of War: A History of the United States Military Strategy and Policy* (New York: Macmillan, 1973), 158–162.

[14] Letter from Wm. H. Rowan to Representative Thomas L. Jones, 9 July 1876, reproduced under the heading, "Noble Sentiments" in *The Daily Critic* (Washington, D.C.) 18 July 1876.

later dramatically consolidated during the Spanish-American War, the impetus for cultural reunification would have been significantly delayed. Combat against a new enemy laid the basis for southern support of national expressions of heroism, while expansion in war allowed the North to bask in the might of Union.

Just as war was pivotal in promoting male warrior heroism, Civil War officers assumed a critical role in promoting northern and southern reconciliation. Union generals, mostly trained at West Point, respected their former classmates and recent adversaries. Possibly only the memories of lost comrades kept them from acquiescing to President Johnson's pro-southern program for reunification and resisting congressional control of a more Radical Reconstruction. Officers trained at West Point formed a class apart from the rank and file, citizen-soldiers. At times ambivalent, they were much more prepared to resume past friendships developed at the academy and forged as comrades-in-arms during the Mexican-American War. Enlisted men, less conflicted by personal and professional relationships, maintained that loyalty to the Union, not valor, should receive the nation's respect.

The rituals accompanying the surrender of General Lee at Appomattox illustrate the shared culture of the officer corps. Horace Porter, a Civil War veteran who recorded his memories of that day, emphasized the pathos of Appomattox and the overtures of reconciliation made by Grant and his officers. When Grant began to commit the terms of surrender to writing:

> He looked towards Lee, and his eyes seemed to be resting on the handsome sword which hung at that officer's side. He said afterwards that this set him to thinking that it would be an unnecessary humiliation to require officers to surrender their swords, and a great hardship to deprive them of their personal baggage and horse, and after a short pause he wrote the sentence, "This will not embrace the sidearms of the officers, not their private horses or baggage."

For the first time, Lee showed a slight change in his demeanor and was "evidently touched by this act of generosity." Expressing different emotions from Grant's officers, Union troops began to fire salutes when news of the surrender reached them. Upon hearing this, Grant immediately sent orders for them to stop and cautioned the men that "the war is over, the rebels are our countrymen again."[15] The officer class closed ranks against demonstrations of a more popular rowdyism, but emotional demonstrations proved hard to contain.

By 1884, officers from both sides were ready to contribute to a series

[15] Horace Porter, "Grant's Last Campaign," *The Century* 35 no. 1 (November 1887): 145–52.

on war recollections that would appear during a three-year period in a popular illustrated magazine, *The Century*. The magazine attracted leading generals from both sides, including Grant and Sherman from the North and Beauregard and Johnston from the South. The series emerged out of its editors' entrepreneurial recognition that the public was ready for a dialogue among former enemies. The editors carefully chose the series' title, "Leaders and Battles," to signal that the magazine did not intend to address either the Emancipation Proclamation or the condition of freedmen. The decision met with great success, increasing the magazine's circulation by 100,000 within a year after the series began.[16]

The magazine featured dignified graphics of heroic generals and romanticized battle scenes. Images of soldiers marching under the Confederate battle flag presented a far cry from cultural representations of only twenty years earlier. At the war's end, gendered imagery and language lauded Union veterans for their masculine exploits as citizen-soldiers, while northern presses caricatured the leader of the Confederacy, Jefferson Davis, as a "President in Petticoats." Davis became the symbol of a feminized Confederacy.[17] Numerous songs, cartoons, and newspaper graphics depicted Davis dressed as a woman in flight before the triumphant advance of manly Yankees.[18] Though the nation praised women for their maternal affection and self-sacrifice, they were still denied the just rewards of citizenship owed to patriots because of their gender. No more demeaning insult could be made of Davis than to humiliate his manhood. Catchy tunes lampooned Davis's capture by describing how "just on the out-SKIRTS of a wood, his dainty shape was seen. His boots stuck out, and now they'll hang old Jeff in Crinoline!"[19]

The Century's editors believed that the time was ripe for reconciliation and condemned as public enemies anyone who attempted to "revive or trade upon the dead issues of the war."[20] Most white southerners mixed acceptance of national reunification with demands for southern autonomy around race relations. By emphasizing valor, rather than treason, white southerners provided the country with an interpretation of the Civil War that obfuscated their fundamental attack on the Union. Northern patriotic groups, who refused to concede the righteousness of fight-

[16] Stephen Davis, "A Matter of Sensational Interest: *The Century* Battles and Leaders Series," *Civil War History: A Journal of the Middle Period* 27, no. 4 (December 1981): 338–43.

[17] Nina Silber, *The Romance of Reunion: Northerners and the South, 1865–1900* (Chapel Hill: University of North Carolina Press, 1993), 29–37.

[18] A front-page graphic of Jefferson Davis dressed as a women appeared in *Frank Leslie's Illustrated Newspaper* (New York), 3 June 1865.

[19] "Jeff in Petticoats" (Chatham, N.Y.: H. De Marsan, n.d.). Song sheet on Jefferson Davis's capture is located in the Virginia Historical Society (Richmond, Va.).

[20] "Soldier and Citizen," *The Century* 30, no. 6 (October 1887): 950. "Let Us Have Peace!" *The Century* 29, no. 4 (February 1885): 638.

ing the war to preserve the Union, proved much more malleable when it came to recognizing the integrity of southern valor and endorsing a nostalgic view of the antebellum South. Officers again led the way. Once the federal government made the decision to recall Union troops from the South in 1877, officers from both sides began to appear at the growing number of Blue and Gray reunions. The occasion of Grant's funeral in 1885 testified to the increased willingness of Confederate officers to publicly endorse national unity. Leading generals from the Union and the Confederacy, reported *The Century*, stood shoulder to shoulder and "mingled their tears in a common grief."[21] At the dedication of Grant's Tomb in 1897, the elite Richmond Light Infantry Blues marched at the head of the contingents from Virginia, with the battalion of black troops bringing up the rear.[22]

The full exoneration of Confederate officers came with the onset of Spanish-American War when, for the first time since secession, the U.S. Army appointed former Confederates to its officer corps. Officers, among the most ready to promote a national dialogue, clearly gained from the expanding role of the military within society. But the most significant influence over negotiating the cultural terms of reunification came from rapidly growing patriotic and hereditary organizations who assumed enormous cultural power over national discourses during the 1890s.

"ONE COUNTRY, ONE FLAG, ONE PEOPLE, ONE DESTINY": PATRIOTIC ORGANIZATIONS AND NATIONAL RECONCILIATION

The victory of the North and the survival of the Union brought about a historic moment in which patriotic culture became a battleground for working out the dramatic implications of post–Civil War change. Between the 1880s and early 1900s, developments within patriotic organizations profoundly influenced how the nation came to see itself. While antebellum society largely turned its back on the past, the period following the 1876 centennial witnessed unprecedented efforts to memorialize past heroes, create symbols, and invent rituals that could stand for the nation. In contrast to the activist role played by the state in nations as diverse as Germany, France, and Japan, the development of patriotic culture in the United States was first initiated by organizations and individuals within civil society.[23]

[21] "North and South," *The Century* 30, no. 6 (October 1885): 965.

[22] Colonel John A. Cutchins, *Famous Command: The Richmond Light Infantry Blues* (Richmond, Va.: Garret & Massie, 1934), 199.

[23] Michael Kammen, *Mystic Chords of Memory: The Transformation of Tradition in American Culture* (1991; New York: Vintage Books, 1993), 290, 293–94.

Facing a heterogeneous and regionally divided nation, patriotic organizations in the North pursued a two-pronged strategy for creating a national community. On the one hand, they worked toward the long range goal of achieving "100 percent Americanism" among the immigrant working classes. But more immediately, they set about to create a transcendent patriotism capable of inculcating loyalty among a population not yet unified into a single nationality. Because the language and meanings of patriotism are subject to definition and redefinition, its torchbearers assumed key roles in the ideological debate over what it meant to be a loyal American.

Uneasy with leaving the mythology and rituals of patriotism to popular and regional constructs, patriotic groups like the Union veterans who formed the Grand Army of the Republic (GAR), dedicated themselves to gaining mass and official support for everything from anthems to holidays, but most important, they promoted enshrinement of the flag as the nation's most sacred symbol. The Grand Army presented themselves as "living testaments" of the immortal struggle to save the Union. Creating patriotic models for the twentieth century, Union veterans paraded on patriotic holidays beneath the tattered flags they had carried into battle. The Grand Army initially dedicated the "nation's Sabbath"—Memorial Day—to "those who sought to preserve the Union, and not those who sought to destroy it."[24]

Yet following the Spanish-American War, the inclusion of Confederate soldiers into official patriotic culture became apparent. In 1903, Confederates held services for their dead at Arlington National Cemetery—the nation's shrine to her martyrs.[25] By 1906, the GAR commander-in-chief revised the official meaning of Memorial Day. It was no longer to be used to demarcate Union veterans from the Confederacy; instead, the commander described the day's purpose in terms of weaving and blending the "peoples of this country, obliterating differences."[26] The Spanish-American War, he concluded, had generated a surge of nationalism that finally verified Lincoln's prediction that "the mystic chords of memory, stretching from every battlefield and patriot grave to every living heart and hearthstone all over this broad land, will yet swell the chorus of the

[24] Grand Army of the Republic (GAR), *Proceedings of the Thirteenth Annual Meeting of the National Encampment, Held at Albany, N.Y., June 17–18, 1879* (New York: Office of the Grand Army Gazette, 1879), 598.

[25] President McKinley believed that the federal government should assume responsibility for the care of Confederate soldiers' graves. Gaines M. Foster, *Ghosts of the Confederacy: Defeat, the Lost Cause, and the Emergence of the New South* (New York: Oxford University Press, 1987), 153–54.

[26] GAR, *Journal of the Fortieth National Encampment, Minneapolis, Minnesota, August 16th and 17th, 1906* (Philadelphia: Town Printing Company, 1906), 97.

Union." The commander encouraged his comrades to place flowers on the graves of former opponents in honor not of their cause but of their valor on the field of battle.[27]

In 1912, the United Daughters of the Confederacy (UDC) further dramatized the move toward cultural reconciliation when they decided to convene their annual convention outside of Dixie. Having assumed the mantel of preserving the "Lost Cause," these southern women came to the nation's capital to lay the cornerstone for a Confederate Monument in Arlington Cemetery. The Daughters of the American Revolution (DAR) invited their southern sisters, many of whom shared joint memberships, to hold their formal ceremonies at Independence Hall. The vice-president of the Daughters of the Confederacy spoke of their dual allegiance. As "Southern women, American women," she explained, they taught their children the "loftiest patriotism—to glory in, to honor and support the Stars and Stripes—yet fold close to their hearts and swear eternal allegiance to a blood-stained banner forever furled."[28]

President Taft agreed to be the featured speaker on opening night. To an overflowing crowd, Taft urged every northern son with "any spark of race pride" to rejoice in the nation's "common heritage of courage and glorious sacrifice." Confederate flags and the Stars and Stripes draped the hall, while immense bouquets of flowers sent from Confederate organizations and the White House greeted the DAR's guests. The U.S. Marine Band underscored themes of national unity by playing "Dixie" and the "Star Spangled Banner."[29] Among the songs notably absent was the familiar Civil War tribute to John Brown.

Initially, Grand Army veterans had been more willing to laud individual Confederates than accept rituals, symbols, or monuments that implied respect for the "Lost Cause."[30] However, in less than fifty years, the memory of the Civil War and the tenets of patriotism had been sufficiently revised to allow Confederates to be remembered as loyal sons rather than as traitors. Veterans from the Grand Army and the United Confederate Veterans laid the groundwork for this cultural reunification at the turn of the century. In the process, each also attempted to define the nation's patriotic "traditions." Four fundamental issues emerged as points of contention: status of Confederate soldiers, historical interpretations of the Civil War, political and veteran rights

[27] Abraham Lincoln, quoted in ibid., 97.

[28] Hilary A. Herbert, Chairman of the Executive Committee of the Arlington Confederate Monument Association, *History of the Arlington Confederate Monument at Arlington, Virginia* (United Daughters of the Confederacy, 1914), 22–23.

[29] *Ibid.*, 19–22.

[30] Stuart McConnell, *Glorious Contentment: The Grand Army of the Republic, 1865–1900* (Chapel Hill: University of North Carolina Press, 1992), 192.

for black Americans, and the place of Confederate symbols within the national culture.

First, Grand Army veterans grappled with the status of former Confederate soldiers: would they forever be denounced as traitors or recognized as brothers who fought with valor for what they believed to be right? Torn between sectional animosity and their ardent passion for Union, Grand Army veterans revisited the debate each year as they prepared to celebrate Memorial Day. Determined to recognize only the graves of Union soldiers, the GAR often clashed with Confederate veterans' intent to honor their dead. Long after the Civil War, Union veterans insisted that they did "not seek to commemorate valor, but patriotism."[31] For many years the northern ritual was known as Decoration Day, and the commemoration of the soldiers in gray was known as Confederate Memorial Day. Each side claimed credit for inventing the holiday. In fact, many southerners believed that General Logan of the Grand Army first got his idea for Memorial Day when he and his wife visited Petersburg in 1865. The often repeated story describes how the couple came upon women of the Confederate Memorial Association placing flowers on soldiers' graves.[32] Across the South, states legally set aside certain days for Confederate Memorial Day.

The exact origins of the day may never be known. What remains significant is how the story was used and remade in the cultural battle for legitimacy between the veterans of the Union and the Confederacy.[33] Celebrations of Memorial Day validated who would be remembered as national heroes and which interpretations of the Civil War would be handed down to future generations. Frederick Douglass understood the invented quality of tradition and endeavored to indelibly link Memorial Day to emancipation and thus mobilize historical memory in the struggle for civil rights.[34] For white southerners, public tribute to fallen comrades vindicated their belief that they were not traitors but part of the American tradition. For northern veterans, the impulse to include Confederates proved difficult. Having survived a war that sacrificed a generation of men, Grand Army veterans felt conflicted.

The acceptance of southern valor emerged slowly. As a selective mem-

[31] GAR, *Proceedings of the Thirteenth Annual Meeting of the National Encampment, June 17–18, 1870*, 598.

[32] George William Douglass, *The American Book of Days* (New York: H. W. Wilson, 1937), 230.

[33] See Wallace Evan Davies, *Patriotism on Parade: The Story of Veterans' and Hereditary Organizations in America, 1783–1900* (Cambridge: Harvard University Press, 1955), 217.

[34] David W. Blight, "'For Something beyond the Battlefield': Frederick Douglass and the Struggle for the Memory of the Civil War," *Journal of American History* 75, no. 2 (September 1988): 1156–78.

ory of the Civil War moved from pondering its causes to stressing moments on the battlefield, aging white veterans on both sides became more
receptive to looking at the communality of their experiences. During
campaigns for veteran pensions, the tendency to idealize citizen-soldiers
also led to judging former Confederates in a more favorable light than
noncombatants.[35] Angered by criticism of veteran campaigns for increased pensions, the editor of the leading northern veteran newspaper
wrote that the main enemy of the Union veteran was not the former
Confederate but the "selfish, cold-blooded, low-minded fellow, who
cared too little for anything outside of his own mean little interests to be
even an active rebel."[36]

Despite sentiments against those who had not fought, a deep ambivalence continued to divide veterans over the terms of reconciliation. A
magazine graphic picturing a Union general with a "bloody shirt"
wrapped around his eyes captured the tension. The caption sardonically
asked when he would stop blinding himself to the spirit of reconciliation:
could he not see "that the Gettysburg of 1887 is not the Gettysburg of
1863!"[37] When a Grand Army comrade proposed making the surrender
of the Confederate army at Appomattox and the freeing of the slaves into
a national holiday, a lengthy debate erupted. Opponents denounced the
proposed holiday on the grounds that it would foster sectional antago-
nism. "We fought for the Nation," declared one veteran, "not for the
North, and we want the Nation undivided in sentiment and loyal to a
common flag." Others in agreement raised the specter of hatred dividing
the United States as it had divided Europe for centuries.[38] Under the
slogan "one country, one flag, one people, one destiny," the 1897 encampment encouraged a rapprochement between northern and southern
veterans.[39] The full change from viewing Confederates as traitors to embracing them as brothers, however, necessitated compromises over the
writing of Civil War history.

The second area of contention centered on whose historical interpretation of the Civil War would be taught to succeeding generations. Grand
Army veterans vigorously demanded that the language and interpreta

---

[35] See Theda Skocpol, *Protecting Soldiers and Mothers: The Political Origins of Social Policy
in the United States* (Cambridge: Harvard University Press, 1992).

[36] "Our Worst Enemies," *National Tribune,* 13 January 1887.

[37] Political cartoon from *Puck* (n.d.), Photographic Files, "Symbols—The North, The
South, and Peace," in Women's History, 4.3, Political Division of the National Museum of
American History, Smithsonian Institution, Washington, D.C. (hereafter cited as NMAH
Political Division).

[38] GAR, *Journal of the Twenty-Sixth National Encampment, Washington, D.C., September
21st and 22nd, 1892* (Albany, N.Y.: S. H. Wentworth, 1892), 213–14.

[39] GAR, *Journal of the Thirty-First National Encampment, Buffalo, New York, August 25th,
26th, and 27th, 1897* (Lincoln, Nebr: State Journal Company, 1897), 55.

tion of the Civil War make it clear that southern "withdrawal" from the Union represented an insurrection.[40] On their part, southern authors insisted on depicting the war as a "heroic struggle for constitutional freedom." The United Confederate Veterans took particular offense at Civil War histories that referred to Confederates as rebels and traitors and lobbied textbook companies to replace the phrase "war of rebellion" with "Civil War between the states."[41] The writing of history became a consciously political act as textbook writers and their censors waged an ideological battle over which interpretation of the Civil War would prevail.

In several cases the Grand Army lobby forced publishers to make revisions. When a "Populist Commission" in Kansas adopted a text that the GAR felt was "devoid of patriotism," the local post wrote up its objections to *Taylor's Model School History* and distributed more than ten thousand copies to influential people throughout the state. New technologies in printing allowed GAR posts to reach far beyond the confines of their isolated communities. Typical of their knack for grass-roots organizing, the post sent two copies of the pamphlet to every teacher, county superintendent, legislative candidate, and prominent man and woman in Kansas. The post organized for five more years until the governor finally appointed a new textbook commission favorable to the Grand Army point of view.[42] The spread of public education added urgency to debates over which historical interpretations were to be taught. Before 1860 only six states required the study of history, but with general approval for tax-supported public education following the Civil War, legislation aimed at controlling textbooks appeared in numerous states. By 1900 twenty-three states had enacted laws requiring the study of history.[43]

As vehement as the northern patriots, the United Confederate Veterans demanded that southern teachers not be expected to "instruct children that their fathers were traitors and rebels."[44] Agitation for a southern viewpoint in history textbooks predated the Civil War when southerners, alarmed by teachers from the abolitionist North, launched a movement for "home education."[45] The education campaign not only allowed Confederate patriotic societies to counter northern condemnations of the South, but it also served as a vehicle to bolster the embattled status of southern patricians against the challenge of discontented black

[40] GAR, *Journal of the Twenty-Sixth National Encampment*, 207.

[41] Bessie Louise Pierce, *Public Opinion and the Teaching of History in the United States* (New York: Alfred A. Knopf, 1926), 149.

[42] GAR, *Journal of the Thirty-Sixth National Encampment, Washington, D.C., October 9th to 10th, 1902* (Minneapolis, Minn.: Kimball Stofer Co, 1902), 252–53.

[43] Pierce, *Public Opinion*, 13, 14–16.

[44] "Patriotic School Histories," *Confederate Veteran* 5, no. 9 (September 1897): 450, 146.

[45] Pierce, *Public Opinion*, 136–37.

and white agrarians. Linking the need for white supremacy with the lessons from the antebellum social order, southern historians hoped to perpetuate Old South values among a new generation.[46] Organized along similar lines to the Grand Army of the Republic, Confederate veterans worked at the national, state, and local levels to ensure that white southern teachers taught from southern texts. The passage of uniform textbook laws in states throughout the South greatly aided their work.[47] Using their gender as a sword more than a shield, the Daughters of the Confederacy drew upon their moral status as mothers to wage a relentless campaign for statewide adoption of histories "just and true" to the "Lost Cause."[48]

Negotiation of a mutually acceptable interpretation of the Civil War did not begin to emerge until professional historians at the turn of the century sought a consensus around a "usable past." Most southern historians grudgingly accepted the Grand Army's demand that the unconstitutionality of secession be recognized. Northern historians, confident that a pro-Union view was correct but increasingly influenced by Social Darwinism, found common ground with their southern colleagues in a shared racism and willingly made concessions around softening—even romanticizing—their pictures of slavery. They condemned Reconstruction for its "excesses" and expressed admiration for General Lee.[49] These patently racist interpretations would not be significantly challenged until the 1930s when W.E.B. Du Bois condemned the degeneration of history into "lies agreed upon." Far from the depiction of Reconstruction leaders as scoundrels whose corruption led to their failure, Du Bois argued that both the North's and the South's fears of black success fueled white reaction.[50]

Local and state organizations from North and South continued their textbook campaigns even after the GAR and the UCV shifted their organization priorities to other projects. By 1904, the national Grand Army of the Republic concluded that their special commission on textbooks had satisfactorily met its objectives.[51] In the years following the Spanish-

---

[46] Fred Arthur Bailey, "The Textbooks of the 'Lost Cause': Censorship and the Creation of Southern State Histories," *The Georgia Historical Quarterly* 75, no. 3 (Fall 1991): 508–11.

[47] Pierce, *Public Opinion*, 163.

[48] UDC, *Constitution of the United Daughters of the Confederacy, 1903* (n.p., n.d.), located in the Virginia State Library and Archives, Richmond, Va.

[49] Peter Novick, *That Noble Dream: The "Objectivity Question" and the American Historical Profession* (Cambridge: Cambridge University Press, 1988), 74–78; Ernst Breisach, *Historiography: Ancient, Medieval and Modern* (Chicago: University of Chicago Press, 1983), 261.

[50] W.E.B. Du Bois, *Black Reconstruction in America, 1860–1880: An Essay Toward a History of the Part Which Black Folk Played in the Attempt to Reconstruct Democracy in America, 1860–1880* (1935; New York: Athenaeum, 1970), 714.

[51] GAR, *Journal of the Thirty-Eighth National Encampment Boston, Massachusetts, 17th and 18th August, 1904* (Chicago: M. Umbdenstock, 1904), 67.

American War, the United Confederate Veterans also slackened their vigilance. "We do not fear the bookmaker now," declared the Confederate veterans in 1910.[52] Several factors led both organizations to conclude that they had accomplished their mission. The Spanish-American War had considerably lessened feelings of sectional recrimination, while publishing companies, mindful of the exigencies of a national market, successfully developed separate lines of textbooks that could meet the scrutiny of the Grand Army in the North and the Confederate Veterans in the South.

The third area of debate, political and veteran's rights for black Americans, proved the most contentious. As white southerners and northerners moved closer to reunification, agitation by black Americans for political rights forced the Grand Army to take a position on whether "whiteness" would define the nation's patriotic brotherhood. On issues of race relations, the Grand Army verbally committed itself to equality by insisting that it would never close its doors to "any deserving comrade on account of his nationality, creed or color." But in practice, the campaign of white veterans who settled in the South to impose a "color line" eventually prevailed. Although small numbers of black veterans joined white veterans in northern Grand Army posts, in southern areas with large black populations the development of separate posts became the general pattern. Following the end of Reconstruction, Union veterans began to organize again, but they refused to jeopardize their positions by supporting integration. Black veterans launched vehement protests over their exclusion from southern Grand Army departments. At first, the alliance between black veterans and their white northern and border state allies held. In 1891, a national Grand Army committee adamantly insisted: "It is too late to divide on the color line. A man who is good enough to stand between the flag and those who would destroy it when the fate of the nation was trembling in balance is good enough to be a comrade in any Department of the Grand Army of the Republic."[53]

A white GAR veteran from Louisiana passionately retorted that if his department opened its doors to black members, "there would be eight or ten or fifteen white men, perhaps, in a Post, perhaps twenty-five and there would be two or three hundred colored men, and it would be the tail wagging the dog." Fearing the mood of the encampment might shift,

[52] United Confederate Veterans (UCV), *Minutes of the Twentieth Annual Meeting and Reunion of the United Confederate Veterans, 1910* (Camp ST., New Orleans: Press of Schumert & Warfield, 1910), 101.

[53] GAR, *Journal of the Twenty-Fifth National Encampment (Silver Anniversary), Grand Army of the Republic, Detroit, Michigan, August 5th, 6th and 7th* (Rutland, Vt.: Tuttle Company, 1891), 250.

a black veteran took to the floor and condemned the hypocrisy of having been comrades and brothers in the field of battle but not in times of peace.[54] In the end, the 1891 national encampment officially rejected the imposition of a color line. Nonetheless, the white Grand Army posts in Louisiana and Mississippi remained unconvinced and unmoved.[55]

At the 1892 Grand Army encampment, the struggle over whether "whiteness" would become a criterion for membership again caused heated debates. Despite the GAR again taking a strong position against the imposition of a color line, white southern posts simply ignored the national policy against segregation. Throughout the 1890s, southern veterans engaged the national Grand Army in a battle of wills. Although the organization remained officially open to all veterans, an increasing number of white members sanctioned or grew indifferent to the racialization of patriotism. Some white veterans turned their undivided attention to expanding veteran pensions; others shared racial resentments toward new immigrants and sympathized with their southern comrades' predicament; still others revised wartime memories to allow for feelings of camaraderie to former foes as they grew older. Grand Army veterans, after all, based their brand of patriotism on the belief that they had preserved the Union, not radically restructured the nation. The movement for reconciliation between the white North and the white South—in which the valorization of battlefield deeds replaced patriotic appeals for democracy and equality articulated during the struggle to end slavery—overwhelmed the alliance between black veterans and their white allies.

Nonetheless, black GAR posts remained active, organizing Emancipation Day ceremonies, holding patriotic concerts in their churches, and decorating their comrades' graves on Memorial Day.[56] On the national level, black posts marched at Grand Army encampments, and Frederick Douglass periodically addressed veterans on emancipation's central place in the war's legacy.[57] At one of the first observances of Memorial Day, Douglass declared:

> We are sometimes asked, in the name of patriotism, to forget the merits of this fearful struggle, and to remember, with equal admiration, those who struck at the nation's life, and those who struck to save it—those who fought for slav-

[54] Ibid., 259–62, 156–57.

[55] Wallace E. Davies, "The Problem of Race Segregation in the Grand Army of the Republic," *Journal of Southern History* 12 (August 1947): 365–66.

[56] "Our Emancipation Day: The Celebration Proposed," *New York Freeman*, 13 December 1884; "Freedman's Natal Day Proudly Celebrated," *The Savannah Tribune*, 6 January 1900; "Veterans Pay Tribute to Their Honored Dead," *The Afro-American Ledger*, 31 May 1913; "Colored Veterans Hold Reunion," *Indianapolis Recorder*, 10 May 1913; "Program for G.A.R. Reunion," *Indianapolis Recorder*, 17 May 1913.

[57] Stuart McConnell, *Glorious Contentment*, 213.

ery, and those who fought for liberty and justice. I am no minister of malice. I would not strike the fallen. I would not repel the repentant, but may my right hand forget its cunning . . . if I forget the difference between the parties to that terrible, protracted and bloody conflict.[58]

Until he died, Frederick Douglass insisted that the Civil War was a "war of ideas, a battle of principles . . . a war between the old and the new, slavery and freedom."[59] While the Grand Army popularized Memorial Day and an interpretation of the Civil War as a battle to preserve the Union, black Americans emphasized the Emancipation Proclamation.

The GAR used a language of consensus, but beneath claims to a universal and inclusive Americanism, racial divisions deepened. The United Confederate Veterans played a critical role in negotiating cultural terms favorable to the white South. Many northerners—disturbed by the growing number of new immigrants whom they regarded as belonging to inferior races—were more than prepared to turn society's "race problem" back to the South. Heartened by pro-southern sentiments, the *Confederate Veteran* reprinted an article from *The Ladies' Home Journal* that praised the South as "the heart of America." Between tyranny and anarchy, read the article, the South remains a place where "men and women are guided in their action by wholesome sentiment, where people live righteously, where the best of our customs are perpetuated," and "where our own language is spoken by all."[60]

The fourth disputed issue, the place of Confederate symbols within national culture, generated passionate debate. Initially, Grand Army veterans adamantly refused to march next to southern veterans still in Confederate uniforms or carrying the Stars and Bars. Emotions ran high on both sides as Confederates lobbied for the return of their battle flags stored in a federal facility with other enemy flags captured by the United States and dating to the War of 1812. Confederate Captain McCarthy argued that the Stars and Bars was not a symbol of the Confederacy, but simply the flag of the Confederate soldier—the "unstained banner of a brave and generous people whose deeds have outlived their country." As such, he continued, "it should not share in the condemnation which our cause received, or suffer from its downfall." In a nation traditionally lacking formal symbols, veterans from each side turned to their tattered banners and infused them with sacred meanings. Confederate veterans re-

[58] Frederick Douglass, "Address at the Graves of the Unknown at Arlington," Arlington, Va., 30 May 1871, Frederick Douglass Papers, reel 14, Manuscript Division, Library of Congress, Washington, D.C. (hereafter cited as Douglass Papers, Library of Congress).

[59] Frederick Douglass, "Speech in Madison Square, New York, Decoration Day, 1878," reel 15, Douglass Papers, Library of Congress.

[60] "The Heart of America," *Confederate Veteran* 3, no. 12 (December 1895): 354–55.

fused to accept cultural defeat and sustained a Confederate tradition in spite of the South's reincorporation into the United States.

"THE LOST CAUSE": CONSTRUCTING A CONFEDERATE TRADITION IN THE NEW SOUTH

Beginning in the late 1880s, at the same time that the Grand Army began to reach the zenith of its membership, a coalition of middle-class forces breathed new life into the Confederate movement. Empowered by the removal of federal troops from the South and the end of national support for Radical Reconstruction, the United Confederate Veterans attracted a mass following. They pressed for sectional reconciliation and in turn demanded northern acknowledgment of southern heroism. The movement, led by a town-based middle class, recognized the benefits of economic reintegration and mobilized veterans of all classes in affirming loyalty to the southern past as they offered new visions of the future.[61] Patriotic and commercial concerns easily merged as southern cities in search of urban renewal saw that an active Confederate culture also meant added revenue. Ready to capitalize on the awakened patriotism, real estate interests and banks promoted building Confederate statues on Monument Avenue in Richmond, Virginia, when all that existed was farm land and maps of vacant lots promising a boon to the local economy.[62]

Unlike the period of the Civil War, the revitalized spread of Confederate monuments and rituals neither resurrected the demand for independence nor served as a basis for rebellion. Instead, the Confederate movement created a model of social order that ritualistically affirmed social unity and deference to authority. Alarmed by threats to white supremacy during Reconstruction, challenged by the revolt of farmers in the Populist movement, and determined to silence the demands of a militant labor force, the United Confederate Veterans hoped that a redefined Confederate culture could mobilize loyalty and defuse competing allegiances.[63]

The United Confederate Veterans believed that only by becoming legitimate members of the nation could they be left alone to handle race

[61] Foster, *Ghosts of the Confederacy*, 112, 108, 80.

[62] Real estate map of projected lots on each side of what was to become Monument Avenue, The Valentine: Museum of the Life and History of Richmond, Virginia (hereafter cited as The Valentine). The intersection of commerce and the construction of the Confederate tradition is also readily evident in the pages of advertisements found in *The Official Souvenir of the Dedication of the Monument to General Robert E. Lee* (Richmond: R. Newton Moon & Co., n.d.), The Valentine.

[63] Foster, *Ghosts of the Confederacy*, 86–87.

relations and preserve the memory of the Confederacy. Broad enough to accommodate a spectrum of viewpoints and interests, veterans swore allegiance to the Stars and Stripes without undermining a more visceral loyalty to the "Lost Cause." Such ambivalent sentiments characterized much of the invention of Confederate traditions. Across the South communities erected monuments to southern generals and privates, thousands participated in Confederate Memorial Days, and cities enthusiastically embraced annual reunions of the United Confederate Veterans.

In cities such as Richmond, Raleigh, Columbia, Atlanta, Tallahassee, Montgomery, Jackson, Little Rock, and Baton Rouge, statues dedicated to Confederate soldiers could be found gracing the grounds of state houses. In the legislative halls hung portraits of Confederate officers painted by the best artists and displayed in the most prominent places. Confederate swords and battle flags were also tenderly preserved in glass cases where everybody could see them.[64] At the dedication of a monument in South Carolina to the Confederate dead, a military demonstration of twenty companies (more than a thousand men) and an audience of eight thousand attested to the vitality of Confederate culture.[65]

Parallel to the creation and consolidation of a national patriotism, Confederate symbols and rituals persisted as part of an autonomous regional culture. The "Lost Cause," never just an idea, gained added substance from the stories, songs, paintings, monuments, and statues generated by the United Confederate Veterans. Although the Confederacy lasted only four years, each succeeding generation used and redefined the relics of Confederate culture. Typical of grass-roots organizing in the 1890s, Sumner A. Cunningham, founder of the *Confederate Veteran* magazine, organized fund-raising drives to raise money for memorials to Sam Davis, the "Boy Hero of the Confederacy." Virtually unknown, the legend of Sam Davis grew as veterans presented him to the South's youth as an example of the "courage and firmness of the Confederate soldier element." Captured by Union troops, Davis was hanged rather than reveal Confederate secrets.[66] Strikingly similar to statues of Sam Davis, many southern towns erected statues of private Confederate soldiers with one leg bent and apparently at ease. A model of propriety and the new social

[64] "A Question of 'Offense,'" *The National Tribune*, 23 June 1887.

[65] "The Lost Cause," *The National Tribune*, 18 June 1883.

[66] Tucker Hill, *Victory in Defeat: Jefferson Davis and the Lost Cause* (Richmond, Va.: The Museum of the Confederacy, 1865), 6–7; "Monuments to the Dead" (United Daughters of the Confederacy, 1914) in *Historical Records of the United Daughters of the Confederacy, Scrapbooks*, 8, compiled by Mildred Lewis Rutherford of Athens, Ga., the historian-general of the United Daughters of the Confederacy, 1911–1916, The Museum of the Confederacy, Richmond, Va. (hereafter cited as The Museum of the Confederacy).

order? Yes, but the casual stance belies a soldier with arms crossed in the quiet defiance of Sam Davis.

Today, memorials to the "Lost Cause" remain, with hundreds of Confederate statues still gracing town squares. In 1889, the Alexandria UCV erected a statue featuring a soldier with his back to the national capital. Rather than looking North, the soldier purposely faces what used to be the Confederate capital in Richmond, Virginia. A substantial contribution for the erection of the statue came from a Confederate commander who donated his government pension from services rendered in the Mexican-American War.[67]

"No Northerners, No Southerners, but Americans All": Popular Imperialism and National Reconciliation

The experience of a new war in which all regions could assert their American-ness against a Spanish and later Philippine "other" affirmed the power of national unity and provided the two veteran movements with dramatic opportunities for reconciliation. The nation's opinion of whether to go to war with Spain over the "liberation" of Cuba had been divided until the sinking of the Maine in the port of Havana on February 15, 1898. The mass presses declared the explosion a direct assault by Spain and agitated for retribution. In April, President McKinley asked Congress to use the Army and Navy to secure Cuba's freedom from Spain. Hearst's *New York Journal* printed full-page images of the Stars and Stripes with headlines announcing: WE'RE FIGHTING FOR HUMANITY, FREEDOM. SHOW YOU'VE NO OTHER FLAG. CUT THIS OUT. DECORATE YOUR HOME.[68] Across the country tens of thousands businessmen, labor associations, and college students organized their own regiments and volunteered their services. States mobilized National Guard units even before receiving an official call to duty. Protective of its position, a fierce rivalry broke out between the Regular Army and National Guard enthusiasts over who would be used in the assault and who would be left behind.[69]

Though most were now too old to reenlist, both Union and Confederate veterans volunteered to march against the "Spanish oppressors." Former Confederates once again served as high-ranking officers. President McKinley made a calculated decision to court the South by awarding

[67] James M. Goode, *The Outdoor Sculpture of Washington: A Comprehensive Historical Guide* (Washington, D.C.: Smithsonian Institution Press, 1974), 214.

[68] *New York Journal*, 1 May 1898.

[69] Graham A. Cosmas, *An Army for Empire: The United States Army in the Spanish-American War* (Columbia: University of Missouri Press, 1971), 93–94.

major generals' commissions to Joseph Wheeler of Alabama and Fitzhugh Lee of Virginia. Intent on increasing southern support for his administration and eager to demonstrate that sectional animosity was a thing of the past, McKinley also awarded numerous brigadier generals' stars to Confederate veterans of less prominence.[70]

McKinley's appointments enthused the South, and applications poured into recruitment offices for the newly organized volunteer army. Regiments from all the southern states filled their quotas quickly, and their numbers compared in strength to units raised in the North, East, and West.[71] Theodore Roosevelt welcomed southern recruits to the Rough Riders—including former Harvard classmates from Virginia and hardened frontier fighters from the Texas Rangers.[72] The military set up camps in the South and suddenly places like Chickamauga Park (Georgia), Huntsville (Alabama), and Tampa (Florida) became meeting grounds for soldiers from the North and the South, as well as the all-black regiments.[73] A martial spirit infused popular culture with thrilling stories of combat. Advertisements in support of the war tax appeared on everything from sleeping car tickets to pieces of chewing gum stamped with "Remember the Maine." When the Virginia troops set out from Richmond, the Lee and Pickett Camps of Confederate Veterans cheered the southern troops, and thousands lined the streets to bid them farewell. The Richmond Blues, now made up of the sons of Confederate veterans, marched to their camp in Florida.[74]

Northern and southern brigades mixed for the first time since before the Civil War in divisions of the volunteer army. Major-General Joseph Wheeler commanded brigades from states as diverse as Arkansas, Alabama, Florida, Kentucky, New York, Tennessee, and Wisconsin.[75] In the North, school children recited "The War Ship Dixie":

[70] Ibid., 93, 149.

[71] Office of the Adjutant-General of the Army, *Correspondence Relating to the War With Spain and Conditions Growing out of the Same Including the Insurrection in the Philippine Islands and the China Relief Expedition, Between the Adjutant-General of the Army and Military Commanders in the United States, Cuba, Porto Rico, China, and the Philippine Islands, From April 15, 1898, to July 30, 1902* (Washington: Government Printing Office, 1902), 1: 583–87.

[72] Theodore Roosevelt, *The Rough Riders* (New York: Scribner's Sons, 1902), 20–21, 32.

[73] Office of the Adjutant-General of the Army, *Correspondence Relating to the War With Spain*, 509–49.

[74] D. D. Christian and W. Asbury, *Richmond and Her Past* (1912; Spartanburg, S.C.: The Reprint Company, 1973) 458–60; Photo, "The Richmond Blues—The American-Spanish War—1898 onto Jacksonville, Fla.," Photo Files, Groups: Parades Military, The Valentine.

[75] Office of the Adjutant-General of the Army, *Correspondence Relating to the War With Spain*, 538–39.

THEY'VE named a cruiser "Dixie"—
that's what the papers say—
An' I hears they're goin' to man her with
the boys that wore the gray;
Good news! It sorter thrills me . . .[76]

In a little less than three months, Spain agreed to sign a peace treaty. "VICTORY!!" declared the *New York Journal* above the wings of an enormous eagle. "COMPLETE! GLORIOUS! THE MAINE IS AVENGED!"[77] The Grand Army rejoiced that the war not only "resulted in arousing the patriotism of our people to the highest conceivable point, but has had the effect of bringing the people of all sections of the country into the most harmonious of relations."[78] Southern newspapers praised Spanish-American War officers, such as Virgil Cook, William Montgomery, and Keller Anderson, for bringing "honor to the whole country, and eminently so in representing the South." The *Confederate Veteran* praised Montgomery for having impeded the advance of Grant's army during the Civil War and then leading the revolution that made it "possible for the white people to redeem Mississippi in 1875." The magazine recognized Colonel Anderson for having survived three wounds during the Civil War before quelling the "mobs" during the "mining troubles" of Coal Creek, Tennessee, between 1891 and 1893.[79] New South heroes stood squarely in the tradition of the prejudices of the old.

Though the nation briefly extolled black soldiers as American heroes during the summer of 1898, the war did not result in any new enthusiasm for expanding the civil rights of black Americans. Instead, the war reinforced racism at home as the nation basked in assuming the "white man's burden." Geo. W. Prioleau, a chaplain in the black Ninth Cavalry, wrote to the *Cleveland Gazette* about the difference in reception given white soldiers and the black members of his own unit. Upon arriving in Kansas City, Missouri, the townspeople invited the white First Cavalry into their homes and furnished them with free meals in the local restaurants. The Ninth Cavalry, whose members had "returned home with victory perched upon their country's banner," were not even allowed to stand up to get a bite to eat at the restaurant counters. "You can call this American

[76] Hon. James Rankin Young, comp., *Reminiscences and Thrilling Stories of the War by Returned Heroes Containing Vivid Accounts of Personal Experiences by Officers and Men* (Chicago: C. W. Stanton Company, 1899), 531.

[77] *New York Journal*, 2 May 1898.

[78] GAR, *Journal of the Thirty-Second National Encampment of the Grand Army of the Republic, Cincinnati, Ohio, September 8th and 9th, 1898* (Philadelphia: Town Printing Company, 1898), 193.

[79] "Confederates Commanding U.S. Regiments," *Confederate Veteran* 6, no. 8 (August 1898): 365–67.

prejudice," wrote Prioleau, but "I call it American hatred."[80] Despite exuberant claims to the triumph of a national spirit, internal divisions and racial boundaries limited those who were recognized as loyal Americans.

Typical of editorial assessments of the war, the *Atlanta Constitution* concluded that it had erased regional divisions and proved that a "national spirit" could "conquer the world in peace, and if need be, hold the world at bay in war."[81] However, reconciliation had its limits. A large number of United Confederate Veterans members took particular offense when, following the Spanish-American War, their organization's historical committee recommended that the U.S. government keep captured or surrendered Confederate flags. "Confederate veterans are unquestionably loyal to this government," countered an enraged veteran, "but they are not satisfied to have it keep our flags." The time has come, he continued, for the North to stop cherishing "trophies" of war. "We love our relics, and we want to keep them ourselves." Others criticized their history committee's report for excessive "fraternalism."[82] Confederate veterans, while willing to show loyalty to the national flag, were not prepared to "surrender their affection" for their Confederate flags.[83]

Each attempt by the United Confederate Veterans to have the United States return captured Confederate flags created a massive public outcry from the Grand Army.[84] However, in the jingoistic aftermath of the Spanish-American War, Congress finally approved the return of the flags without any public opposition.[85] The return of the flags represented not only the new alliance but also popular acceptance of a rewritten Civil War history in which individual valor was separated from the "Lost Cause." Not unlike the cultural adjustments following the Vietnam War, the nation attempted to heal its divisions by separating individual soldiers from the larger political context in which they had fought. No longer held as emblems of treason, it was now left to the white South to determine the Stars and Bars' ideological significance.

In 1899 monuments to the Blue and the Gray began to be erected. The valor of Kentuckians from both Confederate and Union armies was com-

[80] Willard B. Gatewood, Jr., *"Smoked Yankees" and the Struggle for Empire Letters from Negro Soldiers, 1898–1902* (Fayetteville: University of Arkansas Press, 1987), 29, 44–45; George W. Prioleau, Ninth Cavalry to *The Gazette* (Cleveland), 22 October 1898; reprinted in Gatewood, *"Smoked Yankees,"* 82–84.

[81] GAR, *Journal of the Forty-Second National Encampment, Toledo, Ohio, September 3rd and 4th, 1908* (Kansas City, Mo.: John C. Bovard, 1908) 169.

[82] *Confederate Veteran* 7, no. 6 (June 1899): 246.

[83] "The Confederate Flag," *Confederate Veteran* 3, no. 12 (December 1895): 353–54.

[84] GAR, *Journal of the Thirty-Second National Encampment, September 8th and 9th, 1898*, 49–50.

[85] Foster, *Ghosts of the Confederacy*, 154.

memorated on battlefields like Chickamauga. The Kentucky monument dramatized the reunion of brothers by sculpting a Union and Confederate flag crossed, with the staff of each flag grasped in the claws of an American eagle.[86] By 1910, the GAR commander-in-chief declared that the Spanish-American War had been worth the cost because it had united the North and South. "We only needed a common danger to arouse our people," he explained. "No section of our country responded to the call to arms more readily or more enthusiastically than the young men from Dixie." Participation in the war served as the litmus test for judging southern "loyalty and devotion" to the nation. "From that date," the commander concluded, "we had a new Union, no Northerners, no Southerners, but Americans all."[87]

"TO MAKE A NATION": RENEGOTIATING THE MEMORY OF THE CIVIL WAR

After the patriotic outpouring of the Spanish-American War faded, entrepreneurial capitalists, eager to expand national markets, advertised their products in ways that could appeal to both northern and southern audiences. Businesses as diverse as publishers of textbooks and dime novels, to producers of sheet music and flag manufacturers agreed that what was good for business was in the national interest. Widely read magazines and graphics on music sheets began to include General Robert E. Lee among their listing of "American heroes."[88] Flag companies, also eager to capitalize on national sales, advertised "flags of our country" alongside "Confederate flags." The Annin Company, founded in 1847 and the first large-scale flag manufacturer, advertised its firm as "Old Glory Corner" with a front-page photo of its factory flying American flags from all four stories. Yet, in its promotion booklet the badges and colors of Grand Army posts are followed by pages advertising "hand embroidered silk stars" for Confederate flags. On pages featuring "patriotic novelties," Irish-American flag bows appear next to "Confederate Bows—Red & White." And on opposite pages revolutionary flags with

[86] United States Department of the Interior National Park Service, Chickamauga-Chattanooga National Military Park, "National Registrar of Historic Places Inventory, Structure #776, Kentucky State Monument," 1.

[87] GAR, *Journal of the Forty-Fourth National Encampment, Atlantic City, New Jersey, September 22d and 23d, 1910*, 66–67.

[88] Graphic on cover of Jos. J. Kaiser, "March American Heroes" (New York: Jos. J. Kaiser Music Co., 1904), Warshaw Collection, 9.3., Campaign Objects, 1900–1908, Archives Center of the National Museum of American History, Smithsonian Institution, Washington, D.C. (hereafter cited as Archives Center).

the icon of the rattle snake and the motto, "Don't Tread On Me" appear, without intended irony, next to Confederate battle flags.[89] Advocates of "100 percent Americanism" who were dismayed during World War I at the depth of competing loyalties, would have found multiple allegiances existing all along in the catalogue pages of the Annin Flag Company.

In 1912, white southerners felt particularly vindicated as thousands gathered in the nation's capital to cheer the swearing-in of a southern son, President Woodrow Wilson. From the crowd, rebel yells and strains of "Dixie" could be heard.[90] During the following summer, veterans gave the nation a moving image of old men in Blue and Gray once again on the fields of Gettysburg—this time for a joint commemoration of the fiftieth anniversary of the battle. Daily newspapers reported on the "Peace Jubilee." Over fifty thousand veterans attended: 44,714 from the Union, and 8,694 from the Confederacy.[91] Additionally, tens of thousands of soldiers from the Regular Army, Boy Scouts, state and federal officials, and civilians came each day to participate in the activities.[92] Organizers erected thousands of tents, often replicating the camp positions where veterans had fought in 1863. "It is a spectacle to inspire the world," reported the *Philadelphia Evening Bulletin*.[93]

The negotiation of political language and symbolism, as well as geographic space, was readily evident. Railroads brought passengers with ease from the deep South, New England, the Midwest, and the far West. Politically, the terms of the negotiated reconciliation were evident in old Confederates marching in uniform next to the "boys in blue." Tattered Confederate battle flags flew alongside the Stars and Stripes. Tents stretched for miles across green meadows where only fifty years earlier eighty thousand men from the Union Army fought the decisive battle of the Civil War against seventy-five thousand Confederates. The battle signaled the end of the Confederacy and dealt a decisive blow to slavery and secession.[94] Yet, speakers neither mentioned the role of slavery in bringing about the war nor raised the unfinished reconstruction of race relations. Although it would be an overstatement to conclude that the white

[89] *Annin & Co., Makers of Fine Flags* (New York: Annin, 1912), 161, 169, 226–227, 40–41.

[90] *New York Times*, 5 March 1913; *Washington Bee*, 8 March 1913. For a fuller discussion of the South to national leadership, see George Brown Tindall, *The Emergence of the New South, 1913–1945* (Baton Rouge: Louisiana State University Press, 1967).

[91] Charles R. Nitchkey, *Gettysburg 1863 and Today* (Hicksville, N.Y.: Exposition Press, 1980), 113.

[92] Report of the Pennsylvania Commission, *Fiftieth Anniversary of the Battle of Gettysburg*, 60.

[93] *The Philadelphia Evening Bulletin*, 30 June 1913, quoted in ibid., 195.

[94] *The Columbus Citizen*, quoted in ibid., 197; *The Washington Post*, quoted in ibid., 194; *London Telegraph* (England), quoted in ibid., 217.

South won in the cultural arena what it had lost on the battlefield, there was no mistaking the influence of Confederate veterans on the revised memory of the Civil War. No longer a war of secession, orator after orator recast the war as a heroic struggle between brothers whose blood had strengthened and purified the nation. It was neither southern nor northern but American valor that Civil War soldiers had vindicated when they each fought for what they considered to be right.[95]

"It matters little to you or to me now," declared the chairman of the Gettysburg reunion, "what the causes were that provoked the War of the States in the Sixties." What matters, he continued, was that veterans from the Union and the Confederacy had survived to see their sons stand shoulder to shoulder to "sweep San Juan Hill, sink Spanish fleets in Santiago and Manila Bays, and thundering at the gates of Peking, establish our country as a power second to none on earth."[96] The commemoration at Gettysburg served domestic and international purposes. To the nation, the symbolic face of sectional solidarity asserted itself against new divisions occasioned by unprecedented rates of immigration. Internationally, the United States appeared united and ready to serve as the model and judge of the world's nations. In 1913, the Gettysburg reunion celebrated sacrifice to the nation and legitimated the official revision of Civil War history as a great step toward American world power.

Preparations for the fiftieth anniversary of Gettysburg captured the nation's imagination. In 1913, there were ninety-eight films about the Civil War. At first, the films' sympathies went overwhelmingly to the North, but as directors heeded protests from the South they began to feature heroic figures from the Confederacy. A new generation shaped the old contradictions of racism into new cultural forms. Producers quickly found that both northern and southern audiences responded favorably to the depiction of romantic and heroic ideals from the defeated South.[97] Nostalgia for the antebellum South and explicit support for Jim Crow reached new heights in 1915, when D. W. Griffith's film *The Birth of a Nation* became the most popular film of the era.[98] Based on Thomas Dixon's *The Clansman* and drawing upon Woodrow Wilson's *A History of the American People*, Griffith depicted Reconstruction as a time of tor-

[95] Speaker of the House of Representatives, Honorable Champ Clark, quoted in ibid., 137–38.

[96] Chairman of Pennsylvania Commission, Colonel J. M. Schoonmaker, quoted in ibid., 95–96.

[97] Eileen Bowser, *The Transformation of Cinema, 1907–1915*, vol. 2, *History of the American Cinema*, ed. Charles Harpole (New York: Charles Scribner's Sons, 1990), 177–78.

[98] Lary May, *Screening Out the Past: The Birth of Mass Culture and the Motion Picture Industry* (Chicago: University of Chicago Press, 1980), 80–83.

ment and corruption for the white South.[99] Dixon gave a talk about the significance of the film on opening night, telling the audience "that he would have allowed none but the son of a Confederate soldier to direct the film version of *The Clansman*."[100] Mildred Lewis Rutherford, historian-general for the United Daughters of the Confederacy, wrote that the film would do more to bring the North and South together than anything that had happened since the Civil War. "All these years we have been trying to make the North see that we had a grievance, and now that they acknowledge it, we can without bitterness or prejudice discuss our troubles with them."[101]

National culture, never just a point of fixed identity and allegiance, reflected changing relations of power. By World War I, songs, such as "Dixie Doodle," proclaimed that "there are no boys in blue or gray. It's just one country" beneath the "Stars and Stripes of Dixie Doodle and the good ole U.S.A."[102] Northern and southern whites fought side by side in their reforged alliance, yet during World War I black Americans faced the contradiction of being expected to be loyal in Europe at the same time they were treated as second-class citizens in the United States. Lynching continued at home, and the long arm of racism reached over to the battlefields of France. Black Americans fought World War I on two fronts: proving their loyalty in Europe while on the home front linking the demand "to make the world safe for democracy" with the demand "to make America safe for the Negro."[103] Reflecting the mood of the times, the black *Chicago Defender* featured a graphic of the Statue of Liberty that offered "Liberty, Protection, Opportunity, Happiness, For all White Men" and "Humiliation, Segregation, Lynching, For all Black Men."[104]

[99] Woodrow Wilson, *A History of the American People*, vols. 4 and 5 (New York: Harper & Brothers, 1902).

[100] "'The Birth of a Nation': Film Version of Dixon's 'The Clansman' Presented at the Liberty," *New York Times*, 4 March 1915.

[101] Mildred Lewis Rutherford, "Reconstruction and the Ku Klux Klan," from an untitled newspaper, 1914. Found in the *Historical Records of the United Daughters of the Confederacy, Scrapbooks*, vol. 25, complied by Mildred Lewis Rutherford of Athens, Ga., the historian-general of the United Daughters of the Confederacy, 1911–1916, The Museum of the Confederacy.

[102] Raymond Zirkel, "Dixie Doodle: 'You're the Land for Me'" (Columbus, Ohio: Buckeye Music Pub. Co., 1918), DeVincent Collection, 5.1, Box 1, Folder A-D, Archives Center.

[103] *The Crisis*, 14 (September 1917): 216–19, 241–44. For a fuller discussion of black allegiance and identity during World War I, see Cecilia Elizabeth O'Leary, "A Right to the Flag" (Paper delivered to the annual meeting of the Western Association of Women Historians, 1992).

[104] *Chicago Defender*, 28 July 1917.

CONCLUSION

In the period between the Civil War and World War I, the cultural reconciliation between the Union and the Confederacy was evident in films
sympathetic to the antebellum South, in songs that announced "there is
no North or South today," and in military spectacles of aged veterans
shaking hands over the stone wall at "Bloody Angle."[105] National culture
reflected the dominance of the North but with significant concessions to
Confederate culture. From the beginning, former Confederates argued
that southern valor must be respected. Unable to link patriotism with
defense of the Union, the white South maintained that devotion to the
righteousness of their cause, self-sacrifice, and courage on the battlefield
had earned them the title of patriots. Northern veterans eventually acqui-
esced. As long as the South marched under the Stars and Stripes, northern veterans and historians participated in reshaping the memory of the
Civil War to allow their former enemies back into the national
brotherhood.

Black and white Americans who supported Reconstruction struggled
for a different interpretation. To them, the historic memory of the Civil
War and the definition of patriotism were irrevocably linked to principles
of racial equality, democracy, and social justice. They refused to separate
the memory of the war and the moral character of loyalty to the Union
from what it meant to be a patriotic American. Grand Army veterans,
passionately dedicated to the Union, also at first argued that the causes
and goals of the Civil War could not be separated from determining the
patriots and the traitors. Yet by 1913, most northern veterans were prepared to concede that each side had fought heroically for what they
thought to be right.

Nonetheless, contradictions, divisions, and cross-cutting allegiances
remained. Rather than reflecting an essential unity, the Grand Army of
the Republic and the United Confederate Veterans struggled for cultural
reunification for very different reasons. The North demanded the priority of one nation and respect for its most important symbol, the flag. The
Confederate Veterans advocated reunification for economic reasons, but
they simultaneously demanded the right to an autonomous Confederate
culture and control of southern racial relations. A critical term of negotiation was the national abandonment of the cause of Reconstruction. Once
national support for racial equality was removed, black Americans and
white supporters of social justice were effectively silenced within the

[105] Honorable J. Hampton Moore, of Philadelphia, member of Congress, 3rd Pennsylvania District quoted in Report of the Pennsylvania Commission, *Fiftieth Anniversary of the
Battle of Gettysburg*, 168–71.

dominant political culture. Emancipation would continue to be cele-brated by black Americans, but it would not be included among the na-tion's great traditions.

From being a "people in arms," the military, its officers, and veteran organizations assumed their positions as the torchbearers of patriotism; they were committed to keeping the flame alive between wartime mobil-izations. Members of the officer's corps had been among the first to pro-mote reconciliation. Patriotism, traditionally associated with willingness to die for one's country, had to be renegotiated to allow former Confed-erates back into the nation's fraternity. New battles, both within and outside of the nation, provided the arenas for reconciliation. The final conquest of the continent and the subjugation of the Plains Indians per-mitted former Confederates to once again identify with the Regular Army in its struggle for the nation's "manifest destiny." But even more important, the Spanish-American War endorsed "American," not north-ern or southern, valor, as the United States assumed its position as a world power.

Regional, ethnic, and local interpretations of loyalty and the meaning of the Civil War persisted, but official images of patriotism stressed the reunification of the boys in blue and the boys in gray as brothers in a progressive national history. The celebration of martial grandeur and the glorification of the imperial nation-state, popularized by Theodore Roo-sevelt, prevailed over memorials that advocated the expression of per-sonal loss and the centrality of emancipation in the commemoration of Memorial Day. By World War I, official patriotic culture—defined by the ascendance of northern institutions, shaped by the language of mas-culinity, influenced by the rise of a martial spirit, and narrowed by the imposition of racialized criteria and intolerance of domestic opposition—eclipsed competing interpretations.

Chapter 3

LABOR REPUBLICANISM, RACE, AND POPULAR
PATRIOTISM IN THE ERA OF EMPIRE, 1890–1914

ANDREW NEATHER

SPEAKING at a National Civic Federation banquet in New York in
May 1903, John Mitchell told the assembled dignitaries that "if I
believed that there were . . . one thing un–American in the trade
union movement, I would not be a trade unionist. The trade union
movement . . . is an American movement." A conservative like Mitchell, leader of the United Mine Workers, could hardly be expected to
say anything else to such an audience.[1] Yet twenty or even ten years
earlier, a unionist like him would probably not have found it necessary to
indulge in such a rhetorical gesture. That he felt the need was a measure
of increased ideological pressure on the labor movement from around
1900 to conform to a standard of political and economic conservatism
constructed through that peculiarly expansive political idiom, American
nationalism. In this chapter I examine the construction of patriotism in
turn-of-the-century labor movement ideology and its transformation in
the Progressive era. I argue that what is generally known as "labor republicanism" survived in some form until the early twentieth century and
that patriotism represented one of its central organizing concepts—a
form of what Gary Gerstle has called "working-class Americanism."[2]
But in the Progressive era the character and politics of that patriotism
shifted decisively. Republican nationalism collapsed through a combination of internal and external contradictions and pressures; its collapse
gave way to the "Americanism" associated with the aftermath of World
War I, in which patriotism was linked to support for the economic and
political status quo.

Surviving the Knights of Labor's demise in the late 1880s, labor republicanism represented a tradition that was at once richer and more complex than has generally been realized.[3] It was neither very coherent nor

---

[1] As reported in National Civic Federation *Review* 1, no. 2 (June 1903): 8.

[2] Gary Gerstle, *Working Class Americanism: The Politics of Labor in a Textile City, 1914–
1960* (Cambridge: Cambridge University Press, 1989).

[3] I address the subject of labor republicanism at length in my dissertation, "Popular

very precisely derivative of classical eighteenth-century or antebellum republicanism. It had become, rather, a polyglot, contradictory ideology that drew on many other vocabularies of dissent—socialism, popular evangelical Christianity, and liberalism, as well as various more transient reform currents like Bellamyite Nationalism and the Single Tax. Two principal characteristics of this ideology suggest, however, that the term "republican" is still apt: its conception of the citizen-producer, and its nationalism grounded in a republican history.

First, distinctive elements of eighteenth-century republicanism survived in the labor movement's notion of citizenship.[4] Organized workers claimed the mantle of Jeffersonian republicanism primarily through ideals of citizenship. They emphasized the citizen's identity as a producer and consequent equal rights in what Bruce Palmer has called a "moral society of producers."[5] Emphasizing workers' role as the only true "wealth-producers," the "producerist" critique of the inequalities of industrial capitalism also offered an unelaborated labor theory of value.[6] Yet "producerism" was not necessarily anticapitalist: organized workers generally blamed the social and economic inequality they saw around them on the corruption of republican political ideals by greed and commerce. They placed "justice" and "rights" at the forefront of their appeals and demands by emphasizing the citizen-producer's respon-

---

republicanism, Americanism, and the roots of anti-communism, 1890–1925," (Ph.D. diss., Duke University, 1994), chaps. 2–4. See also Leon Fink, *Workingmen's Democracy: The Knights of Labor and American Democracy* (Urbana: University of Illinois Press, 1983); and his "The New Labor History and the Powers of Historical Pessimism: Consensus, Hegemony and the Case of the Knights of Labor," *Journal of American History* 75 (June 1988): 115–36. Other important studies of labor republicanism include portions of Nick Salvatore, *Eugene V. Debs: Citizen and Socialist* (Urbana: University of Illinois Press, 1982), and idem, "Some Thoughts on Class and Citizenship in America in the Late Nineteenth Century," in *In the Shadow of the Statue of Liberty: Immigrants Workers and Citizens in the American Republic, 1880–1920*, ed. Marianne Debouzy (Paris: Presses Universitaires de Vincennes, 1988); Linda G. Schneider, "American Nationality and Workers' Consciousness in Industrial Conflict: 1870–1920, Three Case Studies" (Ph.D. diss., Columbia University, 1975).

[4] A voluminous literature exists on eighteenth-century republicanism: for surveys, see Robert Shalhope, "Republicanism in Early American Historiography," *William and Mary Quarterly* 39 (April 1982): 334–56; Daniel T. Rodgers, "Republicanism: The Career of a Concept," *Journal of American History* 79 (June 1992): 11–38. For labor historians' application of the "republican" interpretive concept to antebellum working-class ideology, see especially Herbert Gutman, "Work, Culture and Society in Industrializing America, 1815–1919," *American Historical Review* 78 (June 1973): 567–71; Sean Wilentz, *Chants Democratic: New York City and the Rise of the American Working Class* (New York: Oxford University Press, 1984), esp. chap. 2.

[5] Bruce Palmer, *Man Over Money: The Southern Populist Critique of Capitalism* (Chapel Hill: University of North Carolina Press, 1980), 9.

[6] On the concept of "producerism" see, for instance, Bruce Laurie, *Working People of Philadelphia, 1800–1850* (Philadelphia: Temple University Press, 1980), 75–79.

sibility to participate in politics and resist unjust laws as the solution to inequality.

The second distinctively republican feature of labor ideology was a patriotism based on a republican interpretation of history. Indeed popular republican nationalism found its greatest coherence in working people's interpretation and use of republican history in struggle. Organized workers constructed a republican patriotism through constant and creative use of a distinctively republican version of the national past: the Revolutionary War, Constitution, Jacksonian democracy, and the Civil War. The organized working class was often composed of English-speaking immigrants or their children, with only a received folk memory of earlier artisanal republicanism; this composition did not lessen the ideology's appeal or usefulness for Americanized immigrants, although it was less relevant for the waves of new immigrants from the 1890s.[7]

Even around 1900, a popular reappropriation of republican history could act as a powerful legitimating component of workers' demands, a countermemory that they constantly employed against employers and government. For unionists, the republican historical experience legitimated their struggle as a patriotic rising of citizens, or "the people," against wealthy "tyrants" or "aristocrats." References to and hagiographic pieces on Lincoln, the founding fathers, and the Revolution were endless. In 1906, printer James Armstrong equated the contemporary views of "plutocracy" with those who held Tory or "open country" sympathies in the Revolutionary War.[8] In 1894, carpenter James O'Mara sounded a typical claim: "government as now administered is no longer that founded by the heroes and statesmen of the Revolution; it is in name, but no longer exists as a government of the people." It followed, for him, that workingmen "must beg their bread or follow the example of their forefathers of 1776 and fight for that which is justly due."[9] These kind of appeals remained extremely common in the labor movement around 1900, even across the political spectrum. Eugene V. Debs frequently

[7] On republicanism's meaning for immigrants, see David Montgomery, "Labor and the Republic in Industrial America: 1860–1920," *Le Mouvement Social* 111 (Avril–Juin 1980): 201–15; and idem., "Nationalism, American Patriotism, and Class Consciousness among Immigrant Workers in the U.S. in the Epoch of World War I," in *Struggle a Hard Battle: Essays on Working-Class Immigrants*, ed. Dirk Hoerder (Dekalb: Northern Illinois University Press, 1986).

[8] *Typographical Journal*, reprinted in *Journal of the Switchmen's Union of North America* 9, no. 2 (December 1906): 76–78. See also, for instance, "Tangle Sixer," letter to *Miners' Magazine* 1, no. 9 (September 1900): 15; Wilert Bateman, letter to *Monthly Journal of the International Association of Machinists* 4, no. 5 (June 1892), 139; AFL statement on Pullman strike, 1894, (Executive Committee records) reel 2, *AFL Records: The Samuel Gompers Era* (microfilm edition, 1979); hereafter cited *AFL Records*.

[9] Letter to *The Carpenter* 14, no. 8 (August 1894): 12.

drew comparisons between labor's struggle and that of the insurgent American colonists against the British. In the wake of the lost Pullman strike of 1894, he called the Declaration of Independence a "strike for liberty" by "patriot strikers": "It was the greatest strike on record, and as a result of the strike conditions were greatly improved and a new nation was born, and England learned that the strikers were not anarchists. . . . In 1894 the battle cry, not of tories and traitors, but of patriotic wage earners, is wages—for without honest wages comes poverty, degradation and slavery, hence the strike."[10] Glassworker Charles Smitley maintained a militantly anti-AFL industrial unionist position; yet he asserted even in 1910 that "we hear much about the heroes of '75 [sic] and '61. They bled and died that we might be free. Instead of maintaining that freedom we have allowed a few individuals to usurp it. It is not too late to regain that freedom. All that is necessary is unity among those who are oppressed."[11] Native-born socialists thus drew on the same historical tradition and inspiration as many labor republicans.[12]

Organized workers' constant invocation of history amounted to an ongoing construction of a mythical master-narrative of republican history, against which the current progress of the nation's political-ethical "mission" could be measured. Even if that narrative was at times fanciful, workers consciously realized the importance of struggling to establish a narrative that put themselves at its center, thus legitimating a particular future course of history, a dreamt-of "workers' republic." The narrative was also unavoidably and self-consciously patriotic, restating and valorizing the United States' uniqueness as a democratic republican alternative to the tyrannies of the Old World.

In workers' renditions of the master-narrative, virtue was being negated, republican ideals had been corrupted, and the people's rights eroded. Yet while such sentiments, like other aspects of republican nationalism, could certainly betoken a militant anticapitalist class consciousness, they did not necessarily do so. Republican views of class struggle were complicated by a belief in "commonwealth," political community based on political ideals rather than class. Thus to lambast plutocrats as royalty showed class consciousness of a kind, to be sure, but not necessarily socialist sympathies.

Despite radical and inclusive aspects of republican citizenship, however, labor republicanism was also severely compromised by its internal

---

[10] Editorial, *Locomotive Firemen's Magazine* 18, no. 9 (September 1894): 872–74.

[11] Letter to *American Flint* (American Flint Glass Workers' Union of North America) 1, no. 3 (January 1910): 21–22. Smitley was from Toledo, Ohio.

[12] See Salvatore, *Eugene V. Debs*; Elliot Shore, *Talkin' Socialism: J. A. Wayland and the Role of the Press in American Radicalism, 1890–1912* (Lawrence: University Press of Kansas, 1988), chap. 2.

racial and gender categories. Organized workers' definitions of the citizen and political participation depended organically on exclusions based on race and gender. In rhetoric, iconography, and symbolic practice they constantly referred to the citizen-worker as "manly" and, even if often implicitly, white.

Republican nationalism was distinctly muscular in its rhetoric; references to "manliness," "manly virtue," and "manhood" saturated the language of male trade unionists.[13] The citizen was almost always assumed to be male—both as an actor in a republican public sphere that was ideally male in its political and institutional life where women were denied suffrage and as "wealth producer" in the male-dominated world of paid work.[14] True manhood was thus highly politicized: it demanded patriotism yet also a struggle to maintain "independence" from power and commerce. Not only work but also collective political action and rights—what the steelworker "Puddler Poet," Michael McGovern, called "manhood's right"—were unavoidably gendered.[15] In this view, patriarchal "rights" represented the promise of the republic as much as did the dream of economic equality.

The inseparability of republican ideals from American patriotism was ensured in significant part by the centrality of gender to both. "Sturdy, virile manhood" was a desirable attribute of republican citizens because it was "essential to the maintenance and perpetuation of free institutions and a republican form of government," wrote Samuel Gompers in 1902.[16] In other words, because the republic's survival depended on maintaining a virtuous citizenry and because citizenship was in turn based largely on maleness, it followed that the destablizing or emasculation of manhood would correspondingly corrupt the republic. Not only the workingman's pride in craft, class consciousness, and role as breadwinner were bound up with masculinity, but his role as a citizen within

[13] The gender implications of labor republicanism at greater length in Neather, "Popular republicanism," chap. 3. See also Alice Kessler-Harris, "Gender Ideology in Historical Reconstruction: A Case Study from the 1930s," *Gender and History* 1 (Spring 1989): 37, and idem., "Treating the Male as 'Other': Re-defining the Parameters of Labor History," *Labor History* 34 (Spring–Summer 1993): 190–91; essays in Ava Baron, ed., *Work Engendered: Toward a New History of American Labor* (Ithaca: Cornell University Press, 1991); Mary H. Blewett, *Men, Women, and Work: Class, Gender, and Protest in the New England Shoe Industry, 1780–1910* (Urbana: University of Illinois Press, 1988).

[14] See Alice Kessler-Harris, "A New Agenda for American Labor History: A Gendered Analysis of the Question of Class," in *Perspectives on American Labor History: The Problems of Synthesis*, ed. J. Carroll Moody and Kessler-Harris (Dekalb: Northern Illinois University Press, 1989), 227.

[15] Michael McGovern, "Where Liberty Should Be and Is Not," *Labor Lyrics and Other Poems* (Youngstown, Ohio: The Vindicator Press, 1899), 42.

[16] Gompers was writing in the context of the 1902 anthracite coal strike. See his *American Federationist* 9, no. 7 (July 1902): 372.

the republic and his patriotism also turned substantially upon such definitions of gender.

Race created similar contradictions at the heart of labor republicans' formulations of citizenship and patriotism. Racial ideology was played out politically in the context of battles to exclude workers of color from unions and to ban Asian immigration. All the railroad brotherhoods and most AFL unions routinely excluded African Americans, Latinos, and Asians. Most southern union locals and a number of international unions vehemently opposed admission of African Americans.[17] In the West organized workers practiced similar exclusions, although there, "Asiatic Exclusion" loomed larger.[18] Many western workers lobbied for legal exclusion of Chinese and Japanese; others organized boycotts against Asian businesses. Such campaigns regularly spilled over into violence, encouraging fights, vandalism, and riots, as in Bellingham, Washington, in September 1907, where white textile workers rioted against "Hindus" employed at the mills.[19]

This racism was undoubtedly in part a function of competition for jobs and of more "irrational" psychological factors. In the South and elsewhere in the twenty-five years before World War I, white workers found themselves competing with both white immigrants and workers of color in a rapidly changing labor market. White southern unionists' drive against admitting African Americans was closely linked to the intensification of "Jim Crow" racism in the South from around 1890. "Irra-

[17] On black workers and the exclusionary and other racist policies of white unions, see, for example, Herbert Gutman, "The Negro and the United Mine Workers of America: The Career and Letters of Richard L. Davis and Something of Their Meaning," in *The Negro and the American Labor Movement*, ed. Julius Jacobson (Garden City, N.Y.: Doubleday, 1988); Paul B. Worthman, "Black Workers and Labor Unions in Birmingham, Alabama, 1897–1904," *Labor History* 10 (Summer 1969): 375–407; Eric Arnesen, *Waterfront Workers of New Orleans: Race, Class, and Politics, 1863–1923* (New York: Oxford University Press, 1991). On the exclusion of Asians, see, for example, Alexander Saxton, *The Indispensable Enemy: Labor and the Anti-Chinese Movement in California, 1865–1920* (Berkeley: University of California Press, 1971); Michael Kazin, *Barons of Labor: The San Francisco Building Trades and Union Power in the Progressive Era* (Urbana: University of Illinois Press, 1987), chap. 6; Gwendolyn Mink, *Old Labor and New Immigrants in American Political Development: Union, Party and State, 1875–1920* (Ithaca: Cornell University Press, 1986), esp. chap. 3. On the exclusion of Latinos, see, for example, Emilio Zamora, *The World of the Mexican Worker in Texas* (College Station: Texas A & M University Press, 1993), esp. chap. 7; Nancy A. Hewitt, "The Voice of Virile Labor: Labor Militancy, Community Solidarity, and Gender Identity among Tampa's Latin Workers, 1880–1921," in *Work Engendered*; Angela Yvette Huginnie, "'Strikitos': Race, Class, and Work in the Arizona Copper Industry, 1870–1920" (Ph.D. diss., Yale University, 1991).

[18] Letter to *Typographical Journal* 39, no. 1 (July 1911): 18.

[19] Seattle *Post-Intelligencer*, 6–8 September 1907. The "Hindus" were probably in fact Sikhs. See Joan M. Jensen, *Passage from India: Asian Indian Immigrants in North America* (New Haven: Yale University Press, 1988), 44–53, 88–89.

tional" factors such as status or sexualized white racial fears and anxieties also undoubtedly played a determinative role. But race was more deeply embedded in labor ideology via the categories of republican citizenship, a holdover from the roots of artisanal republicanism in the antebellum slaveholding republic.[20] The extremely common belief that industrial capitalism was reducing white workers to "slavery" was one example of this racial coding of political and economic rights.[21] Working-class republican language consistently implied a white *polis*: the "citizen" or "brother" was always assumed to be not only male but also white. As well as operating through implicit categories of republican citizenship, race shaped organized workers' understanding of nationality and patriotism more directly. In some contexts of organized struggle, defense of the nation's racial integrity could mean almost the same thing as "patriotism." Californian W. W. Stone wrote that because the Chinese were "moral and spiritual lepers," they posed a threat to not only "Christian civilization" but also the American republic. By contrast "the caucasian," Stone claimed, "rejects this infusion for the pure blood of the manly American. . . . Our sturdy forefathers of Revolutionary times never dreamed of the introduction of such an element into our body politic."[22] John O'Neill of the Western Federation of Miners ridiculed Chinese workers' patriotism with reference to the Spanish-American war: "Was Wah Lee, Ah Fung and Ping Pong on San Juan hill? Were there any pigtails upon the Pacific coast whose patriotism was aroused when the *Maine* was blown up in Havana harbor?"[23]

Some white unionists, like Will Winn, AFL organizer in Columbus, Georgia, also excluded African Americans from such a racially based patriotism. Winn claimed that "as a race, [the negro] does not give evidence of a possession of those peculiarities of temperament such as patriotism, sympathy, sacrifice etc. which are peculiar to most of the Caucasian race, and which alone make an organization of the character and complicity of the modern trade union possible."[24] Such arguments could be used by southern white workers in the context of their efforts to exclude African Americans from jobs. Despite strenuous attempts by some middle-class African Americans to draw attention to their loyal military service in

[20] On the development of racial elements of republicanism up to c. 1880, see David R. Roediger, *The Wages of Whiteness: Race and the Making of the American Working Class* (London: Verso, 1991); Alexander Saxton, *The Rise and Fall of the White Republic: Class Politics and Mass Culture in Nineteenth-Century America* (London: Verso, 1990).

[21] See Roediger, *Wages of Whiteness*.

[22] W. W. Stone, "The Chinese and the Labor Question," in *The Labor Movement: The Problem of Today*, ed. George McNeill (Boston: A. M. Bridgman & Co., 1887), 431–32, 437–38.

[23] *Miners' Magazine* 6, no. 112 (17 August 1905).

[24] *American Federationist* 4, no. 12 (February 1898): 269–70.

Cuba in 1898, their patriotism remained suspect in the eyes of some white unionists.

These facts force us to go beyond the well-proven truism that the early AFL was racist and sexist. The masculinism and white supremacism of labor ideology decisively shaped not only labor's strategies for organizing and legal activism but also organized workers' conceptions of resistance, class, and solidarity. Class solidarity was racialized and gendered: true white republicans resisted the boss, while those who submitted implicitly compromised their "manhood" as well as their status as citizens and nonslaves and thus as whites. And because race and gender were also deeply embedded in organized workers' understanding of patriotism, they opened such an oppositional patriotism up to attack from labor's opponents.

Patriotism proved crucial in the anti-union offensive of organized businessmen, the middle-class press, and the courts from around 1900. Aggressive business organization surged in reaction to the growth of unions and strikes from around 1899 to 1903, with the formation or drastic reorientation of several national industrywide organizations and hundreds of local employers' groups.[25] In particular, these local "Citizens' Alliances" and "Employers' Associations," the principal local face of business activism, proliferated rapidly after 1900.[26] Most prominent of the national groups was the National Association of Manufacturers (NAM), transformed from its earlier role as a lobbying organization on trade issues. Although the NAM did not represent all businessmen and was criticized by some, most were ready to use the NAM's tactics when faced with strikes, and many shared the NAM's basic dislike for unions and socialism. Business activists employed three principal tactics: political activity, including lobbying; propaganda; and local strong-arm intervention.

But beyond the mechanics of business anti-union organizations or vigilante violence, through their changing ideological and rhetorical thrust these business activists also played a central role in altering working-class patriotism. Whatever the exact effectiveness of the NAM and local

[25] See Neather, "Popular republicanism," chap. 5; Bruno Ramirez, *When Workers Fight: The Politics of Industrial Relations in the Progressive Era* (Westport, Conn.: Greenwood Press, 1978); David Montgomery, *The Fall of the House of Labor: The Workplace, the State and American Labor Activism, 1865–1925* (New York: Cambridge University Press, 1987), 57–63, 260–75; Sarah Lyons Watts, *Order Against Chaos: Business Culture and Labor Ideology in America, 1880–1915* (Westport, Conn.: Greenwood Press, 1991), esp. chap. 4.

[26] See George G. Suggs, Jr., *Colorado's War on Militant Unionism: James H. Peabody and the Western Federation of Miners* (Detroit: Wayne State University Press, 1972), esp. chaps. 4 and 7; Arthur Thurner, *Rebels on the Range: The Michigan Copper Miners' Strike of 1913–1914* (Lake Linden, Mich.: John H. Forster Press, 1984), esp. chap. 9; Robert P. Ingalls, *Urban Vigilantes in the New South: Tampa, 1882–1936* (Knoxville: University of Tennessee Press, 1988).

groups in slowing union recruitment, blocking labor legislation, and breaking strikes—and they would appear to have had a definite impact—their ideological successes were even longer lasting and more profound.[27] The business assault on labor depended centrally on the manipulation of the meaning of patriotism and the acceptability of dissent within "Americanism." Although businessmen had long been hostile to unions and socialism, before the 1890s trade unions were not normally or in most parts of the country associated in middle-class opinion with anarchy or socialism. Such radical ideologies were seen as the work of marginal foreigners, in contrast to respectable white American workingmen. A reformulated patriotism involved recasting the political components peculiar to American nationalism; that is, the nation commanded loyalty through its embodiment of a political ideal as well as through the accident of one's birth. The new business version of American patriotism's political component emphasized unquestioning loyalty to government and the law, virtually unlimited business power, and the defeat of socialism.

Business activists used patriotism to cement together the other central components of their ideology, particularly the notion of "free contract" and appeals to social order, thereby elevating such principles as the defining ideals of American liberty. In his speech to the NAM convention in New Orleans in April 1903, possibly the defining statement of the new anti-union campaign, president David Parry called the right of free contract "one of the most sacred and fundamental of American liberty"; he named unions, by contrast, an "un-American institution."[28] At the 1907 convention F. C. Nunemacher of the United Typothetae called for a "campaign of *true* Americanism" and "true patriotism," and then-president James Van Cleave declared that "Americanism must rule America."[29]

---

[27] The NAM's direct, practical impact on union organizing is difficult to gauge, and neither its leaders' bombastic claims nor the AFL leadership's airy dismissals of its effect seems reliable. But the expansion of union membership levelled off sharply after 1904, and unions won significantly fewer strikes—only 32 percent from 1906 to 1911 compared to 54.4 percent from 1898 to 1901: see P. K. Edwards, *Strikes in the United States, 1881–1974* (New York: St. Martin's Press, 1981), 42. And the importance of local CAs in prolonging strikes and reinforcing business and law enforcement action seems clear: see Foner, *History of the Labor Movement, Vol. III: The Policies and Practices of the American Federation of Labor, 1900–1909* (New York: International Publishers, 1988), 58–60; Ingalls, *Urban Vigilantes*, chap. 3.

[28] *Proceedings of the Eighth Annual Convention of the National Association of Manufacturers of the United States of America* (Indianapolis: Century Press, 1903), 17–18; hereafter cited as NAM *Procs.* and date.

[29] NAM *Procs.* (1907), 103, 240. See also, for example, W. C. Shepherd, president of the Employers' Association of Wilkesbarre, "Americanism the Living Issue," *American Industries* 2, no. 22 (1 July 1904): 13; ibid., 3, no. 7 (15 November 1904), 1.

In identifying Americanism and patriotism with individual free contract, business activists also portrayed American values as threatened by forces of disloyalty and disorder—namely, unionists and socialists. John Kirby, a leading Dayton activist and NAM figure, posed a telling question to delegates at the 1903 NAM convention: "Shall lawlessness and anarchy, under the sanction and control of organized labor, or Americanism prevail, and direct [the country's] future?"[30] Later he would go even further by condemning unionists as "those who neither revere nor respect the flag of our country."[31] In 1911, the rabidly anti-union *Los Angeles Times* faked photos purporting to show Gompers standing on the American flag at a Labor Day rally. Released at the height of the trial of the McNamara brothers for blowing up the offices of the *Los Angeles Times* and accompanying press hysteria over union-sponsored violence, the "flag desecration" photos received national attention.[32]

Business activists indeed branded all organized workers as socialist as well as unpatriotic, even when the evidence was indeed thin. For example, David Parry accused labor leaders of being "at heart disciples of revolution," and C. W. Post's *Square Deal* called Gompers "a rabid English socialist."[33] Business activists widened the scope of their criticism to anyone who did not fully support them. The battles over labor-sponsored anti-injunction bills before World War I provide clear examples of this. John Kirby for instance attacked the Hoar-Grosvenor anti-injunction bill of 1903 as the work of a "disloyal and anarchic element . . . the tyrannous and treasonable" and "an insult to all true Americans."[34] In this kind of usage, businessmen placed themselves squarely at the center of the "national interest" and the discursive space denoted by the term "the pub-

---

[30] NAM *Procs.* (1903), 17–18, 202, 211. Similar accusations can be found in dozens of business pieces; e.g. founding resolution of Bloomington, Indiana, Citizens' Alliance, 1903, reprinted in *American Industries* 1, no. 12 (1 February 1903): 3; Anthony Ittner to NAM convention, 1904, in *American Industries* 2, no. 22 (1 July 1904): 9; William H. Speer, New Jersey circuit judge, address to Citizens' Industrial Association of St. Louis, 19 January 1909, in *The Square Deal*, no. 44 (March 1909), 69.

[31] Kirby to NAM convention, 1909, in *American Industries* 9, no. 8 (June 1909): 7.

[32] *Los Angeles Times*, 1 October 1911; see also, for example, *New York Times*, 2 January 1912; *Army and Navy Register*, 30 December 1911, 3, 6, and 6 January 1912, 10. For union reaction, see Gompers press release, 2 January 1912, reel 111, *AFL Records*; also Orion T. Thomas, of Stanton GAR, to Gompers, 24 October 1911, and Gompers's reply, 30 October (telegram); also further Thomas letter, 6 November, reel 74, *AFL Records*; Gompers, editorials, *American Federationist* 19, no. 1 (January 1912): 18–23, and 19, no. 2 (February 1912): 125–31; editorial, *American Flint* 3, no. 2 (December 1911): 24–25; *Coast Seamen's Journal* 25, no. 22 (14 February 1912): 1, 7; editorial, *Weekly Bulletin of the Clothing Trades* 11, no. 12 (12 January 1912): 4; *Miners' Magazine* 12, no. 446 (11 January 1912): and 12, no. 447 (January 18, 1914).

[33] NAM *Procs.* (1903), 20; (1904), 112; *The Square Deal*, no. 37 (August 1908), 91.

[34] *American Industries* 1, no. 11 (15 January 1903): 2–3.

lic"; they marginalized labor and forced unions to constantly reiterate and demonstrate their "moderation" and "loyalty." This redefinition also further alienated dwindling middle-class support for labor.

Workers were not helpless before such attacks: they resented—and challenged—business slurs on their patriotism. Many unionists did consciously recognize the way that employers and government were increasingly using appeals to patriotism to smother opposition. Even in 1895, one labor commentator complained that "the money power" was mounting a new campaign of ideological control, a new brand of officially sanctioned patriotism in which "they are drilling our boys and girls in school, and even in Sunday school, into mimic soldiery; they are raising the flag on public school houses, they are resoluting [sic] against foreign flags being raised on American soil, and, in fact, are exhibiting every phase of the jingo article. . . . So much for patriotism as it stands today."[35] This was the so-called "patriotic boom" of the 1890s, when flag worship and extravagant public displays of patriotism grew to a previously unprecedented scale. Leftist critics saw this kind of ideological campaign as deliberate and cynical, nourished especially through moments of national emergency. During the Spanish-American war, even the conservative *Cigar Makers' Journal* noticed that now "any one who differs with the policy of those who are trying with might and main to foist imperialism and militarism upon the people of our country are accused of being traitors and traducers of the flag."[36] Unionists now frequently countered by accusing employers and scabs of being "unamerican," foreshadowing rhetoric later used against employers' "Kaiserism" and "Prussianism" during World War I.

More important, organized workers continued to try to advance their own dissenting version of national loyalty. From the 1890s many unionists increased efforts to protest their patriotism by trying to respond to or preempt accusations of lacking patriotism by business and the middle-class press. From the mid-1890s onward the large number of extant photos of Labor Day floats and marching unions almost invariably show workers surrounded by flags, floats covered with red, white, and blue decorations, and men like steelworker George Hicks in a Pennsylvania Labor Day parade of 1902, dressed up as Uncle Sam.[37] Examining Labor Day celebrations of the period, Michael Kazin and Steven Ross note a shift from red flags and other militant symbols to national flags and patriotic symbols.[38] American flags and other patriotic trappings became

[35] George Smith, *American Federationist* 2, no. 6 (August 1895): 99–100.
[36] Editorial, *Cigar Makers' Official Journal* 25, no. 1 (October 1899): 8.
[37] Photo in *Amalgamated Journal* 3, no. 51 (18 September 1902).
[38] Michael Kazin and Steven J. Ross, "America's Labor Day: The Dilemma of a Workers' Celebration," *Journal of American History* 78 (March 1992): 1303–04.

more prominent too in other marches, meetings, and social events from the mid-1890s. Even on picket lines unionists made conscious displays of their patriotism. Workers could carry the flag in even the most dangerous of situations, although it did not necessarily act as the protective talisman workers hoped; a number of standard-bearers were gunned down in the twenty years before World War I.[39] All this was in part a product of the "patriotic boom"; but it is important to note the extent to which the symbols of patriotism remained open to dissenting and even radical reinterpretation. San Francisco's unionists used such symbolism while striking against members of the city's newly formed Employers' Association in summer 1901. At a Labor Day celebration dedicated to the strike on September 1, in which an estimated twenty thousand workers marched, the *Coast Seamen's Journal* took pains to note the marchers' orderliness and the fact that "patriotism was the keynote of the parade. Everywhere the nation's flag and the nation's colors were on view. The big silk banners rustled in the breeze; the smaller flags fluttered in every hand. The children carried their tiny symbols of the nation's strength; the women waved them from the walk and window to encourage the breadwinners. Unionism that is founded on patriotism and order cannot be stamped out. . . . There were types of men who go to the front to fight the nation's battles when Patriotism issues its call to arms."

Along the route of the demonstration, marchers made symbolic use of some novel variations on the nationalistic theme; these usages indicated in part an ideological struggle exceeding mere rhetoric. Suggesting a more broadly discursive struggle about the power of particular representations of ideology, they employed a wide variety of written, spoken, and symbolic contestations.[40] To patriotic music, shipyard workers marched with a float in the shape of the battleship *USS Oregon*, inscribed, "We are the men who built the *Oregon*." Three hundred men of blacksmiths' local #168 marched with a float in the shape of a giant anvil; the words "No Traitors" were inscribed on either side, and a second float included a cage containing two eagles.[41]

[39] Marching workers, including flag-bearers, were massacred in a number of incidents; e.g., incident in Hazleton, Pa., *Machinists' Monthly Journal* 10, no. 3 (March 1898); St. Louis, 1905, as recounted in Industrial Dept., Socialist Party, "Violations of the Right of Free Speech, 1905–1914," typescript in box 2, Records Relating to the Commission on Industrial Relations Studies, 1912–1915, in General Records of the Department of Labor (Record Group 174), National Archives, Washington, D.C.

[40] My understanding of the concept of discourse clearly draws on the work of Michel Foucault, notably *The Archaeology of Knowledge* (New York: Pantheon, 1972), esp. pt. 2 and appendix, "The Discourse on Language." For Joan Scott's interpretation of his theory, see *Gender and the Politics of History* (New York: Columbia University Press, 1988).

[41] *Coast Seamen's Journal* 14, no. 49 (4 September 1901), 1–2, 7–10; see also other issues from July to September.

What did such displays mean to the immigrant workers who composed an ever larger proportion of the U.S. working class from the 1890s? The copper strike of 1913–1914 in northern Michigan, a major confrontation involving a mostly immigrant workforce, offers one example of workers' battle for the flag against unequal odds and of immigrants' use of American patriotism.[42] Workers' parades in fall 1913 were invariably led by national flags, which led to direct clashes and literal battles for the flag with troops. One Armenian striker, Gabriel Mahatssin, was arrested and severely beaten by deputies for allegedly "cursing the American flag and American government"; he received a sentence of thirty days in jail.[43]

A more serious incident was repeated on several occasions: a standard-bearer was attacked as he led a parade of about one thousand strikers through the mining village of Calumet on 13 September. Frank King, a twenty-four-year-old Dalmatian immigrant, told congressional investigators that when the strikers' parade met National Guard troops, one militiaman on horseback cut the flag from its staff with his sword, another knocked the eagle from the top, and another bayoneted it. King still hung on to the flag. One soldier demanded the flag, but King told him, "I never give you the flag. I die before I give you this flag out of my hand." The soldier, repeating his demand for the flag, threatened to kill the striker. King replied again, "Kill me. I will die on this flag."[44] At this point in the melee, with troopers beating strikers, "Big Annie" Clemenc seized a flag—perhaps King's—from the ground. Clemenc, the wife of a Croatian miner, was president of the Calumet Women's Auxiliary and a frequent flag-bearer at parades. Like King, she challenged troops to kill

---

[42] The only full-length study of the strike is Thurner, *Rebels on the Range*; see also the U.S. Dept. of Labor's partial account, written in November 1913, in *Strike in the Copper Mining District of Michigan*, U.S. Senate, 63rd Cong., 2d sess., 1914, S. Doc. 381; U.S. House of Representatives, *Conditions in the Copper Mines of Michigan*, parts 1–6 (Washington, D.C.: Government Printing Office, 1914); Larry Lankton, *Cradle to Grave: Life, Work, and Death at the Lake Superior Copper Mines* (New York: Oxford University Press, 1991), chap. 13; William A. Sullivan, "The 1913 Revolt of the Michigan Copper Miners," *Michigan History* 43 (September 1959): 294–314; William Beck, "Law and Order During the 1913 Copper Strike," *Michigan History* 54 (Winter 1970): 275–92.

[43] House, *Conditions*, pt. 2, 941.

[44] Ibid., pt. 3, 1085–88. Militiamen present at the parade testified that they thought the flag was carried only as a weapon and claimed that strikers had tried to spear them with the flags—hardly surprising since troops waded into the crowd first: ibid., pt. 6, 2149–78. For testimony of similar incidents, see ibid., pt. 6, 1090–97, 1112–14, 1119–20, 1128; and the Socialist Party report on the strike, reprinted in ibid., pt. 2, 700; Graham Romeyn Taylor, "The Clash in the Copper Country," *The Survey* 31, no. 5 (1 November 1913): 127, 134; "The Copper Strike," *International Socialist Review* 15 (November 1913): 271.

her to take the flag; she was clubbed and slashed with a bayonet, but the soldiers did not fire through the flag.[45]

There are, however, some difficulties in assessing exactly what immigrant workers understood by such symbolism. What did they understand, beyond the fact that the flag might confer some legitimacy on their actions? Louis Zargnl, a Croatian miner, later explained the multiple meanings of patriotic symbols. After joining the strike, Zargnl was evicted from his company-owned house sometime in fall 1913 and arranged for a cart to move his furniture. It took two loads; as Zargnl finished piling on the second load of furniture, he stuck small U.S. flags left over from the Fourth of July on either side of his pile of belongings. As he told the congressional hearing into the strike, "You know that flag for Fourth of July—I put one on either side, and I say, here, now, that is all." This statement lead to the following exchange:

> REP. TAYLOR: "What flag?"
> ZARGNL: "U.S. flag for July."
> HILTON (a company lawyer): "You were going out in style."
> ZARGNL: "I put one on each side. I know I vote first time for McKinley"
> [Zargnl was a naturalized U.S. citizen].
> HILTON: "You put the flags on because you voted for McKinley?"
> ZARGNL: "Yes; and I put the flag on too, for fun."[46]

Zargnl understood the flag's significance as a national symbol and seemed to connect it with some pride to McKinley's flag-waving campaigns. He was also familiar with the broader use of the flag in American society "for fun"—for frivolous purposes, advertising, and at celebrations of many kinds. And yet he was also a striker, being evicted from his home; vividly aware of the struggles in the streets over the flag, his use of the flags was transparently, if quite subtly, a defiant act.

Certainly for immigrants like Zargnl, as well as those less well acquainted with the patriotic symbolism of American society, patriotism had multiple and contradictory meanings. Although the rhetoric of republicanism meant little to them, they were made quickly aware of the potential of the flag, both as a symbol of state power and the socioeconomic status quo and as something signifying at least broad ideals of justice for ordinary people like themselves. After no more than a few

[45] There is some disagreement over the exact details of the story: see *Miners' Bulletin*, reprinted in *International Socialist Review* 15 (December 1913): 342; Ella Reeve Bloor, "The Woman's Part in the Calumet Copper Strike," *Miners' Magazine* 15, no. 560 (19 March 1914); Taylor, "Clash," 132; Clarence A. Andrews, "'Big Annie' and the 1913 Michigan Copper Strike," *Michigan History* 57 (September 1973): 53–68; Thurner, *Rebels*, 92–97.

[46] House, *Conditions*, pt. 2, 1030. Zargnl was an American citizen.

years of living in the United States, the flag was for these immigrants a site of contested meaning as well as a ubiquitous decorative object. Writing about these kinds of displays in Pullman, Illinois, Larry Peterson notes that "workers appropriated the flag as part of their everyday lives by displaying and photographing it in family and community celebrations of national holidays. . . . The flag was above all a symbol of neighborhood solidarity and workers' desire for a freer life."[47]

But there was an inherent weakness in this kind of working-class patriotism: it inevitably involved an element of accommodation to official versions of national loyalty. The Spanish-American War exposed this particularly clearly. The spectacle of the first New World republic to shake off European rule was now itself imposing colonial rule on subject peoples, an irony not lost on some unionists. Anti-imperialists denounced the Cuban and Philippine wars and the annexation of Hawaii as abandoning republican and democratic principles. While some organized workers bitterly criticized imperialism, many shared some of its fundamental assumptions with the ruling elites who directed colonial policies, notably the racial justifications for empire and patriotic pride in military victories. The internal racial categories of white working-class republicanism and patriotism thus collided with the issue of imperialism in unpredictable ways. Many labor writers, even those against annexations, emphasized the supposed degeneracy and unfitness of people of color for republican government. *Seamen's* editor Walter MacArthur developed one of the clearest and most consistent versions of this argument between 1898 and 1900. He strongly opposed imperial expansion and claimed that "the Filipinos must be judged unfit for the responsibilities of blood relationship to the United States. The Filipinos are a tropic people, and, as such, unless we risk the theory of exceptions, they must continue a subject people."[48] Colonies thus threatened to bring racially "inferior" nonwhites into the republican *polis* itself. Union commentators frequently emphasized that these people of color, simply genetically incapable of citizenship, would thus pollute the republic and nullify its monoracial egalitarian promise.

More often, however, American representations of nonwhite, colonized peoples rarely involved any explicit political comment. Rather, the supposed inferiority of colonized peoples was communicated to workers through photos, cartoons, travelogues, and the ephemera of consumer Americana from cigarette packets to circus posters, helping to build

---

[47] Larry Peterson, "Producing Visual Traditions among Workers: The Uses of Photography at Pullman, 1880–1990," *International Labor and Working Class History* 42 (Fall 1992): 64–65, 61–63.

[48] *Coast Seamen's Journal* 12, no. 8 (23 November 1898).

more subconscious attitudes toward empire. Such representations, in both union and mainstream publications, were, after all, most American workers' main source of information on the parts of the world concerned. The labor press participated enthusiastically in creating such a discourse; it printed dozens of photographic essays and travelogues of Cuba, the Philippines, Puerto Rico, and Hawaii, and of other "exotic" countries in the pre–World War I period, especially from 1898 to 1900. Natives were inevitably portrayed as either dirty and dressed in rags or as lazy and carefree innocents; they were sometimes also eroticized, a sexualization of empire extremely common elsewhere in contemporary American discourse on empire.[49]

Organized workers and middle-class writers alike thus portrayed colonized people of color as at best amusing, harmless, or sexy, at worst lazy, stupid, and vicious; either way they were ripe for the imposition of American "civilization." Although intended primarily for entertainment, such representations of the nondeveloped world and the colonial amounted to more than simply innocent amusement or education. Within the context of the global development of empire, they powerfully reproduced the gaze of the colonizer and bolstered white workers' identification with the racial politics of colonialism.

Moreover, imperial adventures tended to demand a greater patriotism and loyalty to the state. For the most part unionists' patriotic pride took precedence over their outrage against what some saw as the United States' imperial violation of republican principles of self-determination.[50] Popular antimilitarism—in the tradition of the revolutionary era prejudice against large standing armies—existed uneasily alongside celebrations of military prowess. For many unionists, opposition to the war was further compromised by a desire to somehow "support" American troops, if not the more general wartime patriotic ballyhoo. Michael McGovern's flag-waving, vengeful poems, "The Men Who Manned the *Maine*," "The Men Who Guard the Flag," "To Our War Critics" and others, offered no serious possibility of critiquing imperialism, despite his staunch republicanism.[51]

Other workers took part in patriotic demonstrations: the Brotherhood of Locomotive Engineers, for instance, participated in flag raisings in a number of cities. All involved jingoistic speeches by local politicians and clergy and patriotic songs like "The Star-Spangled Banner" and "Colum-

---

[49] See, for example, *The Electrical Worker*, n.s., 5, no. 11 (September 1905): 13–16; *Indiana Labor Bulletin*, 3 October 1913.

[50] For lengthier discussion of labor opposition to empire, see Neather, "Popular republicanism," chaps. 4, 6; I. Dementyev, *United States of America: Imperialists and Anti-Imperialists* (Moscow: Progress Publishers, 1979), chap. 11.

[51] McGovern, *Labor Lyrics*.

bia." And other workers volunteered to fight. Railwayman Charles Maier thought that the war "proved the loyalty of the laboring people to their country and their country's cause. When war broke out, members of organized labor shouldered a gun and marched away to fight for the starry flag"—a position he contrasted with that of unpatriotic anarchists.[52]

These varieties of support for national military aims and officially orchestrated patriotism were, at best, difficult to combine with any sustained critique of imperialism. One railway brotherhood editor typically discussed the situation as one of "Americanism versus Militarism"; yet he also celebrated "the tidal wave of patriotism [that] has again rolled over the country" and the "pluck and grit" of the "born patriots" in the U.S. armed forces.[53]

The problem was that in the context of an imperial nation, such working-class patriotism legitimated imperial policies carried out in the name of national ideals and glory. Working-class republican participation in the orgy of patriotic sentimentalism occasioned by the war was difficult to differentiate, in practice, from more reactionary understandings of national pride. One Barclay, Illinois, coal miner, signing himself "A Union Man," made this contradiction clear as he commented on the unfolding Spanish war in May 1898: "If President McKinley had called for a million men instead of 125,000 he could have them. There are more patriots and brave men to the square mile in this country than in any other country under the sun. . . . The mine workers of this state have given not a few men to invade Cuba, some of whom joined in the war last summer for better conditions of employment and fair wages against the injustice of some coal operators."[54] Such patriotism was not, then, separate from class militancy in unionists' minds; indeed both patriotism and union solidarity were for most of them expressions of the same virtues of republicanism, loyalty, and "manhood."

If patriotism and class solidarity had become this mutually dependent, then class action remained hostage, at some level, to the meaning of American loyalty—a meaning ultimately enforced by those in power. And imperialistic foreign wars from 1898 onward were leading political elites to demand a patriotism more invested with loyalty to the state than to traditions of democratic dissent. As organized workers became more heavily dependent on the same patriotic language and symbols as those in

[52] Letter to *Locomotive Firemen's Magazine* 34, no. 6 (June 1903): 781. See also, for example, C. N. Hughes of San Antonio, letter to *Machinists' Monthly Journal* 12, no. 1 (January 1900): 37.

[53] *Railroad Trainmen's Journal* 16, no. 9 (September 1899): 831–32, and 15, no. 8 (August 1898): 680–81; see also, for example, speech by Gompers to New York Central Labor Union, July 1898, Reel 24 (scrapbook), *AFL Records*.

[54] Letter to *United Mine Workers' Journal* 9, no. 7 (26 May 1898).

power, and as the imperial state came to demand more loyalty for its military actions, it became easier for elites to coopt unionists' views. Thus, however much workers waved the flag, the views of government and business leaders about what was patriotic or American were still the ones that ultimately dominated. And many native-born white workers found themselves in agreement with not only imperialistic wars but also the anti-immigrant animus common in business Americanism. Moreover, the flags and the tradition they symbolized offered neither any real strategy for resistance except voting nor any protection from the company thugs and police.

It is true that a few unionists, mostly socialists of various stripes, denounced patriotism as a diversion from real issues of power and inequality. But most such criticism was directed within the relatively safe context of lambasting "patriotism" in the abstract or distant examples of it as exhibited in European imperialism and war, especially in the dozen years of international tension preceding World War I. It was fairly rare for unionists to reject patriotic images entirely. When they occasionally did—like *Seamen's* editor W.J.B. Mackay's claim that "the stars and stripes symbolize injustice, tyranny, slavery to the seamen of the world"—it was a rhetorical device, almost requiring its audience to suspend their patriotic feelings only momentarily in order to see how bad conditions were.[55] Similarly the satirical version of "My Country 'tis of Thee" (/"Dark land of tyranny"), far from challenging patriotism's basic premises, represented a critique intended to reinvigorate patriotism.

Harsher socialist critiques of patriotism could paradoxically remain compatible with the constant use of patriotic symbolism. The Western Federation of Miners, for example, frequently railed against patriotism: typically, in 1900, president Ed Boyce warned employers, "Conceal yourselves under the folds of the stars and stripes to disguise your true motive. . . . We still remember Johnson's saying: 'An appeal to patriotism is the last resort of a scoundrel [sic].'"[56] Yet the WFM drew particularly strongly on republican-nationalist appeals during the 1903–1904 Colorado mining strikes, a patriotic discourse directly contested by the authorities. A union flyer incorporating the American flag and headed with the words, "Is Colorado in America?" was the pretext to arrest Boyce's successor, Charles Moyer, and secretary-treasurer Bill Haywood

---

[55] *Coast Seamen's Journal* 8, no. 3 (24 October 1894). See also MacArthur's defenses of San Francisco seamen's decision to boycott the city's Fourth of July parades from 1895 to 1898, in the face of intense criticism from the middle-class press: *Coast Seamen's Journal* 8, no. 38 (26 June 1895); 9, no. 39 (1 July 1896); 10, no. 39 (30 June 1897); 11, no. 39 (29 June 1898); handwritten notes, folder 15, carton 1, Ira B. Cross Collection, Bancroft Library, Berkeley, California.

[56] Editorial, *Miners' Magazine* 1, no. 1 (January 1900), 18.

for "flag desecration" in March 1904.[57] The leftist response was to reiterate their version of patriotism: as the Spokane, Washington, *New Time* commented of the employers, "Never let such foul pirates sail under so fair a banner. Let the people who have defended the flag on every field of battle, the working people, save it now from desecration, by taking it from the hands of the corporation freebooters and make it stand for what it was intended, 'life, liberty and happiness.' Socialism is the thing to stop flag desecrators."[58] With the limited range of acceptable political symbols available to workers, patriotism remained the last refuge of not only scoundrels but also socialists.

Patriotism offered organized workers a truncated political vocabulary and a more inherently limited one than the novelty of the business offensive might suggest. At root there remained a problem intrinsic to the nature and appeal of any nationalism: its function as a fictive collectivity. If one's identity as a worker, a unionist, and even a socialist was articulated in part through nationalism, then even if one claimed that national myths had meaning only in the context of a struggle for justice or one's class, the collectivity of nationalism still ultimately implied a positive relationship to bourgeois politicians and capitalists. For those few workers who emphasized class struggle as cancelling out such collective bonds, this aspect of patriotism was not a significant problem. But for the less doctrinaire majority of the labor movement and even the socialist movement, patriotism implied that, at some level, workers were members of the same fictive national "family" as their class opponents. This construct erased difference: both the differences in class power, in favor of ruling elites, and the racial and gender difference within the working class, obscured to the advantage of skilled, white, male workers. To be sure, these tensions in patriotism were played upon and exacerbated by business activists and the state; but it is also important to recognize workers' shaping of their own politics, for workers' class opponents did not simply impose contradictions of patriotism from outside; such contradictions also unfolded dialectically from within working-class consciousness and experience.

The complexities of such ideology in the Progressive era suggest the need for a broader reassessment of the importance of working-class patriotism, a phenomenon generally ignored by labor historians. This ideology can be neither dismissed as some sort of "false consciousness" or mystification nor celebrated as a kind of surrogate socialism. In its Amer-

[57] U.S. Senate, *A Report on Labor Disturbances in the State of Colorado from 1880–1904, Inclusive, with Correspondence Relating Thereto*, 58th Cong., 3d sess., 1905. S. Doc. 122, 229–30, and 230–46 on trials; Suggs, *Colorado's War*, 166, 216 n. 19, and plate of flyer, 36; on Moyer's trial, 166–77.

[58] Reprinted in *Miners' Magazine* 5, no. 43 (21 April 1904).

ican context at least, even for socialists, patriotism was and is a peculiarly coercive ideology. The political alternatives and vocabulary available to Americans—even Debsian socialists—remained inextricably caught up in national myths and pride in America's "unique" system and history— far more so than in, say, Britain or Germany. National pride remained an integral part of organized workers' language of democracy, justice, and political participation. Nationality amounted to more than just a context for the discussion of politics and social justice: it was the bone and mar- row of such debates. Loyalty and patriotism were therefore, inevitably, highly politicized. Questions of patriotism absorbed discursive space, and organizers' energy, in a way that was difficult to avoid. Workers could not ignore businessmen's questioning of their patriotism as a diver- sion from the real issues, although socialists occasionally tried. They had to challenge such questions because the accusations cut to the bone of their politics.

Connecting as it did with powerful currents in labor ideology, business Americanism forced organized labor to direct more energy into a patrio- tism that emphasized loyalty at the expense of the radical anticapitalist currents of republicanism, a shift toward the "100 percent Americanism" of the 1920s. The shift was by no means the end of contestation over the meaning of American patriotism and icons like the flag, as 1990s debates on flag-burning demonstrate. But by 1919, nationalism had come to sig- nify an impossibly wide range of issues and demands, a vague all- purpose touchstone that narrowed the range of acceptable demands for change.

Chapter 4

READING THE FLAG: A RECONSIDERATION OF THE PATRIOTIC CULTS OF THE 1890s

Stuart McConnell

HOW ARE we to explain the sudden onslaught of patriotic agitation that swept the United States in the 1890s? To hear the spread-eagle patriots of that tumultuous decade tell the story, American patriotism had long historical roots. Contemporary celebrants of the flag were fond of tracing the heraldic devices of the national banner back to English, French, or even classical sources and elaborating the details of such things as "the first salute to our flag." Patriotism was eternal; the agitators of the 1890s believed that they were only rousing it from its slumber, a conceit much in keeping with late nineteenth-century thinking about the national "will" or "soul" which Ernest Gellner has dubbed "sleeping-beauty" nationalism.[1] Yet as historians have long known, the icons of American patriotism, far from being timeless, had a relatively weak presence for most of the nineteenth century. The national flag was rarely seen except on ships and during wartime. The army and navy were at a low ebb between 1865 and 1898, reduced in size almost thirtyfold from their Civil War peaks and engaged in constant appropriations battles with Congress. Hereditary societies were few, and the most prominent one—the Society of the Cincinnati—was confined mostly to the Northeast and labored under the suspicion of aristocratic leanings.

A very early version of this essay was delivered as a paper, "The Cult of the Flag in the 1890s," to a session at the 1991 American Studies Association annual meeting in Baltimore. I would like to thank Kirk Savage and David Glassberg for their comments at that time, and John Bodnar, Cecilia O'Leary, and Daniel Segal for advice on revisions. I am also grateful to the Newberry Library for a short-term fellowship that funded some of my research and to James Grossman and the rest of the Newberry lunch seminar for comments.

[1] George Henry Preble, *Our Flag: Origin and Progress of the Flag of the United States of America with an Introductory Account of the Symbols, Standards, Banners and Flags of Ancient and Modern Nations* (Albany, N.Y.: Joel Munsell, 1872), 192, 198–237; Richard H. Titherington, "The Story of Our Flag," *Munsey's* 13, no. 4 (July 1895): 401–2; William Elliot Griffis, "Where Our Flag Was First Saluted," *New England Magazine*, n.s., 8, no. 5 (July 1893): 576–85; Ernest Gellner, *Nations and Nationalism* (Ithaca, N.Y.: Cornell University Press, 1983), 48.

American history was taught in elementary schools only in some parts of the country, and at the university it was a distinctly subordinate part of a classical curriculum.[2]

Only in the late 1880s did this situation begin to change. New hereditary organizations such as the Sons and Daughters of the American Revolution (SAR, DAR) sprouted, and they joined the Grand Army of the Republic (GAR), the new American Flag Association, and such national publications as *The Youth's Companion* and *St. Nicholas* in promoting flags for schools, flag salutes, legal sanctions for flag misuse, and public singing of "The Star Spangled Banner." In 1890, North Dakota and New Jersey made the flying of flags at schoolhouses mandatory; other states soon followed suit. In 1891, delegates to the GAR national encampment began the practice of standing for the playing of "The Star Spangled Banner." In 1897, New York became the first state to bar the use of the flag in advertisements. By 1898 the GAR reported 35,049 schoolrooms with flags, and 26,352 in which the pledge of allegiance to the flag was administered. The army and navy returned to prominence during the Spanish-American War, and military drill for schoolboys briefly became a national craze, endorsed by former President Benjamin Harrison. Professional historians began to concern themselves with teaching American history in schools, and by World War I many states required high school students to complete courses in United States history. In little more than a decade, then, the United States saw the invention—or at least the major retooling—of many of its patriotic traditions.[3]

The conventional explanation of the 1890s patriotic boom relies on three undeniably important factors: mass immigration, industrial unrest, and the Spanish-American War. Strife between foreigners and the native-born, it is argued, combined with class antagonisms and an overseas war

[2] Mary R. Dearing, *Veterans in Politics: The Story of the G.A.R.* (Baton Rouge: Louisiana State University Press, 1952), 472–73; Samuel P. Huntington, *The Soldier and the State: The Theory and Politics of Civil-Military Relations* (Cambridge: Harvard University Press, 1957), 226–30; Wallace E. Davies, *Patriotism on Parade: The Story of Veterans' and Hereditary Organizations in America, 1783–1900* (Cambridge: Harvard University Press, 1957), 1–27; Merle Curti, *The Roots of American Loyalty* (New York: Columbia University Press, 1946), 128; John Higham, *History: Professional Scholarship in America*, 2d ed. (Baltimore: Johns Hopkins University Press, 1983), 4; Laurence R. Veysey, *The Emergence of the American University* (Chicago: University of Chicago Press, 1965), 36–40.

[3] Stuart McConnell, *Glorious Contentment: The Grand Army of the Republic, 1865–1900* (Chapel Hill: University of North Carolina Press, 1992), 228–31; Dearing, *Veterans in Politics*, 405, 408, 472, 474–75; Curti, *Roots of American Loyalty*, 190–91; Scot M. Guenter, *The American Flag, 1777–1924: Cultural Shifts from Creation to Codification* (Cranbury, N.J.: Associated University Presses, 1990), 81–132; Davies, *Patriotism on Parade*, 44–73, 218–22; Peter Novick, *That Noble Dream: The "Objectivity Question" and the American Historical Profession* (New York: Cambridge University Press, 1988), 70–72; Higham, *History*, 19–20.

to produce an unprecedented wave of nativism and patriotism. Still, and without wishing to minimize the obvious significance of nativism, class conflict, and war, I am convinced that the patriotic cults of the 1890s represented something more complex than a simple-minded defense mechanism employed by members of the native-born middle class against intruders. First, there is the matter of timing. The presentations of flags to schools, the worries about American history textbooks, and the founding of the SAR and DAR all date from the late 1880s, well before the most significant wave of immigration, which crested after 1900, had gotten fairly under way and a decade before the Spanish-American War. The school drill craze similarly predated the war by several years, and while legislation protecting the flag from desecration post-dated the flag-waving McKinley campaign of 1896, it was actually part of a negative reaction to that campaign, not a continuation of it.[4]

More important, while the ideologies of nativism, middle-class consciousness, and state patriotism sometimes converge; sometimes they do not. Frank De Roose points out that patriotic sentiments can be employed in opposition to the state as well as in support of it—in arguments that a particular state action is unconstitutional, for example.[5] The same Republican industrialists who employed the flag as an antidote to class strife in the extraordinary election of 1896 found themselves opposed to nativists who invoked "Americanism" as a justification for cutting off the abundant flow of cheap immigrant labor, Populists such as William Jennings Bryan and Jerry Simpson opposed "the interests" but supported the Spanish-American War; disgruntled opponents of the war warned of the dangers of "unassimilable races" in the newly acquired territories.[6] Analytically, nativism, middle-class consciousness, and state patriotism are distinct because each proclaims loyalty to a different object that is then conflated with "the nation": a race or kin group; a particular social class; or a set of political institutions, namely those of the nation-state. Thus even among the native-born, middle-class whites who dominated the patriotic organizations of the 1890s, we may find not simple, undifferentiated patriotism, but a complex mix of loyalties.

[4] Curti, *Roots of American Loyalty*, 191; Randolph I. Geare, "Historic Flags," *New England Magazine* 28, no. 6 (August 1903): 703.

[5] Frank De Roose, "The Study of Patriotism" (occasional paper, University of Illinois Program in Arms Control, Disarmament, and International Security, Champaign, September 1990), 11–13.

[6] John D. Hicks, *The Populist Revolt: A History of the Farmers' Alliance and the People's Party* (Minneapolis: University of Minnesota Press, 1931), 389–90; William Appleman Williams, *The Tragedy of American Diplomacy*, 2d ed. (New York: Dell, 1972), 31; John Higham, *Strangers in the Land: Patterns of American Nativism, 1860–1925* (New Brunswick, N.J.: Rutgers University Press, 1955), 108–10.

In this essay I argue that the patriotic exercises of the 1890s represented a significant break with earlier attitudes toward the nation. Far from being a last-ditch defense of a well-established set of ideas about American citizenship, these activities—the cult of the flag, with which I shall be chiefly concerned, but also such things as school military drill and the hereditary societies—show native-born whites groping toward a new definition of what "American" meant. In so doing, they moved away from earlier, particularistic readings of national loyalty, readings that had been tied to family, locality, and historical incident and toward an abstract national vision that was at once more and less flexible than the particularisms that preceded it.

Any coherent nationalist program has at least two essential components: an ideology of sameness, and an ideology of obligation. An ideology of sameness bounds the nation, limiting its membership to those who are thought alike in some way, while excluding those thought unlike (thus "the French" may include those who speak the French language while excluding those who speak German; "the Japanese" may include those of Japanese parentage but not those of foreign parentage; and so forth). For much of the early nineteenth century, American ideas of "sameness" were predicated on yeoman freeholding—the bundle of attitudes usually labeled "republicanism." Americans were alike socially in their standing as actual or potential owners of property and politically in their standing as independent voters. Exclusions from this definition included those who *were* property or who were otherwise thought dependent; thus in practice, American nationalism was raced and gendered as well, if only implicitly.[7]

An ideology of obligation, as the economist Robert Reich has tren-

---

[7] The best discussion of the symbiotic relationship between republican ideology, slavery, and racism remains Edmund Morgan, *American Slavery, American Freedom: The Ordeal of Colonial Virginia* (New York: W. W. Norton, 1975), 295–337; and see also Daniel Segal, " 'The European': Allegories of Racial Purity," *Anthropology Today* 7, no. 5 (October 1991): 7–9, and Daniel Segal and Richard Handler, "How European is Nationalism?" *Social Analysis* 32 (1993): 1–16. On republicanism, scholarship is now so vast as to be almost unmanageable. The most influential works have been J.G.A. Pocock, *The Machiavellian Moment: Florentine Political Thought and the Atlantic Republican Tradition* (Princeton: Princeton University Press, 1975); Gordon S. Wood, *The Creation of the American Republic, 1776–1787* (Chapel Hill: University of North Carolina Press, 1969); and Sean Wilentz, *Chants Democratic: New York City and the Rise of the American Working Class, 1788–1850* (New York: Oxford University Press, 1984); while useful period interpretations are provided in a special issue of *American Quarterly* 37, no. 4 (Fall 1985). Daniel Rodgers reviews the whole corpus of writing on the subject in "Republicanism: The Career of a Concept," *Journal of American History* 79, no. 1 (June 1992): 11–38. Although Rodgers sees the plethora of scholarship on republicanism as evidence of a trendy interpretation stretched to the breaking point, I am inclined to see it as confirmation of the ubiquity of the republican worldview among native-born whites until late in the nineteenth century.

chantly argued, is a bargain between differently empowered social groups within the bounded nation, an answer to the question: What do members of the nation owe one another?[8] Liberal capitalism, which historians once thought was the essence of the nineteenth-century American worldview, required conationals only to leave each other alone so far as possible. Republicanism, which more recent writers have stressed, implied a stronger sense of civic responsibility, but one usually mediated through such local institutions as the town, the family, or the regiment, with the national state a relatively weak and distant presence. In either case, obligations to conationals were not something processed through allegiance to the national state. The great exception to this pattern was, of course, the Civil War, and it is no accident that aged veterans of the Union Army were among the first and loudest of the patriotic agitators of the 1890s.[9]

By 1890, the small-producer economy that had formed the material basis for the old republican ideology of sameness was clearly in eclipse. As independent proprietorship became harder to sustain, more people went to work as wage laborers. Meanwhile, the national market was drawing more and more formerly isolated places into its orbit, and the national state was growing apace through such instrumentalities as the military pension system.[10] Republicanism's ideology of sameness was now of decreasing relevance; liberalism offered no plausible ideology of obligation (loyalty to the nation as loyalty to self-interest?). How, then, was the national bond to be understood under changed social and economic circumstances?

The cult of the flag in the 1890s was the starting point of some answers that have endured well into our own century. To appreciate the changes

[8] Robert B. Reich, *The Work of Nations* (New York: Alfred A. Knopf, 1991), 58–68, 301–15.

[9] The standard work on liberalism is, of course, Louis Hartz, *The Liberal Tradition in America: An Interpretation of American Political Thought Since the Revolution* (New York: Harcourt Brace, 1955). Robert B. Westbrook points out the liberal state's "problem of political obligation" in "I Want a Girl, Just Like the Girl That Married Harry James: American Women and the Problem of Political Obligation in World War II," *American Quarterly* 42, no. 4 (December 1990): 587–615. On the filtering of national ideals through the figure of the "republican mother," see Linda K. Kerber, *Women of the Republic: Intellect and Ideology in Revolutionary America* (Chapel Hill: University of North Carolina Press, 1980); on Union veterans, McConnell, *Glorious Contentment*.

[10] Charles Sellers, *The Market Revolution: Jacksonian America, 1815–1846* (New York: Oxford University Press, 1991); Robert Wiebe, *The Search for Order, 1877–1920* (New York: Hill and Wang, 1967); Steven Hahn, *The Roots of Southern Populism: Yeoman Farmers and the Transformation of the Georgia Upcountry, 1850–1890* (New York: Oxford University Press, 1983); on state building and the pension system, Theda Skocpol, *Protecting Soldiers and Mothers: The Political Origins of Social Policy in the United States* (Cambridge: Harvard University Press, 1992), 67–151.

that took place in that decade, however, one must first realize that for most of the nineteenth century the national flag rarely inspired the sort of reverence we now associate with it. The design was changed a number of times, and in fact it seems to have been subject to local fiat. Although the flag flew from American ships and military installations from the outset, army regiments continued to carry only their own regimental colors into battle until the Mexican War of 1848. As late as 1889, most schoolhouses did not fly flags, such things as Flag Day and the Pledge of Allegiance were not yet in existence, and the practice of taking off hats and singing at the playing of "The Star Spangled Banner" was followed only in a few localities.

This is not to say that the flag was an unimportant symbol in the early nineteenth century, only that what it symbolized was limited and often local. Even when troops were raised to defend the Union or the Confederacy, they were raised and officered locally. As Don Harrison Doyle and Reid Mitchell, among others, have pointed out, this meant that troops on both sides viewed their national army service in fundamentally local terms. Northerners fought for Jacksonville, or Indianapolis, or Portland, as much as for an abstract Union, while on the southern side, Mitchell argues, fidelity to regimental comrades kept the Army of Northern Virginia in the field long after its Confederate nationalism had evaporated.[11]

To these soldiers, the regimental flag symbolized home and hearth, and in battles during the war it was guarded with an appropriately intense loyalty. The regimental color bearer came to be seen as a special individual. David Eugene Hicks of the Fifteenth New Jersey, for example, "a tall, noble-looking young man," was selected for "his fine soldierly qualities." His early death in battle, the regimental historian recalled, was often mentioned around the campfire. In the Eleventh Maine, Sergeant James Gross was remembered for carrying the colors in his arms after the flagstaff was shot away during a retreat at Deep Run, where the dead fell around him. The lore of the Civil War was replete with legends of soldiers fighting to defend the colors or dying with the flag in their hands.[12]

[11] Don Harrison Doyle, *The Social Order of A Frontier Community: Jacksonville, Illinois, 1825–70* (Urbana: University of Illinois Press, 1978), 227–59; Reid Mitchell, *Civil War Soldiers: Their Expectations and Their Experiences* (New York: Viking, 1988), 16–17; Mitchell, "The Northern Soldier and His Community," in *Toward A Social History of the American Civil War: Exploratory Essays* ed. Maris A. Vinovskis (New York: Cambridge University Press, 1990), 78–92.

[12] Mitchell, *Civil War Soldiers*, 18–20; Alanson A. Haines, *History of the Fifteenth Regiment New Jersey Volunteers* (New York: Jenkins and Thomas, 1883), 57; *The Story of One Regiment. The Eleventh Maine Infantry Volunteers in the War of the Rebellion* (New York: Press of J. J. Little & Co., 1896), 249; Guenter, *The American Flag*, 75–77.

Perhaps the most famous piece of such lore, however, concerned neither a combatant nor a man, and the tale points to a second way in which
the flag was a particularistic symbol. "Shoot, if you must, this old gray
head, but spare your country's flag," Barbara Frietchie tells Stonewall
Jackson in John Greenleaf Whittier's widely recited poem of 1863. It is
true that in "Barbara Frietchie," Whittier was invoking the flag as an
emblem of spread-eagle nationalism, not of localism ("Over Barbara
Frietchie's grave/Flag of Freedom and Union wave!). Still, one reason
the poem became as popular as it did among northern civilians was that
its gray-headed female heroine spoke to another important symbolic
meaning of the national colors: the association of the flag with women,
and especially with family, whose nurturance, under prevailing Victorian
gender conventions, was the special realm of women. During the war, it
was standard practice for women to sew flags for hometown regiments;
in some places they produced so many banners that the favored units
scarcely knew what to do with all of them. Within a few months of
Sumter, the ceremony of flag presentation had taken form: the tendering
of the homemade flag, the thanks of the local captain, the promises of the
troops to acquit themselves like men in defense of home and hearth. In
Kalamazoo, Michigan, for example, the Sixth Infantry received a flag
containing the motto "Do Your Duty" stitched among the stars. In
Niles, Michigan, women of the town presented the local regiment with a
silk banner that "was carried by the regiment through all its hard fought
battles up to and including Fredricksburg, when it had become so tattered by wear, and some forty bullet holes, that it was deemed unservice-
able, and was returned to the donors, who treasure it highly." Women, in
short, had a special relationship with the flag, one reinforced at the local
level through presentation rituals.[13]

During the fighting, the flag took on a third even more particularistic
set of meanings that stemmed from what one might term the particularity of incident. As regimental flags were carried from battle to battle,
they became valued for the special places they had been, the unique
scenes they had witnessed. The Twenty-Fourth Massachusetts, for example, recorded every major engagement through which its flag had
passed by stitching the names of battles to the bunting itself. Other regiments did the same, or they recorded the trials and tribulations of their
flags in regimental histories. Indeed, early general histories of the flag,
such as George Henry Preble's *Origin and History of the American Flag*,

---

[13] "Barbara Frietchie," *The Complete Poetical Works of John Greenleaf Whittier*, Cambridge
ed. (Boston: Houghton, Mifflin and Co., 1894), 342–43; John Robertson, comp., *The Flags
of Michigan* (Lansing: W. S. George and Co., State Printers and Binders, 1877), 33–42. On
the presentation of homemade flags during the war, see also Mitchell, *Civil War Soldiers*,
19–20; and Guenter, *The American Flag*, 79–81.

often read like melodramas, in which individual flags are the protagonists. In these sagas, a flag is born, has adventures and brushes with death, and survives to be venerated in its old age:

> The colors of the Sixteenth Regiment were torn from their standards at the fall of Plymouth, N.C., April 20, 1864, and in part distributed among the officers and men, while the remaining portions were burned, to prevent them from falling into the hands of the rebels. The pieces that were saved were carried through the military prisons at the South, and, finally, on the release of the members who survived, were brought home. These few shreds of the old colors have been kept as sacred souvenirs by their possessors. A few months ago the executive committee of the regiment determined on getting together as many of these fragments as possible, and have them restored, that they might be deposited with the battle-flags at the capitol.[14]

A flag was, in fact, made of these remnants for display at the State House. The fate of the Sixteenth Massachusetts flag was by no means unusual: in the years following the war, individual banners continued to be prized not simply because they were national flags but because of the specific associations they carried. In Philadelphia, for example, the leading GAR post was under constant solicitation from civic societies to loan out its colors for parades, not because these organizations could not obtain flags otherwise, but because the war associations of the veterans' banners made them unique. The banner that had purportedly flown on the *Bonhomme Richard* in 1779 and other "historical" flags were likewise treated as relics, stored away in state capitols or displayed as public treasures.[15] Confederate flags captured by Union troops were so special that when President Grover Cleveland proposed returning them to southern states in 1887, the move was greeted with howls of outrage and had to be rescinded. And when veterans at an 1891 parade in Detroit failed to march with authentic battle flags, a journalist complained: "Flags there were in plenty; but they were as a rule the trumpery pennons of individuals, or the brand-new gaudy banners of the different Posts, and not in the least historical or important."[16]

---

[14] George Henry Preble, *Origin and History of the American Flag*, 2 vols., new ed. (Philadelphia: Nicholas L. Brown, 1917) 2: 563; see also the many similar narratives on 544–88. On the flag of the Twenty-Fourth Massachusetts, see the photos in Alfred S. Roe, *The Twenty-Fourth Regiment Massachusetts Volunteers, 1861–1866* (Worcester, Mass.: Twenty-Fourth Veteran Association, 1907), 449, 563.

[15] Post 2 Minutes, 19 October 1882, Sons of Union Veterans Collection, GAR Memorial Hall and Museum, Philadelphia (among many other examples). On the *Bonhomme Richard* flag, see Guenter, *The American Flag*, 98–101.

[16] *Macmillan's Magazine*, December 1891, 133. On the battle-flag controversy, see Dearing, *Veterans in Politics*, 342–51; and Davies, *Patriotism on Parade*, 257–60.

Such veneration of flag relics has, of course, continued to the present. In the 1890s, however, a new patriotic language began to take shape, in which the flag emerged as a symbol of abstract nationalism. Where previously the flag had carried connotations of locality and familiarity, now it was addressed in almost mystical terms. The reverence of school-children for the flag, GAR Commander-in-Chief William Warner told Union veterans in 1889, should be like that of the Israelites for the Ark of the Covenant. Scot Guenter points out that juvenile fiction of the 1890s sometimes treated the flag as a sort of superhero, rescuing boys from burning buildings or inspiring them to build patriotic shrines.[17] And where once the flag had stood for family and community, it was now praised for its power as a universal symbol. Particularly after the quick U.S. military victory over Spain, the cultists' rhetoric became expansive indeed. GAR Chaplain-in-Chief Frank C. Bruner put it in a prayer that opened the national encampment of 1898:

> Give us greater love for the old flag which has seemed to come from the hand of God itself. We thank thee that thou hast given us this emblem that we are to carry forth for civilization and to make the nations who have been blackened by superstition and darkness, brighter and more beautiful. The evolution of our flag gives a wider truth to humanity. It has become a patriotic school-house, a symbolism of those elements which make good government, justice born of God . . . . A flag for the national capital; a flag for every temple of justice; a flag for every schoolhouse; a flag for all the world. All hail the banner of the free! May it continue to kiss the breeze until distant unborn generations rise up and look on its dancing folds. We pray thee that all the world may be free. We thank thee that we are on a mighty move to bring peace to all the world.[18]

Here and elsewhere, the flag was pictured as a quasi religious symbol with meaning that transcended even national borders.

The flag was not only spoken of more abstractly, but it also began to be treated ritually as an object of transcendent significance. Although "flag etiquette" is largely a product of the twentieth century, the 1890s saw the writing of the pledge of allegiance, the adoption by veterans' organizations of flag codes, and, most important, the elaboration of the ceremony of flag presentation established during the Civil War. In the 1890s, what had been a rather simple ritual, transacted between local women and men, became an elaborate civic affair, girded with marches, patriotic music, and speeches.

The level of abstraction in such ceremonies is perhaps best understood

[17] *Journal of the National Encampment, GAR*, 1889, 41; Guenter, *The American Flag*, 111.
[18] *Journal of the National Encampment, GAR*, q898, 8.

as an attempt on the part of some Gilded Age Americans to describe a "nation" that had always been understood before through the more immediate and concrete social experiences of town and family. As David Kertzer, an anthropologist of political ritual, points out, *every* organization from General Motors to the Ku Klux Klan employs some kind of ritual symbolism because organizations themselves can only be "seen" or represented symbolically. They exist only as constructs to which symbols or symbolic behaviors give life. Michael Walzer describes this phenomenon in another context: "The state is invisible; it must be personified before it can be seen, symbolized before it can be loved, imagined before it can be conceived." The construction of a newer and more abstract flag in the cult of 1890s allowed people to "see" what, from the local angle of 1861, had been only a vague abstraction, namely "the nation."[19]

In some instances, the new cult of the flag annexed and reshaped older, more particularistic readings. Women and family, for example, continued to be central to the meaning of the flag. Now, however, women operated through national patriotic societies such as the DAR, the Women's Relief Corps, and the Colonial Dames of America, or through lobbying campaigns such as Ella Holloway's twenty-four-year crusade to make "The Star Spangled Banner" the national anthem. During this era Betsy Ross was first championed as the legendary "mother of the flag," a title she seems destined to retain despite the efforts of subsequent historians to dislodge her.[20] By the same token, family and flag, once linked through regimental colors, now were connected through mass displays: the "living flag," which became widely popular in the 1890s, schoolhouse flag ceremonies, or patriotic parades in which young children threw flowers to aged veterans.

Sometimes the new flag ritualism could annex the old particularities of

[19] David I. Kertzer, *Ritual, Politics and Power* (New Haven: Yale University Press, 1988), 15–16; Michael Walzer, "On the Role of Symbolism in Political Thought," *Political Science Quarterly* 82, no. 1 (Spring 1967): 194.

[20] On the invention of the Ross legend, see Guenter, *The American Flag*, 101–3. Contemporary sources on Ross include Franklin Hanford, *Did Betsey Ross Design the Flag of the United States of America?* (Scottsville, N.Y.: Scottsville Literary Society, 1921); Preble, *Our Flag*, 192–94; J. Franklin Riegert, *The History of the First United States Flag and the Patriotism of Betsy Ross* (Harrisburg: Lane S. Hart, 1878); and Addie Guthrie Weaver, *The Story of Our Flag, Colonial and National, With a Sketch of the Quakeress Betsy Ross* (Chicago: A. G. Weaver, 1898). On Ross's persistence in American historical memory as the "first mother" of the nation, see Michael Frisch, "American History and the Structures of Collective Memory: A Modest Exercise in Empirical Iconography," *Journal of American History* 75, no. 4 (March 1989): 1130–55, esp. 1146–47. On Holloway, I am indebted to William M. Ferraro, "The National Anthem Act of 1931: The Emergence of a Legal Symbol" (senior thesis in history, Georgetown University, 1982).

locality and incident as well. In 1905, the uneventful return to the South of the same bullet-riddled Confederate battle flags that had caused such a furor in 1887 caused more than one observer to tout them as symbols of a newly reunited nation. "There can be no valid reasons why these tattered and blood-stained relics of a murderous family quarrel should not be returned to the States whose sons fought and died under them," suggested the Cleveland *Plain Dealer*. "The purpose of the war was accomplished when it was universally admitted that the Union is indissoluble."[21] More often, however, the link between locality, incident, and flag was obscured or lost. What emerged instead was a typification: one no longer spoke of particular flags, but of The Flag, in the same way that nineteenth-century orators spoke of The Negro, or The Savage, or The Poor.[22] As Kertzer points out, a truly powerful political symbol must be not only condensed (that is, capable of unifying a diverse set of meanings) but also multivocal (that is, able to be understood in a variety of ways) and ambiguous (that is, finally uncertain and complex, not a declarative statement).[23] Although the cult of the flag did free the national banner from the limiting and particularizing associations more typical of the early nineteenth century, its adherents reconfigured national loyalty in terms that sounded completely univocal and unambiguous: The Flag.

By itself, of course, the typified flag was simply a fetish, as many people at the time realized. "All this blow and bluster about the 'Flag,' the 'Flag,' etc., many times repeated, is merely senseless bosh, and mystifies rather than enlightens and educates," snorted one veterans' newspaper, the *Grand Army Record*, in 1894, "unless the speaker . . . make[s] clear what that emblem represents and is used for." Similarly, the *Independent* complained in 1903 that members of the Sons of the American Revolution "see no difference between an American citizen using a rug with the Star Spangled Banner worked in it, and a Spanish mob trampling the American flag underfoot. . . . This is going nearly as far as the Mohammedans who gather every last scrap of paper lest it should contain the name of Allah and of the ancient Jews who prevented desecration by not writing the name of God at all."[24]

[21] Guenter, *The American Flag*, 103; Cleveland *Plain Dealer*, cited in *Current Literature* 38 (April 1905): 297.

[22] A useful discussion of the concept of typification and a listing of some major theoretical sources appear in Pauline Turner Strong, "Captivity in White and Red: Convergent Practice and Colonial Representation on the British-Amerindian Frontier, 1606–1736," in *Crossing Cultures: Essays in the Displacement of Western Civilization*, ed. Daniel Segal (Tucson: University of Arizona Press, 1992), 83–84, n. 9.

[23] Kertzer, *Ritual, Politics, and Power*, 11.

[24] *Grand Army Record*, September 1894, 5; "The Flag as Fetish," *The Independent* 55, no. 2824 (15 January 1903): 162. In an important sense, of course, such icons can function as the centerpieces of communities of signs, as Benedict Anderson suggests in his discussion of

Most members of the patriotic groups, however, went beyond worship of the flag for its own sake and sought instead to promote it as a symbol of the bond between conationals. To say this, however, is not to say that the would-be patriots all defined the national bond in the same way. With the decline of local, familial, and incidental readings of national loyalty, the flag cultists of the 1890s were forced to return to the core questions of nationalism: What was the nation? What did its members owe one another? Their answers were varied and not always unambiguous.

One way to reconceive the national bond was simply to take the old associations of family and extend them over a wider compass. In the hereditary societies—most important the Sons and Daughters of the Revolution (1889, 1890) but also such smaller orders as the Colonial Dames of America (1891) and the Mayflower Descendants (1897)—the nation was re-envisioned as a kind of extended family, held together by the blood tie of kinship. True Americanism was limited to those who could prove lineal descent from Revolutionary War patriots, with everyone else in the country treated as a sort of guest. The Daughters in particular expended much effort on genealogical research, and engaged in internecine squabbles about such secondary kin designations as "mother of patriots." But others among the ultrapatriots resorted to familial ties as well. Edward W. Tuffley, an English writer, argued in 1883 that the design of the Stars and Stripes had been drawn from the family coat of arms of George Washington, a contention that later writers such as Preble endorsed. Betsy Ross was put forward (by her grandson, appropriately) as the "mother of the flag," a maternal image so persistent that even in our own time, Michael Frisch reports, students often confuse Ross with Martha Washington, the real wife of "the father of the country." Children joined the project through the Children of the American Revolution (1895) and through school exercises such as one concocted for Flag Day in Michigan in 1916, "The Banner Betsy Made," in which boys impersonated Washington and Robert Morris and a girl played Betsy Ross. "It will add interest to this exercise," noted the official authors, "if the girls of the class make the flags in their manual arts class."[25]

Islam in *Imagined Communities: Reflections on the Origin and Spread of Nationalism* (London: Verso, 1983), 20–22, 55–56.

[25] Edward W. Tuffley, *Origin of the Stars and Stripes, Together With an Accurate Account of the Washington Genealogy* (New York: Root and Tinker, 1883), 6–11; Frisch, "American History and the Structures of Collective Memory," 1146–47; *The American Flag in Prose, Poetry and Song* (Lansing: Michigan State Library, 1916), 12. Frisch's collective memory quiz has produced similar results in my own classroom, including one example of the misidentification: "George's wife, Betsy."

If the boundary around the nation was a kinship boundary, then the obligations of conationals were those of family members. Under the prevailing middle-class gender norms of the late nineteenth century, which stressed women's domestic and familial ties, this was clearly a vision with great appeal to women and perhaps partly explains the greater success of the DAR relative to the SAR (the DAR had more than thirty thousand members by 1900, while the SAR had fewer than ten thousand). It was also a vision with a long literary lineage, for as Kathleen Diffley points out, antebellum (and, to a lesser extent, postbellum) fiction typically identified national stability with the preservation of "the old homestead," while political oratory was saturated with references to erring children, sister states, and the national household.[26] Blood ties, however, plainly excluded, as they were intended to exclude, a majority of inhabitants of the United States of the 1890s, including black Americans, who were barred from the DAR whether they had Revolutionary War ancestors or not.[27] Not all the would-be patriots wished to narrow the grounds of national loyalty in quite this way; the GAR, for example, repeatedly resisted efforts to turn that organization into a hereditary order. As the *Independent* put it in 1903, after reviewing public reports of flag misuse: "There is one form of desecration of our national emblems more serious than those mentioned. That is in using them in any way as the distinguishing badge of those self-styled 'patriotic' societies which base their membership on their ancestry or which find their chief occupation in opposing the influence of 'foreigners.'"[28]

A second way of reimagining the national bond was to revert to a model of social obligation nearly as basic as that of the family: the nation as a unit of mutual defense. Among the military drill enthusiasts who suddenly appeared in the mid-1890s, patriotism was equated with the bearing of arms. Although this was an equation long central to American notions of citizenship (as Kimberly Jensen points out in chapter 6 of this volume), the vision of "a nation in arms" usually had been realized only in wartime and even then only through militia units with fundamentally local orientations. The drill units promised a peacetime continuation of mutual military obligation.[29]

[26] Davies, *Patriotism on Parade*, 77; Kathleen Diffley, *Where My Heart Is Turning Ever: Civil War Stories and Constitutional Reform, 1861–1876* (Athens: University of Georgia Press, 1992), 13–39.

[27] Martha Strayer, *The D.A.R.: An Informal History* (Washington, D.C.: Public Affairs Press, 1958), 46–47.

[28] McConnell, *Glorious Contentment*, 202–5; "The Flag as Fetish," 163.

[29] Kimberly Jensen, "Women, Citizenship, and Civic Sacrifice: Engendering Patriotism in the First World War," chap. 6 in this volume. On nineteenth-century militias, Marcus Cunliffe, *Soldiers and Civilians: The Martial Spirit in America, 1775–1865* (Boston: Little, Brown, 1968); Gerald Linderman, *The Mirror of War: American Society and the Spanish-American War* (Ann Arbor: University of Michigan Press, 1974), 60–90; and Robert Rein-

The full-fledged cult of military training that broke out in the 1890s was sometimes sponsored by the patriotic societies, but also by churches, schools, temperance societies, and fraternal organizations. Companies of teenaged boys practiced military drill—with or without arms and uniforms—in Denver, Omaha, Wilmington, Baltimore, and Seattle, as well as in New York City and across New England. A "Baptist Boys Brigade" in 1894 reported one hundred companies outfitted with uniforms, guns, and cartridge boxes containing New Testaments. Six northeastern governors, meeting in New York City in 1895, were treated to military honors, armed marches, and bayonet drills by eight hundred cadets, aged ten to sixteen. In 1896, a reporter for *Munsey's* estimated the membership of a school-based "American Guard" at thirty thousand. The military regimen, said President Benjamin Harrison in 1894, would show schoolboys "the power and beauty there is in a company—moved by one man and as one man," while at the same time ensuring "our strength and safety . . . in a general dissemination of military knowledge and training among the people."[30]

Military obligation was a form of national loyalty accessible even to immigrants; in that sense it was less exclusive than the kinship nation of the hereditary societies. For the institutions sponsoring the drill companies, this inclusivity was a plus. One schoolboy company at the New York governors' review, noted *Harper's*,

> was from a school in the poorer part of the city, and their own hats and caps were so variously ragged that they were marched bareheaded. They came from neighborhoods where there is little in their home environment or associations to induce cleanliness or orderliness, but as they marched by the reviewers with their hands at salute it was seen that those hands were as clean as the shining faces they shaded. Their poor clothing was clean and neat. Their bodies and legs and arms were responding quickly to the training which will make them strong and active.[31]

Similarly, when the GAR's Lafayette Post presented flags to the Rhinelander School in 1897, it was pleased to note "acceptance by Master Hass of the School Battalion."[32]

However, the institutions sponsoring drill companies were dominated

---

ders, "Militia and Public Order in Nineteenth-Century America," *Journal of American Studies* 11, no. 1 (April 1977): 81–101.

[30] "Our Schoolboy Soldiers," *Munsey's* 15 (July 1896): 459–66; Alfred H. Love, "Military Instruction in Schools, Churches and Colleges," *American Journal of Politics* 5 (August 1894): 211; "Military Training in Schools," *Harper's Weekly* 38 (9 February 1895), 127; Benjamin Harrison, "Military Instruction in Schools and Colleges. An Open Letter by Ex-President Harrison," *Century* 47 (January 1894): 468–69.

[31] "Military Training in Schools," 127.

[32] *Ceremony of Flag Presentation to Columbia University*, 110.

by native-born whites, who tended to see them as opportunities to bring order and discipline to an otherwise unruly urban immigrant population. Moreover, a militarized reading of loyalty excluded women, promoted violence, and was much too closely identified with centralized state power for many people raised on the republican militia tradition. "How will it look," lamented critic Alfred H. Love in 1894, "to have one half of the pupils being drilled in military tactics and the other half going on with their studies; in other words, the boys taught that which is destructive and the girls that which is constructive?" Love argued that by promoting military drill "we ape the worst forms of monarchy; and we drift into military despotisms," an objection echoed by the social reform editor Benjamin O. Flower. "The introduction of military training into the common schools of America," wrote Flower, "marked the triumph of the military spirit of despotic Europe over the long-cherished traditions of the republic."[33]

Both the hereditary and military approaches to loyalty took existing small-group loyalties and nationalized them. But at least two other reconfigurations of nationalism among native-born whites in the 1890s proved much longer lasting, and each represented a significant shift in sensibility. The first entailed the embrace of the federal state *as* the nation in its own right. Loyalty to the nation consisted of obedience to the national government or, as it was more often put, obedience to law. This was a new ideology of sameness: Americans were alike in both their fealty to the national state and their association with that state's assertion of power against other states. By the same token, difference was externalized—"non-Americans" were those loyal to other nation-states, not gendered or ancestrally defined Others within the United States. Finally, a new ideology of obligation emerged, predicated on national law as the fairest bargain between individuals, who were for that reason obliged to uphold it uncategorically. "Whatever [the federal] government may desire to do in Oregon," wrote Oregon GAR commander S. B. Ormsby in 1894, "it is our duty to see that it is done."[34]

In fact, this statist model of loyalty proved most appealing to Union veterans. These were men to whom the nation had become "visible" years earlier, as a result of their federal army service. Through the symbolic rituals of training camp, the Union soldiers had given up their peacetime selves and become "new men," "national men," as it were. Donning the uniform, they achieved a species of pro forma equality that swept up pre-

[33] Love, "Military Instruction in Schools and Colleges," 207, 208; Benjamin O. Flower, "Fostering the Savage in the Young," *Arena* 10, no. 57 (August 1894): 428.

[34] General Order #5, Oregon Department Commander S. B. Ormsby, 21 July 1894, Oregon Collection, GAR Papers, Oregon State Library, Salem, Oregon. On the exteriorization of hierarchy, see the discussion in Segal, " 'The European.' "

existing distinctions in the undifferentiated "boys in blue," the title by which Union veterans identified themselves and were identified by others. Those who joined the Grand Army after the war—more than 400,000 of them by 1890—enlisted in an organization that lobbied for national pensions, fought for national textbooks, and loudly supported the national state in its 1898 war with Spain. Starting the war as citizen-soldiers in local militias, the veterans had become, by 1890, staunch defenders of the national state *as a state*. Thus it is no surprise to find veterans in 1892 calling for "obedience to the law under all circumstances" during the Homestead Strike, or cheering Secretary of War Elihu Root's 1902 promise to crush "all elements and conditions against the authority of the government of the United States" in the Philippines.[35]

As the veterans' animus toward the Homestead strikers suggests, a final nationalist vision of the 1890s was that of the flag not as a national family heirloom, a war banner, or an emblem of the state, but as a typification of a particular *sort* of nation—one with a narrow class and ethnic base. In the flag ceremonies, for example, a white, native-born member of one of the patriotic orders was always presenting to Master Hass, to "a Russian girl pupil, five years old," or to the newly annexed inhabitants of Puerto Rico. Members of the patriotic societies appeared theatrically in a position of ownership; the gift of the flag was theirs to bestow upon grateful, symbolically subservient recipients. Similarly, drill company organizers stressed that military training would ensure "obedience and a proper respect for authority" among the urban poor, while forcing "the disputatious . . . to learn that there are conditions when debate is inadmissible." In Worcester, Massachusetts, native-born employers tried to replace the rowdy Irish American Fourth of July with a "safe and sane" holiday under middle-class control. And in many other cities, the native-born led Americanization classes in schools and settlement houses. In each case, immigrants and laborers were on the receiving end of a tutorial relationship.[36]

Under this reading, national loyalty was mediated through ethnic and class hierarchies, with certain groups privileged to dictate the terms of entry to others. The ideology of sameness was one of ethnic and class

---

[35] Washington, D.C., *National Tribune*, 21 July 1892, 6; *Journal of the National Encampment, Grand Army of the Republic*, 1902, 296. I have recounted the GAR's evolution into a nationalist organization at length in *Glorious Contentment*, esp. chaps. 4–6.

[36] T. B. Bronson, "The Value of Military Training and Discipline in Schools," *School Review* 2 (May 1894): 283; Harrison, "Military Instruction in Schools and Colleges," 469; *Ceremony of Flag Presentation to Columbia University*, 110, 111, 114; Roy Rosenzweig, *Eight Hours For What We Will: Workers and Leisure in an Industrial City, 1870–1920* (New York: Cambridge University Press, 1983), 65–90, 153–68; Curti, *Roots of American Loyalty*, 183–87.

similarity: Americanness was defined by such things as light skin, English-language ability, "Anglo-Saxon" ancestry, and social position in the established middle class. Native-born proprietors of such a nation owed other residents instruction and guidance; recipients owed acquiescence to existing ethnic and class relations and "obedience and proper respect" for the authority necessary to maintain them. In short, the flag had lost one set of particularistic associations—those of locality, family, and incident—only to acquire another set—those of ethnicity and class.

Like the statist version of national loyalty, the nativist middle-class one had a long future ahead of it. As Cecilia O'Leary argues in chapter 2 of this volume, the Blue-Grey reunionism of the 1890s, while phrased in terms of national state loyalty, often acted as a cover for white supremacy. Twentieth-century veterans groups such as the American Legion would oversee coercive Americanization campaigns, while the DAR would move beyond genealogical patriotism to discover the menace of communism.[37] Nativists from the Ku Klux Klan of the 1920s to California's English-only movement of the 1980s would continue to wrap themselves in the flag, while the association of flags with corporate capitalism, first made by McKinley in 1896, became so pervasive by 1989 that a Japanese auto company could actually use the Stars and Stripes as a symbol of successful resistance to unionization of its American plants.[38]

A clue to the lasting appeal of the nativist middle-class version of patriotism lies in the social composition of the patriotic organizations themselves. The GAR, for example, was dominated by white members of the middle classes, and while social histories of the early DAR and SAR have yet to be done, it seems very likely that an even more exclusive membership, or at least leadership, pattern prevailed in those organizations.[39] Certainly it did in nationalist groups elsewhere in the world, as evidenced by Geoff Eley's study of Wilhelmine Germany and Pieter Judson's work on Austria. In fact, a number of writers on nineteenth-century nationalism have concluded that members of the petit bourgeoisie were partic-

[37] Cecilia O'Leary, "'Blood Brotherhood': The Racialization of Patriotism, 1865–1918," chap. 2 in this volume; William Pencak, For God and Country: The American Legion, 1919–1941 (Boston: Northeastern University Press, 1989); Strayer, The D.A.R., 132–50; Margaret Gibbs, The DAR (New York: Holt, Rinehart and Winston, 1969), 100–134.

[38] Leonard Moore, Citizen Klansman: The Ku Klux Klan in Indiana, 1921–1928 (Chapel Hill: University of North Carolina Press, 1991); "Defeat at Nissan a Setback, but Not Devastating to UAW," (Harry Bernstein Labor column), Los Angeles Times, 8 August 1989, sec. 4, 1.

[39] McConnell, Glorious Contentment, 53–83; Gaines Foster, Ghosts of the Confederacy: Defeat, the Lost Cause, and the Emergence of the New South (New York: Oxford University Press, 1987) has demonstrated a similar pattern of middle-class leadership for the most prominent Confederate veterans' groups (see esp. appendixes 2 and 3). For the DAR and SAR, the most detailed source remains Davies, Patriotism on Parade.

ularly drawn to nationalist movements, some because they were worried about class dissension, some because their official jobs depended on the support of a national state, some because they had nowhere else to go.[40] Despite the inclusive rhetoric such groups employed, their social bases tended to be rather narrow. All that the American patriotic groups did in the 1890s, it could be argued, was to re-envision the nation as a place that was (or that should be) owned by people like themselves.

This, of course, is the essence of the conventional explanation, with its stress on immigration and industrialization. Yet the phrase "people like ourselves" was not transparent for the native-born Americans who joined the patriotic organizations of the 1890s. Other conceptions of the nation were present as well in the cult of the flag, the hereditary societies, and the drill companies. These, in turn, grew in complicated, and not always mutually reinforcing, ways from older ideologies of sameness: local, familial, mutually defensive, and state-centered. Although such loyalties often reinforced one another in the world of the patriotic societies, they also diverged in such instances as the GAR's resistance to hereditarianism, the flag cultists' difficulty in moving beyond fetishism, or the uneasiness some patriots felt toward the "European despotism" that seemed inherent in a too-well-ordered militia.

In our own time, we have simplified the notion of patriotism to the point that it usually means either unswerving state loyalty or a kind of crude ethnocentrism. Yet it is a mistake to read either of those caricatures back into a decade when national loyalty was still a relatively complicated matter. "People like us" could mean fellow whites, fellow workers, fellow Portlanders, fellow soldiers, fellow blood relatives, or fellow voters; or it could mean several of these at once. The patriotic cults of the 1890s set in motion the process of narrowing national loyalty to the brackish channel in which it now runs. If we are seriously to rethink the meaning of national loyalty, then we must recover some of the complexity that was there before.

[40] Geoff Eley, *Reshaping the German Right: Radical Nationalism and Political Change after Bismarck* (New Haven: Yale University Press, 1980), esp. 125–33 and 166–68; Pieter M. Judson, "Whether Race or Conviction Should be the Standard: National Identity and Liberal Politics in Nineteenth-Century Austria," *Austrian History Yearbook* 22, 76–95. Other authors who argue that members of the petty bourgeoisie are drawn to nationalist movements include V. G. Kiernan, "Nationalist Movements and Social Classes," in *Nationalist Movements*, ed. Anthony D. Smith (New York: St. Martin's Press, 1977), 115–16; Breuilly, *Nationalism and the State*, 316–18; and Eric Hobsbawm, *Nations and Nationalism Since 1780: Programme, Myth, Reality* (New York: Cambridge University Press, 1990), 117–22.

Chapter 5

A CHRISTIAN NATION: SIGNS OF A COVENANT

GAINES M. FOSTER

THE PHRASE "Christian nation," widely used in the nineteenth century, still haunts American political discourse at the end of the twentieth. Although not widely embraced, it surfaces occasionally in the rhetoric of political and religious leaders; even more often, they evoke a special or covenantal relationship between God and the United States. American presidents close speeches with "God bless America" and once a year proclaim a day of national thanksgiving. Long considered part of America's "civil religion," these persistent evocations of Christian nationhood have implications for the study of American patriotism as well. Like civil religion, patriotism may defy precise definition, but it certainly involves a relationship between citizens and their nation. As part of that relationship, the nation serves as a source of identity and, at times, promotes or even demands certain behavior. Traditional religions also provide identity and promote behavior, so patriotism and religion can conceivably come into conflict with a concomitant loss in the authority of either, or both. Therefore, many believers want, in fact on some level need, their nation and their religion to be in harmony. Because so many Americans have considered themselves Christian, this need for a harmony of values and identity helps explain the persistence of the term "Christian nation" in American religious and patriotic discourse.

The term, of course, can carry and has carried a variety of meanings. In perhaps the simplest and most widely used definition, the United States is a Christian nation because most of its citizens are Christians. James Bryce, the English observer of post–Civil War America, pointed out that, "though not the legally established religion," Christianity remained "the national religion. So far from thinking their commonwealth godless, the Americans conceive that the religious character of a government consists in nothing but the religious belief of the individual citizens, and the conformity of their conduct to that belief." A more rigorous definition of Christian nation requires that not just the people but also the government observe Christianity. The United States, under this definition that some Christians endorse, is a Christian nation only in so far as the government's laws and actions conform to standards of Christian morality. Still another definition is evoked when the United States is called, to use Bryce's words again, "a special object of Divine favor" or in more familiar terms, God's chosen nation, the New Israel, or a Redeemer nation. These phrases often refer only to a myth of origin, a belief that God directed the creation of the United States as a society for all the world to emulate. For some Americans, though, the belief that their nation is "a special object of Divine favor" rests on the existence of a covenantal relationship between their nation and their god, one that not only sacralizes its past but is also expected to shape its behavior in the present. In this chapter I explore only this final conception of "Christian nation"—that is, the existence of a continuing covenantal relationship.[1]

Historians have made a strong case for a belief in such a covenant during the American Revolution. One of the first things that the Continental Congress did, historian Perry Miller pointed out more than thirty years ago, was to declare "'a day of publick humiliation, fasting, and prayer,'" assuming that "a national confession of sin and iniquity, then a promise of repentance" might move God to influence Britain to grant a redress of grievances. Similar jeremiads by colonial ministers, Miller concluded, sustained the Americans through the long battle for independence. Confession of sin followed by a return to right behavior, within the covenantal tradition important in many colonial faiths, promised God's favor and eventual victory. When victory came, as other historians have argued, similar thinking became part of a tradition of civil millennialism. This identification of God with the nation persisted despite the fact that Americans wrote a thoroughly secular constitution. It never evoked the aid of the deity and said little about religion.[2]

In the early nineteenth century, the federal government further outraged many Christians by transporting the mail and, worse, opening post offices on Sundays. Between 1810 and 1830, many Christians protested these practices, in part because they sought to uphold the covenant, to have their nation honor God by keeping the Fourth Commandment. Congress, however, refused their request. The committee report defending Sunday mails reaffirmed the importance of the separation of

[1] James Bryce, *The American Commonwealth*, 2 vols. (London and New York: Macmillan and Co., 1889), 2:560–61. In the early twentieth century, the notion of a Redeemer nation was expanded into another definition of Christian nationhood, one that rendered the United States responsible for bringing Christian civilization and order to the world.

[2] Perry Miller, "From the Covenant to the Revival," in *The Shaping of American Religion*, vol. 1 of *Religion in American Life*, ed. James Ward Smith and A. Leland Jamison (Princeton: Princeton University Press, 1961), 322–68, quotations on 322. Ruth H. Bloch, *Visionary Republic; Millennial Themes in American Thought, 1756–1800* (New York: Cambridge University Press, 1985) is an example and contains citations to the literature on the tradition of civil millennialism.

church and state, the necessity of protecting the religious rights of all Americans, Christian or not, and criticized the very idea of religion in government. The petitioners, the report read, "assume a position better suited to an ecclesiastical than to a civil institution."[3]

Congress also declined, somewhat paradoxically, requests to end its own and the military's employment of chaplains. An 1853 report, explaining its decision, acknowledged that most chaplains came from the Christian denominations, denied that such employment constituted an establishment of religion, and attributed it to "the fact that we are a Christian people[,] . . . that almost our entire population belong to or sympathise with some one of the Christian denominations." Throughout the antebellum period, the assumptions that a Christian people made America a Christian nation and that God had established a covenant with the American people seemed to suffice. It did so in no small measure because the nation itself remained inchoate. American nationalism and identity rested, as John Higham has argued, primarily in shared ideologies, with Protestantism one of the most central.[4]

When the Civil War broke out, Americans again sought to involve the government in the national covenant. The Confederacy formalized the relationship, explicitly invoking "'the favor and guidance of Almighty God'" in the preamble to its constitution. The Union never went so far, but Congress did adopt resolutions requesting President Abraham Lincoln to issue proclamations of prayer, fasting, and humiliation. Lincoln did so, invoking the covenantal notion of repentance to secure divine blessing on the cause. His language echoed that of the revolutionary years. So too did the behavior of many northern church leaders, who preached jeremiads in which they called on Americans to repudiate the sin of slavery and other failings. During the same years, Thanksgiving day came to be officially recognized, and Congress voted to allow the motto "In God We Trust" on the nation's coins.[5]

---

[3] Richard R. John, "Taking Sabbatarianism Seriously: The Postal System, the Sabbath, and the Transformation of American Political Culture," *Journal of the Early Republic* 10 (Winter 1990): 517–67; U.S. Congress, Senate, Committee on Post Offices and Post Roads, *Petitions Relating to Mails on Sunday*, 20th Cong. 2d sess., 19 January 1829, Senate Miscellaneous Doc. 46 (serial set 181), quotation on 2.

[4] U.S. Congress, Senate, Committee on the Judiciary, 32d Cong., 2d sess., 19 January 1853, S. Rept. 376 (serial set 671), 3; John Higham, "Hanging Together: Divergent Unities in American History," *Journal of American History* 61 (June 1974): 10–18.

[5] Marshall L. DeRosa, *The Confederate Constitution of 1861: An Inquiry Into American Constitutionalism* (Columbia: University of Missouri Press, 1991), 53–54; *Congressional Globe*, 37th Cong., 1st sess., 1861, 365, 382, 427, 430, 454; *Congressional Globe*, 38th Cong., 1st sess., 1864, 3350, 3374–75, 3481. For copies of the proclamations, see Roy P. Basler, ed., *The Collected Works of Abraham Lincoln*, 8 vols. (New Brunswick: Rutgers University Press, 1953), 4: 482–83, 7: 431–32. James Moorhead, *American Apocalypse: Yankee Protestants and the Civil War, 1860–1869* (New Haven: Yale University Press, 1978), 47. On Thanksgiving, see Merle Curti, *The Roots of American Loyalty* (New York: Columbia

From the end of the Civil War until the First World War, a period historians have usually slighted in studies of both civil millennialism and Christian nationhood, fundamental changes occurred that prove crucial to evaluating the validity of the covenantal ideal. First, the people, with whom the covenant was assumed to be established and whose faith Bryce and Congress presumed made the nation Christian, began to change. Science and a newly aggressive free thought challenged faith, the very notion of unbelief became more accepted, and turn-of-the century immigration brought Catholics and Jews in unprecedented numbers. The impact of these developments may not have been as sweeping as historians have sometimes made them. These social changes challenged the "Protestant establishment," but Christianity remained a powerful force within the nation, in part because of Catholicism's growing influence.[6]

More important and less often discussed, the nation itself changed. Before the Civil War Americans referred to the nation in the plural—"the United States" are—but after Appomattox United States came to take a singular verb, a grammatical shift that symbolized a real one: the nation had become an entity as never before. The changing conception of nationhood only started there, however, as Americans began to conceive of this entity in new ways. Many abandoned the idea of a government resting on a social compact or a legalistic conception of Union and embraced an "organic theory of the nation," in Merle Curti's phrase, in which the nation became "a superperson that has gradually developed much as other organisms and individual personalities grow." Although during the early years of the nation the "keyword" had been "People," in Daniel T. Rodgers's formulation, moralists later spoke of "Government" and political theorists of the "State." In their thinking a state was deliberately made by no one and certainly not by God, but it "was a unity, a moral 'person,' whose will radiated outward into what men called law." As World War I approached, the powers that radiated outward became far more pervasive. A bureaucratic state emerged that made the national government more real and important in the lives of Americans than their ancestors at the time of the Revolution could have imagined.[7]

To say, as Bryce did when the changes were still in progress, that America was Christian because its people were, no longer sufficed. The "nation" had become more than its people and more than their shared

---

University Press, 1946), 135–36; on coins, see 60th Cong., 1st sess., H. Rept. 1106, 1–3; cited in note 19.

[6] A recent account of this story is in Robert T. Handy, *Undermined Establishment: Church-State Relations in America, 1880–1920* (Princeton: Princeton University Press, 1991).

[7] James M. McPherson, *Abraham Lincoln and the Second American Revolution* (New York: Oxford University Press, 1990), viii; Curti, *Roots of American Loyalty*, 173–99, quotation on 174; Daniel T. Rodgers, *Contested Truths: Keywords in American Politics Since Independence* (New York: Basic Books, 1987), 80–175; quotation on 160.

beliefs. Yet many Christians still sought harmony between their patriotism and their religion. Not surprisingly, then, during these years some American Christians sought to provide a firmer definition of the term "Christian nation." Congregational minister Benjamin F. Morris, former Supreme Court Justice David J. Brewer, and other observers published books that proclaimed the nation "Christian" and defended this assertion by pointing to the role Christianity played in American history, references to God in colonial charters and national documents, practices such as employing chaplains, and court cases upholding Sunday laws.[8]

Other Americans, who did not necessarily object to such definitions of "Christian nation," wanted to go further. Some fought to keep the nation's population not only Christian but Protestant; others sought national laws that conformed to Christian morality. And in a related campaign, the one investigated here, Christian reformers sought to formalize the covenantal relationship between God and the United States. Three organizations campaigned for some sort of formalization of the relation between God and the emerging nation.

The National Reform Association, a small group but influential far beyond its numbers, formed during the Civil War. Its leaders and members came from several denominations, but its heart and soul lay in, and most of its support came from, the Reformed Presbyterian Church. Its communicants proudly traced their roots to the Covenantors of Scotland and, like their Scottish forebears, affirmed that the state was a moral individual, answerable to God and standing in God's judgment—an extreme, theological version of the redefinition of the state that many accepted during the late nineteenth century. Two other groups, which did not embrace the National Reform Association's position that the state was a moral individual, shared its goal of recognizing the authority of God in government. Reform Association doctrines had influenced Wilbur F. Crafts, a Methodist minister who became a Sabbath reformer and then, in 1895, a self-proclaimed "Christian lobbyist" in Washington. His organization, the National Reform Bureau, secured petitions and lobbied in favor of a host of religious causes. Even more influential, indeed the most important group of all, was the Woman's Christian Temperance Union (WCTU). The WCTU worked with Crafts, whose wife was active in the group, and, especially in the decade after 1884, with the National Reform Association. In 1893 the WCTU's national convention passed a resolution praising the National Reform Association "whose

---

[8] Benjamin F. Morris, *Christian Life and Character of the Civil Institutions of the United States, Developed in the Official and Historical Annals of the Republic* (Philadelphia: George W. Childs, 1864); David J. Brewer, *The United States as a Christian Nation* (Philadelphia: John C. Winston Company, 1905). For a discussion of these and other such books, see Handy, *Undermined Establishment*, 11–14.

aim is identical with that of this organization, to enthrone Christ the King of the cloister, the camp and the court." The following year, however, WCTU leaders considered but rejected a proposal to merge the two associations, at least in part because of disagreements with the National Reform Association's doctrines on the state. Nonetheless, in 1895, the WCTU national convention again expressed its "hearty sympathy to our brothers of the National Reform Association, whose efforts are parallel to ours on many lines."[9]

WCTU leaders' rhetoric revealed the similarities in goals. Perhaps the strongest statement came in 1887 when WCTU President Frances E. Willard proclaimed that her organization: "has one vital, organic thought, one all-absorbing purpose, one undying enthusiasm, and it is that *Christ shall be this world's King.*" Later in the same speech, Willard called on the Prohibition Party, which she and the WCTU had endorsed, to add to its platform a declaration that "Christ and His law" are "the true basis of government and the supreme authority in national as well as individual life." She challenged her members to secure this goal, and in each of the next three years the WCTU passed variously worded resolutions that acknowledged "God in Christ is the King of Nations, and as such should be acknowledged in our government; and His Word made the basis of our laws." Within a very few years, Willard moderated such extreme demands for God in government, but others within the WCTU did not.[10]

Despite slightly different agendas and visions of what they meant by

[9] My observations on the National Reform Association are based primarily on my own study of its records and magazine, *The Christian Statesman*. There are now several accounts of the association; the most helpful are Gary Scott Smith, *The Seeds of Secularization: Calvinism, Culture, and Pluralism in America, 1870–1915* (Grand Rapids, Mich.: Christian University Press, 1985), 53–73, and Stewart Olin Jacoby, "The Religious Amendment Movement: God, People and Nation in the Gilded Age," (Ph.D. diss., University of Michigan, 1984). On Reform Association influence on Crafts, see "Volume Twenty-Six— No. 1," *The Christian Statesman* 26 (1 October 1892): 8, and for more on Crafts and his bureau, Wilbur F. Crafts, *Practical Christian Sociology: A Series of Special Lectures Before Princeton Theological Seminary and Marietta College* (New York: Funk & Wagnalls Company, 1895), pp. 6–15, which has a biographical sketch by Joseph Cook. For a history of the WCTU, see Ruth Bordin, *Women and Temperance: The Quest for Power and Liberty, 1873– 1900* (Philadelphia: Temple University Press, 1981). On relations with Craft, see esp. *Report of the National Woman's Christian Temperance Union, at the Twenty-Fourth Annual Meeting, At Buffalo, New York, October 29th to November 3d, 1897* (Reel 5 of the Woman's Christian Temperance Union Papers, Microfilm Edition of Temperance and Prohibition Papers published by the University of Michigan), 155, 157; hereinafter cited, *WCTU Convention Minutes*, date, (reel #). See also for the NRA, "Worker's Field Notes," *Christian Statesman* 18 (2 October 1884): 5; *WCTU Convention Minutes*, 1884, 105 (reel 1); 1885, 46 (reel 1); 1893, 43–44 (reel 4); 1894, 44 and 66 (reel 4); 1895, 50 (reel 4).

[10] *WCTU Convention Minutes*, 1887, 71, 75; 1888, 7; 1889, 61–62; 1890, 54 (all on reel 3). For later statements, see *Minutes*, 1896, 395–96 (reel 4); 1901, 78 (reel 6).

putting God in government, the WCTU, National Reform Association, and Craft's Reform Bureau, as well as some individuals not affiliated with any of the three, shared a desire to force the nation to confront what it meant by the term "Christian nation." To do so, these groups championed a host of reforms. Many of their members favored international arbitration; most worried about the plight of workers. The Reform Association took a stand against lynching and, on occasion, in support of hand-gun control. But in their combined efforts and, especially, through their lobbyists in Washington, these groups focused not on matters of social justice but on failings of personal morality. Perhaps these sins seemed a more direct affront to God and therefore a more immediate threat to a national covenant. Far from satisfied with a definition based solely on past influences or popular acceptance of Christianity, these groups sought to establish a real covenantal relationship, one in which the government itself acknowledged Christ and His authority. Their crusade failed, leaving a clear historical record that the nation had considered and rejected a more formal relationship.[11]

In the most direct attempt to formalize the idea of the covenant, the National Reform Association and its allies sought to amend the preamble of the U.S. Constitution so as to read, "We, the people of the United States, acknowledging Almighty God as the source of all power and authority in Civil government, our Lord Jesus Christ as the Ruler of nations, and his revealed will as of supreme authority in civil affairs, in order to form a more perfect union." Supporters of such an amendment had sent petitions to Congress before the Civil War, but during the years from 1863 to 1865 and then again between 1869 and 1874 the newly formed National Reform Association made a concerted effort to secure its passage. The first involved both an appeal to President Lincoln and petitions to Congress; the second centered on the presentation of a much larger petition to Congress. Jews and religious liberals, the latter led by Francis E. Abbot, sent counterpetitions. On both occasions, the congressional committees that received these pleas for and against the Christian amendment declined to act. In 1865 Senator Lyman Trumbull, speaking on behalf of the Committee on the Judiciary, asked to be discharged from further consideration of the petitions because the Constitution already recognized "the existence of a Supreme Being" through its requirement for an oath of office and in its promise of the free exercise of religion. Nine

---

[11] For examples of unaffiliated individuals, see Thos. M. C. Birmingham, *Scriptural Politics the Way to National Salvation.* 2d ed. (Nashville: printed for the author by the Publishing House of the Methodist Episcopal Church, South: 1890); Robert Ellis Thompson, *De Civitate Dei: The Divine Order of Human Society* (Philadelphia: John D. Wattles, 1891).

years later, the Committee of the Judiciary in the House also tabled the petitions, but this time with Benjamin F. Butler arguing that the Constitutional Convention and early congresses had refused similar proposals. The founders, Butler maintained, feared any union of church and state and believed "with great unanimity that it was inexpedient to put anything into the Constitution or frame of government which might be construed to be a reference to any religious creed or doctrine." Trumbull referred to older definitions of Christian nationhood; Butler reaffirmed the idea of a totally secular federal government; neither would even consider an amendment that formally acknowledged a covenant.[12]

In the late 1880s, the National Reform Association renewed its agitation for a Christian amendment. Not surprisingly, the nation's leading agnostic, Robert G. Ingersoll, published a scathing attack on the movement, but others within the Christian tradition criticized it as well. "This is a Christian nation in a general and loose sense of the term, because the greater part of the people are really or nominally Christian," proclaimed an article in the *Universalist Quarterly* that same year, "but it is not at all a Christian government." Despite such attacks, the attempt to amend the Constitution went further this time than it ever had before. In 1894 and again in 1896, Elijah A. Morse, a Republican from Massachusetts in the House, and William P. Frye, a Maine Republican in the Senate, entered resolutions proposing a Christian amendment. In both years, Congress held hearings on the measure, at which proponents made their case, but so too did opponents, especially leaders of the Seventh Day Adventist Church. After the 1894 hearings, newspaper response from around the country proved negative, and probably even most Christians opposed the amendment. Certainly Congress did not favor any such formalization of a covenant. Its proponents received a mildly hostile response during the hearings, and no committee in either house reported the resolution.[13]

---

[12] The wording of the amendment changed slightly over time; quotation here is from a petition, filed in Petitions and Memorials, Committee on the Judiciary (Sen54A-J19.2), 54th Cong., Records of the U.S. Senate, Record Group 46, National Archives. Petition from Jews introduced by Charles Sumner in the Senate, U.S. Congress, *Congressional Globe*, 38th Cong., 2d sess., 1865, 742; from liberals by Sumner in Senate, *Congressional Record*, 43rd Cong., 1st sess., 1874, 432. Trumbull quoted, *Congressional Globe*, 38th Cong., 2d sess., 1865, 1272; Butler in Committee on the Judiciary, *Acknowledgement of God and the Christian Religion in the Constitution*, H. Rept. 143 (serial set 1623), 43rd Cong., 1st sess., 18 February 1874, 1. L. C. Kessler, "District of Columbia: Annual Convention Reports," *Union Signal* 20 (15 November 1894): 10, reports that the general officers of the WCTU signed a petition in support of the National Reform Association constitutional amendment.

[13] Robert G. Ingersoll, "God in the Constitution," *The Arena* 1 (January 1890): 119–30; S. A. Whitcomb, "Christianity in Relation to the Constitution of the United States," *Universalist Quarterly and General Review*, n.s. 27 (October 1890): 441–57, quotation on 447; *Congressional Record*, 53rd Cong., 2d sess., 1894, H. Res. 120, 1439; S. Res. 56, 1374;

Yet another attempt to put God in the Constitution occurred between 1907 and 1910, and this time proponents, to the annoyance of the Reform Association, offered a more inclusive reference to the deity. In one resolution entered, Congressmen Morris Sheppard, a prohibitionist from Texas, proposed that only the phrase "In the name of God" be added to the Constitution's preamble. Sheppard appeared before a congressional committee on behalf of his proposal, but once again no bill was reported. A fifty-year crusade to acknowledge a dependence on God in the Constitution not only failed, but it never even reached the floor. Not only Jews and free thinkers but also most Christians apparently opposed it.[14]

The removal of a reference to God from America's money, however, met a very different fate. In 1905 President Theodore Roosevelt asked the renowned sculptor Augustus Saint-Gaudens to design a new set of coins for the nation. For artistic reasons, Saint-Gaudens left off the phrase "In God We Trust," which had appeared on many American coins since the Civil War. When the public learned of the design, all hell, or perhaps better, all heaven broke loose, as many Christian groups protested. In the next Congress, nine different bills were entered requiring that the motto "In God We Trust" appear on coins. Acknowledging this tremendous public pressure, the committee studying the bills recommended that the phrase be restored to the coins on which it had previously appeared. Its report included the observation that "as a Christian nation" we should do so "'as an outward and visible form of the inward and spiritual grace,' which should possess and inspire American citizenship, and as an evidence to all the nations of the world that the best and only reliance for the perpetuation of the republican institution is upon a Christian patriotism, which, recognizing the universal fatherhood of God, appeals to the universal brotherhood of man as the source of the authority and power of all just government." When the bill reached the House floor, similar,

---

Congressional Record, 54th Cong., 1st sess., 1895, S. Res. 28, 168; H. Res. 28, 184; H. Res. 157, 3374; "The Hearing at Washington," Christian Statesman 27 (17 March 1894): 8–9; "National Reform," Christian Statesman 27 (7 April 1894): 1; U.S. Congress, House, Hearing Before the Committee on the Judiciary, House of Representatives, March 11, 1896, on H. Res. 28, Joint Resolution Proposing An Amendment to the Constitution of the United States (Washington, D.C.: Government Printing Office, 1896); "God in the Constitution," Public Opinion 17 (12 April 1894): 46–47; Isaac A. Cornelison, The Relation of Religion to Civil Government in the United States of America: A State Without A Church, But Not Without A Religion (New York: G. P. Putnam's Sons, 1895), 233.

[14] Congressional Record, 60th Cong., 1st sess., 1908, H. Res. 187, p. 6640; 61st Cong., 1st sess., 1909, H. Res. 17, 105; 61st Cong., 2d. sess., 1910, S. Res. 86, 2938; H. Res. 17, (HR61A-B2), Bills and Resolutions Originating in the House, 61st Cong., Records of the House of Representatives, Record Group 233, National Archives; Clippings in Scrapbook #11, 15, 73, Morris Sheppard Papers, Barker Texas History Collection, Center for American History, University of Texas, Austin, Texas.

though somewhat more cogent, statements were made. Charles C. Carlin of Virginia, who had served on the committee, again invoked the idea of a Christian nation. Ollie M. James of Kentucky did as well; he added that the motto spoke "the language of the fathers. Belief in a Supreme Being is breathed in the Declaration of Independence, lives in the Constitution, hallows the oath we take at the bar of this House." Gustav Kustermann of Wisconsin did dissent, suggesting that true religion needed no such advertising and expressing a preference for keeping religion in the people's hearts rather than on their coins. Few agreed. The bill passed the House with only five negative votes, and the Senate did not even bother to conduct a debate before concurring. Roosevelt, who had already expressed his approval, soon signed it.[15]

By putting God on their money, one could argue, Americans paid higher homage than they would if they had put God in their Constitution. The differing congressional responses to the two crusades nevertheless seem important. Putting God in the Constitution threatened to be more than a symbolic act. It could conceivably have made the Bible the basis of law, prevented anyone but Christians from holding office, and necessitated other fundamental changes. It certainly would have formalized the covenantal relationship. Congress never even seriously considered such an acknowledgment, but it leapt at the chance to reaffirm a comparatively meaningless sign of a covenant. "In God We Trust" on the nation's coins required the government to do nothing; it raised no religious standard of behavior. Like other signs of a covenant, though, it still suggested to Christians, especially those who voted, that some sort of special relationship existed between their nation and their God and reassured them that the government and their religion remained in harmony.[16]

Congress showed a similar penchant for signs over action when agitation for Sabbath legislation, relatively dormant in Washington since the

[15] On the coins themselves, see Homer Saint-Gaudens, "Roosevelt and Our Coin Designs: Letters between Theodore Roosevelt and Augustus Saint-Gaudens," *The Century* 99 (April 1920): 721–36. For examples of protests see *WCTU Convention Minutes*, 1907, 66–67 (reel 7); "In God We Trust," *Christian Statesman* 42 (January 1908): 1, and clippings in Scrapbook #10, 145, and Scrapbook #11, 3, in Sheppard Papers, Austin. U.S. Congress, Committee on Coinage, Weights, and Measures, *To Restore the Motto 'In God We Trust' To the Coins of the United States*, H. Rep. 1106 (serial set 5225), 26 February 1908, quotations from 1 and 2; *Congressional Record*, 60th Cong., 1st sess., 1908, 3384–91, 6189, and 6893; James quoted on 3385. The *Washington Post* reported that other legislators opposed the measure but "took to the woods" when a recorded vote was ordered. See *Post*, 17 March 1908, 4.

[16] I have chosen to use signs rather than symbols with Paul Tillich's distinction between the two in mind. Signs only point to something else, according to Tillich; symbols participate in the reality to which they point. My argument goes a step further, of course, by arguing that these signs point to something that, in the final analysis, really is not there. Tillich, *Dynamics of Faith* (New York: Harper & Brothers, 1958), 41–42.

early 1830s, revived in the 1880s. Led by the National Reform Association, the WCTU, Crafts, and toward the end of the decade by the American Sabbath Union (a group formed to focus the influence of various denominations), many American Christians called for legislation against what they considered the great trinity of Sunday sins—Sunday mails, Sunday trains, and Sunday newspapers. Sabbath reformers operated from varied motives. Workers and some of their unions primarily sought a shorter work week; other advocates considered Sunday laws a means to protect worship and to support morality and order. Many Sabbatarians, however, assumed the existence of a covenant and believed that the national government needed to uphold its terms by recognizing the "Lord's day." "The nerve centre of a Christian nation is the Sabbath—the sign between God and Man," Josephine C. Bateham, the WCTU's leading Sabbath reformer proclaimed in 1887. Seven years later, when Sunday practices had not improved and political action had failed, Bateham interpreted financial disaster, forest fires, and strikes as God's attempts to discipline the nation. Clearly, Bateham and no doubt many of her WCTU followers saw federal recognition of the Sabbath as part of the keeping of the covenant. Crafts, at least on occasion, made that link even more direct. Among the many reasons to keep the Sabbath, he explained, is "deference to the authority of Him who is acknowledged by the chaplain's prayer as the Lord of nations as well as of persons." Not just individuals but the state must "respect the law of God and the Christian sentiments of the people."[17]

Bateham, Crafts, and the other reformers organized a massive petition drive and personally lobbied Congress. In response, the Senate Committee on Education and Labor, in April 1888, held hearings on Sunday legislation. Unable to attend, Bateham sent a letter admitting that most petitioners sought Sabbath legislation "first of all . . . because God commands it, and His commands are disobeyed at our peril." Nevertheless, she quickly added, "we confine ourselves to asking it on humanitarian grounds." Crafts directed the hearings, and he and several others testified in support of an expansive law. The committee took no action, though, saying no bill was actually before it. The following month, New Hampshire senator William Henry Blair—an ally of the WCTU, later an officer in Crafts's Reform Bureau, and a champion of all forms of Christian legislation—entered a bill: "To secure to the people the enjoyment of the

[17] Roy Z. Chamlee, Jr., "The Sabbath Crusade: 1810–1920," (Ph.D. diss., George Washington University, 1968); Dennis L. Pettibone, "Caesar's Sabbath: The Sunday-Law Controversy in the United States, 1879–1892," (Ph.D. diss., University of California at Riverside, 1979); *WCTU Convention Minutes*, 1887, xxv (reel 2); 1894, 374 (reel 4); Wilbur F. Crafts, "Shall the World's Fair Observe the American Sabbath?" *Christian Statesman* 25 (4 December 1891): 2.

first day of the week, commonly known as the Lord's day, as a day of rest, and to promote its observance as a day of religious worship." It sought to ban on Sunday in the territories, District of Columbia, and other areas under federal authority virtually all labor and public recreation, opening post offices or transporting most mail, peacetime military drills and parades, and interstate shipment of goods, with a few exceptions such as perishable foods.[18]

The Senate held even larger hearings on this bill, with Crafts, Bateham, a National Reform Association representative, and others in favor of Sunday legislation testifying, but this time Seventh Day Adventists and others opposed to Sunday legislation had their say as well. The opponents condemned what they considered an attempt to create a theocracy and overthrow a long tradition of separation of church and state. Proponents, stressing the need for rest and respect for religious worship, occasionally slipped and offered religious rationales as well. Despite senators' seeming support at the hearing, the committee never reported the bill. During Congress's final meeting of the session, an attempt to discharge the bill from committee and pass it failed. Passage of Blair's bill would have involved a radical change in both the government and the economy because it would have ended most interstate commerce on Sunday, which no doubt goes far toward explaining why it never got out of committee. But Congress had also declined to consider making a covenantal relationship legal and real, which the bill would also have done.[19]

As with the move to keep God on coins after failing to put God in the Constitution, Congress quickly followed its refusal to write the Lord's Day into federal law with passage of a less meaningful gesture toward Sunday celebration. With the World's Columbian Exhibition, or Chicago World's Fair as it was also known, scheduled to open in 1893, many Christian crusaders who had fought for the Blair bill wanted to ensure that the fair would not operate on Sundays. After appeals to the fair's directors failed, the crusaders in 1892 launched a massive petition and lobbying campaign designed to force Congress to close the fair on Sunday. When Congress considered an appropriation to help underwrite its costs, legislators friendly to the Sabbath cause in-

---

[18] U.S. Congress, Senate, *Notes of a Hearing Before the Committee on Education and Labor, United States Senate, Friday, April 6, 1888,* . . . , S. Misc. Doc. 108 (serial set 2517), quotations on 2; S. Bill 2983, *Congressional Record,* 50th Cong., 1st sess., 4455; U.S. Congress, Committee on Education and Labor, *Sunday Rest Bill,* S. Misc. Doc. 43 (serial set 2615), 17 January 1889, 1–2. The title is taken from the list of Senate bills in the index to the *Congressional Record,* 50th Cong., 1st sess. The same title appears in the hearings, but a slightly different title appears on 4455.

[19] *Sunday Rest Bill, Congressional Record,* 50th Cong., 2d sess., 2 March 1889, 2640.

troduced a proviso making Sunday closing a requirement for receiving federal aid.[20]

Opponents of this move condemned the idea, citing the tradition of separation of church and state, the rights of workers to attend the fair on their day off, the fair's contribution to educational and moral uplift, and the potential for riotous behavior by bored visitors denied entry to the grounds on Sunday. Clearly some in Congress, particularly those from the Midwest, worried less about riots than possible loss of revenues. Congressional proponents of the Sunday closing countered with a host of arguments. Congressman Elijah Morse, who entered his resolution to put Christ in the Constitution a short time later, invoked the covenant. "I believe," Morse maintained, "the happiness and prosperity of any city or nation, great or small, before Christ or since Christ, can be measured by their [sic] regard and reverence for the holy Sabbath day." Having "confessed ourselves a Christian nation by stamping upon our coin, . . . 'In God We trust,' . . . ," he continued, "Shall we now insult the Almighty by national sanction of a disobedience of the fourth commandment." A senator also referred to the United States as a Christian nation, called on Congress to acknowledge that fact by closing the exposition, and reminded his fellow lawmakers that not to do so would "grieve tens of millions of people." Many other legislators seemed to have their constituents on their minds; the multitude of petitions that Congress had received came up more than once in the debate. One House member confessed to a reporter that he and his colleagues would vote for Sunday closing out of "'a fear that, unless we do so the church folks will get together and knife us at the polls next; and—well, you know we all want to come back, and we can't afford to take any risks.'" They did not; after considerable maneuvering and a conference to resolve differences between the House and Senate, Congress made its grant of funds to the fair dependent on Sunday closing.[21]

---

[20] There are many accounts of the fair. Reid Badger, *The Great American Fair: The World's Columbian Exposition & American Culture* (Chicago: Nelson Hall, 1979), offers a handy introduction; Pettibone, "Caesar's Sabbath," 256–77, provides an overview of the closing fight.

[21] *Congressional Record*, 52nd Cong., 1st sess. 4690–94, 4714–17, 5941, 5993–6004, 6038–40, 6042–53, 6096–6108, 6148–62, 6223, 6294, 6365–80; Morse quoted Appendix, 302–3; senator on 5999. House member, quoted in *Chicago Daily Post*, 9 April 1892, cited in *American State Papers and Related Documents on Freedom in Religion*, ed. William A. Blakely 4th ed. (Washington, D.C.: Published for the Religious Liberty Association, 1949), 302. The vote to close the fair on Sunday did not follow straight party lines in either house, although as might be expected Republicans voted more consistently in favor of closing than did Democrats. In the House of Representatives 63 percent of the Democrats, 91 percent of the Republicans, and 100 percent of the Populists voting voted for closing; in the Senate 57 percent of Democrats, 71 percent of Republicans, and 100 percent of Populists voting voted

The *Christian Statesman*, the National Reform Association's major magazine, hailed this action as the "Greatest Moral Victory Since Emancipation," and Crafts maintained that it signified "that the official recognition of the law of Christ in our land is the same yesterday, to-day, and forever." But soon the victory seemed less complete. The fair at first complied, then reopened, only to close again in the face of a boycott by some Christians. Later, lawsuits forced the fair to open its gates once again, but attendance remained disappointing. Nevertheless, a precedent had been set; several subsequent fairs voluntarily closed on Sunday, and those that accepted federal funds, such as the St. Louis World's Fair and the Jamestown Exhibition, had to agree to close on Sunday as a condition for receiving the money.[22]

The federal government had again adopted a sign of Christian nationhood, the closing of fairs on Sundays, even as it had rejected a more substantive recognition of a covenantal relationship, Blair's comprehensive Sabbath legislation. After their congressional victory on the fair, Christian forces revived a version of Blair's bill, but it again failed to attract much support. Attempts to enact a comprehensive Sunday law for the District of Columbia fared little better. In 1912 Congress did close post offices on Sunday, in effect ending all but special deliveries. Collection, processing, and shipping of mail continued, though, so this hardly proved a covenantal keeping of the Sabbath. Moreover, congressional debates suggested that the rights of post office workers had as much or more to do with its passage than reverence for God or the Fourth Commandment.[23]

Indeed, the whole tenor of the discussion of Sunday legislation seemed surprisingly secular. The titles of the bills introduced in Congress offered one indication. Some mentioned the Sabbath or the need to protect a day for worship, but few included the Blair Sunday bill's reference to the Lord's Day and the promotion of worship. Most simply referred to Sunday, or the "first day of the week, commonly called Sunday," and emphasized rest rather than worship or duty to God. Even Sabbath reformers couched their case for Sunday legislation in secular terms;

---

in favor of closing. Representatives and senators from the Midwest were more likely to vote against Sunday closing than lawmakers from other regions.

[22] "Sabbath Closing of the World's Fair—The Greatest Moral Victory Since Emancipation," *Christian Statesman* 25 (30 July 1892): 8; Crafts, *Practical Christian Sociology*, 195; Badger, *Great American Fair*, 93–94. For a debate over the Saint Louis Fair, see *Congressional Record*, 56th Cong., 2d sess., 2874, 3177–80, 3326–28. Chamblee, "Sabbath Crusade," 325–26, points out that the practice ended in 1915, when reformers failed to stop the Panama-Pacific Exhibition in San Francisco from opening on Sunday.

[23] This discussion rests on a search of the *Congressional Record*. Chamblee, "Sabbath Crusade," 335–40, discusses the last battle against Sunday mails.

Crafts's book, which became the virtual bible of the movement, carried the title "The Sabbath For Man," hardly an affirmation of keeping the Sabbath as part of a covenant with God. Crafts believed Christians had to be able to justify Sunday laws even to those who would not accept a religious rationale. Bateham made much the same point: "'All our arguments for the bill are based upon the *civil* Sabbath, not because we do not appreciate the religious aspect of the case, but because we think that it has nothing to do with a bill before Congress, which must be sustained by other than religious considerations.'" Therefore, Sabbath crusaders often stressed the importance of one day's rest in seven for the health and efficiency of all people and claimed to be defending the rights of laborers. Or they championed an "American" as opposed to a continental Sunday, an appeal that sometimes carried latent anti-Catholicism, but primarily sought to enlist American patriotism in behalf of religious observance. Such appeals, as one student of this crusade has contended, involved a certain amount of hypocrisy on the part of the Sabbatarians. Though not unconcerned about the rest of laborers, reformers acted primarily from religious motives. Looked at another way, the strategy of Crafts, Bateham, and their allies constituted an acknowledgment by those who wanted to put God in government that as yet no real covenantal relationship existed and that only secular arguments mattered in governmental debates.[24]

The failure to put Christ in the Constitution or to enact meaningful federal Sunday legislation suggested that the God-in-government forces judged rightly. Faced with their demands, Congress never even seriously debated formalizing the nation's relationship with God. During the crucial era in which a national government, a true nation-state, emerged, legislators refused to make it anything other than a secular one. They had no desire to undermine the separation of church and state. Nor did lawmakers appear willing to alienate unbelievers or the most active pressure group opposed to both the amendment and Sunday laws, Seventh Day Adventists, conservative Christians who recognized Saturday as the Sabbath. To keep their other Christian constituents happy, though, legislators did vote to preserve certain signs of a covenant. They and others often proclaimed the United States a Christian nation; indeed, the term itself probably became the most pervasive of these signs. Legislators also insisted that the World's Fair be closed on Sunday and that "In God We Trust" stay on the coins. And as Mark Twain observed, it wouldn't have sounded "any better if it were true." Indeed, the idea of a covenantal

[24] Wilbur F. Crafts, *The Sabbath For Man: A Study of the Origin, Obligation, History, Advantages and Present State of Sabbath Observance*, 6th ed. (New York: Baker & Taylor, 1892); Bateham quoted in untitled editorial *Christian Statesman* 22 (4 July 1889): 2; Pettibone, "Caesar's Sabbath," esp. 354.

relationship, the idea of a Christian nation, served as a "creative fiction," to use the term historian Edmund Morgan applied to popular sovereignty. This fiction allowed Christians to believe that loyalty to God and nation was in harmony, allowed them to reconcile their Christian beliefs with their patriotism, all without entangling the state in a true covenantal relationship. The fiction not only reassured Christians, but it also fostered patriotism by strengthening the state. Signs of a covenant helped legitimatize the emerging nation by clothing it in religious sanction.[25]

Although few seemed to notice, World War I exposed the fiction and revealed how the covenantal thinking seen during the Revolution and the Civil War had all but disappeared. Just as there are said to be no atheists in foxholes, there appear to be few secularists in a wartime Congress. The United States declared war in April 1917; a resolution to set aside a day of prayer was entered in Congress that August and passed in October. By invoking America's status as a Christian nation, the legislation offered only hints of the old-time covenantal religion. The resolution called for a day of prayer, not to confess sin and become worthy of God's favor, but to pray "for the success of our armies and victory for our cause." Moreover, the House committee report recommending its passage simply, but no doubt devoutly, declared the resolution "in accordance with the practices, customs, and character of this country" and "proper, appropriate, and fitting." President Woodrow Wilson's proclamation also cited the nation's past practice and obedience; he then asked for divine blessing on the nation's just cause. In April 1918, perhaps chastened by the involvement of Americans in combat, a second resolution was passed. Although hardly a call for repentance, it at least mentioned humiliation. And this time, Wilson's proclamation even admitted the people's "sins and shortcomings."[26]

Later, Congress considered another, more serious attempt to invoke the covenant, a plan to set aside a time each noon to pray for victory, an idea first proposed by a Roman Catholic in California. This resolution passed the Senate, but it never made it to the House floor. Some Protestants apparently feared its association with the Roman Catholic practice

[25] Twain quoted in Milton Rugoff, *America's Gilded Age: Intimate Portraits from an Era of Extravagance and Change, 1850–1890* (New York: Henry Holt and Company, 1898), 344. Edmund S. Morgan, *Inventing the People: The Rise of Popular Sovereignty in England and America* (New York: W. W. Norton & Company, 1988), esp. 13–15.

[26] Senate Concurrent Res. 12, 1917, *Congressional Record*, 65th Cong., 1st sess., pp. 5957, 6935, 7807; U.S. Congress, Committee on Military Affairs, *Day of Prayer for the Success of the American Armies*, H. Rept. 160 (serial set 7254), 24 September 1917; Senate Concurrent Res. 19, 1918, *Congressional Record*, 65th Cong., 2d sess., 4372, 4463; Arthur S. Link, ed., *The Papers of Woodrow Wilson*, 69 vols. (Princeton: Princeton University Press, 1983–84), 44: 399–400; 47: 598–99.

of the "Angelus." At least one senatorial opponent also argued that it would do no good: "We shall win this war, . . ." said Charles S. Thomas of Colorado "by utilizing and mobilizing every active physical, economic, and social agency against our enemies and by persistent effort. All the prayers of all the peoples on earth in our behalf will be impotent if we fail to exercise our very best efforts in all directions for victory." Even the rhetoric of the resolution's defenders did not hark back to nineteenth-century conceptions of a covenant, but the language anticipated that of Norman Vincent Peale and "New Age" thought in the twentieth. A "resolute determination to win" is one of the most important components of victory, contended Robert L. Owen of Oklahoma, "and the ringing of the angelus at 12 o'clock every day, calling every man and woman of this land to pray to God for victory will fix victory and the idea of victory and purpose of victory in the American heart even more strongly and broadly than it is now fixed." Similarly, Californian James D. Phelan argued that even scientists felt "that when a large body of people concentrate their minds on a given purpose it is helpful even to those who doubt and scoff."[27]

Not only the comments of legislators but also the rhetoric of many religious leaders revealed diminished covenantal thinking. As did their forebears in the Revolutionary and Civil wars, most rallied to the cause, but few delivered jeremiads against the sins of the nation. Rather the majority portrayed the battle as one between good and evil. Billy Sunday, baseball star turned evangelist, put it simply: "'If you turn hell upside down, you'll find 'Made in Germany' stamped on the bottom.'" Even Shailer Mathews, dean of the Divinity School of the University of Chicago, who offered a more sophisticated analysis in a series of lectures on religion and patriotism, portrayed the war as a battle between the godly and the ungodly.[28]

Clearer echoes of the old covenantal notion—that in order to deserve God's blessing and victory the nation must repent and become faithful—could still be heard in the land. Prohibitionists, for instance, occasionally spoke of the sin of drinking the way northern ministers during the Civil War had the sin of slavery. One Montana woman believed that God would never give the United States the victory as long as it fostered that "terrible evil." Richmond P. Hobson, a former congressman and ardent

---

[27] Senate Joint Res. 164, *Congressional Record*, 65th Cong., 2d session, 8602–3, 8672–75, 9035, 10097; Thomas quoted on 8673, Owen on 8675, and Phelan on 8602–3, 8673. *Congressional Record*, 65th Cong., 3d sess., 168.

[28] Ray H. Abrams, *Preachers Present Arms* (New York: Round Table Press, 1933), and John F. Piper, Jr., *The American Churches in World War I* (Athens: Ohio University Press, 1985). Sunday quoted in Abrams, p. 79; Shailer Mathews, *Patriotism and Religion* (New York: Macmillan Company, 1918).

prohibitionist, prayed: "in this fateful hour" help "us at home . . . to purify our land of the Great Sin of drink and hasten the day when we shall be worthy and ready in thy high blessing in victory to our arms." Probably as often, though, prohibitionists enlisted patriotism in the cause of temperance. Anna A. Gordon, who had been Willard's personal secretary and during World War I served as president of the WCTU, spoke of "Patriotic Teetotalism" and claimed: "Total abstinence and prohibition can both be recommended to the American people as articles not 'made in Germany.'" When the federal government undertook wartime prohibition and a war on prostitution—crusades that could easily have been justified as attempts to bring the nation into harmony with God's law to secure his support for victory—other rationales predominated. Proponents and legislators championed the attack both on prostitutes and liquor as necessary to ensure better fighting men and more efficient use of wartime resources. In addition, they maintained that the government had a responsibility to protect the morals of the "boys" sent off by their parents to fight the war. In such contentions, as in Gordon's call for "Patriotic teetotalism," the state seemed a greater, or at least more immediate, source of authority than God.[29]

Not all Christians supported the American cause in World War I or even accepted the signs of a covenant. Many premillennialists had given up on the United States and anticipated the Second Coming. Most Christians, though, did seem to accept the creative fiction and appeared satisfied with only signs of a covenant. These may have sufficed because the battle for a Christian nation on other fronts, the identity of the people and the behavior of the government, appeared to be going well. At the request of some of the same groups that fought for a covenantal relationship, but of others as well, Congress had ensured that the new state that was emerging outlawed the mailing of pornography and information on birth control, stopped the interstate transportation of both lottery information and women for purposes of prostitution, and, most important, enacted prohibition. Campaigns to preserve a Christian population, though nowhere near as successful, still went well. Congress had waged a long campaign against polygamy and the Church of Jesus Christ of Latter-Day Saints before finally helping bring Mormons into closer conformity with American religious norms. Campaigns to limit the immigration of Cath-

---

[29] "A Montana Mother," to Thomas J. Walsh, Box 303, Thomas J. Walsh Papers, Library of Congress; Ledger, Notes #3, 76–77, in Box 5 (of Acc. 61961, add. 1) Richmond P. Hobson Papers, LC; *WCTU Convention Minutes*, 1917, 82 (reel 9). Comments on the crusade against prostitution and for wartime prohibition are based on my readings of the debates in Congress and other sources.

olics and Jews continued and shortly after the war resulted in stringent limits on immigration.[30]

Perhaps such victories made the signs, the fiction, more easily believed, but in any case for decades the fiction persisted and sufficed. Throughout the 1920s, battles over prohibition and evolution as well as Protestantism's own internal war over modernism diverted attention. Depression and another world war did as well. In the years after World War II, a revolution in morals continued, the courts dictated a more stringent separation of church and state, and the influence of non-Protestant faiths and unbelievers increased. By the 1970s, conservative Christians believed that a secular elite had abandoned Christian values and that the courts and Congress had forsaken all vestiges of moral law. Because of their patriotism, nourished in part by their belief in the signs of a covenant, and their assumption that most Americans agreed with them, in part a perpetuation of the old ideal of a Christian people, they still thought of the nation as "theirs." Many of these disgruntled Christian patriots therefore set out to reclaim it, to make the United States a Christian nation in fact, not just in fiction.

The story of how the nation reacted to the movement to force an acknowledgment of a covenantal relationship during the years between the Civil and First World wars, in some ways as much a time of national creation as the Revolution or the Civil War, provides little support for the current quest. At the turn of the century, the government of a redefined nation rejected any but a secular conception of itself and, when asked, refused to make its relationship with God either real or substantial. It did, however, embrace the signs if not the reality of a covenant. Confidence in those signs may help explain the sense of betrayal and frustration that has marked conservative Christians' renewed culture war for a Christian nation.

[30] Timothy P. Weber, *Living the Shadow of the Second Coming: American Premillennialism, 1875–1982*, enl. ed. (Chicago: University of Chicago Press, 1987), 105–27.

Chapter 6

WOMEN, CITIZENSHIP, AND CIVIC SACRIFICE: ENGENDERING PATRIOTISM IN THE FIRST WORLD WAR

KIMBERLY JENSEN

O N 8 NOVEMBER 1917, seven months after the United States entered World War I, a group of New York women physicians representing the Medical Women's National Association sent a resolution to President Woodrow Wilson assuring him of their patriotic support. The United States was at war and the government needed the skills, labor, and support of a nation comprised of diverse groups of people in various occupations and with various skills. At the Medical Women's National Association meeting that July women physicians had organized a war service committee called the American Women's Hospitals (AWH) to lobby for the acceptance of medical women as officers in the army's Medical Reserve Corps. And women had just achieved the right to vote in New York State. Accordingly, the members of the AWH Executive Committee and Council sent a resolution to Wilson charged with the language of civic responsibility and patriotism:

> WHEREAS, the privilege and responsibility of full citizenship has been extended to the women of New York State and
> WHEREAS, the physicians of the American Women's Hospitals residents in New York State realiz[e] what full citizenship means, especially now in time of war, therefore, be it
> RESOLVED, that our first official act of business as enfranchised citizens be to forward to the President of the United States our pledge of undivided loyalty.[1]

The medical women of the AWH constructed this public pronouncement of loyalty with care. By making this strategic statement at the mo-

---

[1] The resolution, signed by Rosalie Slaughter Morton as chair of the American Women's Hospitals, the War Service Committee of the Medical Women's National Association, may be found in the minutes of the Executive Committee and Council Meeting of the American Women's Hospitals, 8 November 1917, box 30, folder 292, American Women's Hospitals Records, 1917–1982, Accession no. 144, Archives and Special Collections on Women in Medicine, Medical College of Pennsylvania, Philadelphia, Pa.

ment of winning the vote, they emphasized that enfranchisement conferred a higher level of citizenship on New York's women. Therefore, as more complete citizens, women in the state could now offer a higher degree of loyalty to the nation than was possible before they held the right to vote, and the possibility of further service to the state engendered a more complete patriotism for women. This explicit connection between women's increased civic participation through the vote and an increased capacity for civic loyalty suggested two related civic claims. At the same time that they were sending this pledge of loyalty to Wilson, medical women were leading the fight for commissions as military medical officers. For them, "full citizenship" meant the right of equal access to officer status and service as professionally prepared physicians, and wartime exigencies made the possibility of acceptance imaginable, even possible. This was "what full citizenship means, especially now in time of war." In addition, their rhetoric emphasized their belief in a social contract of citizenship: loyalty and service in exchange for full recognition of female citizenship and women's equality in American society. If a loyal citizen fulfilled her patriotic responsibilities, she would, in return, receive the privileges of citizenship and full membership in the state. Women physicians used the words "privilege" and "responsibility" in their resolution to convey both sides of this social contract of citizenship; full citizenship meant the privilege of civil rights when women fulfilled their "responsibility" by serving the state during wartime.

Loyalty was an act for citizens, but Americans were in the process of redefining the concept of citizenship to fit the conditions and concerns of modern life. Many equated citizenship with the process of "Americanizing" immigrants as record numbers of people migrated to the United States from different shores. Others saw it as the process of "elevating" the laboring classes to middle-class norms of "good citizenship" through codes of proper behavior. The Progressive Era's emphasis on urban and political reform demanded civic attentiveness and activism. For Theodore Roosevelt, Leonard Wood, and other concerned men of their class and generation, training for good citizenship would reinvigorate and remasculinize America. Enfranchisement and the strengthening of female citizenship were key goals of the women's rights movement, and by 1917 women in thirteen states had achieved full voting rights. Many Americans of color were working to combat the legal, social, and economic effects of disfranchisement.[2] At the same time the links between the re-

[2] For background on these issues, see John Bodnar, *The Transplanted: A History of Immigrants in Urban America* (Bloomington: Indiana University Press, 1985); Ronald Takaki, *Strangers from A Different Shore: A History of Asian Americans* (New York: Penguin Books, 1989); Nell Irvin Painter, *Standing at Armageddon: The United States, 1877–1919* (New York: W. W. Norton, 1987); Nancy Cott, *The Grounding of Modern Feminism* (New Haven: Yale University Press, 1987); Peter Filene, "Men and Manliness," in *Him/Her Self:*

sponsibilities of citizens and the obligations of the state to those citizens were being strengthened in the American discourse about civic identity. These reciprocal obligations were particularly significant during wartime. From 1900 to 1918 the nation's popular magazines published some four hundred articles on citizenship and patriotism, and Yale University sponsored an extensive, widely reprinted lecture series on the meaning of citizenship. This public discourse about citizenship focused, above all, on participatory citizenship by emphasizing the duty and the privilege of citizens to act in support of the nation.[3]

When Americans juxtaposed wartime needs with this debate about the nature of citizenship, loyalty became currency—the medium by which individuals and groups pledged their service in exchange for civic and social recognition. The disfranchised debated the meaning of supporting the wartime call of a nation that preached but did not practice full democracy. Woodrow Wilson's government, constructing loyalty as "100 percent Americanism" with the goal of eradicating differences in belief and ethnicity in America, insisted on absolute support of the war effort and government programs.[4] But a high premium on loyalty provided social space within which those who could prove themselves loyal might be able to claim the rewards of patriotic service.[5] From this matrix of participatory citizenship and loyalty some women constructed an ideology of full female civic identity beyond suffrage that included the obligation of service to the state in time of war. Active defense of the state would complete the spectrum of women's civic duties and privileges and recast a limited female citizenship into civic equality with men. Women could then claim the rewards of equal service and loyalty in social, economic, and professional terms. This was not the only approach women activists took; indeed women formed the foundation of the peace movement in this period.[6] But these women, whom I call institutional feminists, had

Sex Roles in Modern America, 2d ed. (Baltimore: Johns Hopkins University Press, 1986); Anthony Rotundo, "Passionate Manhood: A Changing Standard of Masculinity," *American Manhood: Transformations in Masculinity from the Revolution to the Modern Era* (New York: Basic Books, 1993), esp. chap. 10; and John Pettigrew, "Modern Traditions of Service: Nationalism and Citizenship in Pre-World War I American Political Culture" (paper presented 8 January 1995 at the annual meeting of the American Historical Association, Chicago).

[3] See the *Readers' Guide to Periodical Literature* (Minneapolis: H. W. Wilson Company, 1905–1919), vols. 1–4.

[4] For more on this campaign, see David M. Kennedy, *Over Here: The First World War in American Society* (New York: Oxford University Press, 1980).

[5] In a similar vein, John Bodnar contends that patriotism "embodies both official and vernacular interests." See Bodnar, *Remaking America: Public Memory, Commemoration, and Patriotism in the Twentieth Century* (Princeton: Princeton University Press, 1992), 18.

[6] Barbara Steinson's *American Women's Activism in World War I* (New York: Garland Press, 1982) provides useful information on their activities.

worked primarily for equality within institutions; they sought to redress inequality by access to education, professional positions, and recognition. Their theoretical approach to advances within institutions meant that they transferred this easily from one institution to another: from the goals of access to equal position and pay within the medical profession or political equality through the vote, for example, to participation in the institution of the military itself. Indeed, their very language was the rhetoric of equal access and institutional advancement. They did not seek to transform the paradigm of citizenship that equated full civic status with military service. Rather, they sought equal access to that service to fulfill the requirement of citizenship as it stood.

Institutional feminists in the World War I era sought equal access to military service in the context of shifting ideas about women's place as well as in broad transformations in American society. Women and their organizations were at the forefront of Progressive Era social reform, and privileged women were gaining access to higher education and to professions such as medicine and business in rising numbers. Women of color challenged segregation in the South and West in education and employment, and middle-class Americans began to embrace patterns of sexuality that had been part of working-class culture. The New Woman—sexually free, economically independent, physically unshackled—was a feature of film and fiction as aspects of "new womanhood" were becoming a choice for some real women as well. The movement for women's empowerment included a variety of perspectives on the manner in which to challenge women's inequalities, among them rights-based, liberal feminists, who emphasized suffrage and political power and entrance into male institutions; cultural feminists who emphasized women's difference from men and male institutions; socialist feminists who placed class issues as central to the analysis of women's inequality in American society.[7] In addition to the discourse about the nature of citizenship noted above, the U.S. military was becoming a "modern" institution. World War I was the first protracted campaign in which women's traditional services to armies—nursing, laundering, cooking—were now part of a supplies and service bureaucracy. The military could be seen, and was seen by the institutional feminists I study in this chapter, as another institution to be entered. Yet the military is an institution like no other, and some supporters of women's advancement hesitated to call for full inclusion in an institution whose purpose was to wage war. World War I and the discourse of women's service was layered over these potentially conflicting views within the women's movement and social and cultural shifts in American society.

[7] For background, see Cott, *Grounding of Modern Feminism*; Josephine Donovan, *Feminist Theory: The Intellectual Traditions of American Feminism* (New York: Ungar, 1985); and Sara Evans, *Born for Liberty: A History of American Women* (New York: Free Press, 1989).

Wartime also offers powerful reasons for many people to insist on the stability of "traditional" gender relations. Opponents to women's military service in World War I believed that such service would violate all the rules of gender relations and the "passionate manhood" embodied in military service.[8] As scholars Judith Stiehm, Jean Elshtain, and Robert Westbrook demonstrate, women have signified the things for which men fight; they are not the comrades with whom men fight.[9] And while women were achieving many goals in the struggle for equality, a powerful backlash threatened their goals through hostility to organized women, the continued double burden of working women, satirization of intellectual women, and the demonization of women who enjoyed same-sex relationships during this period. Wartime claims for increased institutional access fell into this oppositional context as well. Resistance to women's claims for military service was often part of the discourse of popular culture, expressed through what Patricia Hill Collins calls "controlling images." For women in this study, a variety of "controlling images" to restrict women independent of male control—from sexual Jezebels to "mannish lesbians"—operated to counter the claims of women for equality through military service.[10]

The experiences of medical women whose ideals of patriotic service also included equality in their profession, African American women who claimed racial equality through service with volunteer agencies, and women who claimed that the obligation and the right to bear arms to defend the state would complete the role of the female citizen demonstrate the complexities of the social contract of citizenship for women in this period. These women sought to define their loyalty and thereby to engender patriotism in ways that included strengthened civic equality for women during and after the war. Yet powerful constraints against women's equality and the complex institutional and cultural role of the military in American culture engendered a competing vision of women's wartime roles.

[8] See Rotundo, *American Manhood*, and Pettigrew, "Modern Traditions of Service."

[9] See Judith Hicks Stiehm, "The Protected, The Protector, The Defender," *Women's Studies International Forum* 5 (1982): 367–76; Jean Bethke Elshtain, "On Beautiful Souls, Just Warriors and Feminist Consciousness," *Women's Studies International Forum* 5 (1982): 341–48; Elshtain, *Women and War* (New York: Basic Books, 1987); and Robert Westbrook, " 'I Want a Girl, Just Like the Girl That Married Harry James': American Women and the Problem of Political Obligation in World War II," *American Quarterly* 42 (December 1990): 587–614.

[10] Patricia Hill Collins, *Black Feminist Thought: Knowledge, Consciousness, and the Politics of Empowerment* (New York: Routledge, 1991). See also George Chauncey, Jr., "From Sexual Inversion to Homosexuality: The Changing Medical Conceptualization of Female 'Deviance,' " in *Passion and Power: Sexuality in History*, ed. Kathy Peiss and Christina Simmons (Philadelphia: Temple University Press, 1989), 87–117; Alice Kessler-Harris, *Out to Work: A History of Wage-Earning Women in the United States* (New York: Oxford, 1982).

Women physicians made their wartime claims for equal opportunity in the context of a broader history of struggle for access to educational, professional, and organizational opportunity in the field of medicine.[11] In the years after the Civil War American women struggled for increased access to medical education and practice. As Regina Morantz-Sanchez explains insightfully, women physicians faced the dilemma of "sympathy" versus "science." Many found their practice limited to the care of women and children based on their supposed "sympathetic" natures as women. Some welcomed this as a recognition of female traits in medical care while others chafed at the limitations such categorization placed on their professional development in the growing specialty fields based on scientific research. In spite of these important problems the decade of the 1910s was a time for optimism for many medical women. As the nation entered the war, women physicians could point to progress in both educational opportunity and occupational variety. In 1910 women physicians reached a peak of approximately 6 percent of the medical profession (about 6,000 women practitioners), and a 1916 study showed that 1,313 American women physicians in active practice were specializing. Two-thirds did so in what were considered women's specialties such as obstetrics and gynecology; one-third were making inroads into fields considered to be male territory.[12] But there were still many reforms to be made, especially in access to medical education for women of color and in internship and professional opportunities for all women. Here the medical profession mirrors the patterns studied by Margaret Rossiter for women in the sciences. After women achieved some access to medical education, institutional gatekeepers such as the American Medical Association raised the stakes for professional success to include internships, hospital residencies, and research publications.[13]

Many women physicians joined their AWH colleagues in linking wartime service and an enhanced civic role with institutional goals of equality with male colleagues in the medical profession. Physician Mary Sutton Macy asserted that "medical women as a body" were "better equipped to do practical service than any other one class of women," in America.[14] As Dr. Frances C. Van Gasken told students and faculty at the

[11] Two standard texts on these developments are Regina Morantz-Sanchez, *Sympathy and Science: Women Physicians in American Medicine* (New York: Oxford, 1985), and Mary Roth Walsh, *Doctors Wanted, No Women Need Apply: Sexual Barriers in the Medical Profession, 1835–1975* (New Haven: Yale University Press, 1977).

[12] See Mary Sutton Macy, M.D., "The Field for Women of Today in Medicine," *Woman's Medical Journal* 27 (March 1917): 49–58.

[13] See Margaret Rossiter, *Women Scientists in America: Struggles and Strategies to 1940* (Baltimore: Johns Hopkins University Press, 1982).

[14] Mary Sutton Macy, M.D., "American Medical Women and the World War," *American Medicine* 23 (May 1917): 322–28.

opening of the first college session at the Women's Medical College of Pennsylvania since the U.S. entry into the war:

> Today we are overlooking the Promised Land . . . it is for *you* to enter this Promised Land, this land of equal opportunity. . . . [I]t does not take a prophet to read the writing on the wall for the woman of today. In letters of light it says to her: "Come on! Here is work! Here is opportunity! Here is equality of reward!" The war that has opened "Pandora's Box" has also set free Hope. And, when the "world is made safe for democracy," Democracy will be made safe for women. . . . The demand for women physicians is, and will be, a constantly increasing one.[15]

Medical women constructed their case for inclusion in the army Medical Reserve Corps based on their professional skills and their loyalty as citizens throughout the period of the war. Hundreds signed petitions to the war department. The American Women's Hospitals (AWH) sent several women's medical units abroad, and some eighty women physicians served abroad with voluntary organizations such as the Red Cross. Fifty-five American medical women worked as civilian contract surgeons with the Army Medical Corps, eleven of them overseas. Women from Colorado and Oregon constructed test cases for women's service as medical officers.[16] Mary Bates, a Denver gynecologist who spearheaded the Colorado test case spoke for her colleagues when she argued that the real issue at hand was "the rights of citizenship as applied to women."[17] Physician Rosalie Slaughter Morton, who headed the AWH for the Medical Women's National Association, conducted a census of the 5,287 women physicians of the country to determine who was willing to provide wartime medical service for the military and the government.[18] Almost one-third (1,816, or

[15] Frances C. Van Gasken, M.D., "Introductory Address, Woman's Medical College of Pennsylvania, Delivered at the Opening of the College Session, September 19, 1917," *Bulletin of the Woman's Medical College of Pennsylvania* 68 (December 1917): 3–5; quotation on 3–4.

[16] For more on these activities and claims, see Kimberly Jensen, "Uncle Sam's Loyal Nieces: American Medical Women, Citizenship, and War Service in World War I," *Bulletin of the History of Medicine* 67 (Winter 1993): 651–71, based on, among other sources, the American Women's Hospitals records, the *Census of Women Physicians* published by the American Women's Hospitals in New York in 1918, and records from women's medical journals. See also Jensen, "Minerva on the Field of Mars: American Women, Citizenship, and Military Service in the First World War" (Ph.D. diss., University of Iowa, 1992). And see Ellen S. More, "'A Certain Restless Ambition': Women Physicians in World War I," *American Quarterly* 41 (1989): 636–60.

[17] See Mary Elizabeth Bates, "A Most Interesting Report of Work of Colorado Medical Women's War Service League," *Woman's Medical Journal* 28 (February 1918): 39–40; quotation on 40.

[18] The information that follows is taken from my analysis of the database I created from the *Census of Women Physicians* (New York: America Women's Hospitals, 1918).

31 percent) of the medical women of the country in 1917–1918, active and retired, signified their willingness to provide war service.

Because the *Census* also contains data on graduation year and institution, state of residence, and professional affiliation, we may construct a social profile of these women physicians to consider their possible motivation for registration. Age and state of residence do not seem to have been decisive factors in the pattern of war service registration, nor does the institution from which women graduated seem to have made a difference. But professional organizational affiliation does affect the war service registration patterns in the *Census*. Of medical women who were members of the American Medical Association 41 percent signed up for war service; 59 percent of the members of the Medical Women's National Association registered; and 63 percent of those women who were members of both the AMA and MWNA registered for war service, twice the average for the *Census* as a whole.[19] Only 24 percent of the women with no professional affiliation registered for war service. These figures indicate that those medical women most concerned with women's professionalization, those active in organizations, and those believing that they had the most to gain in a bid for equality with male colleagues registered for war service. It is not surprising that those women who were members of the Medical Women's National Association, which was organized to speak for medical women as a class, as well as the American Medical Association, which represented the profession as a whole but was an organ of male power, had the highest percentage of war registration as a group. Their affirmation of the social contract of citizenship and their institutional feminist approach to military service linked their efforts with other women seeking access to military service for present and future gains in the civic and professional arenas.

Secretary of War Newton Baker, government officials, and many male physicians resisted and rejected women physicians' claims for equal wartime service as officers in the medical corps.[20] Even though the language of the requirements for entrance into the Medical Reserve Corps specified the service of professionally prepared citizens in gender-neutral language, the Judge Advocate General of the Army rejected all appeals by basing his decision on lack of precedent and his concern that women as medical officers would be in command of men.[21] And when male allies

---

[19] By 1918 new members of the Medical Women's National Association were also required to be members of the American Medical Association, but the original constitution did not have this requirement. Therefore, in the 1918 *Census* some women list MWNA membership without membership in the AMA.

[20] Baker "did not approve of commissioning or enlisting women in the military service." See Anita Newcombe McGee, "Can Women Physicians Serve in the Army?" *Woman's Medical Journal* 28 (February 1918): 26–28.

[21] See U.S. Judge Advocate General's Department (Army), *Opinions of the Judge Advo-*

presented women's claims for commissions at the June 1918 national meeting of the American Medical Association, the delegates ruled in favor of the principle of "equal rank and pay for equal service" but drew the line for complete support of commissions with the caveat that the "very character of military service and women's natural limitation for such service must require wise discrimination in their employment in war work."[22] Like many other male workers in wartime who support women's "equality," many male physicians at the AMA convention were interested in maintaining standards and pay levels for jobs that they believed would remain in the hands of men.[23] The AMA delegates recommended their resolutions to the general membership for action, but before that organization could respond the war was over, taking with it many expediencies that had made the arguments for medical women's military service possible.

A nation away, white women working for the war effort in New Mexico also used the concept of loyalty to describe the meaning of their wartime actions. Alice Corbin Henderson gave her perspective as part of New Mexico's Anglo elite in her report of women's state activities during the war years. "Although the state is bilingual," she wrote,

> there was never the least question of disloyalty or of anything but complete willingness and a desire to be of service on the part of New Mexico women. Nothing could have been more inspiring than the deep earnestness of the English, Spanish, and Indian speaking women who met over the canning kettle, or across the Red Cross table where a common impulse moved them and a common purpose obviated any need of an interpreter—the will to win the war! In New Mexico certainly it has been amply demonstrated that racial variety is indeed no barrier to national unity, when democracy and not autocracy is the government practiced.[24]

Henderson based her vision of loyalty on the social goal of assimilating diverse ethnicities in a common cause. Using language as a symbol of

---

cate General, vol. 1, 1 April 1917 to 31 December 1917 (Washington, D.C.: U.S. Government Printing Office, 1919), 126–27.

[22] See "Proceedings of the Chicago Session: Minutes of the Sixty-Ninth Annual Session of the American Medical Association, Held at Chicago, June 10–14, 1918," Journal of the American Medical Association 70 (1918): 1855, 1870; and "Report of Reference Committee on Legislation and Political Action," 1858.

[23] See, for comparison, Ruth Milkman's study of auto and electrical workers in World War II. Ruth Milkman, Gender at Work: The Dynamics of Job Segregation by Sex during World War II (Urbana: University of Illinois Press, 1987).

[24] Alice Corbin Henderson, "The Women's Part," in New Mexico in the Great War, ed. Lansing B. Bloom Historical Society of New Mexico Publications in History, vol. 3 (Santa Fe: El Palacio Press, 1927); copy at the Center for Southwest Research, University of New Mexico, Albuquerque, New Mexico.

difference, Henderson asserted that the "will to win the war" obviated—
that is, did away with, or prevented—the need for an interpreter between
"English, Spanish, and Indian speaking women." Her statement reflects
the "100 percent American" ideology that permeated wartime rhetoric
and programs. In this view, ethnic and racial diversity was dangerous
because it might work against national unity, and diversity needed to be
managed and controlled through patriotic loyalty.[25]

Many American women of color expressed a different view of wartime loyalty. For them, danger came from racism, not diversity. Patriotic
support of and service to the state could be an act of loyalty to the nation
not as it was, but as it might become—a democracy that delivered on its
promises of civic equality to all citizens. Black nursing leader Adah
Thoms believed that when Woodrow Wilson called the nation to arms
with the goal of making the world safe for democracy he opened the
door for such an interpretation of wartime loyalty. "Whether he meant to
include us or not makes no difference; we are included," she told an
audience of African-American medical professionals in August 1917.[26]
Thoms worked for the acceptance of black women in the Army Nursing
Corps throughout the war and claimed victory when eighteen African-
American women were accepted for stateside service in army camps during the influenza epidemic in the fall of 1918.[27]

Addie Waites Hunton, one of three African-American women who
worked with black troops in France through the YMCA during the war,
believed that if black women, whose "souls and bodies" bore the brunt of
racism and sexism in America,[28] engaged in war service in the midst of
this oppression, they would offer a renewed vision of civic sacrifice and
citizenship. Such loyal service would challenge the nation to shed its racism by protecting the rights of all citizens. This would be, in Hunton's
words, "the best there is in citizenship," representing the "highest quali-

[25] For more on Mexican American women in this context, see George J. Sanchez, "'Go
After the Women': Americanization and the Mexican Immigrant Woman, 1915–1929," in
Unequal Sisters: A Multi-Cultural Reader in U.S. Women's History, ed. Ellen Carol Dubois
and Vicki L. Ruiz (New York: Routledge, 1990), 250–63.

[26] "Greetings to the National Medical Association—Delivered by Mrs. Adah Bell
Thoms, R.N.—at Philadelphia, August 30, 1917," *Journal of the National Medical Association*
10 (January–March 1918): 52–53.

[27] See Jensen, "Minerva on the Field of Mars," 316–44, and, among other sources Adah
B. Thoms, *Pathfinders: A History of the Progress of Colored Graduate Nurses* (1929; rpt. ed.,
New York, 1985); Darlene Clark Hine, "The Call That Never Came: Black Women
Nurses and World War I, An Historical Note," *Indiana Military History Journal* 8 (January
1983): 23–27; and Hine, *Black Women in White: Racial Conflict and Cooperation in the Nursing
Profession, 1890–1950* (Bloomington: Indiana University Press, 1989).

[28] The quotation is on p. 282 of Addie Hunton's essay "Negro Womanhood Defended,"
The Voice 1 (July 1904): 280–82.

ties of mind and soul."[29] Hunton, a Brooklyn educator and clubwoman, and Washington, D.C., businesswoman Amanda Gray led dozens of African-American women who held administrative posts with the YWCA and the YMCA in army camps in the United States and in France during the war. Gray and Hunton were educated and involved in African-American community uplift organizations and women's clubs— part of the group that Evelyn Brooks Higginbotham terms the "Female Talented Tenth."[30] Hunton and her associates Kathryn Johnson and Helen Curtis went to France with the YMCA to work in service canteens in areas where black troops were stationed. Amanda Gray joined twelve other black women as administrators of YWCA hostess houses for sol- diers of color and camp workers in U.S. training camps.[31]

For African-American women *virtue* as a prerequisite for citizenship held an incisive double meaning. In their quest for equal citizenship Am- anda Gray and Addie Hunton entered war service not only to demon- strate public or civic virtue in the classical sense of "devotion of one's self to the public good,"[32] but they also wished to demonstrate the sexual virtue of black women. Beginning with the slave trade, those who en- countered and enslaved black women identified them as libidinous, sexu- ally promiscuous Jezebels, and this persistent mythology continued to define African-American women after the official end of enslavement in what Patricia Hill Collins calls "controlling images."[33] For generations black women individually and in organizations on the community and

[29] See Addie Hunton's contribution to "Votes for Women: A Symposium by Leading Thinkers of Colored America," *The Crisis* 10 (August 1915): 188–89, for these remarks.

[30] Evelyn Brooks Higginbotham, *Righteous Discontent: The Women's Movement in the Black Baptist Church, 1880–1920* (Cambridge: Harvard University Press, 1993). Aside from organizations within ethnic and racial communities, the YMCA and the YWCA offered the greatest opportunity for wartime service for many nonwhite women, in large part because of the decades-long struggle of women of color for leadership roles in these groups. For an example of community organizations, see Hine's discussion of the wartime activities of the Circle for Negro War Relief in *Black Women in White*, 104–7. See Paula Giddings, *When and Where I Enter: The Impact of Black Women on Race and Sex in America* (New York: Bantam, 1984), 155–58, for the YWCA.

[31] For more on Hunton and her associates, see Addie Waites Hunton and Kathryn Johnson, *Two Colored Women with the American Expeditionary Forces* (Brooklyn: Brooklyn Eagle Press, 1920), and various accounts in the *New York Age* and *The Crisis* for this period. Amanda Gray served at Camp Sherman, Ohio. For more on the service of all these women, see Jensen, "Minerva on the Field of Mars," 399–446.

[32] For an analysis of the classical definition of *vertu* and its meaning in Western thought, see J.G.A. Pocock, *The Machiavellian Moment: Florentine Political Thought and the Atlantic Republican Tradition* (Princeton: Princeton University Press, 1975), 88.

[33] See Collins, *Black Feminist Thought*, esp. chap. 4, "Mammies, Matriarchs, and Other Controlling Images." For a discussion of the origins of the Jezebel stereotype and its consequences in the antebellum period, see Deborah Gray White, *Ar'n't I a Woman? Female Slaves in the Plantation South* (New York: Norton, 1985), 27–46.

national levels have worked to counter these stereotypes and their consequences.[34] During World War I, Hunton, Gray, and their colleagues did
all they could to exemplify sexually virtuous womanhood in their wartime service, and through their administrative posts with voluntary organizations they worked to control the behavior of African-American soldiers and to construct a proper public image of that behavior. Sexually
virtuous womanhood as well as civic virtue were each integral parts of
their claims to the rights of citizenship.

But another controlling image of black women that persisted from
enslavement—the black woman as "mule of the world," Mammy, domestic servant, worker for whites—proved as powerful and far reaching
in its consequences as the controlling image of Jezebel.[35] While elite black
women claimed the right to serve and work for wartime goals as essential
demonstrations of their patriotic citizenship, black women working in
some southern communities saw this "right" turned to a duty in the
"work-or-fight campaign" that was used to control the lives of black
women in familiar patterns of economic and social subordination.

Black women did experience some changes in their work patterns during the war years. As part of the migration from the South to northern
cities, some were able to work in factories, and others received higher
wages as white women left domestic work for factories and clerical jobs.
Between 1916 and 1921 some 500,000 African Americans—about 5 percent of the total black population of the nation—left the South for work
in the North and Midwest. Although most African-American women
workers remained in domestic and personal service, the wartime demand
for labor opened jobs for thousands in industry.[36] These choices—
combined with geographic mobility and higher wages and increased op-

[34] See Darlene Clark Hine, "Rape and the Inner Lives of Black Women in the Middle
West: Preliminary Thoughts on the Culture of Dissemblance," *Signs* 14 (Summer 1989):
912–13; and Lynda F. Dickson, "Toward a Broader Angle of Vision in Uncovering Wom-
en's History: Black Women's Clubs Revisited," *Frontiers* 9 (1987): 62–68. These themes are
also discussed by Paula Giddings in *When and Where I Enter*, esp. in chap. 5, "Defending
Our Name," and chap. 6, " 'To Be a Woman, Sublime': The Ideas of the National Black
Women's Club Movement." Stephanie Shaw's work helps us to see that this work and this
focus was part of a long tradition of African American women's activism, not an adoption
of white women's club work during the Progressive Era. See Stephanie J. Shaw, "Black
Club Women and the Creation of the National Association of Colored Women," *Journal of
Women's History* 3 (Fall 1991): 10–25.

[35] White discusses the Mammy stereotype in *Ar'n't I a Woman?* 46–61. She notes on 60–
61, "They are black images but, being almost as old as the images of Eve an the Virgin
Mary, they are also universal female archetypes." See also Collins, *Black Feminist Thought*,
for the Mammy stereotype.

[36] See Jacqueline Jones, *Labor of Love, Labor of Sorrow: Black Women, Work, and the Family
from Slavery to the Present* (New York: Basic Books, 1985), 152–95, and Maurine Weiner
Greenwald, *Women, War, and Work: The Impact of World War I on Women Workers in the
United States* (Ithaca: Cornell University Press, 1980), esp. 22–27.

tions for African-American men—disrupted work patterns in southern communities. Jacqueline Jones reports that some "nervous white southerners" believed that the "entire supply of black labor was about to disappear overnight."[37]

Some southern civic and business leaders, combining their desire for a stable black work force with the rhetoric of the government's "work-or-fight" campaign, attempted to force African-American women to remain in low-paying domestic and personal service work. During the war, government officials encouraged workers to keep up production by declaring that their work was just as important to the war effort as was the work of the soldiers in France. Empowered by the rhetoric and emotionalism of this work-or-fight campaign, southern business and civic leaders attempted to regulate the personal behavior and mobility of black citizens with local ordinances requiring residents to work during the wartime emergency—ordinances reminiscent of the slave codes and the black codes that followed the Civil War.[38]

Black women seem to have been particular targets for this campaign. Some white leaders complained that African-American women "living on allotments received on account of drafted relatives refused to work."[39] The editor of the Jackson, Mississippi, newspaper justified the town's new ordinance requiring signed work cards for African Americans by claiming that black "cooks and servants" refused to take work in white homes. Labor cards and enforced labor in the home of whites would "help" these women observe their civic duty as loyal citizens to work to win the war. It would also, he said, relieve the "servant problem" of "some of its terrors."[40] African American women who refused to work for less than wartime wages were also vulnerable to the work-or-fight campaign, as the case of Mildred Anderson of Memphis demonstrates. Memphis newspapers reported in October 1918 that Anderson "boasted to 'white folks' that she wouldn't work for less than $5 a day" and that she had "refused several offers of $5 a day to work." As a result, she was arrested for disorderly conduct and loitering, fined ten dollars, and sentenced to work at the Shelby County workhouse. Judge John Fitshugh told her, "'I'll give you a job at 40 cents a day in the workhouse,'" when he handed down her sentence.[41]

[37] Jones, *Labor of Love, Labor of Sorrow*, 157. Jones does not discuss the "work or fight" episode. See also James W. Johnson, "'Work or Fight' Laws for Women," *New York Age*, 2 November 1918, 4.

[38] For more on the codes, see Eric Foner, *Reconstruction: America's Unfinished Revolution, 1863–1877* (New York: Harper & Row, 1988), 199–201, 208–9.

[39] "Abuse of the 'Work or Fight' Slogan," *New York Age*, 28 September 1918, 4.

[40] The article is reprinted in "Washington Officials Deny Report Women Can Be Made Work [sic]," *New York Age*, 16 November 1918, 1 and 2; quotation on 2.

[41] Johnson reports this incident in "'Work or Fight' Laws for Women," 4.

African-American leaders and the black press responded with outrage and action, and various government officials repudiated the connection between the work-or-fight idea and enforced labor for African-American women.[42] But employers and civic officials could still attempt to use statutes against loitering and disorderly conduct to punish women who transgressed the boundaries of racial work patterns in southern communities. The case of the work-or-fight campaign against African-American women workers illustrates in a compelling way that civic identities for women of color are particularly fragile and that racism reaches across class lines to contain and twist claims for the rewards of citizenship based on patriotic service.

In addition to women who tied loyal service to the state in wartime to professional issues and to goals for racial as well as gender equality, some women negotiated the space offered by loyal support of the war to claim the obligation and right to bear arms. As civilians faced the realities of war in Europe these women called for the right to bear arms to defend themselves and their homes should war come to America. For these women, the "Rape of Belgium" was more than a metaphor: from shop floors to drawing rooms they discussed reports of the sexual violation of Belgian women and children at the hands of German soldiers.[43] Some women took specific steps to arm themselves and to form groups for home defense. A suffrage group in Old Orchard, Maine, led by Lurana Sheldon Ferris organized the Women's Defense Club in 1916 to teach women "to shoot, and shoot straight." The club eventually provided shooting instruction to thousands of women in several regions of the country, so that, according to Ferris, "if American women are ever called upon to defend their homes, their children, and themselves, they will not be as helpless as were the Belgian women."[44]

Ferris was careful to link the actions of women at arms to patriotic defense of the state. "We are teaching patriotism and courage," she asserted. "Certainly patriotism, with efficiency in shooting, or even the ability to load a gun, is a combination that makes either a man or a woman a national asset in time of trouble." As a suffrage activist, Ferris made it clear that the right to bear arms was part of the fabric of female citizenship: "Whether we vote or not," she concluded, "we are going to

---

[42] See "Washington Officials Deny Report," Johnson, "'Work or Fight' Laws for Women," and "Abuse of the 'Work or Fight' Slogan."

[43] See, for example, *New York Times*, 1 September 1914, 2; "The Case of Belgium," *The Outlook* 108 (30 September 1914): 239–40; Louis L. Seaman, "Where Hundreds of Thousands are Suffering," *Independent* 80 (5 October 1914): 18; and "Women in War Time," *The Suffragist*, 3 October 1914, 2.

[44] "Women in a Defense Club," *New York Times*, 17 February 1916, 5.

shoot."[45] Yet there is an implicit, subversive reading of women's loyalties in time of war within this construction of patriotic service. The Belgian state and Belgian men had failed to protect the women of that neutral nation from violation. They had failed to uphold the traditional gender bargain that cast men and the male-dominated state in the role of protectors and women as the protected.[46] American women could not entrust the final protection of their bodies to their own government or their own men; therefore, they had the right to bear arms to defend themselves and their homes, the core of the state itself.

Other women joined Ferris in organizing women's defense and rifle groups in the years before the United States entered the war in 1917, including the five-hundred-member American Women's League for Self Defense that held cavalry drills in the streets of New York City and drill practice in New York's armory building.[47] Following U.S. entry into the war, groups of American women followed the example of Russian women who formed a regiment known as the Russian Women's Battalion of Death to fight in the world war and defend the Kerensky government in the Russian Revolution. The *Woman Citizen* reported that women from Oklahoma and Texas, "wives of soldiers in the Regular National Army and National Guard" were organizing their own Battalion of Death "to serve in any way the War Department asks—in trenches if necessary."[48] *The Suffragist* reported in the same month that women's regiments'were being formed in Texas, Indiana, and Florida.[49]

These rifle and defense groups and the women's regiments are only the most visible examples of a grass-roots movement of American women to promote the female use of guns during the World War I era. A close reading of the journal of the American Rifle Association, *Arms and the Man*, from 1914 to 1919 reveals that thousands of women nationwide joined rifle and revolver clubs at indoor and outdoor ranges and for trapshooting (firing at clay targets), a phenomenon that the editors of the journal and various contributors believed was "stimulated by the U.S entrance into the war."[50] *Arms and the Man*, the *New York Times*, and *Stars and Stripes*, the

---

[45] See "The Women's Defense Club," letter to the editor of the *New York Times* from Lurana Sheldon Ferris, Old Orchard, Maine, 27 March 1916, *New York Times*, 31 March 1916, 10, and also her letter of 18 February 1917, sec. 7, 4.

[46] For these categories, see Stiehm, "The Protected, The Protector, The Defender"; Elshtain, "On Beautiful Souls, Just Warriors and Feminist Consciousness"; and Elshtain, *Women and War*.

[47] For a detailed discussion of these groups, see Jensen, "Minerva on the Field of Mars."

[48] "American Battalion of Death," *Woman Citizen* 1 (13 October 1917): 372.

[49] "Women May Fight for Democracy Abroad," *The Suffragist*, 6 October 1917, p. 3.

[50] See *Arms and the Man*, 4 August 1917, 378; "Trapshooting Attracts Both Sexes," *Arms and the Man*, 1 March 1917, 458; "About Women Shots," *Arms and the Man*, 19 January 1918, 338; and Peter B. Carney, "Target Smashing Stimulated by Entrance of U.S. in War," *Arms and the Man* 15 December 1917, 237.

newspaper of the American Expeditionary Forces in France, provide evidence for the existence of thirty-nine women's rifle and defense groups for this period around the country, with total membership numbering in the thousands. Like the women's regiments, several of these groups, including the American Women's League for Self-Defense and the New York Rifle Club, offered their services to the government. As the instructor for the New York Rifle Club, June Haughton, summed it up: women "are in the munitions shops, in the mines, in the fields, and in various branches of manual and military service. Why not the battlefield?"[51]

While the U.S. government did not accept the services of these women-at-arms (only some fifteen thousand women were placed as telephone operators and in clerical positions, especially under Josephus Daniels in the Navy and Marine Corps), some Americans accepted women bearing arms at home and abroad as proof that women as a class were full citizens who deserved the vote. Such observations, plentiful in suffrage journals, were not limited to their pages. Popular journals such as the *Literary Digest* and the *Delineator*, and newspapers like the *Tulsa World* that picked up an International News Service series on "Women and the War" joined the *Woman Citizen* and *The Suffragist* in carrying stories of women bearing arms and observing that these women had crossed an important conceptual boundary of citizenship.[52]

Another strategy used by suffrage supporters was to turn the fighting-for-voting argument on its head to dramatize the cultural links between military service and citizenship. In November 1917 the *Woman Citizen* featured Alice Foley's poem "In the Subway":

Six fat slackers sat so smug,
Behind their papers slinking,
While a tired shop-girl "strap-hung" above
Was thinking, thinking, thinking—
If six fat slackers have the right to vote
Because they can carry a gun,
Should the six fat slackers still have the vote
When they *will not* carry one?[53]

The *Tulsa Daily World* reported that a Texas woman suggested that men who avoided going to war should not be allowed to vote because "a

[51] "Rifle Range for Women" *New York Times*, 25 December 1916, 9.

[52] See, for example, "Warrior Women," *Literary Digest* 50 (19 June 1915): 1460; "The Battalion of Death," *Delineator*, January 1918, 3; G. Kay Spencer, "Women in the War," *Tulsa Morning News*, 22 October 1917, 8; "Another Phantom Laid," *Woman Citizen* 1 (4 August 1917): 162; and "Russian Women and the Ballot," *The Suffragist*, 12 December 1914, 2. Not all suffrage supporters, of course, supported women taking on what they believed was male militarism.

[53] Alice Foley, "In the Subway," *Woman Citizen* 1 (3 November 1917): 439.

favorite argument of people opposed to women suffrage is that women should not be allowed to vote because they cannot bear arms."[54]

Extending these claims of the rights of citizenship through defense of the state, some women working in munition factories supported their claims for the vote by arguing that their physical production of bullets and life-threatening work for the war qualified them as soldiers eligible for the ballot. In early summer of 1918 women workers from the Bethlehem Steel Plant at Newcastle, Delaware, and from the Bartlett-Hayward munition plant in Baltimore, Maryland, came as representatives to present their case to President Woodrow Wilson and members of the Senate while the suffrage amendment was pending in Congress.[55] The government "admits that we face the risk of injury and death as soldiers face it, but it does not recognize us as citizens of the country as soldiers are," they assured the senators and told them of their determination to be "recognized as citizens of the government we are working to defend and equals of the men who fight with the arms we make for them."[56] Women working in munitions plants were exposed to hazardous chemicals and risked death in explosive conditions. These health risks were graphically evident: the effects of the powders made the skin of the women's hands and faces turn yellow and their hair turn a bright orange. "They do not need the arm bands bearing the words 'munition maker' which they wear in Washington, in order to distinguish them from ordinary people," editors of *The Suffragist* reported.[57]

When President Wilson refused to give the women an audience the munitions women constructed a symbolic stage for the representation of their claims of loyalty and physical sacrifice for the state in the outer offices of the White House. Each day they came to inquire when the president would see them, and they waited during office hours for a chance to speak with him. Knitting socks for soldiers was one of the most recognized signs of female patriotism on the home front. The arresting sight of a group of women with bright yellow skin, orange hair, and arm bands quietly knitting socks for soldiers outside the presidential offices drew the immediate attention of many "prominent people" who

[54] "Shooting and Voting," *Tulsa Daily World*, 23 September 1917, sec. 3, 8.

[55] See Eleanor Taylor, "Munition Workers Wait for Audience with the President," *The Suffragist*, 1 June 1918, 10–11; and Gladys Greiner, "Maryland Munition Workers Appeal to President," *The Suffragist*, 15 June 1918, 7.

[56] The letter from the Baltimore women to senators in reprinted in "The Appeal of a Munition Worker," *The Suffragist*, 8 June 1918, 7.

[57] See "Munition Workers Wait," 10; Florence Bayard Hilles, "A Suffragist Makes Munitions" *The Suffragist*, 25 May 1918, 7; and John D. Barry, "Munition Workers as Political Factors," reprinted from the 3 June 1918 ed. of the *San Francisco Bulletin* in "Comments of the Press," *The Suffragist*, 22 June 1918, 12; quotation in "Munition Workers Wait," 10.

"streamed in and out" of the area. Secretaries had to answer constant inquiries about the women and admit that they had not been granted access to the president, which added publicity to the cause. The women returned to their jobs after several weeks, but they had made their statement. *The Suffragist* reported dramatic increases in support for women's enfranchisement at munition factories in many locations across the country.[58]

The woman at arms threatened gender relations and women's roles in America at the same time that she symbolized their changing status. While government officials subdued potential female soldiers by refusing their services, the creators of some forms of American popular culture conquered them through ridicule, satire, and by constructing cautionary tales about their ultimate downfall. In 1918 *Stars and Stripes* published a poem "I Loved an Amazon"; it is written in the voice of a soldier on leave who is dismayed to find that his wife has joined a women's defense and drill group.

> I hastened home to find my child
> Alone, unfed, provoked and riled.
> My wife I found—my search was long—
> The center of a female throng.
> That voice, with love once soft and low,
> Was shouting, "Right by section—HO!"
> A lady by me in the street
> Said, "Ain't their uniforms just sweet?
> That khaki's dear as precious stones—
> Their tailors charged them 80 bones!"
>
> With that I gazed upon my wife—
> Oh, saddest moment of my life!
> A campaign hat with brim slouched down
> Was crushed upon those tresses brown.
> My pride and joy! Her swan-like neck
> A flannel shirt conspired to wreck.
> A figure, once like that of Venus,

[58] See "New Jersey Munition Workers Appeal to the President," *The Suffragist*, 29 June 1918, 11, 14; and "New Jersey Munition Workers Demand Federal Suffrage," *The Suffragist* 14 September 1918, 8, for examples. For other examples of the politicization of women's physical appearance, see Jacquelyn Dowd Hall, "Disorderly Women: Gender and Labor Militancy in the Appalachian South," *Journal of American History* 73 (1986): 354–82, and Amy Swerdlow, "Ladies' Day at the Capitol: Women Strike for Peace versus HUAC," *Feminist Studies* 8 (1982): 493–520.

Looked like a sack. (That's just between us.)
The swish of dainty skirts was now
No more; instead were—khaki trou!

Bring on the war with bang and clatter,
With blood and thunder—that's no matter,
But let no band, lest anger blind me,
Strike up, "The Girl I Left Behind Me!"[59]

Neurologist Graeme H. Hammond, a noted specialist in nervous disorders, dismissed the female soldier with a rhetorical twist of the knife in an interview for the *New York Times Magazine*, "When Women Fight." Of course women would make good soldiers, he told journalist George McAdam. Any married man could attest to their combativeness. And, Hammond stressed, "all women in their hearts have struck men with bayonets." Hammond proposed that allowing women to be soldiers would be a great benefit to society: the physically defective women would perish, and the fit would survive to create a better white race.[60]

Popular journalists capitalized on the public's fascination with the members of the Russian Women's Battalion of Death. Popular women's magazines like the *Delineator*, *Ladies Home Journal*, and *Good Housekeeping* carried stories about them and emphasized their patriotic service to Russia. The editors of the *Delineator*, for example, featured an idealized portrait of a female soldier standing guard over Russia on the cover of its January 1918 issue. But the stories also emphasized that while the battalion members were fighting to save their country they did so at the expense of their "femininity"; indeed, they crossed the boundaries of heterosexuality to lesbianism. In his extensive report on the battalion, "The Soul that Stirs in 'Battalions of Death,'" William Shepard reported: "In the minds of all the girl soldiers I found a fine scorn [of male soldiers] mixed with a mischievous enjoyment." This, he reported, was the downfall of the battalion. Reports of the rape of some battalion members and their disbanding at the fall of the Winter Palace made the cautionary tale complete.[61] Photographs of battalion members with shaved heads, wearing male uniforms and carrying guns, reinforced the construction of the female soldier as the mannish lesbian. At a time when physicians

[59] Fairfax D. Downey, "I Loved an Amazon," *Stars and Stripes* 1 (8 March 1918): 2.

[60] George McAdam, "When Women Fight," *New York Times Magazine*, 2 September 1917, 3, 14. Hammond was the son of William A. Hammond, surgeon general for the Union during the Civil War.

[61] William G. Shepherd, "The Soul That Stirs in 'Battalions of Death'" *Delineator* 92 (March 1918): 5–7, 56.

were medicalizing homosexuality and defining lesbians and gay men as deviant, and when lesbianism represented the ultimate threat of the movement for women's autonomy,[62] these representations of the female soldier were powerful weapons in the arsenal of opposition to all women's wartime claims for military service.

Women physicians, African-American women in volunteer agencies, and women in citizen militias and defense groups focused on the social contract of citizenship to make their claims for increased civic participation and equality during the First World War. In their view, the wartime era seems to have represented the meeting of two vital currents. The first of these encompassed the collective accomplishments of women in the late nineteenth and early twentieth centuries in suffrage, community reform, and professional advancement. These achievements engendered a strengthened civic identity for women. The second current was the wartime context that imbued citizens' loyalty and service to the state with enhanced meaning and potential; therefore, these women argued, as more powerful citizens they could offer a more powerful loyalty and patriotism to their nation during this crucial time, and in so doing they could claim rewards of equality in civic, racial, and professional terms. As institutional feminists they conceived of the military primarily as an institution and sought entrance in rights-based arguments that echoed suffrage, professional, and community activism in other arenas. Yet they sought entrance to an institution like no other and thereby challenged powerful boundaries of gender at the intersections of race, sexuality, and class as well as the intimate connections between military service and masculinity. They exposed what Theodore Roosevelt feared about the war in general—"volcanic fires" beneath the "smiling surface of civilization"—and threatened to bring about an eruption that would change the geography of social relationships forever.[63] Women physicians whose vision of complete female citizenship included full equality with male colleagues in their profession, African-American women who encountered powerful controlling images as they challenged democracy's promise through patriotic service, and women who claimed the right to bear arms and confronted the gender bargain of protection for women from the state all encountered fierce resistance and did not achieve their ultimate goals. Yet many women active in pressing these claims celebrated the victories—partial recognition of patriotism, rewards within

[62] See, for example, George Chauncey, Jr., "From Sexual Inversion to Homosexuality," and Carroll Smith-Rosenberg, "The New Woman as Androgyne: Social Disorder and the Gender Crisis, 1870–1936," in *Disorderly Conduct: Visions of Gender in Victorian America* (New York: Oxford University Press, 1985), 245–96.

[63] Theodore Roosevelt refers to the war in this way in *America and the World War* (New York: C. Scribner's Sons, 1915), 2.

professional and local communities, and pathbreaking work that would direct women's claims in World War II for full inclusion. When Congress ratified the Nineteenth Amendment in 1920, the recent claims made by women for equal opportunity in the military in the "war to end all wars" made the franchise moderate in comparison. The women I discuss in this chapter demonstrate the will and tenacity of the people to shape the national construction of citizenship and the rewards of loyalty in ways that fit *their* definitions and needs, even when they challenge and contradict opposing values of the state.

Chapter 7

PATRIOTISM IN ORANGE: THE MEMORY OF
WORLD WAR I IN A MASSACHUSETTS TOWN

DAVID GLASSBERG AND J. MICHAEL MOORE

TOWN BY TOWN in the 1920s and 1930s, Americans unveiled monuments to their friends, sons, and brothers who died in World War I. Retired artillery and statues of doughboys joined Civil War soldiers and cannon on town squares in a landscape of patriotic sacrifice equating national loyalty with martial valor. But the monument unveiled to the eleven men from Orange, Massachusetts, who died in World War I was different; the twelve-foot-high bronze depicts a seated, weary veteran recounting the horror of his war experience to a young boy. Inscribed in the granite base is the slogan, "It Shall Not Be Again."

How did this monument come to be built? What did it mean in the life of the community? What new meanings has the monument acquired since its dedication in 1934? Through the "biography" of this unusual monument, we can explore the problematic relationship between the creation, institutionalization, and dissemination of a memory of war and how Americans identify themselves with the nation-state.[1]

The connection between war and national identity has alternatively fascinated and repelled generations of writers. The earliest studies of nationalism in the aftermath of the First World War analyzed the powerful emotional connections formed between a people and their government as the result of war experience. Focusing on the collective psychology of the homefront during wartime, many of these studies equated feelings of national unity with the herd instinct. Psychological explanations for nationalism grew more prominent with the growth of fascism in the interwar years.[2] In his analysis of Memorial Day ceremonies in Newburyport,

[1] Phrase "biography of a monument" borrowed from James E. Young, "The Biography of a Memorial Icon: Nathan Rapoport's Warsaw Ghetto Monument," *Representations* 26 (Spring 1989): 69–106.

[2] Scholars sought to distinguish patriotism, a healthy love of country, from nationalism, a dangerous belief in the superiority of one's country to other countries. See, for example, Carlton J. H. Hayes, *Essays on Nationalism* (New York: Macmillan, 1926). The scholarly critique of nationalism after World War I is analyzed in Merle Curti, *Roots of American*

Massachusetts, in the 1930s, W. Lloyd Warner concluded that "it is in time of war that the average American living in small cities and towns gets his deepest satisfactions as a member of his society." "The public commemoration of war," Warner added, seeks to "recapture feelings of wellbeing when society was most integrated and feelings of unity most intense."[3]

More recently, scholars seeking to explain the connection between war and nationalism have relied less on questionable assumptions about the unity of the homefront in wartime than on the invention of a collective memory of the war experience and the role that government plays in insuring that citizens recall the war experience in similar ways. The memory of war, disseminated nationally, forms a crucial element in the construction of an imagined community through which disparate groups envision themselves as part of a collective with a common past, present, and future. Historians of modern Europe have explored how governments after World War I created war memorials, holidays, and rituals to link service in war and service to country and how the myth of the war experience and cult of the fallen soldier became powerful symbols helping the modern nation-state consolidate control over its citizenry.[4]

Historical studies of how governments created a national memory of war leave unanswered questions that the initial generation of scholars raised about the apparent spontaneity and emotional depth associated with nationalism. If the myth of the war experience was a top-down phenomenon, communicated from an elite to masses, then why did the masses buy it? How did it connect with the everyday world of family and local community that social historians have insisted are most important? The question is especially vexing for the United States, where the ability of the federal government to disseminate a national memory of war was

---

Loyalty (New York: Columbia University Press, 1946), and Weston Gladding Donehower, "Conflicting Interpretations of American Patriotism in the 1920s" (Ph.D. diss., University of Pennsylvania, 1982). The most famous of the psychological studies of nationalism that emphasized the importance of an enemy out-group for maintaining in-group solidarity is Theodore Adorno, et al., *The Authoritarian Personality* (New York: Harper & Row, 1950). For a summary of Adorno and other early psychological literature on nationalism, see Leonard Doob, *Patriotism and Nationalism: Their Psychological Foundations* (New Haven: Yale University Press, 1964).

[3] W. Lloyd Warner, *The Living and the Dead* (New Haven: Yale University Press, 1959), 274, 276.

[4] See George L. Mosse, *Fallen Soldiers: Reshaping the Memory of the World Wars* (New York: Oxford University Press, 1990); Eric Hobsbawm, "Introduction" and "Mass Producing Traditions," in *The Invention of Tradition*, ed. Hobsbawm and Terence Ranger (New York: Cambridge University Press, 1983); and Raphael Samuel, "Introduction," in *Patriotism: The Making and Unmaking of British National Identity*, ed. Samuel, 3 vols. (New York: Routledge, 1989).

relatively limited. At first glance, World War I, which involved national mobilization, the mixing of recruits from across America in the same military units, and even the dissemination of the same graphic images nationally via government agencies such as the Committee on Public Information, would seem tailor-made to study the construction of a national memory of war. Yet while the U.S. government could largely control the representation of war as it happened, it could not control how the war was remembered in towns and cities across America. Once the mobilization ended and the troops came home, different memories of war converged in the arena of the town. The story of Orange, Massachusetts, and its monument demonstrates the need for citizens both to rethink our assumptions about patriotism and collective memory in the interwar period and to study the process through which a public memory of war is created, institutionalized, disseminated, and changed over time.

Orange is a small industrial town located on Millers River in north-central Massachusetts. Never an especially prosperous town, its population of approximately 5,500 hardly changed in the forty years from the turn of the century until World War II.[5] As in other American towns, at the declaration of war in April 1917 the men and women of Orange organized a host of local committees to support the war effort, the local manufacturers obtained government contracts to produce war materials, and the young men went off to fight.

Many of Orange's young men fought in the Great War as members of their local state guard unit, Company E of the 104th Infantry Regiment, Twenty-Sixth (Yankee) Division. The unit shipped out to France in October 1917; it received the Croix-de-guerre for its heroism while attached to the French army at the battle of Apremont in April 1918 and saw extensive action with the American Expeditionary Force in the summer and fall of that year. Unlike most American soldiers in World War I, drafted into units scattered throughout the army, the men of Company E fought alongside men from their hometown and region; their distinctive war experience served as a source of identity and solidarity for them when they returned to Orange after the war.[6]

The men returned to Orange in April 1919 amid a public debate about

---

[5] *Historical Atlas of Massachusetts*, ed. Richard Wilke and Jack Tager (Amherst: University of Massachusetts Press, 1991), 143.

[6] The nucleus of the 104th U.S. Infantry was made of several Western Massachusetts State Guard Units that had seen service in Mexico in 1916 and thus was ready to go to France before most other regular army divisions could be formed or trained. James H. Fifield, *The Regiment: A History of the 104th U.S. Infantry, AEF* (Springfield, Mass., 1946), 2–14.

the proper way to honor them and memorialize their deeds. Some in town proposed the erection of a stone shaft or triumphal arch, in keeping with the late-nineteenth-century commemorative traditions suggesting that symbolic memorial art could promote idealism and influence the behavior of present and future generations of viewers.[7] A monument, argued a letter to the local newspaper, would "stand for generations to come, an object lesson in patriotism and loyalty to country." Another writer extolled the particular value of the plaque such a monument would hold. "The present and future generations to come will be proud to point to certain names and say, this is my son, this is my father; that's my grandfather's name. They served their country in the World War."[8]

But there were others in Orange openly disdainful of the prospect of the traditional monument. The local paper editorialized that "no better dead memorial can be provided than a big marble shaft or statue toward which small boys in after years can shoot small stones and snowballs and aged people can sit complacently about and by squinting their eyes through strong lenses satisfy their curiosity in reading the names of those who responded to duty."[9] Echoing national trends, this group in town preferred a "living memorial," such as a community building, gymnasium, or park, that could honor the veterans' spirit of service while also providing something useful to the town.[10]

Debate was heated. After four special town meetings, in May 1919 the town voted to create a new memorial park by clearing a rundown section of town between the railroad tracks and Millers River.[11] Much of the

[7] The American Federation of Arts, an organization of professional artists, strongly endorsed the creation of symbolic world war memorials to promote idealism and combat what they saw as materialism and literal-mindedness of Americans. The federation organized a monuments committee within a week after the armistice to advise local communities and published guidelines in its journal *American Magazine of Art*. A list of committee members and their guidelines appears in "War Memorials," *American Magazine of Art* 10 (March 1919): 180–83. Fifteen artists elaborated on the federation's position in a special issue of the *American Magazine of Art* (May 1919). The artists had more success influencing the design of American battle monuments overseas than in towns back home. On overseas, see G. Kurt Piehler, "The War Dead and the Gold Star: American Commemoration of the First World War," in *Commemorations: The Politics of National Identity*, ed. John Gillis (Princeton: Princeton University Press, 1994), 168–85. On American traditions of monumental art before the world war, see Michele H. Bogart, *Public Sculpture and the Civic Ideal in New York City, 1880–1930* (Chicago: University of Chicago Press, 1989).

[8] Orange *Enterprise and Journal*, 31 January 1919, 2; *Enterprise and Journal*, 28 February 1919, 2.

[9] *Enterprise and Journal*, 28 February 1919, 2.

[10] Recreation organizations especially pushed the "living memorial" idea nationwide; see the series of pamphlets distributed by Community Service, Inc., an offshoot of the Playground and Recreation Association of America, titled *Community Buildings as War Memorials* (1919).

[11] The town voted to borrow $30,000, which represented the owners' asking prices for

argument in favor of the park centered on local businesses wanting to create a town common near the railroad station to greet visitors, a strategy popular with village improvement societies throughout New England; merchants also saw the plan as providing additional parking space for their stores.

Although space was reserved in the park for a World War monument, the decision for the park left many recently returned veterans feeling used and left out. One veteran stated, "The boys did not relish the idea of being used as a lever by the townspeople to obtain something they could get in no other way"; he added that the new park "would serve more as a benefit to the townspeople than the servicemen."[12] The former soldiers' feeling of separation from the rest of the town was reinforced when in November 1919 the first anniversary of the armistice came and went unobserved by the townspeople.

But by then, the veterans had their own organization to perpetuate the memory of World War I in town. With the help of $2,600 that the town had originally set aside, but never used, for a welcome-home celebration, the veterans founded a local chapter of the American Legion in August 1919. Post membership soon exceeded one hundred, and the Legion's prominence within the community grew.[13] By May 1920, the Legionnaires had taken over the headquarters of the Grand Army of the Republic (the northern Civil War veterans' organization) and assumed direction of the town's annual Memorial Day celebration; the former soldiers transformed the focus of the observance from the Civil War dead to those of World War I while keeping intact the old rituals such as the visit to schools and children decorating soldiers' graves. In 1922, the Legion made the commemoration of November 11 into a public event for the first time; they organized a short parade to the newly landscaped memo-

---

the three parcels that would become the park. The assessed value of the sites was approximately half that amount; because the law did not allow the town to pay more than 25 percent over assessed value, the town offered $19,500 and took the parcels by eminent domain.

[12] *Enterprise and Journal*, 21 November 1919, 2.

[13] By 1920 there were sixty thousand American Legion members in Massachusetts, the highest total of any state in the United States. William Pencak, *For God and Country: The American Legion, 1919–41* (Boston: Northeastern University Press, 1989), 67. The prominence of the Legion also grew with its members' social prominence in town. Among the first post commanders was Howard Warren, manager of Minute Tapioca Company. Of the ninety-four membership cards that survive from 1923, sixty-seven listed occupation; of those, 29 percent listed occupation as merchants or professionals, 36 percent skilled craftmen, and 33 percent semi-skilled factory workers. This compares with approximately 20 percent, 24 percent, and 56 percent for each occupational category in a sample of the 1920 Orange city directory. Membership cards, American Legion Post 172 Legion Hall, Orange, Massachusetts. *Orange City Directory 1920* (New Haven: Price and Lee, 1920).

rial park during the day and hosted an Armistice Day Ball at night. Although the Legion could not convince local businesses to close that day, many observed three minutes of silence at 11:00 A.M.—a silence that was enforced in one local foundry in 1925 when three workers who did not stop work were forced to kiss the American flag.[14] At the open house before the Legion ball the following year, a speaker reminded his audience of the importance of observing the day: "Armistice Day is not a holiday, but let us not forget the great thrill of eight years ago when the Great War came to an end, let us not forget those 'buddies' who never came back. Ex-servicemen, mothers, fathers, friends, be with us on this night. We don't forget."[15]

The former soldiers' desire to remember and to be remembered kept the idea of a permanent memorial alive. When the state returned $3,100 in unspent veterans' bonus money to the town in 1926, the veterans insisted that it be earmarked for a memorial in the vacant park.[16] The town committee appointed to recommend a design heard from ten different firms that manufactured war memorials.[17] But because the committee wanted "a memorial designed especially for Orange, rather than a stock model which may be seen anywhere," committee members sought to commission an original bronze statue by John T. Hardy, who in the nearby town of Templeton had created a memorial doughboy in combat gear holding a rifle in one hand while bending over to place a wreath on the grave of a fallen comrade. When the Orange monument committee approached Hardy to create a similar mourning statue for Orange, the

[14] Two did so, one who refused was dunked in water. "So into the Tank He Went," *Enterprise and Journal*, 13 November 1925.

[15] *Enterprise and Journal*, 5 November 1926, 4.

[16] Between 1919 and 1924, Massachusetts collected a poll tax of $5 to be used for a bonus to Massachusetts World War I veterans. Perhaps the passage of the federal bonus bill in 1924 allowed the Legionnaires to designate that their state bonus be used for a town memorial; their decision might also reflect that Legion members were more affluent than the average veteran. On the struggle over the federal bonus bill, see Pencak, *For God and Country*.

[17] While the Orange memorial committee records are lost, we know the type of monument several commercial firms had available. American Doughboy Statues of Spencer, Indiana, touted "The Spirit of the American Doughboy," a realistic life-size bronze with rifle in one hand, grenade in the other, stepping over barbed wire. The firm's promotional brochure reprinted an endorsement by the American Legion and a testimonial letter from Sergeant Alvin York. In addition to the life-sized doughboy for towns, the studio also sold a twelve-inch size for home and office. Most of the sixty towns listed in the brochure as "some of the many communities" that purchased the statue were in the Midwest, but several were in New Jersey, Pennsylvania, New York, and Vermont. "The Spirit of the American Doughboy," Memorials File, Microfilm # 89–14013, American Legion Library, Indianapolis. According to T. Perry Wesley, editor emeritus of the Spencer, Indiana, *Evening World*, the statue also was erected in Bethel and Canaan, Connecticut. T. Perry Wesley, correspondence with author, 30 January 1995.

sculptor wanted more than double the money the veterans had available (fig. 1).[18]

Frustrated, the veterans moved ahead with less expensive alternatives. In November 1929, the veterans unveiled a large wooden frame containing photographs of the eleven men from Orange who had died in the world war grouped around a silk embroidered emblem of the coat of arms of the United States (fig. 2).[19] In 1931, the Legion persuaded the town to memorialize its eleven war dead in public by placing bronze markers at eleven intersections around the town, "as near as possible to a spot which the man whose memory it perpetuates passed in his daily life."[20] Turning to Memorial Park, in August 1932 the Company E Veterans Association dedicated a boulder "to the buddies who never returned."[21] Former company members from throughout western Massachusetts attended the Saturday evening dedication ceremony and then stayed overnight for a clambake. Two months later, in October 1932, the newly organized Damon-Spooner Veterans of Foreign Wars Post added a French 88-millimeter World War cannon to the landscape of the park, with a plaque reading "In memory of her departed comrades."[22]

The veterans wanted the markers, boulder, and cannon as permanent reminders of their war experience. What did this experience mean to Orange's world war veterans? We do not know what motivated the men of Orange to go to war in 1917—what combination of sense of duty to nation and boredom with small town life. But we do know how their experience was retroactively explained in the decade following the war. Even before World War I had ended, the town had transformed the soldiers into model citizens and patriotic exemplars, sliding them into the social role that had been occupied by the thinning ranks of Civil War

---

[18] *Enterprise and Journal*, 4 March 1927, 9.

[19] *Enterprise and Journal*, 8 and 15 November 1929.

[20] *Enterprise and Journal*, 1 May 1931, 1.

[21] *Enterprise and Journal*, 25 August 1932, 1. This was not the first memorial to go into Memorial Park; in May 1932, the American Legion accepted a spruce tree as a community Christmas tree from the Women's Club. It is significant that Memorial Park was considered space for veterans, who accepted the tree on behalf of the town, even though the tree was not explicitly a world war memorial. On the use of natural features such as boulders for war memorials in western Europe, see George L. Mosse, *Fallen Soldiers: Reshaping the Memory of the World Wars* (New York: Oxford University Press, 1990). Of the eleven men who died from Orange, five belonged to Company E. We do not know what percentage of Orange veterans served in Company E, but Company E veterans dominated the veterans organizations active in preserving the memory of World War I in Orange.

[22] *Enterprise and Journal*, 13 October 1932. The local VFW post was approximately half the size of the American Legion; many VFW members belonged to the Legion as well. The post was named after Henry Damon and Ralph Spooner, both of whom died at Apremont. The cannon was dedicated by May Spooner, Ralph Spooner's mother.

FIGURE 1. John T. Hardy's War Memorial sculpture for Templeton, Massachusetts. (Photo by J. Michael Moore)

FIGURE 2. Photo memorial in American Legion Hall, Orange, Massachusetts. (Photo by David Glassberg)

veterans.[23] Orange's veterans did not shy away from this patriotic role or the national iconography that went with it—the photographic memorial hanging in the Legion Hall intertwined the pictures of the men with the American eagle, and veterans hoped to add a flagpole to Memorial Park with a plaque to Gold Star mothers. But the focus of their efforts to mark the landscape, like their other public activities of the early 1930s— encouraging military training for youth, sponsoring drum corps, organizing Memorial Day and Armistice Day ceremonies—was as much to reinforce the former soldiers' camaraderie with one another and their special position in the community as to promote national loyalty among their fellow citizens.

The Legion's increasing public activities in the 1930s gain additional meaning when placed in the context of the Great Depression; the Company E clambake and boulder dedication took place six weeks after federal troops routed the bonus marchers in Washington. Not only did the former soldiers forego their bonuses that year, but in March 1933 the

[23] On the GAR's origination of the role of patriotic veteran, in the decades after the Civil War, see Stuart McConnell, *Glorious Contentment: The Grand Army of the Republic, 1865–1900* (Chapel Hill: University of North Carolina Press, 1992).

Government Economy Act also slashed veterans benefits by 40 percent. As the Depression worsened, Legion membership offered veterans an important source of personal identity and mutual economic support as well as a base from which to retain their claim on civil society.[24] Veterans of the early 1930s had reason to fear that their special position in town would be lost as the story of what they did in the war was forgotten and their direct testimony was replaced with books and films about the war.[25]

Thus as Orange's veterans dedicated the boulder and cannon on the perimeter of Memorial Park in late 1932, they left room at the center for a more imposing monument—one that unmistakably would embody the veterans themselves and their central place in town life as well as the centrality of their story over others about the war. In 1933, as the Depression deflated prices, the former soldiers launched yet another effort to realize their long-sought goal of a doughboy statue for Memorial Park.

By the early 1930s, however, the veterans were not the only group in town keeping alive the memory of the war. In a reflection of national trends, pacifist activities in the community veritably erupted, many directed toward using the memory of the world war to transform the traditional rituals that connected war and patriotism.

Among the earliest centers of pacifist sentiment in Orange were the churches, where Arthur Blair, pastor of the Universalist Church from 1922 to 1931, regularly wove antiwar themes into his sermons.[26] In 1924, on Armistice Day, Blair called for the town to "make war on war psy-

[24] Although there is no record of Orange veterans participating in the bonus march, the Massachusetts American Legion invited bonus march leader Walter Waters to be the keynote speaker at its 1932 state convention. Pencak, *For God and Country*, 203. The American war veterans sense of entitlement from civil society seemed to parallel those of Great Britain, as described in Eric J. Leed, *No Man's Land: Combat and Identity in World War I* (New York: Cambridge University Press, 1979), and Stephen R. Ward, "Land Fit For Heroes Lost," in *The War Generation: Veterans of the First World War*, ed. Stephen R. Ward (Port Washington, N.Y.: Kennikat Press, 1975), 10–37. Some evidence suggests that Legion membership grew in importance in the Depression as a source of business connections; after ignoring "occupation" on membership cards through the 1920s, members almost unfailingly filled it out in the 1930s. Paralleling the national pattern, a substantial proportion of members of the Orange American Legion post were merchants or in sales. In a 1938 national survey of Legion members, Pencak found one-quarter were retail shop owners; in Orange in 1934, the percentage was 26 percent. Pencak, *For God and Country*, 81. American Legion Post 172, Membership Cards.

[25] We know that mass media versions of the war such as *What Price Glory?* (1927) and *The Lost Squadron* (1932) played in the movie theaters of Orange and the nearby town of Athol, though it is unclear how they shaped the memory of the war.

[26] At 250 members, the Universalists were among the largest Protestant denominations in Orange in 1932; others were Swedish Lutheran (252), Congregationalist (200), Methodists (200), and Baptists (172), with 700 Catholics in town. *Enterprise and Journal*, 4 February 1932.

chology," including the elimination of children's toy guns and soldiers.[27] Blair, active in the town's commemoration of World War I, chaired the war memorial committee in 1926 and spoke at the dedication of the memorial street markers in 1931.

Another center of antiwar sentiment was the high school. Civics and Government teacher Henry Littlefield, only twenty-four years old in 1929 and fresh from New York University, encouraged students to question the results of the armistice, the system of war reparations, and the role of arms manufacturers.[28] In an article in the school paper, which was later reprinted in the town paper, Principal Dwight Davis provoked the imagination of the students who would view the 1931 Memorial Day parade:

> As you watch the parade swing from the old town hall down East Main Street toward the cemetery, I hope that you will see more than the veterans, old and young, more than the members of the various organizations who will be marching there. I hope that you will see shell-torn, mud-spattered, bleeding humanity as it was on the fields of France. While the band is playing a stirring march, I hope that you will hear the cry of suffering humanity as God has heard it through all the wars of the ages. I hope that in some way you can sense the awful futility of war as a means of settling national disputes.[29]

Local pacifist sentiments gained further public expression in September 1931, when two representatives of the Massachusetts chapter of the Women's International League for Peace and Freedom (WILPF) drove into Orange with petitions calling for the total disarmament of all nations. Those who took copies of the petition for circulation in Orange included ministers from the Congregational, Universalist, and Methodist churches, as well as representatives from the Orange Women's Club, the Millers River Grange, and, interestingly, the Catholic Women's Club.[30]

[27] *Enterprise and Journal*, 14 November 1924.

[28] Interview with Henry W. Littlefield, Bridgeport, Conn., 14 July 1993.

[29] *Enterprise and Journal*, 29 May 1931.

[30] This was an offshoot of the national peace caravan that traveled from Hollywood, Calif., to Washington, D.C., between June and October 1931. "Disarmament Caravan Reaches Orange," *Enterprise and Journal*, 4 September 1931, 7. See the records of the Massachusetts WILPF in WILPF Papers, U.S. Section—Massachusetts, Box 8; also Peace Caravan materials in Box 4. WILPF Papers, Peace Collection, Swarthmore College Library. In addition, Massachusetts WILPF mailed more than one thousand kits to teachers, including holiday programs for schools developed by the National Council for the Prevention of War. "List of Material for Work with Boys and Girls, 1931," National Council for Prevention of War Educational Department Papers, Peace Collection, Swarthmore College Library, micro reel 41.32. Holiday suggestions also appear in a book by the head of the NCPW education department Forence Brewer Boeckel, *Between War and Peace: A Handbook for Peace Workers* (New York: MacMillan, 1928).

In spring 1932, the twenty-four-year-old Wallace Fiske replaced Blair as both pastor of the Universalist Church and a member of the town monument committee. The young minister wasted no time in letting the veterans know how he felt about the war. On the Sunday before Memorial Day in 1933, Fiske began his sermon with a recollection of being in grammar school and seeing soldiers returning home from the world war "broken in body and mind and spirit." He went on to implore the veterans in his congregation to join him in teaching that war was horrible and futile: "You who tasted battle know that war is not music and flags and clean uniforms. It is filth and suffering and death. Let us join our energy then to tear away the mask and see war as it really is, a death dealing monster. [Let the memory of the war dead serve as an] 'inspiring influence' in a peacetime war on poverty, . . . ignorance, superstition, vice, oppression, and exploitation."[31] Fiske, severe in his condemnation of the Great War, claimed that the veterans knew "that every nation lost the war" and that it had established none of the principles for which it was fought. As a member of the town monument committee, Fiske wanted the residents of Orange to face this fact squarely. But would the veterans support a monument to the futility of their effort? Could a monument honor the men while condemning the war?

Fiske sat down with the other two members of the committee, Herbert Macdonald, owner of a local jewelry store, and Cora Bangs, prominent member of the Daughters of the American Revolution chapter and former chair of the Women's Club, to review the proposed monument designs collected by the American Legion over the years and to solicit new ones.[32] As in 1926, the committee placed a high priority on originality; there would be no duplicate of the design elsewhere. To avoid the problem they had encountered with Hardy, they let sculptors know in advance that they only had $4,300 to spend. The committee received numerous sketches, including a design by Paul St. Gaudens, nephew of Augustus Saint-Gaudens, consisting of a large stone tablet with a bronze relief of a draped figure holding a wreath above an honor roll, with a broken sword below. The inscription read "Let the Word Be Peace." The back of the tablet displayed an American eagle over a dedication "to the men of Orange who gave their lives for their country" (fig. 3).[33] But this symbolic memorial, in the allegorical style of an earlier generation, was not the figurative statue that the veterans wanted.

Unhappy with the proposals it received, the committee began to de-

---

[31] *Enterprise and Journal*, 1 June 1933, 1.

[32] Interview with Wallace Fiske, West Hartford, Conn., 4 April 1991.

[33] We found the Paul St. Gaudens (1900–1954) sketch, with Wallace Fiske's mailing address, in the "Peace Monuments and Symbols, 1932–" folder, Swarthmore College Peace Collection, Swarthmore, Pa. But no record of the design, or correspondence with Fiske, appears in the Paul St. Gaudens Papers, Dartmouth College Library, Hanover, N.H.

FIGURE 3. Paul St. Gaudens' sketch for proposed Orange World War Memorial. (Peace Monument and Symbols Collection, Swarthmore College Peace Collection)

velop a monument design of its own. Fiske sketched a soldier and boy—a scene perhaps recalled from his own youth—and refined it with the help of the other committee members and the sculptor Joseph P. Pollia. The forty-year-old, Boston-trained sculptor had a number of pieces in the area by 1933.[34] Among them were Spanish-American war monuments in

[34] Pollia had made his living as a sculptor of war memorials in the New York City area since the middle-1920s. His first commission in western Massachusetts came in summer

Stoneham and Greenfield, Massachusetts, unveiled in 1928 and World War I statues in Barre and Franklin, Massachusetts, unveiled in 1929. The Spanish-American memorials, modelled on "the hiker" statues nationwide, showed a soldier with a rifle striding through a field. The Barre world war memorial depicted a doughboy thrusting forward his bayonet (fig. 4). The Franklin doughboy stands in prayer, with his gun at rest. Pollia had a well-deserved reputation in western Massachusetts for the quality of his doughboy statues, but none of them hinted at the design he would execute in Orange.

The Orange World War I monument contains no helmets, no rifles, no bayonets (fig. 5). It depicts the soldier not on the battlefield, but back in his community. The seated soldier, wearing his service hat, boots, and leggings, gives the impression that he has just arrived home. At his side stands a young boy, a book under one arm. One imagines the insistence of the boy to hear "all about" the war, without even allowing the soldier time to get out of his uniform. Viewed from the front the soldier's expression appears stern, but from the vantage of the boy, to whom his gaze is turned, it appears compassionate and concerned. His right arm is extended in a gesture, the hand half-opened as he relates his story to the child. The bronze tablet on the front of the granite base suggests the soldier's words, "It shall not be again." A shrouded figure, reminiscent of St. Gaudens's design, frames the tablet and crushes underneath its feet the weapons of modern war. Eleven stars, representing the eleven men from Orange who died in the war, float in the background. On the rear of the base is a plaque, "Dedicated in Memory of Those of Orange Who Served Their Country During the World War, 1917–19."[35]

1928 when Massachusetts United War Veterans invited him to create a memorial in Greenfield marking the thirtieth anniversary of the Spanish-American war. Biographical references to Pollia (1893–1954) pieced together from Boston Museum of Fine Arts Scrapbooks, 3: 9, 56; 10: 58, 118; 11: 29; 13: 122; 17: 120; as well as *Who Was Who in American Art*, ed. Peter Hastings Falk (Madison, Conn.: Soundview Press, 1985), 489; Mantle Fielding's *Dictionary of American Painters, Sculptors, and Engravers*, 2d ed., ed. Glen B. Opitz (Poughkeepsie: Apollo Books, 1987), 733.; *Who Was Who in America*, 3 (1951–1960): 692.

[35] Space was left on the sides of the base for an honor roll plaque listing all Orange residents who served in World War I. A list of names for an honor roll had been compiled immediately after the war; the "final list" of names was published in May 1919. But when the Legion met to consider the plaque in 1934, shortly before the monument was finished, members voiced concern about some names that had been included. In a debate that lasted until midnight, the Legion decided that the plaque would retain the names of soldiers and Red Cross nurses but not the names of those who served in Salvation Army, YMCA, or Merchant Marine, those who had been dishonorably discharged, and those from surrounding towns who did not live in Orange. *Enterprise and Journal*, 8 March 1934. Despite the mention of nurses, none of the 241 names printed in 1919 was a woman, an omission that suggested the larger absence of women's role in war commemoration. On the gendered memory of war, see the "Introduction," in *Behind the Lines: Gender and the Two World Wars*,

FIGURE 4. Joseph Pollia's War Memorial sculpture for Barre, Massachusetts. (Photo by J. Michael Moore)

Although the monument suggests the ease of communicating the veteran's experience across generations, the boy's posture suggests that he is reacting angrily to what he is hearing. Clinging to the textbook stories of martial valor and heroism, pugnaciously thrusting out his fist, the boy's initial reaction to the eyewitness account of the soldier is to hold on to the happier stories with which he has grown up. The confrontation between the soldier, reluctant but nevertheless determined to tell the tale of what war is really like, and the boy, drawing back from the soldier while cling-

ed. Margaret Randolph Higonnet, Jane Jenson, Sonya Michel, and Margaret Collins Weitz (New Haven: Yale University Press, 1987).

FIGURE 5. Orange War Memorial. (Photo by Hames Brothers, 1936; Richard Chaisson collection)

ing tenaciously to his storybook version, gives the monument enormous power. At the same time that it conveys its message against war it dramatizes the need for the message—to educate the children.

The Orange monument was unique in its depiction of a returning soldier in the classic "educator" statue pose of an adult teaching a youth.[36] But it shares a kinship with a number of memorials erected in the United States and Europe in the 1920s and 1930s that emphasize the human cost of war. Americans and Europeans dedicated figurative mourning statues—mourning comrades such as John Hardy's doughboy monument at Templeton, Massachusetts, or Albert Toft's in Streatham in England; mourning parents, such as the one Käthe Kollwitz sculpted in memory of her son in Belgium; even mourning wives and children, such as in Compiegne, France, or in Gentioux, where a sculpture of an orphan with clenched fist stands by a shaft listing the names of the war dead (fig. 6).[37] These memorials contrast sharply with the late-nineteenth-century memorials that emphasized the greater national cause for which the soldiers fought.

Orange dedicated its new world war monument on Memorial Day 1934; the unveiling was inserted into the annual holiday program, between the main exercises in town hall and the march to the Civil War monument in the central cemetery. Arthur Lundgren, former American

[36] Thanks to Karal Ann Marling for information about "the educator" as a genre of public sculpture.

[37] An excellent image of Albert Toft's world war memorial in Streatham, dedicated "to our glorious dead" in 1921, appears in Derek Boorman, *At the Going Down of the Sun: British First World War Memorials* (York: Ebor Press, 1988). On the funereal aspects of British war memorials, see Thomas Laqueur, "Memory and Naming in the Great War," in *Commemorations*, ed. Gillis, 150–67. Although many figurative statues appear in World War I monuments in Great Britain, many more monuments contain allegorical and religious imagery, especially crosses, a feature seldom found in American or French memorials. Besides Boorman's photo book, other sources for images of World War I memorials in Britain are Colin McIntyre, *Monuments of War: How to Read a War Memorial* (London: Robert Hale, 1990), and Alan Borg, *War Memorials: From Antiquity to the Present* (London: Leo Cooper, 1991), which despite its title focuses primarily on the 1919–1939 period. Käthe Kolwitz's "Mourning Parents" sculpture in memory of her son Peter, who was killed in the war, is described in Robert Cowley, "The Mourning Parents," *MHQ: Quarterly Journal of Military History* 3 (1990): 30–39. The most extensive research on World War I memorials in France appears in Antoine Prost, *Mentalités et Idéologies*, vol. 3, *Les Ancienne Combattants et la Société Française, 1914–39* (Paris: Presses de la Fondation nationale des sciences politique, 1977), 48–50. Prost's typology of war memorials, ranging from most nationalistic to pacifistic, also appears in his chapter "Les Monuments aux Morts," in *La Republique*, vol. 1, *Les Lieux de Mémoire* ed. Pierre Nora (Paris: Presses de la Fondation nationale des sciences politique, 1984), 195–225. A comparative treatment of war memorials appears in a special issue of *Guerres Mondiales et Conflits Contemporains* 167 (July 1992). It includes essays in French on Britain, France, Italy, Australia, New Zealand, as well as an introductory essay in English by K. S. Inglis, "War Memorials: Ten Questions for Historians," 5–21.

FIGURE 6. War memorial, Saint Bertrand de Comminges, in the Basque region of France. (Photo by Anne Rearick)

Legion Post commander and chair of the board of selectmen, accepted the statue on behalf of the town and laid the wreath at the base of the monument. Fiske, delivering the main address in Memorial Park, proudly put the monument in the context of the times: "With representative clergymen of every denomination speaking against participation in armed conflict and refusing to consider any idea of aid or assistance in another war, with college students rioting against military instruction, with college professors teaching and preaching against excessive military preparation, the feeling is spreading among laymen that War Memorials which they propose to erect should reflect the new spirit."[38]

Why did the American Legion—known nationally for its opposition to pacifist ministers—accept the monument?[39] How did Fiske, a new-

[38] Pollia, conveniently ignoring his earlier commissions, declared at the dedication that he never liked to see the "machinery of war memorialized in bronze" and never included weapons in his memorials. "World War Monument Dedicated," *Enterprise and Journal*, 31 May 1934, 1.

[39] Four weeks before the dedication, the American Legion Americanism Commission meeting in Indianapolis passed a resolution "that we decry and deplore the unwarranted,

comer to town and barely ten years old in 1918, gain the authority to design it? Clearly the distance between the ministers and the Legion at the local level was not as great as historians have supposed. Former Legion commander Howard Warren belonged to the Universalist church and served as its treasurer. Fiske, the Universalist minister, was also president of the Kiwanis Club that year. Henry Littlefield, the high school teacher who the month before the monument dedication supervised a contest for the best essay on "The Part Played By Armaments Industries in Making Wars" (with a first prize of $25 and book autographed by Senator Gerald Nye), also organized the town's George Washington bicentennial celebration and historical pageant dedicated to the Civil War veterans of the GAR. Historians who came of age in the 1960s are accustomed to seeing polarization between antiwar groups and a local patriotic establishment, but clearly in Orange in the 1930s they shared common ground.

It is also likely that Legion members were not the militarists one might expect from reading the literature produced by the national headquarters. In a national survey of Legion members later in the 1930s, 44 percent felt World War I was a "mistake," even though 38 percent described their own time in the military as a "great experience."[40] Perhaps the Pollia statue spoke against war in ways that the veterans could not, given the expectations of civilian society concerning manliness and war.[41]

---

unpatriotic, and subversive pacifistic activities of so many individuals and organizations over the country, particularly those following a religious calling" (2 May 1934, American Legion Library, Indianapolis). There is no evidence that the national American Legion was aware of the monument. In July 1935, Thomas Owens, national historian of the American Legion, sent a request to state historians for information and photographs of war memorials. The Massachusetts survey lists several western Massachusetts towns, including the state memorial at Mt. Greylock, but nothing built after 1933. Microfilm, 90–14019, American Legion Library, Indianapolis.

[40] A summary of the 1939 veterans' survey appears in Pencak, For God and Country, 44. On the veterans and American foreign policy, see Donald J. Lisio, "The United States: Bread and Butter Politics," in The War Generation: Veterans of the First World War, ed. Stephen R. Ward (Port Washington, N.Y.: Kennikat Press, 1975), 38–58. For a contemporary argument that Legion members had diverse political opinions not expressed by their national leaders, see Sylvanus Cook, "The Real American Legion," The Nation 125 (7 September 1927): 224–25.

[41] There was sizable antimilitary sentiment among British and French world war veterans. On the French, see Antoine Prost, In the Wake of War: Les Anciens Combattants and French Society, trans. Helen McPhail (Oxford: Berg, 1992). This translation, which condenses his three-volume French work, includes more of Prost's material on veterans' politics than on memorials. Of course, the principal work arguing for the antimilitarism of English world war veterans is Paul Fussell's The Great War and Modern Memory (New York: Oxford University Press, 1975). There is little evidence that Orange's world war veterans shared the alienation of the lost generation of British writers or even of American counterparts such as Ernest Hemingway or John Dos Passos. But their focus on their buddies and

But the most likely reason that the veterans endorsed Fiske's design was that they saw Pollia's statue not as an antiwar statement as much as a portrait of themselves in the community. This was, after all, the same organization that promoted military training for youth. Despite the rhetoric of "unmasking horror of war," the monument shows the soldier returning home intact, a handsome likeness occupying a central place in the park established for that purpose fifteen long years ago. Although the veterans might have been disappointed that Pollia's doughboy was not laying a wreath at the grave of fallen comrades, like Hardy's statue in Templeton, it depicted him in another activity, educating youth, which Legion members felt important.

The dedication of the monument in 1934 must be seen as part of a continuum of activities through which Orange and its former soldiers recalled the world war of 1917–1919. The month before the dedication, the Legion put on the play "Buddies" at Town Hall and read installments of the diary of an Apremont veteran published in the local newspaper. The local veterans' commemoration of Apremont culminated the following year when the entire 104th division, not only Company E, held its reunion in Orange. A poem published on that occasion, "Your Pal at Apremont," concluded that although the former soldiers might come to know famous men, millionaires, and movie stars, "the friends worthwhile and true, are the happy smiling few, who shared with you the Hell at Apremont."[42] If the veterans' commemorative activities sought to put words in the mouth of the monumental soldier in Memorial Park, then it was likely to be tales of his buddies at Apremont—a Hell—not pacifist abstractions about war.

The compromises and ambiguities of that Memorial Day in 1934, cast in bronze, have remained with the monument long after the popular pacifist sentiment of the early 1930s subsided. Very soon after the dedication, local newspapers boasted that Pollia's memorial had put the town on the map. In the mid 1930s, brief profiles of the Orange monument appeared in the *Boston Herald, Christian Science Monitor, New York Times,* the *WPA Guide to Massachusetts,* and of course journals of national peace organizations. The statue made the cover of the *Church School Journal* for November 1936. These articles described Pollia's statue as a peace monument, emphasizing its antiwar message, and quoted praise from prominent pacifist clergy John Haynes Holmes and Harry Emerson Fosdick as

---

insistence on a figurative statue rather than the kind of allegorical nationalistic monument prevalent at the turn of the century does suggest the break with earlier idealistic traditions of memorializing war that Fussell argues.

[42] *Enterprise and Journal*, 25 April 1935. Several monuments to the 104th's role in the battle of Apremont exist in western Massachusetts, including Apremont Square in Springfield and a monument in Westfield.

well as Eleanor Roosevelt and former Navy secretary Josephus Daniels.[43] That these nationally known figures liked the monument is not surprising; more significant is that their comments were reprinted in the same local paper that elsewhere attacked the New Deal as socialist and the pacifist church groups as "tearing down" America.[44] Orange was still the same town that voted three to one for Alf Landon in 1936. But for better or worse, Orange through its monument had become "internationally known." And the local paper, by reprinting comments from afar, reinforced the monument's inscribed meaning as a "peace statue" as well as established a new meaning for it as a local tourist attraction—an attraction the local chamber of commerce tried to capitalize upon in 1945 in its bid to get the United Nations to locate its headquarters in Orange.[45]

By the late 1930s, as war broke out in Asia and Europe, local residents found other meanings in the statue and its slogan, "It shall not be again." A cartoon in 1937 printed a picture of the statue with the "It shall not be again"—and added a "we wonder?" (fig. 7). Speaking on 11 November 1938, the first year that Armistice Day was a federal holiday, Methodist minister Ernest Lyman Mills lamented the nation's lack of military preparedness in 1917 and vowed "we must not be caught napping again." The following year the Orange newspaper editor, taking an isolationist tack, explained the appropriateness of the ceremonies in front of the statue whose message warned that "this country should refrain from

[43] See "Adorns Front Page," *Enterprise and Journal*, 30 August 1934; "Local Monument Gets Wide Recognition," *Enterprise and Journal*, 12 November 1936, 1, 3; "Orange Memorial is Unique in Absence of War Feeling," 28 May 1938, Chaisson Scrapbook. (Note: Many newspaper citations come from a scrapbook kept by Richard Chaisson, who recorded the date, but not always the paper and page number, of the articles he clipped). It is unclear how widely the Orange monument was known in peace circles in the 1930s. While a photo and press release about the Orange monument appear in the "Peace Monuments and Symbols, 1932–" file of the Swarthmore College Peace Collection, the monument does not appear in any educational materials on "peace symbols" that Zonia Baber prepared for distribution by the Women's International League for Peace and Freedom in the late 1930s. See Baber, "Peace Symbols," *Chicago Schools Journal* 18 (March–June 1937): 151–58.

[44] "Time to Teach Americanism," *Enterprise and Journal*, 14 May 1936, 2; "In Memory of Those Who Served," *Enterprise and Journal*, 28 May 1936, 2. These editorials appeared in midst of debate in local newspaper over Jehovah's Witnesses and flag salute. Editor Roy French attacked the religious sect as unpatriotic; Wallace Fiske wrote to the paper (30 April 1936) in defense of the Witnesses, which prompted the editorial response attacking "those who don't believe anyone should salute the flag if they don't choose to and those who think a religion which preaches such stuff should be tolerated." *Enterprise and Journal*, 28 May 1936, 2.

[45] "Orange Internationally Known," *Enterprise and Journal*, 3 June 1937; "Presenting Orange, Massachusetts, as a Site of the Permanent Seat of the United Nations Organization," December 1945, ms. in Athol Public Library, Athol, Mass. Meanwhile, Pollia also capitalized on the fame his monument brought by securing commissions for statues of Philip Sheridan, Stonewall Jackson, and Babe Ruth.

FIGURE 7. "It Shall Not Be Again—We Wonder?" editorial cartoon, Orange *Enterprise and Journal,* 11 November 1937.

solving Europe's troubles." Then in 1940, with France on the verge of surrender to Nazi Germany, a Memorial Day editorial pointedly stated that "it shall be again if it is necessary to preserve our independence, our liberty and our democracy."[46]

In the decade after World War II, Pollia's statue in Memorial Park lost its particular association with World War I veterans as the commemorative ceremonies around it mentioned service in all wars, a phenomenon paralleled at the national level in 1954 when Congress changed the name

[46] "We Wonder" cartoon appeared in *Enterprise and Journal,* 11 November 1937; "Twenty Years After, Preparedness Again," *Enterprise and Journal,* 17 November 1938, 3; "Armistice Day Will Be Observed on Saturday," *Enterprise and Journal,* 9 November 1939, 1; "Another Memorial Day," *Enterprise and Journal,* 30 May 1940, 2.

of Armistice Day to Veterans Day.[47] But as these public ceremonies diminished in size through the 1950s, and the passing seasons turned the memorial's bronze to a weathered green, it seemed to fade into its park surroundings, with little of the political meanings that it had been given in the 1930s.

Such apoliticalness would change in the following decade, during the Vietnam War. Veterans organizations sought to bolster the patriotic associations of Memorial Park by renaming it Veterans Memorial Park and enlisting the Boy Scouts in a townwide campaign for a flagpole, which was dedicated Memorial Day, 1966. At the same time, peace activists rediscovered the statue. In 1971, the Athol-Orange Peace Action Committee tried to enter into the patriotic rituals of the town by joining the Memorial Day ceremonies. Denied a place in the procession (on the grounds that it would be "inappropriate on Memorial Day and not in the best interests of the town of Orange" and might cause "a serious public safety hazard"), the seventy-five protesters held their vigil at Pollia's World War I monument in Memorial Park, standing in silence before the statue that itself commemorates the act of communication about war across generations (fig. 8).[48]

Since the 1970s, while the monument has remained "a favorite of pacifist groups" the same veterans organizations who dedicated the statue in 1934 now seem distant from it.[49] On Memorial Day, 1991, four months after peace groups held vigils at the Pollia statue to protest the Gulf War, the veterans' procession to the Civil War monument in the town cemetery paused for ceremonies before the honor roll erected for veterans of World War II, Korea, and Vietnam in front of the town library, but

[47] A speaker on Armistice Day in 1948 placed the customary wreath on the "peace monument" (as it was described in the local paper), a gesture he saw as underscoring the "importance of keeping America militarily strong in order to prevent World War III." A Universalist speaker on Veterans Day in 1956 pointed to the statue as a symbol of humankind's desire for peace, but he did not allude to either the Great War, contemporary events, or even World War II. *Enterprise and Journal*, 11 November 1948; "Cyril Brubaker Stresses Peace in Veterans Day Address," *Enterprise and Journal*, 15 November 1956.

[48] "Peace Vigil Permit Denied," Greenfield *Recorder*, 27 May 1971; "Peace Vigil at Orange Monday OK'd," Worcester *Telegram*, 29 May 1971; "Court Ruling Clears Orange Peace Vigil," Worcester *Gazette*, 29 May 1971; "Peace Vigil Is Held in Orange," Worcester *Telegram*, June 1971; "Hundreds Turn Out for Ceremonies," *Enterprise and Journal*, 2 June 1971, 1, 9; "Orange Honors Its Own War Dead in Own Way," 2 June 1971, Chaisson Scrapbook.

[49] The quotation is from "War Has No Winners," *Orange Oracle*, June 1984, 4. In 1984, the Rural Peace Coalition persuaded the Junior Women's Club to commemorate the fiftieth anniversary of the statue by sponsoring an essay contest for high school students on "How to Obtain Peace in 1984" and publishing the winning entries in the local paper. "Essay Contest at Mahar," *Orange Oracle*, May 1984, 4; "Peace in 1984," *Orange Oracle*, June 1984, 3.

FIGURE 8. Peace vigil in Orange Massachusetts, Memorial Day, 1971. (Richard Chaisson collection)

passed by the World War I statue in Memorial Park twice without stopping.[50] Although Legion members continue to hold Veterans Day ceremonies in Memorial Park in which children play a prominent role, in effect reenacting the scene cast in bronze in the statue; the women of the Universalist Church, not the veterans, have assumed the primary role in caring for the monument against deterioration from vandalism and the weather.[51]

[50] In 1984, the Rural Peace Coalition and the Pioneer Junior Women's Club proposed adding a Memorial Day stop at the World War I statue in honor of its fiftieth anniversary, but the groups confessed they were "not sure" how the proposal would be accepted by the American Legion. Letter from Mary-Ann DeVita Palmieri to Joanna Fisher, 15 March 1984, in Richard Chaisson collection. As it turned out, the parade was canceled that year on account of rain. Pacifist vigils in Orange during the Gulf War described in "Weekly Vigils Begin in Orange," Worcester *Telegram & Gazette*, 22 January 1991; "100 Walk Out on Classes in Protest of War," Springfield *Union-News*, 17 January 1991.

[51] As further evidence of the veterans' neglect they never attached the World War I honor roll to the statue; it was found in 1993 in the attic of the Legion hall. This neglect might change if the proposal to move the World War II, Korea, and Vietnam honor rolls to Memorial Park—as proposed in 1984 as part of a grant to the state for park renovation—is

While the memorialization of World War I, the source of Orange's fame in the 1930s, has now all but disappeared from the public life of the town, elements remain within the Legion Hall. The memorial picture of the eleven soldiers who died in World War I hangs on the wall of the new hall, along with numerous World War I era photographs of the buddies at camp, the Last Man's Club, and the charter membership roll—all relics significant to the members' identity as legion members. Interestingly, the walls of the Legion Hall contain practically nothing from World War II or later wars.

The political interpretations that surface during times when issues of war and peace are foremost on the minds of Orange residents constitute one set of meanings for the statue in Memorial Park. But another set of meanings surrounds the statue; they are inscribed not through the organized activities of various political groups but through day-to-day interaction with the townspeople. Three years after the dedication in 1934, the local newspaper ran a picture of Pollia's statue depicting the veteran handing the youth a tax bill, complete with the caption "It shall not be again" (fig. 9). In 1956 the caption accompanied a photograph of the monument in the snow, wondering if this was the last of the season.[52] Over time, the soldier and boy in the statue have come to symbolize not only national issues of war and peace but also the townspeople themselves.

Unlike war memorials that depict death and sacrifice on the battlefield, the Orange doughboy is down to earth; you can talk to this doughboy, and he talks back. The returning soldier talking to the young boy is talking to all children; by embracing the civilian child he is embracing the town. And over the years the town has embraced back. During the Gulf War, we observed the soldier with a yellow ribbon and an American flag, as if in an effort to finish off Pollia's statue, to supply what was missing in the 1930s. The monument serves as an icon through which local residents can express their concern about family members in the service and hope for their safe return, as well as a prompt through which residents recall their own service. Fifty years after the monument dedication of 1934, Kenneth Richards remembered identifying at the time with the boy in the statue: "Expecting a heroically postured soldier depicted in the heat of battle, my childish concepts were disappointed when the statue was unveiled." But then his reminiscence linked the statue with his own military service: "Years later when I returned from World War II, I saw that me-

---

ever implemented. "Orange Competing for Park Rehabilitation Grant," Greenfield *Recorder*, 2 August 1988.

[52] Tax bill cartoon appeared in *Enterprise and Journal*, 3 June 1937, 1; snow photo appeared 20 March 1956, Chaisson Scrapbook.

FIGURE 9. Adult handing youth tax bill, editorial cartoon, Orange *Enterprise and Journal*, 3 June 1937.

morial in a different light." He then identified with the seated soldier telling the child about war's inhumanities. Richards's story reminds us of what we do not know about the memory of war in Orange—what real veterans tell their children about their war experience.[53]

The statue may have come to represent not only the promise of the safe return of local residents in the service but also the continuity of the town itself. In a town with declining industry after World War II (Orange is

[53] Kenneth Richards, *Memories of a Small Town Yankee* (Athol: Millers River Publishing Company, 1985), 39. We do have the story of Robert P. Collen, whose uncle Oscar was one of the eleven men from Orange who died in World War I. Robert Collen recalled growing up in the 1930s in a family of "America Firsters" bitterly opposed to American intervention in World War II (until Pearl Harbor). He also recalled that local high school students who wanted to join the military during World War II were required to read through a book of explicit World War I photographs before being allowed to enlist. Collen mentioned that he is still interested in the history of World War I, more so than that of World War II, and has taught his children and grandchildren songs popular during the war. Interview with Robert P. Collen, Orange, Mass., 15 December 1994.

now the sixth poorest in the state in per capita income), the statue of man and boy, sometimes explained as a "father and son," may stand for generational continuity—the iconographic message of father and son symbolizing the endurance of the town.[54] Unlike World War I mourning memorials that depicted the disruption of the family, Pollia's monument reflects its origins in both the pacifist sentiment of the 1930s and the Great Depression; much like the images of mother and child in Depression photography, the statue can be read as a family scene. The boy's clenched fist—common in Depression iconography for determination to survive—may be especially important to local residents in the context of the industrial flight of the 1970s and 1980s.[55] This is one son who is not leaving the town. The seated veteran has come to embody loyal service to nation and town and local residents' commitment to maintaining the town's way of life for their children.

The story of the World War I memorial in Orange prompts us to rethink the many meanings for patriotism lost and found in twentieth-century America. The particular form of the monument and its identity as a "peace statue" were the result of an unusual intersection of events and feelings in the early 1930s. Had the statue been built either a few years earlier or later it would have looked quite different. The monument offers a permanent record of feelings in the 1930s that a town could honor its warriors but not their war, of national efforts to construct rituals around the memories of war that would promote a nonmilitaristic love of country. Orange's ministers saw the seated veteran educating the child about the horror of war as a patriotic act, just as patriotic as his fighting in battle. This memory of war that combined pacifism and patriotism was all but extinguished after World War II, as evidenced in town officials' response to antiwar activities as unpatriotic during the Vietnam era. As Armistice Day gave way to Veterans Day, so went the memory that Congress originally set aside the holiday in 1938 as "a day to be dedicated to the cause of world peace."[56] Indeed, the Orange story points to the multiplicity of other activities in the 1930s that sought to expand the boundaries of patriotic belief and behavior only to see those boundaries constrict in the aftermath of World War II.

[54] Henry Littlefield recalled the statue as a returning soldier comforting the son of one killed in combat and said that it symbolized how the members of the community cared for one another. Littlefield interview, Bridgeport, Conn., July 14, 1993. The 1989 statistic on Orange's per capita income relative to other Massachusetts towns appears in *Massachusetts Municipal Profiles, 1993–94*, ed. Edith R. Horner (Palo Alto: Information Publications, 1993).

[55] On the clenched fist as a common image in the Great Depression, especially its advertising, see Roland Marchand, *Advertising the American Dream: Making Way for Modernity, 1920–40* (Berkeley: University of California Press, 1985).

[56] U.S. Congress, *Statutes at Large*, 75th Cong., 3d sess., 13 May 1938, 351.

The memorialization of World War I in Orange also suggests much about the nature of "collective memory." Pollia's monument was not an expression of the town's collective memory of World War I but rather an expression of what James Young has termed a "collected memory," a process by which discrete memories converge in a common memorial space and are assigned a common meaning.[57] Through the 1920s and 1930s, local veterans were given privileged positions in narrating their version of the war and assigning meaning to Memorial Park, but they did not have a monopoly on the memory of the war. What made Orange unusual was that its veterans were not the only ones who seized the right to narrate the war experience: young men such as Littlefield and Fiske, as well as women, also had a large say in the design of how the war would be remembered. The ministers and veterans had different ideas about the meaning of the monument; the design embodied a compromise, not a common vision. Pollia's statue became a site where veterans and others projected their meanings onto the statue—much as a later generation would do with the Vietnam Veterans Memorial in Washington. War memorials tend to be ambiguous to satisfy competing factions at the time of their completion. As multivocal embodiments of compromise, the monuments invite the different factions to read their own meanings into what they see.

We can see that as the memory of a war changes with time, the meaning of the war memorial also changes. In an often quoted passage, critic Robert Musil observed that monuments inevitably repel viewers as the causes they commemorate become less important.[58] But in Orange, during the past sixty years, local residents continually attached new meanings to the memorial. Today memories of living with the monument have displaced the memory of the war it commemorated. No one in Orange remembers either World War I or how the monument arrived; yet they are eager to hear the story. The fact that no other town has such a statue now seems its most important attribute. The symbolic battle over Memorial Park during the Vietnam era shows that the original antiwar message has not always loomed large in Orange since the monument's dedication, but neither has it disappeared.

The story of the Orange monument also suggests the importance of figurative war memorials in the twentieth century. Professional artists concerned with how Americans would memorialize World War I had nothing but harsh words for the Civil War soldier monument, and they

[57] James E. Young, *Texture of Memory: Holocaust Memorials and Meaning* (New Haven: Yale University Press, 1993), xi.

[58] Robert Musil, "Monuments," in *Posthumous Papers of a Living Author*, trans. Peter Wortsman (Hygiene, Colo.: Eridanos Press, 1987), 61–64. Musil's essay was originally published in 1936.

heaped contempt on the commercial doughboy statues that proliferated in America of the 1920s. The contempt for figurative memorials continued after the Second World War—Iwo Jima is one of only a handful of figurative World War II memorials—and erupted with the placement of the Frederick Hart statue by the Vietnam Veterans Memorial in Washington, along with the new statue of women veterans by Glenna Goodacre unveiled in November 1993. Contemporary art critics condemn the Hart and Goodacre statues as degrading the original intent of Maya Lin's wall of names.[59] But these critics miss an important aspect of a war memorial by insisting on aesthetic purity. Paid for by veterans, Lin's wall serves as a powerful memorial to those who died in Vietnam, but it has no representation of the veterans themselves—those who fought and survived. Like the World War I veterans in Orange, many Vietnam veterans rejected the idea of an abstract memorial standing alone; their powerful drive for a figurative memorial suggests that they wanted realistic figures to testify to the reality of their experience, to narrate their deeds in some sort of enduring way. The surprising number of Vietnam veterans memorials across the country that incorporate figurative statues suggests the continuing importance of a documentary rather than abstract style in war memorials. Perhaps this is especially so for wars such as World War I and Vietnam where, unlike World War II, veterans feared neglect and little consensus existed in society concerning the results of their efforts.[60]

The variety of commemorative styles collected on the Mall in Washington returns us to our initial question concerning the connection between the memorialization of war and identification with the nation-state. War memorials are designated common spaces for shared memories, sites that create the illusion that the residents of a town, region, or nation have a common past, present, and future. Creating a "common" memory of war is important in forming a national identity, creating an overarching frame-

---

[59] See Maria Sturken, "The Wall, the Screen, and the Image: The Vietnam Veterans Memorial," *Representations* 35 (Summer 1991): 118–42. For a critique of the Goodacre and Hart statutes together, see Christopher Knight, "Politics Mars Remembrance," *Sacramento Bee*, 7 November 1993, Forum sect., 1, 6. Knight's critique originally appeared in the *Los Angeles Times* "Calendar" section.

[60] A survey of approximately three hundred Vietnam War memorials in 1988 showed that figurative statuary, especially black and white soldiers in a "buddies" pose, was common, though representations of a black assisting a white soldier, as in memorials in Wilmington, Dela., and Phoenix, Ariz., seem more common than vice versa. Among the nonfigurative memorials of the 1980s, many combined World War II, Korea, and Vietnam into a single memorial; this combination suggests not only attempts to associate Vietnam and Korea with the more popular earlier war but also perhaps how the Vietnam veterans' push for recognition stimulated World War II veterans' belated efforts to memorialize themselves. Jerry L. Strait and Sandra S. Strait, *Vietnam War Memorials: An Illustrated Reference to Veterans Tributes Throughout the United States* (Jefferson, N.C.: McFarland and Company, 1988).

work into which particular and diverse local interests can be inserted.[61] Yet the U.S. government in the interwar years seemed to have a limited role in directing this practice, especially when compared to other nations. Other than establishing battlefield cemeteries overseas and the Tomb of the Unknown Soldier in Arlington, the government neither built war memorials of its own, nor subsidized local memorials, nor supplied a list of names for the honor rolls (as in France), nor officially attempted to guide memorial design (as in Great Britain). When Orange's veterans in 1934 asked the federal government for a list of Orange residents who served in World War I for their honor roll, they were turned down. With a comparatively weak federal presence, no single World War I experience emerged as the official one, and the meaning of national patriotic symbols employed in local war memorials such as Orange varied greatly with local context. Local political culture rather than the dictates of the nation-state shaped war memorial practices in the United States to a far greater degree than in other countries, although recent research shows local and regional variation in war memorial practices in European nations as well.[62] This would remain true in the aftermath of World War II, but Cold War orthodoxy and the popularity of the Allied cause made local memorials that questioned national purpose in war less likely to be built until the post–Vietnam era.

Constructed largely as an expression of the camaraderie of the doughboys of Company E and the fear that their deeds would be forgotten in the Depression, and modified by the desire of local pacifists to teach a lesson about war, the Orange World War I monument recalls not the militant 100 percent Americanism and ideological purity traditionally associated with veterans' groups but rather a kind of patriotism from the ground up, one that uses the symbolism of stars, flags, and the war dead to address local concerns and diverse but powerful emotions close to home. The statue of the returning soldier connects the sacrifice of war not for the abstract nation-state but rather for the town's real way of life

---

[61] On the importance of patriotic symbols as mediating between local and national, vernacular, and official interests, see John Bodnar, *Remaking America: Public Memory, Commemoration, and Patriotism in the Twentieth Century* (Princeton: Princeton University Press, 1992).

[62] On the factors making for uniformity versus diversity in France, see Antoine Prost, "Mémoires Locales et Mémoires Nationales: Les Monuments de 1914–18 en France," *Guerres Mondiales et Conflits Contemporains* 167 (July 1992): 41–50; Daniel Sherman, "Art, Commerce, and the Production of Memory in France After World War I," in *Commemorations*, ed. Gillis, 186–211; and David G. Troyansky, "Monumental Politics: National History and Local Memory in French Monuments aux Morts in the Department of the Aisne Since 1870," *French Historical Studies* 15 (Spring 1987): 121–41. For an example of how local circumstances shaped monument-making in England, see K. S. Inglis, "The Homecoming: The War Memorial Movement in Cambridge, England," *Journal of Contemporary History* 27 (October 1992): 583–605.

and its children. Equating protection of America with that of buddies, family, and hometown would prove an important theme in the patriotic literature of World War II.[63]

[63] On equating the protection of America with that of hometown and family during World War II, see Robert Westbrook, "I Want a Girl, Just Like the Girl That Married Harry James: American Women and the Problem of Political Obligation in World War II," *American Quarterly* 42 (December 1990): 587–614, and Westbrook, "Fighting for the American Family: Private Interests and Political Obligation in World War II," in *The Power of Culture: Critical Essays in American History*, ed. by Richard W. Fox and T. J. Jackson Lears (Chicago: University of Chicago Press, 1993), 194–221.

Chapter 8

DREAMING IN BLACK AND WHITE: AFRICAN-AMERICAN PATRIOTISM AND WORLD WAR II BONDS

Lawrence R. Samuel

I N 1944, an elderly African-American woman in Los Angeles, with no sons or daughters to enlist in the armed forces, sold her $15,000 home and used the entire proceeds to buy war bonds. That same year, the following ad appeared in a New York newspaper: "Colored girl, War bond worker, will cook and serve dinner any Sunday for anyone who will buy or pledge $1,000 up in War Bonds, Box 2424, Times-Union." Also in 1944, Jim Kearse, a black man serving a life sentence for murder in Columbia, South Carolina, was presented with the nine war bonds he had purchased while in prison.[1]

What motivated these and many other African Americans to demonstrate such extreme support for the war effort? Why did the federal government aggressively pursue the African-American market, and why did African Americans eagerly respond? How did African Americans view their racial and national identities in relation to such a patriotic cause? These and many other questions arise when considering the intersection of the federal government's World War II bond drives and African American identity and experience. The promotion of war bonds to African Americans is primary evidence of Philip Gleason's claim that "cultural pluralism in all its ambiguities and complexities is the crucial legacy of World War II in respect to American identity." As a site of cultural pluralism, the federal government's targeting consumer groups defined by race in promoting the sale of bonds during World War II is an opportunity for a closer study of the dynamics of minority loyalty.[2]

---

[1] "1944 Report of Inter-Racial Section," William Pickens Papers (Box 19), Schomberg Center, New York Public Library, New York City; hereafter, references cited as Pickens Papers.

[2] Philip Gleason, "Americans All: World War II and the Shaping of American Identity," *The Review of Politics* 43, 4 (1981): 518.

As more scholarly attention is devoted to World War II and the postwar era, revisionist historians are increasingly debunking the notions that World War II was "the Good War" and the postwar years represented blanket homogeneity and consensus. The war was believed to be good because it represented an opportunity to defeat fascism, defend and renew the faith in American democracy, restore the American economy, and reap the benefits of a new and improved consumer ethic. All these goals contributed to preserving and advancing the "American Way of Life," a form of secular religion fusing personal aspirations, nationalism, and consumerism. With the war positioned as a defense of the "American Way of Life," a domestic ideology of nationhood was clearly defined and easily understood. Rhetorically grounding the war in terms of pluralistic democracy rested any fears or suspicions remaining of unchecked consumer capitalism and offered those outside the (white) power bloc a rationale to support the consensus.[3]

Against this backdrop is the popular belief that blacks' broad support of the war, like that of most Americans, demonstrated patriotism and loyalty to their country and focused on winning the war overseas. This is a logical conclusion: African-American displays of patriotism often looked very much like those of whites, and blacks had a special personal interest in an Allied victory, given overt Nazi racism. However, while African Americans were indeed displaying a mainstream version of patriotism in their support for the war, this represents only one-half of the "Double V," the victory over enemies both abroad and at home that the leading black newspaper, the *Pittsburgh Courier*, called for in February 1942. Although it was a relatively short-lived campaign, the Double V was for most African Americans the clearest and most compelling articulation of their attitudes regarding the war. Equally significant, the very existence of the Double V suggests that World War II's underpinnings of a unified and harmonious society joined together to fight a common enemy present a faulty or at least only partial foundation. The other half of the V, victory over enemies at home, demands further attention in the continuing effort to redefine the Good War and recover important narratives of the present's past.[4]

[3] Gary Gerstle, "The Working Class Goes to War" (paper presented at American Historical Association Conference, Chicago, March 1992); Studs Terkel, *"The Good War": An Oral History of World War Two* (New York, Pantheon Books, 1984); Richard Polenberg, "The Good War? A Reappraisal of How World War II Affected American Society," *The Virginia Magazine of History and Biography* 100, no. 3 (July 1992): 295–322; for a thorough interpretation of postwar consensus history, see Godfrey Hodgson, *America in Our Time* (New York: Random House, 1976).

[4] John Morton Blum, *V Was For Victory: Politics and American Culture During World War II* (New York: Harcourt Brace Jovanovich, 1976), 208; for an interesting discussion of the "Double V" in Hawaii, see Beth Bailey and David Farber, "The 'Double V' Campaign in

An important and generally ignored opportunity to add to our understanding of the social history of World War II is the defense (and after Pearl Harbor, war) bond. A closer analysis of the cultural dynamics of what can be considered the most successful consumer product in history—World War II bonds—reveals multiple versions of patriotism defined by the social divisions of age, gender, ethnicity, and race. In this chapter I focus on the latter; the sale and purchase of a bond to and by whites was generally an act of patriotism revolving around a "Single V": defeat the enemy abroad to restore the "American Way of Life" at home. War bond sale to and purchase by African Americans, however, reveal a more complex version of patriotism reflective of both sides of the Double V, the defeat of enemies both abroad and at home. Blacks' enthusiastic "consumption" of war bonds was thus not only a mainstream display of patriotism but also an independent attempt to achieve equality in America by gaining greater social and economic power. With virtually all other avenues of socioeconomic progress closed off to blacks in the early 1940s, bonds represented a rare opportunity by which to improve their individual and group lot in American society. For African Americans, then, an additional political agenda attached to bonds; they were a vehicle of not only national unity but also difference through the pursuit of equal rights. This pursuit of greater socioeconomic power, I argue, was neither exclusively separatist or assimilationist in nature; rather, it was a complex negotiation between African Americans' racial and national identities.[5]

The defense bond was a direct descendent of the Treasury's rather fledgling bond program in existence since the Revolutionary War. The Treasury offered bonds to finance all major wars, as well as the purchase of the Louisiana Territory, the building of the Panama Canal, the acquisition of Alaska, and the completion of the first transcontinental railroad. World War I's Liberty Loan campaign had failed in many respects; variable-rate Liberty Bonds fell in value, which caused many bond holders to lose money. But the Treasury learned from the program that bonds could generate national loyalty. In March 1935, in an attempt to induce Americans to save and bolster their confidence in financial institutions, Secretary of the Treasury Henry Morganthau spearheaded the introduction of U.S. Savings Bonds, government securities designed to meet the investment needs of the ordinary citizen. While on a 1934 trip

World War II Hawaii: African Americans, Racial Ideology, and Federal Power," *Journal of Social History* 26, no. 4 (Summer 1993): 817–43.

[5] For examples of how independent African-American consumerism can operate, see Lizabeth Cohen, *Making a New Deal: Industrial Workers in Chicago, 1919–1939* (Cambridge: Cambridge University Press, 1990), 147–50. For a study of the dynamics within an urban black economy, see Joe William Trotter, Jr., *Black Milwaukee: The Making of an Industrial Proletariat, 1915–45* (Urbana: University of Illinois Press, 1985).

to Europe, Secretary Morganthau was impressed with government-sponsored savings programs in Scandinavia, France, and England and envisioned that a similar program could entice Americans to start saving again. Furthermore, by broadening the base of public debt by attracting small savers, Morganthau believed, the government would rely less on large private investors and commercial banks. With savings bonds, however, Morganthau also saw an important side benefit: by literally buying shares in America, citizens would probably become more interested in and supportive of national policy. Understanding the potential ideological role of bonds led to Morganthau's vision of bonds as a vehicle for a more unified and harmonious America preceding and during World War II.[6]

Through the late 1930s, the Treasury Series A–D or "baby" bonds performed respectably but hardly spectacularly in the security marketplace. As America's entry into the war approached and debt increased rapidly, however, the Treasury foresaw that a more aggressive program could serve various economic purposes, specifically, defray a portion of the war debt, slow of price inflation, and "store" surplus funds for the future. For the consumer, bonds provided the seeds for postwar economic prosperity, this pointed to nothing less than the revival of American democratic capitalism. Secretary Morganthau, who believed many Americans did not fully grasp the country's stake in the war, was convinced that defense bonds and specifically bond drives could play an even larger and more important role as "a potentially unifying factor in a time of great public discord and uncertainty." Americans were divided along the lines of both domestic and foreign affairs, in large part a function of the economic strain of the Depression. Many Americans were opposed to involvement in the European war, and polls showed that most Americans thought the war would be short. By the time President Roosevelt went on the radio in April 1941 to ask Americans to "join [him] in 'one great partnership'" by purchasing defense bonds, it was clear that the Treasury's program had an ideological purpose in addition to an economic one. As Secretary Morganthau expressed it, the government would "use bonds to sell the war, rather than vice-versa."[7]

The flagship product of the Treasury's defense bond program was the new Series E, priced at 75 percent of face value and returning a then

[6] U.S. Treasury Department, "A History of U.S. Savings Bonds" (Washington, D.C.: Government Printing Office, 1963); U.S. Treasury Department, "A History of U. S. Savings Bonds," 1987; Jarvis M. Morse, *Paying for a World War: The United States Financing of World War II* (manuscript, 1971), 34.

[7] "A History of U.S. Savings Bonds," 1987, 8. For a close study of the social influence of war bonds, see Robert K. Merton, *Mass Persuasion: The Social Psychology of a War Bond Drive* (New York: Harper & Brothers, 1946); Morse, *Paying for a World War*, 3.

respectable 2.9 percent interest rate. When held to full maturity of ten years, a bond purchased for $18.75, compounded semi-annually, would be worth $25.00. Five denominations were initially offered: $25, $50, $100, $500, and $1,000; with two larger denominations, $5,000 and $10,000, were offered later. E Bonds, issued only to individuals, could not be transferred or sold, evidence of the Treasury's focus on the small investor. Equally important to the investment aspects, however, bonds offered a safe haven for cash until the emergency was over. The failure of thousands of banks during the Depression obviously made many Americans consider alternative places to store their cash, the purchaser's inability to exchange or sell the bonds was a strong selling point as cash reserves began to build during the boom prewar and war years. "Investing in the future while the present was out of stock" the dominant consumer ethos; thus, defense bonds became the sensible way to store extra cash and demonstrate one's national loyalty at the same time. For smaller investors, particularly children, the government offered saving stamps in denominations of 10 cents, 25 cents, and 50 cents, $1, and $5. Besides being an ideal program to sell the war to children, the aim of the Treasury's "School at War" program, savings stamps represented the idea that the defense program was for "Everyman," not tailored to the interests of big business. The ability to convert stamps into bonds when reaching the $18.75 level gave many smaller investors a goal, a key principle of savings programs.[8]

Upon its introduction, the Series E bond was received favorably by the press and public. *Women's Home Companion* considered the 2.9 percent annual return to be the "best available on any obligation of comparable value." *Collier's* was somewhat less enthusiastic, but still endorsed the bond: "2.9 percent a year . . . isn't wildcat interest but few other investments and almost no savings banks are paying any better nowadays." In designing the "new and improved" bonds, the Treasury knew that they would have to differ substantially from both World War I Liberty Bonds and the Series A–D savings bonds. Most important from the consumer's standpoint, the Series E's fixed interest rate contrasted with the variable rate of Liberty Bonds. The Treasury wanted to protect the small investor against the kind of financial risk associated with Liberty Bonds, which had caused many to lose faith in government securities. Additionally, to encourage investors to hold onto the bonds until full maturity intermediate redemption yields were reduced sharply from the earlier savings bonds, and the limit on annual bond purchases was reduced from $10,000 to

[8] "A History of U.S. Savings Bonds," 1987; for a detailed look at the role of elementary school and specifically social students during World War II, see Sherry Lynn Field, "Doing Their Bit for Victory: Elementary School Social Studies During World War II" (Ph.D diss., University of Texas at Austin, 1991).

$5,000. Finally, Series E bonds, issued only to individuals, could not be transferred or sold; if lost or stolen, the bonds could be replaced. All these changes were measures the Treasury intentionally took to discourage larger investors from monopolizing the bond program. The Series E was, essentially, created as a security considered "boring" to the professional investor.[9]

Unlike savings bonds, which were offered for sale only at post offices, Morganthau worked closely with the financial community to make defense bonds available at banks. With the cooperation of groups from management and labor, particularly from the insurance industry, the Treasury's Defense Savings Staff also orchestrated a payroll deduction plan for the purchase of defense bonds, which proved to be the source of a huge amount of bond revenues. The development of the defense bond program illustrates the workings of a well-oiled machine, striking an unprecedented alliance among business, labor, and the state. As a symbol of and instrument for the power bloc, bonds acted as the central rallying point for these groups to join together for the common goal of selling the idea of the war to all Americans. As the tangible fusion of nationalism and consumerism, the World War II bond played an integral role in forging the "American Way of Life" in both wartime and postwar society.[10]

A fundamental part of the selling of the war and its underlying ideology of the "American Way of Life" related specifically to promoting bonds to African Americans. Much "great public discord" that Secretary Morganthau observed resided in African Americans' growing protest against pervasive racial oppression and discrimination. European ethnic groups became increasingly assimilated through the New Deal era, but American society had essentially remained racially split. The build-up for the war had brought prosperity for most Anglo-Americans, but the fifteen million African Americans were largely excluded, the target for discrimination by both the armed forces and private industry. Blacks were offered war-related jobs in large numbers only when the labor shortage reached a critical stage in 1943, and even then they received more menial, lower-paying positions. Richard Polenberg summarizes African Ameri-

[9] "Our National Bargain," *Women's Home Companion*, January 1942, 2; "Better Buy Some Bonds," *Colliers*, 3 May 1941, 74; Morse, *Paying for a Wold War*, 30.

[10] "A History of U.S. Savings Bonds," 1987. For a discussion of the activities of the Defense Savings Staff's sister organization, the War Advertising Council, see Frank W. Fox, *Madison Avenue Goes to War: The Strange Military Career of American Advertising, 1941–45* (Provo: Brigham Young University Press, 1975); Robert Griffith, "The Selling of America: The Advertising Council and American Politics, 1942–1960," *Business History Review* 57, no. 3 (Autumn 1983): 388–412; and Mark H. Leff, "The Politics of Sacrifice on the American Home Front in World War II," *Journal of American History* 77 (March 1991): 1296–1318.

cans' status on the eve of Pearl Harbor as bound by color, with "economic subordination, political disenfranchisement, legal insecurity, and social inferiority" the norm.[11]

This pervasive racial climate prevailed despite African Americans' fight for equal rights leading up to the war. During World War I, blacks had demonstrated strong support for the war effort, but postponed what W.E.B. Du Bois called their "special grievances" for the sake of national unity during the emergency. The disruption of the struggle for equal rights during the crisis ultimately worked to blacks' disadvantage; their alignment with the national cause did little or nothing in terms of gaining greater civil rights, at least through the war itself. Upon America's entry into World War II, black leaders vowed not to slow their fight for equality as their predecessors had done a generation earlier. With German Nazism cast in government propaganda as the antithesis to the American founding principles of pluralistic democracy, black leaders saw an opportunity to convincingly demonstrate the contradictions between America's rhetorical democracy and African American experience. African-Americans hoped the Roosevelt administration and whites as a whole would see the parallels between Nazi racism and America's own oppression directed to fellow Americans based on skin color and move toward a truly democratic society.[12]

In *V Was for Victory*, one of the earlier and best attempts to expand our vision of "the Good War," John Morton Blum summarily captured what Gunnar Myrdal called in 1944 "the American dilemma"; he suggested that "World War II posed a special test of the ability of American culture to accommodate to its inherent pluralism." Unlike World War I, fought essentially as an Anglo-Saxon war, World War II was fought on the grounds of defending New World pluralism against Old World totalitarianism and racism. Although the war against Japan had its own virulent form of racism that made the issues more complex, America's awareness as a pluralistic nation had advanced immeasurably between the wars, largely a function of the great migration to northern cities by southern blacks and the rise of ethnic groups in the Democratic party. Finally, because World War II was fought on the premise of protecting the inalienable rights of individual freedom and liberty, exceptions of race or ethnicity became increasingly difficult to defend. The Treasury's bond promotion—a broad pluralistic tone and direct appeals to African Amer-

---

[11] Richard Polenberg, *One Nation Divisible: Class, Race, and Ethnicity in the U. S. Since 1938* (New York: Viking Press, 1980), 24.

[12] Blum, *V Was for Victory*; Neil A. Wynn, "The Impact of the Second World War on the American Negro," *Journal of Contemporary History* 6 (May 1971): 42–54; Harvard Sitkoff, "Racial Militancy and Interracial Violence in the Second World War," *Journal of American History* 58 (December 1971): 661–81.

icans and European immigrants and ethnic groups—reflected an ideological shift between the wars.[13]

As President Roosevelt prepared his speech in the days before 30 April appeal for "one great partnership," James L. Houghteling, director of the Treasury's National Organizations Division, called William Pickens, field director of the NAACP. Houghteling asked Pickens to join the Treasury staff to go "about the business of selling the idea of buying bonds and supporting the present war effort" by heading the Division's Inter-Racial Section. The administration believed that a dedicated effort to reach the nation's fifteen million African Americans was necessary to fulfill the ideological objectives assigned to the Treasury's bond program. Consistent with the administration's hiring "experts" as a means of scientifically managing the war, William Pickens was hand-picked to lead the section because he was considered uniquely qualified to sell the idea of the war to African Americans and motivate them to purchase bonds. A press release announcing his appointment emphasized that Pickens "speaks the language, thinks the thoughts, lives the lives of his own people. . . . Because he knows and understands them, Negroes believe in him."[14]

Beyond the rhetoric of his ability to effectively communicate with blacks, William Pickens was the obvious choice to head the Inter-Racial Section because of his moderate position expressed over a thirty-year career within the African American academy, black press, and NAACP. During his tenure as an author, worldwide lecturer, faculty member of three black colleges, and contributing editor of the Associated Negro Press for twenty-five years, Pickens subscribed to and delivered an integrationist philosophy for African Americans. Since 1920 he had been field secretary and then director of the NAACP, an organization devoted to helping blacks advance within or in conjunction with the white power bloc. Houghteling was naturally attracted to Pickens's connections to the black bourgeoisie, but Houghteling also recognized that Picken's ideology was ideally suited to further the administration's goal of easing racial dissension by bringing African Americans into the consensus fold. It was traditional for Republican administration's to name African Americans to the position of Register of the Treasury, a practice that stopped in 1916. Houghteling's confidence in Pickens was so great, however, that Pickens was the first black official to be appointed to an official Treasury post in

[13] Blum, *V Was for Victory*, 147; Gunnar Myrdal, *An American Dilemma: The Negro Problem and Modern Democracy* (New York: Harper & Brothers, 1944); for the most thorough examination of racism directed at Japanese during World War II, see John W. Dower, *War Without Mercy: Race and Power in the Pacific War* (New York: Pantheon, 1986).

[14] "1944 Sketch of the Inter-Racial Section"; "William Pickens in the U.S. Treasury," Treasury press release, 9 September 1941, Pickens Papers.

twenty-five years. Additionally, while Pickens had held key positions of power within the black community, his motivation to take the post was perceived as free from direct political overtones: "When he speaks to [African Americans] of the part they can play in the Defense program, they will listen to him without the suspicious fear lest they be 'taken in' by a smooth speaking, self-seeking smart politician."[15]

The Inter-Racial Section was part of the Defense Savings Staff's National Organizations Division, which was created to direct bond programs to particular segments of the population. Market segmentation techniques developed between the wars led the National Organizations Division to target women with its "Women at War" program, children with its "Schools at War" program, and even grandmothers with its Grandmothers War Bond League. By targeting historically marginalized and disenfranchised groups such as women, youth, seniors, white ethnics, and blacks, the National Organizations Division was the Treasury's primary resource to create a stronger and more unified society, both militarily and ideologically, through bonds. Although some Treasury officials suggested it be called the Negro Organization Section, Houghteling determined "the Inter-Racial section is better and in all points satisfactory," as the chosen name implied the cooperation and harmony the administration was trying to achieve, at least symbolically. As with the Treasury's special effort to reach women, the Inter-Racial Section was designed to work in concert with rather than independently from the general bond program.[16]

The Inter-Racial Section's fundamental strategy in selling bonds was to meet with and address audiences across the country, while promoting the war and bonds through a well-orchestrated public relations program. Weekly black newspapers fully supported the aims of the Inter-Racial Section; all the principal papers devoted space to the section's press releases, which usually consisted of a portion of a recent Pickens speech. These papers included the *Pittsburgh Courier*, the *Baltimore Afro-American*, the *Chicago Defender*, the *Chicago Bee*, the *St. Louis Argus*, the *New York Amsterdam Star News*, the *Norfolk Journal and Guide*, the *New York Age*, the *Kansas City Call*, the *California Eagle*, and the *Philadelphia Tribune*. The one African American daily, the *Atlanta World*, was an enthusiastic supporter, Pickens wrote in 1944, "Its editors have seen eye to eye with executives of the section of the Treasury devoted mainly to pushing the sale of war bonds among the readers of that paper." The key to winning space in the black press was good relations with the Associated Negro Press, which "consistently sent [the Inter-Racial Section's] material to

15 "William Pickens in the U.S. Treasury."
16 Ibid.

many scores of Negro papers all over the country, and in that way has helped our publicity immensely."[17]

As with the Defense Savings Staff's general bond program, borrowing the services of entertainers and sports celebrities was a key component of bond drives. For African American audiences, black celebrities, visible symbols of having achieved the American Dream, held particular power in selling bonds. The most celebrated African American actors and musicians of the day, including Cab Calloway, Marian Anderson, Paul Robeson, Lena Horne, and Count Basie, frequently made appearances at bond rallies. Capitalizing on the ability of these stars to promote bonds to audiences both black and white, the Inter-Racial Section formed a music committee consisting of an all-star cast of leading African American notables such as Langston Hughes, W. C. Handy, and Duke Ellington. The committee's stated mission was to "choose the best patriotic song composed by Negroes and to devise adaptation of Negro spirituals," as in Secretary Morganthau's personal request for Cab Calloway to compose a war bond song in jive. "Combining jive-talk lyrics with a contagious melody," as the Inter-Racial Section's 1944 Report put it, Calloway's "Backin' 'em Back" urged bondholders to "stash your bonds away," explained by the report as jive for "hide your bonds for safekeeping."[18]

The Treasury leveraged the broad appeal of the most popular black entertainers of the war years through appearances that reached a racially mixed audience. Duke Ellington, perhaps the most visible African-American promoter of bonds, played many bond benefits that were broadcast on network radio, an indication of Ellington's power as a spokesperson to both blacks and whites.[19] African American sports figures also played an integral role in bond drives, often in conjunction with white athletes. Ethnic and racial teamwork—what may be called "platooning" after its popularization in films of and about World War II—was a common theme in the selling of bonds, summarily captured by Joe Commiskey, a columnist for the *Washington Post* in August 1944:

> This is the week when we all should take a deep bow to a couple of Negro kids named Jack and Montgomery. They are the two who drew better than $35,000,000 War Bonds at the Madison Square Garden gate and drew nothing but blood for their services. . . . If the Treasury is smart it will try to duplicate last week's show a thousandfold. Somehow, the Stars and Stripes and what we're fighting for runs in a solid pattern right through the whole thing. The

---

[17] "1944 Sketch of the Inter-Racial Section."

[18] Ibid.

[19] "Ellington and Lunceford Bands Set for Coca-Cola Spotlight," *The People's Voice*, 21 November 1942. Duke Ellington Archives, Archives Center, National Museum of American History, Smithsonian Institution.

Jew (Mike Jacobs) will put it on. The Irish (the managers) will say "Yes." The fighters (mostly Negro) will wait for the bell. And all of them will come out swinging. And together. Isn't that the whole idea?[20]

Joe Louis, the world heavyweight champion during the war years, frequently donated the proceeds from a fight to either the bond program or military relief funds. An example of Joe Louis's personal experience of the Double V was captured by Irwin Rosee, a publicist who traveled with Louis when the boxer made appearances at bond drives. Rosee remembered, "Another black man came up to Joe one day and said, "Why'd you join the Army? This is a white man's country and a white man's war?' And Joe said, 'Lot of things wrong in America, but Hitler ain't gonna fix it.'"[21]

One of William Pickens's first tasks for the Inter-Racial Section was to determine to whom the program should be targeted. With deep roots in and connections to the NAACP and black colleges, Pickens knew that the most effective and efficient strategy was to tap into the existing network of local, regional, and national black institutions and organizations. "For three months," Pickens said in August 1941, "I have been gathering into the Treasury lists of Negro organizations in various communities." Working through the solid African American infrastructure of schools, business leagues, churches, fraternal societies, and other organizations and institutions offered the greatest chance to gain black support for the war by lending more legitimacy to appeals. This approach also localized the national program in individual communities and offered economies of scale. Perhaps most important, however, these institutions and organizations, bridging the gap between a largely disenfranchised African-American population and the power bloc, thus served as models for blacks aspiring to share in the American dream. As the power bloc constituency of the African American community, these organizations' members were most likely to align with the consensus ideology and contribute to a trickle-down effect toward those blacks who held more resistant and conflicting views. Thus the "black bourgeoisie" held the key to selling the war and bonds to the African-American community at large through its influence in leading at the local level.[22]

As a former college professor and dean of Morgan College, Pickens understood the importance of having the African-American academy

[20] Joe Commiskey, *Washington Post*, 5 August 1944, in "1944 Sketch of the Inter-Racial Section."

[21] Ira Berkow, "Sports of the Times; Tyson is a Boxing Exception," *New York Times*, 4 February 1992, sec. B (Sports Desk), 7.

[22] Defense Savings Staff press release, 20 August 1941. Excerpt of Pickens speech to the National Medical Association of Negro Doctors, Chicago, 20 August 1941, National Archives; Edward Franklin Frazier, *Black Bourgeoisie* (Glencoe, Ill.: Free Press, 1957).

support the administration's goals. Pickens and his assistant, Jesse O. Thomas, visited most black colleges and universities in the early months of the Inter-Racial Section's existence; they rebutted isolationists' and pacifists' arguments and persuaded administrators and faculty to support the defense effort. With the exception of a few intellectuals who refused to accept the "idea of the war," such as then Howard University law student Pauli Murray, the academy wholeheartedly endorsed the administration's objectives and bond program. As Pickens wrote in 1944, "Most of these schools are headed by patriotic and far-seeing Negro men and women and they took hold of the stamp-buying, bond-buying program with alacrity and zeal." Interestingly, the African-American academy's strong support for the bond program contrasted that of the broader university community, as most college students and faculty were notoriously poor bond buyers and sellers.[23]

The Inter-Racial Section also focused on the business arena in its efforts to leverage the existing infrastructure of the black bourgeoisie. Besides certain key industries, such as insurance and banking, the Negro Business League, an association of African-American business leaders, became a prime target audience for the Inter-Racial Section. For Pickens, the Negro Business League was an obvious target because it served as a shining example of the promise of American democracy. "The life of the Negro Business League and the progress of Negro business men for the last forty years," he told the league in August 1941, "these are an index of the true character of this democratic country." Those in business deserved particular attention, Pickens believed, because of their ability to understand and explain why bonds represented such an important economic opportunity for African-Americans. "It is you and your comrades," he told the same audience, "who can bring to the attention of colored people and all people the manifold meaning of the program of the United States Treasury to unite American citizens in defense savings; for the good of the investor, his fellow-countrymen and his country's future."[24]

Pickens understood that business leaders would recognize the value of bonds for not only their country but also themselves. As he wrote in 1944, "[African-American] business institutions and social clubs have deposited the money saved in their treasuries and have publicized the pro-

[23] "1944 Sketch of the Inter-Racial Section"; Jarvis M. Morse, a Treasury official during the war, reasoned that "the lack of enthusiastic response from colleges was in some cases due to the fact that many college students had no funds to invest. Meager college response to the Treasury's program was also due to academic preoccupation with the intellectual rather than the practical aspects of citizenship."

[24] Defense Savings Staff press release, 9 August 1941; excerpt of Pickens speech to National Negro Business League, Memphis, 29 August 1941; National Archives.

gram among their members, not only for patriotic reasons but in order to better the basis of their organizational strength in the postwar period which lies just ahead."[25] Prominent African-American business leaders themselves spoke of the dual benefit that bonds could provide for investors. C. C. Spaulding, president of the North Carolina Mutual Life Insurance Company, for example, reiterated Pickens's pitch for bonds: "The American people, and most especially the Negroes, have shown commendable loyalty and foresight by the manner in which they have cooperated with the Government in each of the six war loan drives. . . . Let us continue to show patriotism in a practical way, and benefit personally at the same time."[26] Here was a prime instance of the Double V in action, African-Americans supporting the war through the purchase of bonds not only to defeat the enemies abroad but to also achieve socioeconomic progress for themselves, thereby defeating enemies at home who would otherwise stand in their way. The ways in which the Double V played out in bond drives indicate that within African-Americans' definition of patriotism during World War II was a strong awareness of racial identity and difference; the opportunity for social and economic advancement through bonds represented a true test of America's democratic principles.

In addition to educational institutions and business organizations, religious groups represented the third major audience the Inter-Racial Section targeted in its mission to sell the war through bonds to African Americans. The two largest black churches, The National Baptist Church and the Negro Methodist Church, not only boosted the spirits and morale of African-American soldiers and their families during the war but also endorsed bonds and actively sponsored drives. Pickens, noting the contribution made by Negro churches, suggested that the church clearly recognized bonds as representing a unique means of economic advancement for African Americans: "Great church conventions and conferences of all denominations have welcomed the presentation of patriotic messages and addresses by leaders of the Inter-Racial Section and have urged upon their membership the purchase of the war securities, both as a patriotic act and as a sound investment."[27]

With the church such a presence in many African-American lives, Pickens not surprisingly made bond appeals along religious lines. Just as some members of our American democracy were not very democratic, Pickens argued, some members of Christian churches were not very Christian. If one would not abandon his or her faith because of some

[25] "1944 Sketch of the Inter-Racial Section."
[26] Treasury Department press release, N-1486, National Archives.
[27] "1944 Sketch of the Inter-Racial Section."

suspect congregation members, why should one lose faith in America because of a few bad apples? The church was still the church of all its members, both good and delinquent, and America was still the country of all its citizens, both tolerant and prejudiced. By using such analogies to which audiences could personally relate, Pickens effectively overcame the many obstacles inherent to selling a war to some dissatisfied customers.[28]

By the time of America's entry into the war, populist New Deal ideology was being recast as what was good for corporate America was good for the American people, but presenting bonds in the interests of the small investor still had special resonance to an audience whose members were largely on the bottom rung of the economic ladder. Pickens's rhetoric, heavily steeped in the anti–big business sentiment of the New Deal, echoed when he told the National Baptist Convention, "The government wants the people and their own organizations, rather than the big money interests, to get the security, and the good interest on these investments." While the "Everyman" theme was central to selling bonds to all Americans, Pickens emphasized why they were a particularly good investment for African Americans. "It seems that our Government might have had a disadvantaged minority, like the Negro, when they planned these bonds," Pickens told an Atlanta audience in July 1941. "No loan shark or cunning creditor can come between the simplest citizen and his Government and get that citizen's money. Neither the gambling syndicate nor the numbers king has a chance, so long as the United States Government holds that money." Presenting the government as a paternalistic guardian of money that otherwise might be lost to predators was a selling strategy the Treasury did not use for a predominantly white audience.[29]

As pitched to African Americans, the puritanical ethic of saving now for future financial security offered particular salience. The administration considered African Americans to have poor thrift habits and be generally financially irresponsible, a view that shaped the ways in which the Treasury targeted bonds to blacks. For the general public, bonds were positioned as an investment for the good life, but for blacks, they represented opportunity for advancement. Bonds were positioned as a unique chance for blacks to gain a foothold in the emerging abundant and prosperous society; they thus operated as a carrot for improved socioeconomic status, the operative currency of civil rights: "I hope that the

[28] Defense Savings Staff press release, 15 July 1941; excerpt of Pickens speech to the Summer School Teachers and the Public, Atlanta University, 15 July 1941; National Archives.

[29] Defense Savings Staff press release, 12 September 1941; excerpt of Pickens speech to the National Baptist Convention, Shreveport, 11 September 1941 and the National Baptist Convention, Cleveland, 12 September 1941; Atlanta University speech, 15 July 1941; National Archives.

colored people of Rochester will stand way up front in buying bonds during the Third War Loan. It is not only an honorable and patriotic thing, but it is a shrewd matter of business for the colored people of the United States to have as much of their money as possible in the hands of the Government, especially in the period following the war."[30] Often turning this theme upside down in standard advertising fashion, Pickens stressed that without buying bonds, "colored people . . . would be further toward the rear end of the line than they are going to be when this war is over."[31]

Perhaps Pickens's most compelling argument for blacks to join the cause was to stress the longevity of African Americans in the New World and their long history of defending America in all its wars. John Schaar suggests that the core of patriotism is a love for one's homeplace, and in this sense it was vital that Pickens convince African Americans that their homeplace was indeed America. "Our Afro-Americans started coming here in 1619, twelve years after the Whites came to stay," Pickens reminded audiences across the country. "Averaging the groups," he continued, "the oldest American man, next to the American Indian, is the American Negro." The corollary to establishing the nation as the African–American homeplace was emphasizing the past, present, and future role of the Negro in American democracy and national defense. "The Negro also helped to create and always defend this nation; he was a soldier with George Washington," Pickens maintained. "This is the Negro's country in the realist sense and the one he must defend, in order to defend his own future and his posterity." Although bond pitches to white audiences occasionally addressed Americans rallying around previous crises, Pickens relied heavily upon this "homeland" theme to appeal to African Americans' patriotic values grounded in historical sense of place.[32]

Despite the obvious contradictions between American's claims to democracy and its treatment of African Americans, the Inter-Racial Section's efforts to promote war bonds through such powerful symbols as community motivated many African Americans to support the war. In his *Imagined Communities*, Benedict Anderson aptly describes how the concept of community can make marginalized groups venerate the symbol of a nation and fight on its behalf: "[A nation] is imagined as a *community*, because, regardless of the actual inequality and exploitation that may

[30] Letter from Pickens to Mr. and Mrs. Howard W. Coles of Rochester, New York, 20 September 1943, Pickens Papers.

[31] Letter from Pickens to Pauli Murray of Howard University, Washington, D.C., 21 July 1944, Pickens Papers.

[32] John Schaar, "The Case for Patriotism," *American Review*, no. 7 (May 1973): 62; Atlanta University speech, 15 July 1941; National Archives.

prevail in each, the nation is always conceived as a deep horizontal comradeship. Ultimately it is this fraternity that makes it possible, over the past two centuries, for so many millions of people, not so much to kill, as willingly to die for such limited imaginings."[33] Recognizing African Americans' legitimate desire to be full members of the imagined American community, the administration wove a dream of justice into war bond promotion and stirred blacks' national loyalty, effectively drawing upon their human and financial resources. As they did for individuals and social groups, bonds became incorporated into the daily life of many communities, fused with public and popular activities. Bond rallies located within the civic or public sphere brought people literally and ideologically together, just as Secretary Morganthau believed they would. For African Americans, whose lives often revolved heavily around the public sphere, bond rallies represented a source of civic and racial pride. Acting as a vehicle for national unity, bonds also acted as an instrument of difference, a way to proclaim racial separateness within a patriotic cause. African-American bond rallies within large communities were thus the largest scale evidence of the Double V in action, where bonds assist in defeating enemies both abroad and at home.

Activities grounded in both consumer and popular culture were thus often used as sites for African-American community bond drives. For the Seventh War Loan, for example, $450,000 in war bonds were sold at the "Fashion Rhapsody" in Chicago. More than two thousand African Americans attended the fashion show, which was "filled with high grade entertainment and modeling" by acts such as the Club de Lisa Dancing Chorus and Sammy Dyer's Kiddies. In Washington, D.C., almost $750,000 was raised at the twenty-four Lichtman Theaters through the first six war loans. The general manager of the chain, Graham Barbee, believed that it was the individual theater managers, all of them African Americans, who were most responsible for Lichtman surpassing its quota. He viewed these twenty-four men as soldiers, fighting the war at home by selling war bonds through clever promotional schemes. "The boys on the theater front—the managers—," Barbee said, "[get] the credit for seeing the plans mature. They do the job."[34]

Bond drives became linked with community celebrations, a merging of national, local, and racial pride. A June 1945 bond rally held in conjunction with American Negro Day in Buffalo, New York, was such a multi-identity celebration. Bond drives frequently became part of or employed parades, the most visible public demonstration of support for the war. On 4 July 1943, in Atlanta, the city's Council of Negro Women and

---

[33] Benedict Anderson, *Imagined Communities* (New York: Verso, 1983), 16.
[34] Treasury Department press release, N-1501, N-1496, National Archives.

Service Group War Bond Committee held a huge parade and bond rally, described by one observer as a "far-reaching demonstration by Negroes in high and low stations of life." "While other communities are torn by strife and dissension," the reporter continued, "Atlanta Negroes are sponsoring successful rallies to show their faith in the American way of life and its people." In large urban bond drives that included parades, the participation of African-American military units was often a cause for great celebrations. Along Chicago's Michigan Avenue, also in July 1943, a U.S. Treasury Salute to Victory Parade "drew a crowd of an estimated 300,000 persons, both races." Units of African-American military police, WACs, and sailors marching in the parade, one reporter wrote, "added the necessary color to the military process at a huge War Bond Rally held in [Chicago's] Washington Park, netting the U.S. Treasury $350,000." As part of the "Fashion Rhapsody" bond rally in 1945, musicians from the black military units based in Fort Des Moines, Iowa, and Truax Field of Madison, Wisconsin, also marched along Chicago's streets to great community response. African-American bond drives appeared to reach a higher level of enthusiasm when black military troops were represented in parades; their presence served as the clearest proof of blacks' contribution to the war effort.[35]

Moreover, the incentive to name a piece of military equipment after a prominent African American provided a great boost to bond drives involving black communities. Making a direct connection between the "war" on the homefront and the one overseas was an effective strategy to motivate Americas to purchase bonds. A $2-million-bond drive in May 1943, for example, was presented to blacks as an opportunity to name a cargo ship the *Frederick Douglas* [*sic*]. The *Frederick Douglas* would in fact be the third such ship to be named after a prominent African American (all of them with a black ship master); the first was the *Booker T. Washington*, and the second the *George Washington Carver*. Harlem also had a quote of $2 million for the Third War Loan in October 1943; its goal was to purchase a Flying Fortress bomber to be named the *Harlem Express*. Simultaneously, prisoners at the District Reformatory in Lorton, Virginia, were also raising money to go towards the purchase of a Flying Fortress. Coincidentally, they too were considering the name *Harlem Express*, although the convicts were also open to the names *Haile Salassis* [*sic*] and *Life-timer*.[36]

Meanwhile, citizens of Birmingham, Alabama, were taking a more sober approach to the purchase and naming of an airplane. The black

[35] Treasury Department press release, N-1529, National Archives; "1943 Report of Inter-Racial Section," Pickens Papers.
[36] "1943 Sketch of the Inter-Racial Section."

community made $300,000 in bond purchases allocated for a B-24 Liberator bomber to be christened *The Spirit of Ellsberry*, in honor of Julius Ellsberry, an African-American citizen of Birmingham killed at Pearl Harbor. During the same drive, African-American citizens of Kansas City were raising $250,000 in bonds to purchase, as the slogan went, "A Brown Bomber for our Brown Flyers." Many African Americans were employed at defense plants in Kansas City, where they built the very planes that they were raising money to "purchase" with war bonds. The slogan referred to the color of the airplanes and the black flying squadrons training at various Air Force bases around the country. Again, a connection between homefront efforts and military operations overseas was made through the purchase of war bonds.[37]

Sometimes the sale of bonds became entwined with religious rituals, where racial identity was yet another dimension associated with the event. In New Orleans in September 1943, thousands of African-American Catholics incorporated the Third War Loan into their annual celebration honoring a seventeenth-century monk, St. Peter Calves, the "Apostle of the Negroes." The bond drive, held at St. Monica Church, was coordinated to coincide with the birthday of the patron saint. For the same drive in Washington, D.C., Elder Lightfoot Solomon Michaux, a renowned African-American evangelist, turned the first half of a large outdoor religious meeting into a bond rally. "Color was lent to the processional," the Treasury reported, "when the 'Happy Am I Choir' [of] 156 men and women, garbed in white satin robes, marched to the center of the stadium . . . singing songs dedicated to the war effort." A month later in South Boston, Virginia, the Independent Order of St. Luke held a Negro War Bond Auction, with all proceeds from the sale going towards the purchase of bonds. Such case histories illustrate the extreme fluidity inherent in war bonds, the sale of which was seemingly capable of fitting into virtually any existing American ritual.[38]

Finally, in Memphis in December 1943, another $300,000 in bonds was dedicated for a Consolidated Liberator bomber, *The Spirit of Beale Street*. During the Second War Loan, African-American citizens of Memphis had raised an equivalent sum for the Flying Fortress *Memphis Blues*, but it had been shot down and destroyed. This effort for the Third War Loan demonstrated the resolve Memphis blacks had toward participating in the war effort, and they stood as an exceptional example of civic and racial pride. Popularly attributed as the birthplace of the blues, an African-American art form, Memphis's Beale Street was a perfect sym-

[37] Ibid.
[38] Ibid.

bol to commemorate the contribution African Americans were making to win a Double V, victory both abroad and at home.[39]

By the war's end, when bonds were labeled "Victory Bonds," many in the press had begun to refer to the Treasury's bond program as "the greatest sales operation in history." Because bond sales were recorded only by geography, however, there were and are no reliable statistics regarding African Americans' or any other particular group's contribution to the bond program. Early in the war, some banks in the South would stamp bonds sold to blacks "Negro" or "Colored," but this practice was soon disallowed because it violated the democratic intent of the program. The government's refusal to record purchases by demographics such as gender, age, religion, or race was an intentional measure taken to ensure the program remain voluntary and nondiscriminatory. William Pickens himself regularly commented on this aspect of the bond program in reports to his superiors and as part of speeches to various audiences. "No full report of the part which colored citizens have so far borne or will yet bear in the war finance progress is possible," he wrote in his Report of the Inter-Racial Section for 1943. "In our democracy," he continued, "any citizen of any race or color has the privilege of buying his bonds through all the issuing agencies. No records are made by race." To Treasury officials, however, there was little doubt African Americans were backing the war effort on all fronts, including the bond program. As Ted R. Gamble, national director of the War Finance Division, stated in 1944, "When the record of this war effort shall have been written, it will show that Negroes not only fought the enemy in the front lines of the battle overseas, but met him on the homefront on the assembly lines and the bond-purchasing lines." A year later, in response to some hefty praise awarded by the Treasury to African Americans for their contribution to the bond program, William Pickens said simply, "Negroes are merely doing their share. They too are stockholders in the greatest corporation the world has ever known—America."[40]

Despite the absence of accurate sales figures, it is clear that African Americans were eager supporters of the Treasury's program based on the many reports of individuals, groups, businesses, and communities purchasing bonds. Equally clear was the presence of a distinct racial component to African-American investment in bonds, an additional variable in the selling and buying of bonds to and by African Americans. Although

[39] Ibid.

[40] "Often described in the press as 'the greatest sales operation in history.'" From War Finance Division Special Release, 13, 15 February 1946, Pickens Papers; Morse, *Paying for a World War*, 210; "1943 Sketch of the Inter-Racial Section"; "1944 Sketch of the Inter-Racial Section"; Treasury Department press release, N-1593, National Archives.

the net result was the same—purchase of a bond—the administration's aim and that of the African-American people often differed within the context of the consumer culture of bonds during World War II. The federal government used bonds as an ideological and financial tool by targeting African Americans to ease racial unrest, galvanize all Americans around the war effort, and broaden the emerging consensus. America's pluralistic democracy could be espoused, without giving up perceived power through the enforcement of antidiscrimination laws. African Americans were offered war-related jobs in significant numbers only when it served the administration's needs; likewise, extending an offer to blacks to join the consensus was done to meet hegemonic objectives.

Despite the administration's objectives, however, African-Americans enthusiastically purchased bonds to demonstrate their national loyalty, take action against an exponentially more racist regime, and gain greater equality by improving their socioeconomic status. Bonds were sold to and purchased by African Americans because they were in fact the best opportunity to achieve the Double V and carve out a piece of the American Dream. In the middle stood William Pickens, advocate for both the Roosevelt administration and the African-American community. An ideological power struggle was at work, although all parties saw the purchase of bonds as the means to winning the struggle.

Viewing the significant African-American investment in war bonds as a display of ideological alignment with the power bloc consensus or basic act of patriotism is an incomplete and inaccurate conclusion. African Americans purchased bonds as an act of empowerment and means to strengthen their individual and group racial identities in addition to their national one. Although the government was selling war bonds to African Americans in an attempt to defuse a separatist ideology (i.e., to have them literally and figuratively "buy into" the war), African Americans were purchasing bonds for reasons that both supported and redefined the administration's aims. Uncovering such evidence leads to a conclusion that the formation of the consensus society during World War II was more multidimensional than we have been taught; in fact some of its most compelling stories can be found within the bonds of affection.

Chapter 9

IN THE MIRROR OF THE ENEMY: JAPANESE POLITICAL CULTURE AND THE PECULIARITIES OF AMERICAN PATRIOTISM IN WORLD WAR II

ROBERT B. WESTBROOK

THERE IS NOTHING like a war to concentrate the minds of citizens on the meaning of patriotism, national identity, and political obligation. When our country is at war and we ask "why we fight," we are seeking not only an understanding of the war aims of a particular war but also a deeper and more general awareness of just what binds us to (or alienates us from) our nation state. Wartime is one of those rare occasions on which the political theory implicit in our institutions and practices is made explicit and becomes a widely shared concern. In the middle of a war, we come to recognize as we often do not on less crisis-ridden occasions that, as Michael Sandel has put it, "we live some *theory*—all the time."[1]

Sometimes we find ourselves at war with an enemy living quite a different theory, and this discovery sharpens our sense of the peculiarities of our own theory. The more alien the political culture of an enemy nation is, the more it may goad us to self-consciousness and the more theoretical such self-reflection may become. In such a situation, we may well not only make theoretical arguments for "why we fight" but also think in second-order fashion about our political theory itself. In the face of an enemy we find especially difficult to understand, our thinking can take a "meta-theoretical" turn. The more remote the thinking of our enemy, the more likely that our lived political theory will not just inform our patriotism but will itself become a mark of our national identity.

Arguably, no enemy has ever afforded Americans a more alien political culture against which to measure themselves than that of Japan in World War II.[2] This view, at least, was widely held at the time. During the war,

[1] Michael Sandel, "The Political Philosophy of Contemporary Liberalism" (ms.), 2.

[2] The Vietnamese might have provided a comparable challenge had the enemy in the War in Vietnam been seen, in the first instance, as Vietnamese rather than Communist.

Hitler seemed far more explicable to most American commentators than the foe in the Pacific. Americans would do well, the editors of *Fortune* warned typically in 1942, not to allow superficial similarities between the Nazi and Japanese regimes to obscure the wider moral gulf that divided the United States from the Asian enemy. "Whereas Nazi terrorism is the result of a conscious, calculated science of annihilation, on the excuse of the ends justifying the means, and is backed up at every step by long-winded moralizings, the Japanese brand is unhampered by ethical claptrap." Or, at least, the editors conceded, unhampered by familiar ethical claptrap:

> The unfathomable combined influence of Buddhism, Confucianism, and the primitive Shinto on the Japanese has reduced the importance of the individual to little or nothing. The ancient compulsions for unlimited self-sacrifice, the exaltation of the community over the individual, of rulers over law, and of death over life, have numbed the sense of intellectual and moral discrimination and made the Japanese indifferent to suffering—his own or others'.

The Nazis, this argument implied, could easily be judged evil in conventional terms, but the Japanese operated beyond American, that is Western, conventions of good and evil. The Nazis were bad Germans, to be judged by standards Americans shared with good Germans, but the Japanese were another matter. They were, as an entire people, living in a different ethical universe from Americans. There could be no distinctions between good and evil Japanese because good and evil did not mean the same things to the Japanese as they did to Americans (and good Germans). Hence, *Fortune* concluded, war with Japan afforded an especially difficult moral challenge. "We must be prepared," the magazine said, "to fight everywhere and anywhere—on the lofty and dangerous terrain of philosophy and ethics, no less than on the conventional battlegrounds of classic strategy."[3]

This essay analyzes the battle Americans waged on this lofty and dangerous terrain, focusing on their attempts to understand and describe Japanese political culture, particularly the conceptions of political obligation and patriotism embedded in it. But my interest is less in these descriptions themselves than in the way in which they served implicitly, and sometimes explicitly, to help Americans understand their own conceptions of political obligation and patriotism. For behind efforts to understand "why they fight" lay an attempt to grasp better the decidedly different reasons "why we fight."

---

[3] "The Japanese," *Fortune*, February 1942, 53, 52.

NATURE'S NATION

But first I must provide a few necessary, preliminary words about the strangeness of American national identity. Since the founding of the United States, many have contended that the dominant conception of American national identity is rooted in classical liberalism and is, when compared with other nationalisms, a most peculiar notion. For most nations, as Samuel P. Huntington has recently argued, "national identity is the product of a long process of historical evolution involving common ancestors, common experiences, common ethnic background, common language, common culture, and usually common religion." But American civic identity has lacked such ascriptive elements and has required only a subscription to the ideals of liberal democracy: "liberty, equality, individualism, democracy, and the rule of law under a constitution." American nationalism, peculiarly voluntaristic and creedal, is rendered even more peculiar by the fact that the ideals of the "American Creed" are often said (despite the adjective) to embody universal, even natural, rights. Thus, even though nationalism would seem by definition to be a claim to particularity, American nationalism in its liberal formulation argues somewhat paradoxically for a nationalism that transcends particularity. The United States is less a nation among nations than an exceptional place where human beings can enjoy those rights and liberties to which they are entitled, whatever their particular identities may be. America is "Nature's nation."[4]

One important consequence of this liberal understanding of American national identity is a thin sense of political community and a set of inadequate—and, to some critics, incoherent and wholly unpersuasive— arguments by liberals for political obligations to the national state. Political obligation would seem to require moral and affective ties to a particular political community, but liberals have found such ties difficult to establish within the confines of their individualistic, voluntaristic, contractual, and instrumental understanding of the relationship of citizens to the state. However, liberal nationalism, oxymoron though it may be, has often served as a bulwark against the terrors that the deep particularism of other nationalisms has generated both within and without national borders.[5]

---

[4] Samuel P. Huntington, *American Politics: The Promise of Disharmony* (Cambridge: Harvard University Press, 1981), 23, 14. See also Liah Greenfeld, *Nationalism: Five Roads to Modernity* (Cambridge: Harvard University Press, 1992).

[5] A solid overview of the debates over political obligation is John Horton, *Political Obligation* (Atlantic Highlands, N.J.: Humanities Press, 1992). On liberalism's difficulties

War, the greatest test of political obligation, has put a liberal nation such as the United States at something of an ideological disadvantage in mobilizing its citizens to fight. Unable to draw on the strong arguments for political obligation available to the leaders of nonliberal nations, American political leaders have often attempted to mobilize their citizenry with appeals to ethical values transcending any particular political community (the supposedly universal ideals of liberal democracy) or to nonpolitical private moral obligations. The state appears not as the embodiment of a particular political community but as either the guarantor of *human* rights or the protector of an essentially *private* sphere. As I have contended elsewhere, these sorts of appeals to transnational values (such as Franklin Roosevelt's "Four Freedoms") and nonpolitical obligations (such as those of men to women and parents to children) were preeminent during World War II.[6]

Few contemporary historians continue to contend, as some once did, that liberalism is all there is to the story of the making of American national identity. As Rogers Smith has effectively argued, liberal conceptions of American national identity and citizenship have always competed with more particularistic republican and ethnocultural traditions that have afforded, for better or worse, a thicker sense of political community and more compelling arguments for political obligation. Americans have in war and peace used each of these traditions and often articulated various amalgams of the three. Moreover, a good case can be made that, during the late nineteenth and early twentieth centuries, an ethnocultural understanding of American national identity was hegemonic and not terribly different from the nastier nationalisms seldom identified with the

---

with political obligation, see Carole Pateman, *The Problem of Political Obligation: A Critical Analysis of Liberal Theory* (Berkeley: University of California Press, 1985); A. John Simmons, *Moral Principles and Political Obligations* (Princeton: Princeton University Press, 1979); and Michael Walzer, *Obligations* (Cambridge: Harvard University Press, 1970). Other treatments of political obligation friendlier to liberalism include Philip Abbott, *The Shotgun Behind the Door: Liberalism and the Problem of Political Obligation* (Athens: University of Georgia Press, 1976); Harry Beran, *The Consent Theory of Political Obligation* (London: Croom Helm, 1987); Steven M. DeLue, *Political Obligation in a Liberal State* (Albany: SUNY Press, 1989); Richard Flathman, *Political Obligation* (New York: Atherton, 1972); George Klosko, *The Principle of Fairness and Political Obligation* (Lanham, Md.: Rowman and Littlefield, 1992); J. Roland Pennock and John W. Chapman, eds., *Political and Legal Obligation* (New York: Atherton, 1970). For a forceful defense of liberal nationalism, see Yael Tamir, *Liberal Nationalism* (Princeton: Princeton University Press, 1993).

[6] Robert B. Westbrook, "'I Want a Girl Just Like the Girl that Married Harry James': American Women and the Problem of Political Obligation in World War II," *American Quarterly* 42 (1990): 587–614; and "Fighting for the American Family: Private Interests and Political Obligation in World War II," in *The Power of Culture: Critical Essays in American History*, ed. Richard Wightman Fox and T. J. Jackson Lears (Chicago: University of Chicago Press, 1993), 194–221.

United States. But, as Smith concedes, by World War II the liberal tradition again held the upper hand, though the other traditions were not without significance. Thus, Americans scrutinized Japanese political culture largely through the lens of liberalism.[7]

THE JAPANESE ANTHILL

In the wake of Pearl Harbor, American newspapers and magazines not only provided reports from the battlefront but also periodically published feature articles that sought to explain Japanese nationalism to their readers. *Fortune* even devoted most of two issues to an effort to understand what its editors termed the "paradoxes of behavior that have twisted the Japanese mind for centuries." Many of these features were written by journalists and scholars such as Hugh Byas, Gustav Eckstein, Karl Löwith, Helen Mears, Joseph Newman, Willard Price, and Otto Tolischus who had spent time in Japan before the war, and former ambassador to Japan, Joseph Grew, was a regular contributor to this literature as well. Government agencies such as the Office of War Information employed experts, such as anthropologist Ruth Benedict, to study the Japanese character, and military intelligence officers provided soldiers and sailors with lectures and pamphlets on the political culture of the enemy. Documentary filmmakers such as Frank Capra not only instructed Americans in their own war aims but also provided them with such films as *Know Your Enemy—Japan* and *The Enemy Japan* designed to instruct them in the ways of their adversary. Thus, a relatively popular discourse on Japanese political culture was a significant feature of American public life during the war.[8]

Although those Americans who sought to explain Japanese nationalism to their fellow citizens were not without their differences of opinion, the striking thing about their work is a handful of shared themes. At the core of this American wartime commentary on Japanese national identity was the perception of the Japanese as an extraordinarily "collectivist" people, a people devoid of individuality—"photographic prints off the same negative," as Capra put it in *Know Your Enemy—Japan* (1945). "From childhood up," Willard Price told the readers of *National Geo-*

[7] Rogers Smith, "The 'American Creed' and American Identity: The Limits of Liberal Citizenship in the United States," *Western Political Quarterly* 41 (1988): 225–51; "One United People: Second Class Female Citizenship and the American Quest for Community," *Yale Journal of Law and the Humanities* 1 (1989): 229–93; and "Beyond Tocqueville, Myrdal, and Hartz: The Multiple Traditions in America," *American Political Science Review* 87 (1993): 549–66.

[8] "The Way of the Gods," *Fortune*, April 1944, 123.

graphic Magazine, the Japanese "are taught that the individual is of slight importance. . . . Japan has no rugged individualism. She has a rugged collectivism." According to *Fortune,* "in their individual lives, the Japanese have little opportunity for self-expression, simply because they do not exist as individuals at all. They exist as a unit of a family, as an object of the state, as a part of a group to which they are always subordinate."[9]

Such collectivism, commentators argued, was reflected in the extraordinary solidarity among the Japanese people. "It would be harder in Japan to cut between rulers and people than in any other country in the world," argued Gustav Eckstein. "Emperor, military leaders, and people will rise or go down to defeat together." Unlike Germany, Japan had not sent legions of dissenting emigrants to Allied shores. "The difference between German sheep and Nazi wolves is easily exposed," remarked Hugh Byas. "It is demonstrated by the testimony of many eminent Germans who have fled from the tyranny which they denounce. No such evidence can be produced in the case of Japan."[10]

Amidst this solidarity, Americans discerned a troubling, unreflective loyalty to the state. The Japanese, Byas noted, are "steeped in an ethical training which makes loyalty to country its deity." For those so trained, "national unity is an end in itself. The state says to them, 'Thou shalt have no other gods beside me.'" As William Henry Chamberlain saw it, "The slogan, 'My country, right or wrong,' would be alien to a Japanese—he simply could not conceive that his country could be wrong." The Navy instructed American sailors on their way to Japan to meet the defeated enemy in the fall of 1945 that "the words the Japanese hears from the cradle to the grave are 'obey,' 'obey,' 'obey.'"[11] Several features of Japanese political culture were most commonly singled out for comment by American critics in search of the peculiarities of Japanese nationalism: (1) the claims for the divinity of the emperor; (2) the familial ideology in which worship of the emperor was embedded; and (3) the "fanaticism" this ideology produced among Japanese soldiers wedded to it.

American readers and American troops preparing to face the Japanese were repeatedly treated to a retelling of the story of the mythic descent of Emperor Hirohito from the sun goddess Amaterasu, who sent her son to

[9] Willard Price, "Unknown Japan," *National Geographic,* August 1942, 244; "Way of the Gods," 125. On Capra's film, see William J. Blakefield, "A War Within: The Making of *Know Your Enemy—Japan,*" *Sight and Sound* 52 (1983): 128–33.

[10] Gustav Eckstein, "The Japanese Mind Is a Dark Corner," *Harpers,* November 1942, 665; Hugh Byas, "The Japanese Problem," *Yale Review* 32 (1942–1943): 456. See also Joseph C. Grew, *Report from Tokyo* (New York: Simon and Schuster, 1942), 14.

[11] "Way of the Gods," 128; Byas, "Japanese Problem," 456; Jesse F. Steiner, *Behind the Japanese Mask* (New York: Macmillan, 1943), 105–6; William Henry Chamberlain, "Who Are These Japanese?" *American Mercury* 54 (February 1942): 157; *Guide to Japan* (CINPAC-CINCPOA Bulletin No. 209–245, 1 September 1945), 42.

rule over the Japanese before the dawn of recorded history. They were alerted to the fact that this myth and the religion of State Shinto or "emperor-worship" which grew up around it constituted an "invented tradition" that dated from the Meiji Restoration of 1867 and the subsequent efforts of Meiji elites to develop an ideology with which to forge national unity. Nonetheless, most American commentators argued that the Japanese masses firmly believed in the divinity of their emperor and that less credulous Japanese elites at least kept up the appearance of belief in order that the masses would continue their worship. As the editors of the *Christian Century* described this "blasphemous theory":

> The Japanese constitution declares that the emperor is "sacred and inviolable." His office is not an organ of the state. The line of Japanese emperors, "unbroken from ages eternal" since the first emperor descended from Amaterasu Omikami, the sun goddess, existed before the nation and gives the state its being. The only powers exercised by the people, according to the theory on which the government of Nippon is built, are those derived from the emperor. In nearly two thousand years, the history of Western nations affords no parallel to the powers claimed by this ruler. The theory of the divine right of kings had not half the sweeping presumption of the thesis on which the Japanese god-emperor bases his authority. While there have been times when the point was not pressed with the relentless fury now in evidence, since 1931 it has not been possible for anyone in the Sunrise Kingdom to express doubt that the emperor is a god, entitled to blind and absolute obedience from his subjects, who are themselves demi-gods by reason of their relationship to him.[12]

The worship of the emperor sustained a powerful form of patriotism, which was its intended purpose. Strictly speaking, Chamberlain observed, "emperor-worship, as practiced in Japan, is not a religious cult, as we understand the term, but rather a mood of super-patriotism, of a salute to the flag with an added element of religious awe and sanction." The emperor was, above all, "a bond of national unity."[13]

Much of the power of the emperor's cult, American commentators argued, lay in the manner in which it was bound up with Japanese loyalty

[12] "Half-Gods After the War," *Christian Century*, 9 December 1942, 1520. See also "The Control of H. Fujino," *Fortune*, April 1944, 155–59, an effective parable about the complicity of a skeptical Japanese businessman in nationalist ideology. For a meticulous account of the Meiji invention of the imperial tradition, see Carol Gluck, *Japan's Modern Myths: Ideology in the Late Meiji Period* (Princeton: Princeton University Press, 1985). On invented traditions generally, see Eric Hobsbawm and Terence Ranger, eds., *The Invention of Tradition* (Cambridge: Cambridge University Press, 1983).

[13] Chamberlain, "Who Are These Japanese?" 159. See also Carol Bache, *Paradox Isle* (New York: Knopf, 1943), 122; Hugh Byas, *Government by Assassination* (New York: Knopf, 1942), 295–325; and Willard Price, *Japan and the Son of Heaven* (New York: Duell, Sloan and Pearce, 1945).

to the family. "Very few Japanese," Chamberlain reported, "conceive themselves outside the framework of the family, with its authority and obligations for the stronger and more successful and its dependence and limited protection for the poorer and weaker." Moreover, the Japanese state was conceived ideologically as a "family state," with the obligations of citizenship modeled on those of filial obligation. The extended Japanese family was a hierarchical pyramid enclosed with a familial national pyramid with the emperor at its apex.[14] The emperor was not only divine; he was quite literally the "father" of his country. Military intelligence officers in training in Maryland were instructed that

> Japan is one big household, with the Emperor as its head, recipient of the filial piety and obedience traditional to the Japanese family. The Emperor is thus the basis of national unity in terms of religion and the family system. . . . And in theory, at least, this religious and unique quality operating in Japanese life makes for social solidarity, a sense of common welfare and mutual dependence, with a minimum of self-interest and strife such as characterizes ordinary nations.[15]

"The Japanese are still essentially a clan," Eckstein argued. "What material for a fanatic nationalism. What material for an army. Obedience is an instinct. Submission is nature."[16]

No aspect of Japanese conceptions of political obligation attracted more bewildered commentary from Americans than what was commonly termed the suicidal "fanaticism" of the Japanese soldier. Articles with titles such as "Perhaps He Is Human," "Japan's Fanatics in Uniform," "Japan's Soldiers: Unsoldierly Yet Fanatic," "Japan Digs In to Die," "Must We Butcher Them All?" and "These Nips Are Nuts" were regularly featured in popular magazines.[17] Again and again Americans read accounts such as this by *Time* correspondent Robert Sherrod, who

---

[14] Chamberlain, "Who Are These Japanese?" 160.

[15] U.S. War Department, Military Intelligence Training Center, Camp Ritchie, Maryland, *Orientation for the Pacific Theatre* (typescript, 1944), 21; copy in the World War II Collection, Manuscripts and Archives, Yale University.

[16] Gustav Eckstein, "The Center of Japanese Power," *Harpers*, April 1943, 509, and "Japanese Mind Is a Dark Corner," 665.

[17] Robert Sherrod, "Perhaps He Is Human," *Time*, 5 July 1943, 28–29; Mark J. Gayn, "Japan's Fanatics in Uniform," *Science Digest*, March 1942, 10–14; Hallett E. Abend, "Japan's Soldiers: Unsoldierly Yet Fanatic," *New York Times Magazine*, 11 January 1942, 12; Mark J. Gayn, "Japan Digs In to Die," *Saturday Evening Post*, 28 October 1944, 9–10; William L. Worden, "Must We Butcher Them All?" *Saturday Evening Post*, 9 December 1944, 26; and Herman Kogan, "These Nips Are Nuts," *American Magazine*, February 1945, 33.

described Japanese soldiers choosing death and a "twisted" sense of honor over life and the shame of capture:

> The results of Jap fanaticism stagger the imagination. The very violence of the scene is incomprehensible to the Western mind. Here [Attu] groups of men had met their self-imposed obligation, to die rather than accept capture, by blowing themselves to bits. I saw one Jap sitting impaled on a bayonet which was stuck through his back, evidently by a friend. All the other suicides had chosen the grenade. Most of them simply held grenades against their stomachs or chests. The explosive charge blasted away the vital organs. Perhaps one in four held a grenade against his head. There were many headless Jap bodies between Massacre [Bay] and Chichagof [Harbor]. Sometimes the grenade split the head in half, leaving the right face on one shoulder, the left face on the other.[18]

American reporters acknowledged that such suicidal behavior may well have resulted from not only ideological fanaticism but also the fears of Japanese soldiers that they would, as their superiors told them, be horribly tortured by their American captors. But ideological explanations dominated the reporters' accounts. As *Time* put it, "Inside, the Japanese soldier is as tangled as the wires behind a telephone switchboard. From birth he has been taught the glory of dying for the Emperor. He knows what the manual says: 'To die participating in the supreme holy enterprise of mankind (war) must be the greatest glory and the height of exaltation.'"[19]

Efforts to explain Japanese patriotism varied. Occasionally, critics characterized the Japanese state with dehumanizing metaphors linking it to the social organization of collectivist insects such as ants and bees. "Japan is not a nation of individuals," Byas said, "but a hive of bees working, buzzing, and fighting collectively in defense of the hive." But despite the use of such racially inflected metaphors, strictly racial explanations of Japanese political culture were largely absent from the popular literature on Japanese politics, which was marked by relatively little of the overt racism that was such a prominent feature of images of the Japa-

---

[18] Sherrod, "Perhaps He Is Human," 28.

[19] "Portrait of a Japanese," *Time*, 12 January 1942, 18. See also John Goette, *Japan Fights for Asia* (New York: Harcourt, Brace, 1943), 36–51; "Jap Lieutenant: Picture Diary of His Life," *Life*, 19 June 1944, 47–48; "How Japs Fight," *Time*, 15 February 1943, 24–26; Robert Sherrod, "Nature of the Enemy," *Time*, 7 August 1944,: 33; W. J. Clear, "Close-up of the Jap Fighting Man," *Reader's Digest*, November 1942, 124–30; William Munday, "Diary of a Dead Jap," *Collier's*, 25 July 1942, 5; "Jap Soldier: Range of Japanese Military Psychology," *Newsweek*, 9 November 1942, 19–21; and "Life and Death of a Jap Soldier," *Science Digest*, February 1945, 75–79.

nese in American wartime propaganda generally.[20] More widespread were ahistorical cultural explanations that built on the work of "culture and personality" anthropologists such as Benedict, Geoffrey Gorer, and Margaret Mead. These arguments often linked Japanese political culture to the nation's child-rearing practices, and they were sometimes popularized crudely in such reductionist arguments as one linking Japanese character and politics to severe toilet-training practices.[21]

But the preeminent explanation of Japanese political culture was less anthropological than historical, an argument that might perhaps best be termed the neomedieval or neofeudal thesis. According to this argument, Japan was a nation best understood as a mixture of modern and pre-modern elements in which the latter held the upper hand. After centuries of feudalism and isolation, Japan's opening to the West following the confrontation with the "black ships" of Commodore Matthew Perry in 1853 was a carefully controlled embrace of modernity. The Meiji restoration had not so much smashed hundreds of years of Japanese feudalism as revamped the nation as a peculiar neofeudal regime. "The ghost of feudalism," Douglas Haring observed, "still stalks Japan. One asks constantly whether it be a ghost at all." The supreme authority of the emperor was purely symbolic; Hirohito remained, as his predecessors had been, the instrument of elites who ruled through him. Once the tool of medieval shoguns, the emperor was now the vehicle of a "feudally minded military clique." The emperor, Joseph Newman said, was a "lonely man who plays the part of god behind his feudal prison in the heart of Tokyo."[22]

Everywhere in Japan, Haring remarked, one could find the "inner dreams" of feudalism encased in the trappings of modernity. Japanese soldiers armed with the latest weaponry nonetheless fancied themselves latter-day *samurai* and devoted themselves to an updated version of the

[20] Hugh Byas, *The Japanese Enemy* (New York: Knopf, 1942), vii–viii. The beehive metaphor was one of Ambassador Grew's favorites as well. See "The Future of Hirohito: Why Emperor Is Spared," *United States News*, 6 April 1945, 20. The best treatment of the Pacific war as a race war is John Dower, *War Without Mercy: Race and Power in the Pacific War* (New York: Pantheon, 1986).

[21] See "Why Are Japs Japs?" *Time*, 7 August 1944, 66, reporting on Gorer's research. Ruth Benedict's treatment of Japanese character was more complex and subtle than that of Gorer and others who received wider publicity during the war. Her *Chrysanthemum and the Sword* (Boston: Houghton Mifflin, 1946), based on her wartime research but not published until after the war, quickly became the most influential American study of Japanese character and culture. But as Richard Minear has argued, even Benedict was guilty of a largely ahistorical treatment of Japanese culture. See Richard H. Minear, "The Wartime Studies of Japanese National Character," *Japan Interpreter* 13 (Summer 1980): 36–59.

[22] Douglas Gilbert Haring, *Blood on the Rising Sun* (Philadelphia: Macrae, Smith, 1943), 68; Joseph Newman, *Goodbye Japan* (New York: L. B. Fischer, 1942), 37.

code of *bushido*, which required their unstinting, self-sacrificing devotion to the emperor. The apparent concessions Meiji elites and their successors had made to modern democracy—a popular electorate, a constitution, and parliamentary government—produced a false front, a "Potemkin democracy," thinly disguising an oppressive regime of elite rule, thought control, and terror. At the same time, the Japanese had embraced the industrial revolution, mimicking Western science and technical rationality and adopting "automobiles, western clothes, baseball, the movies, chewing gum, electric light, airplanes, machine guns, and battleships." In short, capitalism and modern technology had in Japan been grafted onto a recast yet ancient political order. As Helen Mears summarized this argument, Japanese elites—now headed by the nation's military leaders—had produced a "fusion of the new and old Japan into a tightly meshed machine that can use the mechanical power of the Twentieth Century along with the dynamic of an ancient mythology."[23]

In nearly every narrative of the history of Japanese political culture offered by American commentators, the long insular regime of Tokugawa feudalism (1603–1867) figured as the decisive period in Japanese national development. American accounts repeatedly rendered the Tokugawa centuries as the moment at which the Japanese missed out on the revolutions in thought and practice that had freed the West from the shackles of medievalism. As a Navy pamphlet put it, "From about 1600 to 1853, while the western world was experiencing the Renaissance, the Reformation, the growth of political and economic democracy, the effect of scientific inquiry and research—great movements and developments which have shaped our thinking and molded our behavior—Japan was locked up in complete isolation."[24]

Liberal democracy, on this account, was the boat on the progressive stream of modern political history that the Japanese had failed to catch, and nothing better explained the peculiar character of Japanese political culture than the liberal-democratic revolution that had not happened in Japan. The Tokugawa shoguns had chosen to close Japan off from Western influence at just the moment when the West had the most to offer. As a result of this misguided isolationism, *Fortune* argued, "the spirit and mind [of Japan] were frozen in the mold of medievalism."

---

[23] Haring, *Blood on the Rising Sun*, 70; *Guide to Japan*, 32, 33; Helen Mears, "Japan's 'Divine' Mission," *Nation's Business*, December 1942, 20–21. It is perhaps worth noting that this argument that the enemy had combined modern industrialism with a premodern ideology was an argument some prominent American intellectuals made about Germany during World War I. See John Dewey, *German Philosophy and Politics* (New York: Holt, 1915), and Thorstein Veblen, *Imperial Germany and the Industrial Revolution* (New York: Macmillan, 1915).

[24] *Guide to Japan*, 33.

The tragedy of Japanese political history, the Navy pamphlet contended, was that "the complete elimination of all foreign influence, at a period when the western world was learning freedom, liberty, and the importance of developing individual personality, enabled the Japanese rulers to force the Japanese into a common mold." The Japanese, a *New York Times* reporter remarked, had been left "outside modern thought," that is, outside liberal values and "all that has gone into the making of the European and American mind with respect to group relations and the relations between constituted authority and the individual." Japanese political history, as these Americans saw it, was not just different; it was anomalous—a case of arrested development measured against the liberal-democratic norm.[25]

Much of the persuasive power of American descriptions and explanations of Japanese political culture derived from their use of Japanese self-descriptions of that culture. When the Japanese declared that they were "100 million hearts beating as one," Americans took them at their word, and Japanese manifestos such as the *Cardinal Principles of the National Polity* (1937), *The Way of the Subject* (1941), and *The Way of the Family* (1942), which described the Japanese state and Japanese nationalism in much the same fashion as American critics, were widely quoted. Hugh Byas, for example, quoted excerpts such as this from a 1938 document of the Japanese Department of Justice to impress upon his American readers the depths of Japanese statism:

> [All human beings] are born from the state, sustained by the state and brought up in the history and traditions of the state. Individuals can only exist as links in an infinite and vast chain of life called the state; they are links through whom the inheritance of ancestors is handed down to posterity, making possible continued growth and development in the future. . . . Individuals participate in the highest and greatest value when they serve the state as parts of it. The highest life for the Japanese subject is to offer himself in perfect loyalty to the Imperial throne so that he may participate in its glorious life.[26]

In this fashion, American reporters transformed positive Japanese self-descriptions of and prescriptions for communitarian solidarity into a negative portrait of a premodern state afflicted by irrational myths and a herdlike collectivism. As historian John Dower has said, Americans "accepted Japanese emphasis on the primacy of the group or collectivity at

---

[25] "The Japanese," 56–57; *Guide to Japan*, 44–45; Nathaniel Peffer, "Fatalism—Their Strength, Their Weakness," *New York Times Magazine*, 14 December 1941, 7.

[26] Byas, *Government by Assassination*, 266. Otto Tolischus appended a translation of the whole of *The Way of the Subject* to his book on Japan. See Tolischus, *Tokyo Record* (New York: Reynal and Hitchcock, 1943), 405–27.

face value, and used this as prima facie evidence that the Japanese were closer to cattle or robots than to themselves."[27]

I have refrained from any attempt to judge the accuracy of American representations of Japanese political culture. But Dower, for one, has complained that these representations confused ideology and reality:

> It was not that the Japanese people were, in actuality, homogeneous and harmonious, devoid of individuality and thoroughly subordinated to the group, but rather that the Japanese ruling groups were constantly exhorting them to become so. Indeed, the government deemed it necessary to draft and propagate a rigid orthodoxy of this sort precisely because the ruling classes were convinced that a great many Japanese did not cherish the more traditional virtues of loyalty and filial piety under the emperor, but instead remained attracted to more democratic values and ideals. . . . In other words, what the vast majority of Westerners believed the Japanese to be coincided with what the Japanese ruling elites hoped they would become.[28]

Undoubtedly much is to be said for this complaint, although I believe Dower underestimates both the sophistication of some of the American commentary and the degree to which orthodox ideology did indeed take hold among Japanese citizens and soldiers. But for my purposes, the issue may (thankfully) be left to Japanese historians. For even if Americans constructed a distorted and (negatively) idealized picture of Japanese political culture, this picture served effectively as a mirror in which their own idealized conceptions of political obligation and patriotism were reflected back to them.

POLITICAL OBLIGATION, THICK AND THIN

As I noted, two arguments for "why we fight" were particularly significant in American public discourse during World War II. By and large the representatives of the American state and other propagandists urged the nation's citizens to support the war effort for two reasons: to preserve the presumably universal human rights and liberties of liberal democracy threatened by Axis aggression; or to discharge a set of essentially private moral obligations to individuals and interests similarly threatened—commitments to families, children, parents, friends and neighbors, and generally to an "American Way of Life," defined as a rich and rewarding private sphere of experience.[29] Both these arguments were "thin" argu-

[27] Dower, *War Without Mercy*, 30.

[28] Ibid., 31.

[29] In addition to my articles cited in note 6, see Charles F. McGovern, "Selling the American Way: Democracy, Advertisers, and Consumers in World War II" (paper deliv-

ments for political obligation because neither advocated obligations to a particular political community; at most, loyalty to the American state was conceived as an instrumental virtue, a means for the discharge of obligations that lay elsewhere. Strictly speaking, Americans were seldom asked to work, to fight, or to die for their country. Their leaders instructed them in obligations defined either as those transcending the particularity of the nation-state or those residing in a private, nonpolitical realm of particularity. In both cases, "thicker" Japanese conceptions of political obligation served as an effective foil with which to highlight the virtues of this anorectic, liberal nationalism.

"The Japanese challenge not only the power of the West," *Fortune* declared, "but its fundamental creeds." Above all, Japanese political culture was an affront to the liberal democratic values of liberty and equality that defined American civic identity. As Americans saw it, the nation-state was properly conceived as a voluntary, contractual arrangement among free, rights-bearing individuals, designed above all to protect individual life and liberty and advance the pursuit of private happiness. The American nation was founded in a revolutionary break with an oppressive state that threatened human rights and in the constitution of a new nation that would preserve them. The Japanese state, however, was designed to limit the freedom of ordinary men and women in the interests of a neofeudal elite. According to this idealized liberal argument, American patriotism was less loyalty to the American nation than loyalty to transcendent liberal principles of which that nation was the instrument. Japanese patriotism was unthinking loyalty to a state that violated these principles at every turn, a view any Japanese "fascist" would gladly confirm. Magazines like *Fortune* could readily find quotations from such figures as Baron Hiranuma expressing contempt for liberalism and its values. "No dust shall be allowed to becloud the radiance of the Imperial way," Hiranuma warned, "and what I call dust is represented by liberalism and individualism, which are both opposed to our traditional customs."[30]

By American lights then, most Japanese were less citizens than subjects. In the United States, the legitimacy of the state and political obligation rested in theory on popular consent rather than the "will of heaven," against which there could be no appeal. In America, citizens jealously guarded their freedom and granted the state only those powers that would render this freedom more secure. In Japan the power of the state rested not on the consent of the governed but on their unwavering obe-

---

ered at the National Museum of American History, Smithsonian Institution, Washington, D.C., 23 June 1987).

[30] "The Japanese," 169, 168. See also Gustav Eckstein, *In Peace Japan Breeds War* (New York: Harper, 1943), 132.

dience to a hierarchy of authorities. Cut off from the riches of the liberal tradition, the Japanese were "a people without a conception of their own slavery."[31]

For Americans national identity was secondary to "life, liberty, and the pursuit of happiness"; indeed, to be an American was to make national identity a means to pursue these universal values. But for the Japanese, a particularistic national identity seemed an end in itself, an end to which they appeared more than willing to sacrifice life, liberty, and happiness. Liberalism afforded a vision of a national state constituted by free individuals who preexisted the social contract that underlay their government; in the organic conception of state and society articulated by the Japanese, the state constituted its subjects, subjects who had no existence prior to or apart from their national family.

Americans found this thick, organic, self-constituting nationalism mystifying and even depraved. As Karl Löwith put it with decided understatement, "It is difficult for us to understand why the ultimate values for the Japanese mind have never been 'life, liberty, and the pursuit of happiness,' but rather loyalty, a free disregard of life, and an honorable death." What made the suicidal behavior of Japanese soldiers so appalling to Americans was its roots in a theory of political obligation they regarded as premodern, antiliberal, and hence inhuman and irrational. Americans could well understand and celebrate soldiers like their own who bravely risked their lives in battle. But they could neither understand nor even begin to appreciate soldiers of whom it seemed inappropriate to say they risked their lives because they did not regard their lives as their own to risk; Japanese soldiers seemed to prefer death to the dishonor that defeat would bring to their nation. Such behavior, as American commentators saw it, was not just another way of thinking about political obligation but rather its perversion, not another way of conceiving of human life but a repudiation of its fundamentals. Japan, Price declared, "lacks respect for human life. We believe in living for our country. The Japanese believe in dying for their country."[32]

The thick particularism of Japanese nationalism contrasted sharply with not only American commitment to transnational liberal principles but also the private particularism that was integral to mobilizing Americans for World War II. Japanese arguments for political obligation to an organic state struck Americans as either too particular (because nonliberal) or not particular enough (because too political).

This latter contrast is best illustrated by the differences between the

---

[31] "The Japanese," 169.

[32] Karl Löwith, "The Japanese Mind," *Fortune*, December 1943, 242; Price, "Unknown Japan," 244.

familial ideology of the two nations. The Navy claimed that "the family, rather than the individual as in our country, is the basic unit in Japanese life," but this claim about the United States is countered by a considerable body of evidence to the contrary.[33] For example, the following lines from the memoir of a Japanese soldier reprinted in *Time* magazine might easily have been written by one of his American adversaries (a similarity *Time* implicitly acknowledged in offering the story as evidence that the Japanese soldier might after all be "human"): "A soldier offered me his shovel. I took it and unconsciously traced the characters Father and Mother in the soft sand. Then I erased them and wrote the names of my wife and children. I touched the good-luck omen my mother had given me and I thought of her prayers for my safety."[34] Americans no less than the Japanese conceived of the war as a war for the defense of the family. The American liberal state and its allies in Hollywood and the War Advertising Council did not rest content in their mobilization efforts with the thin universalism of transcendent moral principles but relied heavily on appeals to the more concrete moral obligations of the private sphere, and no obligation ranked higher in American war propaganda than the obligation to protect the family.[35]

Yet fighting for the family meant two profoundly different things in the United States and Japan. Löwith explained the difference:

> The Japanese family is not a family in our sense, i.e., a man, his wife, and their children, separated from the parents and grandparents. The Japanese family is not an individual unity but the center and substance of state and society, including parents and grandparents. The grandfather is the head of the family while the grandson is the guarantee of an uninterrupted ancestor cult. . . . The source and climax of the whole family and ancestral system is the Imperial family, which derives from the Sun Goddess. The "big house" (*Oyake*) of the Imperial family is the principal house from which descend all the "small houses" (*Koyake*) of the people. [National] loyalty and filial piety are in the same line and connected by the ancestor cult. Every Japanese child bows at the beginning of his classes in the direction of the Imperial palace in Tokyo just as he pays respect to the tablets of the family shrine. Fatherland and Imperial house are for the Japanese the same. Hence the social and moral foundations of the Japanese "patriotism" are very different from what we call patriotism, nationalism and imperialism.[36]

Thus, while Americans thought of themselves as a "state of families," an aggregate of idealized, bourgeois nuclear families, the Japanese conceived

---

[33] *Guide to Japan*, 33. See also Byas, *Japanese Enemy*, p. 37.

[34] "Portrait of a Japanese," 18.

[35] Westbrook, "Fighting for the American Family."

[36] Löwith, "The Japanese Mind," 240.

of themselves as a "family state," an organic whole in which the nation was quite literally a single extended family. Political obligation was "the extension of the filial piety to the Imperial family, supported by tradition and emotional appeal."[37]

Americans saw in Japanese political culture an illegitimate expansion of the deepest and most abiding of private obligations. To some, the Japanese family state even made Japanese nationalism "much more substantial and total than that of the totalitarian states."[38] More than willing themselves to conceive of the state as an instrument for discharging private obligations to one's family, Americans were baffled by a people that seemed unable (like good liberals) to draw a clear line between private and public spheres or to distinguish the body politic from the family circle.

THE ALLURE OF SOLIDARITY

There were few relativists in the foxholes of American commentary on Japanese political culture during World War II. The Japanese were not merely different; they were abominable. Their political culture not only had to be understood but also destroyed. On occasion, critics of Japanese political theory could give vent to a rhetoric of annihilation less common among those who regarded the Japanese as a neofeudal historical sport than among those who saw them as an inferior race of monkeys or vermin. Japan, Willis Lamott argued, must be subjected to a defeat in which "the whole fabric of modern Japanese spiritual and ethical life would be torn to shreds." The only way to deal with Japan's dangerous philosophy would be to inflict "a defeat of such an overwhelming and disastrous nature as to reorient the nation and set it upon the task of building its life upon totally different bases." Given their "savage" way of thinking, Otto Tolischus argued, the Japanese must be subjected to "ideological extermination."[39]

Nonetheless, a certain grudging admiration for Japanese political culture and the solidarity it produced occasionally crept into American views of the enemy. *Fortune* may have been wholly ironic in bemoaning the fact that "submissiveness is a Japanese weapon that our war engineers cannot reproduce," but others were willing to lament without irony the superior ideological resources the Japanese had to hand. "The enemy has

---

[37] Ibid., 241. I have borrowed the terms "family state" and "state of families" from Amy Gutmann, *Democratic Education* (Princeton: Princeton University Press, 1987), 22–33.

[38] Löwith, "The Japanese Mind," 240.

[39] Willis Lamott, *Nippon: The Crime and Punishment of Japan* (New York: John Day, 1944), 8; Otto Tolischus, "The Savage Code that Rules Japan," *New York Times Magazine*, 6 February 1944, 37.

discovered a part of man that our materialists don't think about very much," Emmet Lavery observed, "the thing some of us call a soul. True, we appeal to it somewhat in our churches and in our schools. But does our spiritual dynamic move our people to the degree that the spiritual dynamic of the enemy has moved the Germans and the Japanese?" The Japanese had the advantage of "love of country plus a high pressure form of political mysticism." Even Tolischus saw the "savage code" of the Japanese as a two-edged sword, for Japanese leaders had been able "to instill in their followers a faith which is fiendish enough to produce the foul deeds now being recorded but also strong enough to inspire the loyalty, the courage, the endurance, the toughness and fanaticism" with which the Japanese were fighting.[40]

Americans were alert to the need for solidarity in wartime and to the special difficulties that an "individualistic" people like themselves had in sustaining such a collective spirit. They were not inclined in ordinary circumstances to think in terms of "We-All," but they knew it might not be a bad idea in the midst of a total war (fig. 1). Sometimes, they were even willing to entertain the notion of their nation as a single family, "one fighting family . . . 130,000,000 of us," as a General Electric advertisement put it. Representing the United States as a family state did, to be sure, prove extraordinarily difficult to do. It was impossible to do so photographically because, unlike the Japanese, Americans had no conventional rituals of family-state solidarity to offer the camera. At best, one could only paint pictures of the state of families and try to pass them off as something thicker. The GE ad, for example, featured six separate panels of six different families engaged in wartime production and conservation. And most activities depicted in the ad were organized by the market, an institution designed to produce collective goods in the absence of self-conscious collective solidarity. Other graphic representations suffered from the absence of any convincing American iconography of the family state. Portraits of a national family headed by Uncle Sam appeared occasionally, but it was difficult to imagine, let alone represent, a political theory rooted in avuncular authority. Nonetheless, such ventures in family-state thinking do suggest an American appreciation of a thicker patriotism than that which liberalism afforded them.[41]

An attraction to a thicker patriotism was evident as well in the per

[40] Emmet Lavery, "The Enemy in Perspective," *Commonweal*, 19 November 1943, 114; Tolischus, "Savage Code," 36.

[41] General Electric, "This Fight Is a Family Affair," *Life*, 24 August 1942, 14–15. I had intended to reproduce this ad, but I was denied permission by a GE representative who was worried that a reference in it to the bombing of Pearl Harbor by the "Japs" would offend the Japanese, with whom, I was assured, GE now has a very congenial relationship. For a discussion of some graphic representations of an American family state headed by Uncle Sam, see my "Fighting for the American Family," 207, 212, 216.

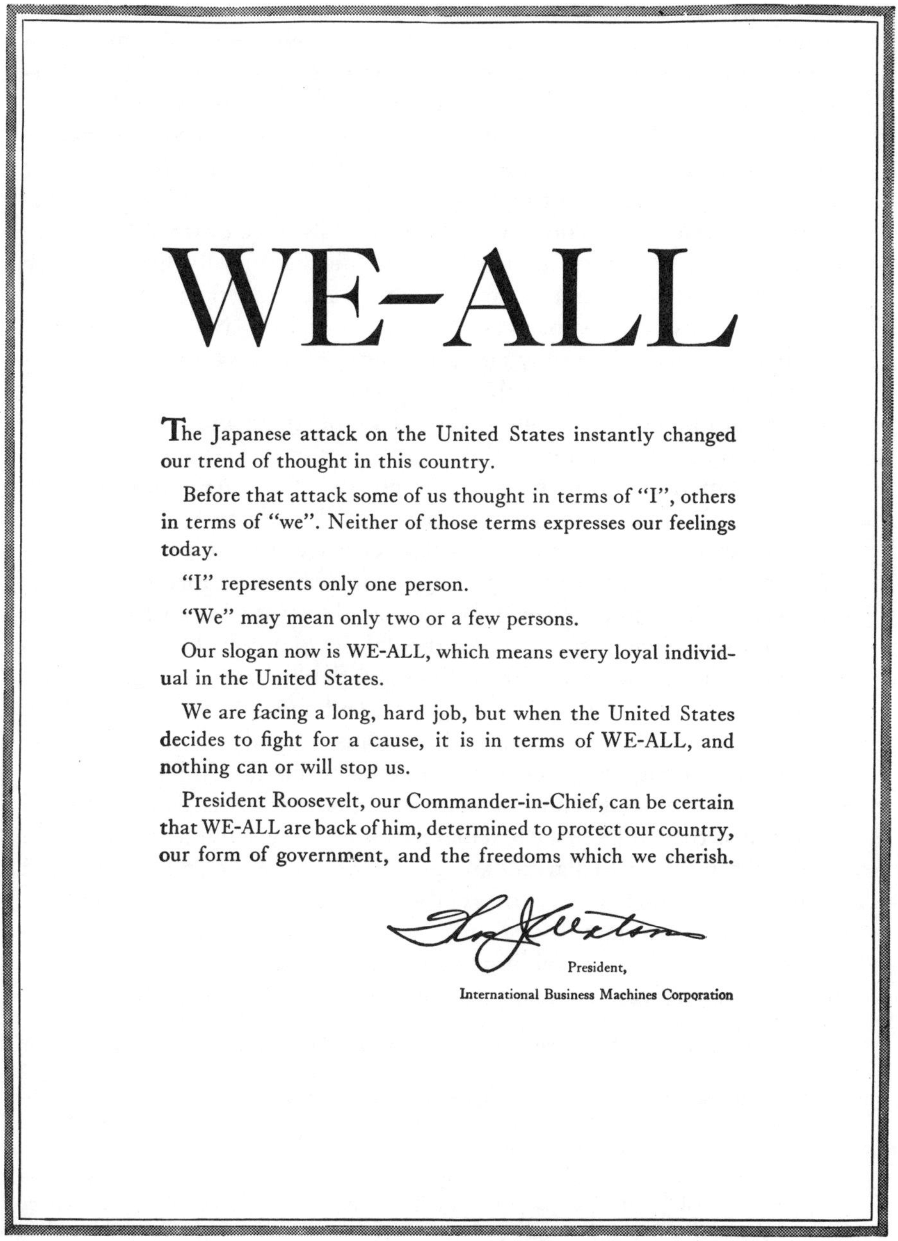

WE-ALL

The Japanese attack on the United States instantly changed our trend of thought in this country.

Before that attack some of us thought in terms of "I", others in terms of "we". Neither of those terms expresses our feelings today.

"I" represents only one person.

"We" may mean only two or a few persons.

Our slogan now is WE-ALL, which means every loyal individual in the United States.

We are facing a long, hard job, but when the United States decides to fight for a cause, it is in terms of WE-ALL, and nothing can or will stop us.

President Roosevelt, our Commander-in-Chief, can be certain that WE-ALL are back of him, determined to protect our country, our form of government, and the freedoms which we cherish.

President,
International Business Machines Corporation

FIGURE 1. IBM advertisement, *Time,* 10 January 1942, 51. (Courtesy of IBM)

sistence of republican and ethnocultural notions of American identity during the war. Only rarely does one find vaguely neorepublican representations of the practice of democratic citizenship as not merely instrumental to the protection of universal liberal ideals or to the discharge of private moral obligations but as an end in itself and one constitutive of American identity.[42] Far more often, the War in the Pacific was conceived as a race war, and propagandists appealed to white American solidarity in the face of a yellow peril. Such appeals were difficult for representatives of the American state itself to make officially because they were allied with the Chinese, anxious not to alienate African Americans, and eager to distance themselves from Nazi racialism. Nonetheless, government officials did employ an ethnocultural understanding of American citizenship to legitimate the internment of Japanese-American citizens. Ironically, no Americans advanced a more lucid and consistent case for a liberal understanding of American national identity than those Japanese-Americans who resisted the efforts of the American state to deny them their rights on particularistic racial grounds.[43]

Yet whatever the attractions of a thicker patriotism and a more genuinely political conception of their obligations to the war effort, few Americans were willing to purchase enhanced solidarity at the expense of their own individual liberties. Whatever the defects of a thin, liberal nationalism, they paled in the face of the oppression that the thickly "collectivist" Japanese state visited upon its subjects. And thin liberalism and thick authoritarianism seemed to most Americans the only alternatives. One can abstractly imagine a thicker, yet nonetheless liberal, American nationalism in which liberal ideals are conceived not as transcendent, universal rights but as the values of a particular national polity, rooted not in human nature but in the particularities and peculiarities of American history and culture.[44] But that would make the United States a nation among nations—and no longer nature's nation. This alternative was a possibility that few Americans were willing to entertain during World War II and one that remains difficult for many to swallow fifty years later.

[42] See my discussion of Norman Rockwell's painting, *Freedom of Speech*, in "Fighting for the American Family," 218–21.

[43] For a full sampling of appeals to racial solidarity, see Dower, *War Without Mercy*, 77–200. On racial arguments for internment and liberal arguments against it, see Peter Irons, *Justice at War* (New York: Oxford, 1983).

[44] Such a thicker liberal nationalism might, for example, be said to characterize the "anti-foundational," historicist, and benignly "ethnocentrist" liberalism of philosopher Richard Rorty. See Rorty, *Contingency, Irony, and Solidarity* (Cambridge: Cambridge University Press, 1989), 44–69, 189–98; *Objectivity, Relativism, and Truth: Philosophical Papers, Volume 1* (Cambridge: Cambridge University Press, 1991), 175–210; and "The Unpatriotic Academy," *New York Times*, 13 February 1994, 15.

Chapter 10

"GOOD AMERICANS": NATIONALISM AND DOMESTICITY IN *LIFE* MAGAZINE, 1945–1960

WENDY KOZOL

IN 1957, Americans responded to news about the Soviet Union's orbiting satellite Sputnik with a mixture of fear and embarrassment. Tangible evidence of Soviet technology intensified anxieties about the possibility of a missile attack. The Soviets' stunning achievement also humiliated American political leaders who had repeatedly lauded U.S. technological superiority, thus implicating the space race in the anticommunist hysteria pervasive in the post–World War II period. It was, therefore, with more than a little sigh of relief that *Life* magazine reported in January 1959 that the United States had successfully launched an Atlas ICBM in orbit around the earth.[1] The photo–essay hails the successful orbit as "America's unique peaceful Christmas gift to itself and the world." Amid lengthy explanations of American technology, one two-page layout visualizes the "free world's" dependence on this technological power through photographs of people at home and abroad listening to President Eisenhower's radio announcement.

Of these pictures, the only full-page color photograph shows fireman Ed Oleksiak seated on the couch with his wife and daughter, listening to the radio. His son and two neighborhood boys sit on the floor in front of them and play with toy missiles. Oleksiak wears his uniform, which identifies his paramilitary status as a male protector not only of his family but of the (local) state as well. The young boys in the foreground enact, like the father, the masculine drama of protection and military prowess. This emblematic photograph visualizes the American families that military technology was intended to protect.

In pictures like this one, *Life*'s figuration of the family had profound consequences for its representation of national issues. *Life* was the most popular general magazine of the period with an estimated readership of

---

This essay is drawn from Wendy Kozol, *Life's America: Family and Nation in Postwar Photojournalism* (Philadelphia: Temple University Press, 1994) by permission of Temple University Press.
[1] "The Big Bird Orbits Words of Peace," *Life*, 5 January 1959, 10–23.

twenty million.[2] Although television was fast becoming the dominant form of visual entertainment, the networks did not commit resources to news programming for much of the period. *Life* was the main source of visual news for Americans during the 1940s and 1950s; thus, the magazine played a crucial cultural role through its representation of postwar society.

From its inception in the late 1930s, *Life* relied on photographic codes of realism to depict the news. The magazine's attention to the middle-class family, however, emerged during the postwar years as part of a cultural and social shift toward domesticity, most visible in the impressive statistics of the baby boom and the rise of middle-class suburban prosperity. *Life*'s readers themselves participated in these social changes, for they were typically white, middle-class, married, and active consumers.[3] Yet, to infer that the news simply reflects social reality ignores the role of cultural discourses in constructing and mediating perspectives on that reality. News discourses, especially the compelling realism of photography, do more than reproduce social conditions, for they privilege certain values at the expense of others. *Life* frequently explained abstract or complex problems, issues, or events through metonymic portraits of "real" people, a technique that the magazine adapted from earlier news traditions. Ordinary characters function effectively as representatives in news reporting because, even though they are "strangers," their easily recognizable social roles make them deeply familiar.[4] Photographs of the family, presented as incidental trivia or as evidence of individual responses to crises, transformed actual events into symbolic meanings by drawing on the cultural values circulating in the society. In its news coverage of the Atlas satellite, then, the Oleksiaks are the metonymic signifier of the America that needs military protection. This study considers the photo essays in *Life*'s news section, "The Week's Events," that used "ordinary" families to represent the newsworthy concerns of postwar America.[5] As we see, from 1945 to 1960 the camera's presumably objec-

[2] See *N. W. Ayer & Son's Directory of Newspapers and Periodicals* (Philadelphia: N. W. Ayer and Son, [annual volumes] 1945–1960).

[3] *Life* commissioned a number of marketing surveys to gather demographic data about their readers. See e.g., *Life Study of Consumer Expenditures*, conducted for *Life* by Alfred Politz Research Inc. (New York: Time, Inc., 1957).

[4] John Fiske, *Television Culture* (New York: Routledge, 1987), 291–93, discusses the news as metonymy; see also Allan Sekula, "Invention of Photographic Meaning," in *Thinking Photography*, ed. Victor Burgin (London: Macmillan: 1982), 84–109, for a similar discussion of the metonymic function of the photographic image. For a discussion of the news convention of "vox pop" or voice of the people, see John Hartley, *Understanding News* (London: Methuen, 1982), 90, 109.

[5] For a larger study of family imagery in *Life* during the postwar period, of which this essay is a part, I examined "The Week's Events" section as well as advertisements and letters to the editors for all issues of *Life* from 1936 to 1960. In addition, I analyzed all

tive gaze mapped out a selective cultural space that privileged one way of life as representative of the nation.

Benedict Anderson defines nations as imagined communities because "members of even the smallest nation will never know most of their fellow-members, meet them, or even hear them, yet in the minds of each lives the image of their communion."[6] Anderson's formulation that communities are defined by "the style in which they are imagined" is useful for interpreting the ability of media like *Life* to envision nationhood. "Style" here refers to the politics of representations that construct national identity. In examining the origins of nationalism, Anderson argues that the advent of print capitalism, especially the novel and the newspaper, "provided the technical means for 're-presenting' the *kind* of imagined community that is the nation."[7] Through reading, people could "imagine" shared experiences with thousands of other readers they would never meet. If print literacy supported the emergence of the concept of nation, then visual media have even greater capacities to visualize social norms and ideals that form national identities. This is evident in *Life*'s photographs of people in London, New York, and San Francisco, all of them listening to the radio announcement about the Atlas satellite; they construct an imagined community of the "free" or "Western" world with shared concerns about the Cold War.

Using the fireman and his family to represent American reactions to Cold War militarism reveals the hegemonic power of the news to align social identities with political concerns. Although the text claims that all Americans worried about the Soviet military threat, the pictures in the photo essay show only white people. During the postwar years, military and political leaders worried that sites of nuclear production like Los Alamos, New Mexico, and Livermore, California, were most vulnerable to attack. These locations had large Native American and Latino populations, but they were not included in *Life*'s portrait of the Cold War. The absence of people of color in this news coverage exposes racist currents in anti-communist rhetoric. Moreover, photographs of families like the Oleksiaks conflated the heterosexual imperatives central to domesticity with national identity. Examining the role of the family in news about the public sphere reveals, then, how family portraits visualized "bonds of affection" based on a politics of exclusion and privilege.

---

special issues devoted to a single topic. See Kozol, *Life's America: Family and Nation in Postwar Photojournalism* (Philadelphia: Temple University Press, 1994).

6 Benedict Anderson, *Imagined Communities: Reflections on the Origin and Spread of Nationalism*, rev. ed. (London: Verso, 1991), 6–7. Among the growing theoretical literature on nationalism, see also Anthony D. Smith, *The Ethnic Origins of Nations* (Oxford: Basil Blackwell, 1986); and E. J. Hobsbawm, *Nations and Nationalism Since 1780: Programme, Myth, Reality* (Cambridge: Cambridge University Press, 1990).

7 Anderson, *Imagined Communities*, 25.

As John Bodnar points out, the twentieth-century triumph of state liberalism was pivotal to the history of patriotism.[8] The statist dimensions of liberalism that the New Deal consolidated intensified as a result of pressures first from World War II and then later the Cold War, as well as the economic boom fostered by successful state intervention. *Life*, along with other popular media, were instrumental in promoting a vision of patriotism that glorified state power. Central to this patriotic vision was an ideal of masculine dominance both at home and abroad. But patriotism in the postwar years also depended on the image of the nuclear family because integral to the ideal of masculine authority is a division of public and private spheres. Patriotic representations of the nation did more than evacuate women from public arenas, for these images depended on ideals of domesticity to define both spheres. In this chapter I examine one popular site that promoted bonds of affection based on this patriotic ideal of a unified nation. We see the centrality of domesticity not only in images that claimed to represent "America" but also in news coverage of the most masculine of public political concerns, the Cold War.

Nationalistic rhetoric structured Cold War ideologies that polarized the world into factions of good and evil. Patriotism was defined as much by social conventions and cultural ideals as by militaristic actions such as risking one's life for one's country. Most clearly, any criticism of the government was defined as unpatriotic, a definition that often extended to criticism of the "American way of life." Patriotism, conversely, aligned dominant ideals about social behavior with political objectives. Rather than reflecting or recording reality, *Life*'s photo essays created an imagined community through pictorial realism that naturalized a particular social form—the middle-class nuclear family—into an ideal that symbolized America. In so doing, this imagined community also regulated social relations and denied diversity at a time when anticommunist campaigns made differences politically dangerous. In claiming the power to represent the world, *Life* promoted a way of life through patriotic imagery that exemplified what it meant to be American.

PATRIOTISM AND *LIFE'S* Family Ideal

Life's 5 January 1953 cover photograph depicts a woman kneeling with her arms around two blond-haired girls who are leaning on the bottom of a window sill. Standing behind them, a man in a business suit holds a toddler seated on the cross piece of the window frame. Looking out of a

---

[8] See John Bodnar's introduction to this volume.

large window, this neatly groomed white family smiles at the camera. The frame connotes a domestic setting, yet the building is unfinished without a window in the frame. By itself, this picture does not provide information about the specific type of home but underneath the window frame, the caption states: "Family Buys 'Best $15,000 House.'" The cost of the house confirms a reading of the family as affluent while the unfinished building suggests progress; the future appears bright for this family. On a yellow banner cutting diagonally across the page, the headline connects this vision of familial intimacy to the newsworthy concerns of postwar America as it announces the topic of this special issue: "The American and His Economy."

Conventional American patriotic symbols include the Minute Men of Lexington and the soldiers raising the flag at Iwo Jima. On the surface, family photographs appear to belong to a private sphere outside political and military worlds of masculine patriotic actions. Yet, photographs like "The American and His Economy," in a similar symbolic fashion, articulate codes of behavior and cultural ideals central to the nationalistic project underlying patriotic expressions, that is to create a unifying and unified ideal of the nation.

The home, for instance, was a prominent symbol in *Life*'s portrait of America. In its Modern Living and Design sections, *Life* featured model suburban homes as the new architectural ideal. Merging editorial and advertising material in these sections, *Life*'s America was a nation of middle-class homeowners. News stories supported this consumer aesthetic by reporting on developments in suburban living. Locating "The American" in a suburban home visually narrates a postwar pattern of white migration out of urban centers. During the 1950s, 64 percent of the nation's population growth occurred in the suburbs.[9] Photographer Nina Leen's cover photograph connects domesticity to suburban living at a time when home loan and taxation policies supported private enterprise efforts to create unprecedented opportunities for working-class and middle-class white Americans to inhabit single-family detached suburban homes. At the same time, an ascendant ideology of domesticity based on strictly divided gender roles pervaded American life, involving such areas as hiring decisions in industry and child-rearing practices. Leen's composition repeats the patriarchal gender divisions basic to this postwar domestic ideology through the man standing above his kneeling wife and children. The woman's supportive embrace of her children encodes her maternal responsibilities while the man's looming protectiveness identifies him as the patriarchal breadwinner. *Life* makes the connec-

[9] Steven Mintz and Susan Kellogg, *Domestic Revolutions: A Social History of American Family Life* (New York: Free Press, 1988), 184.

tions between middle-class status and patriarchy explicit in the title that labels the economy "his"; her role apparently is only one of support.

Although they represented an ideal, labeled as such by the generic "The American," the people who posed for this picture were not actors. *Life* presents Dale and Gladys Welling, the "real" family who recently bought one of these houses, as evidence of actual families living the American Dream. In this way, the magazine legitimizes *Life*'s association of the U.S. economy with a particular social group by individualizing the representation.

Migration, of course, took on different meanings for people of color moving from rural poverty into urban slums. Between 1950 and 1970, five million African Americans, largely from the South, moved into central cities.[10] In addition, millions of immigrants facing poverty and unemployment came to the United States during this period, often through recruitment programs designed to supply cheap labor for agriculture and other industries. For instance, more than four million Mexican workers immigrated through the *Braceros* program.[11] New arrivals to urban areas frequently confronted racial discrimination, low wages, and other social dislocations. The extremely varied consequences of mobility during the postwar years created upheavals in people's economic, political, and social lives. The special issue on the economy addresses white mobility but ignores this other story of migration. Instead, this issue reproduces a discourse of racism by narratively excluding people of color who were physically barred from moving into the suburbs.[12]

Life connected the political economy with a particular social class through photographs of white, nuclear families enjoying the postwar economic boom. The magazine actively promoted the consumer spending and government economic policies that fostered the preconditions for an unprecedented rise in the American standard of living that lasted until the 1960s. Government and business leaders sought to control the instabilities endemic to capitalism through economic stimulation and structural modifications to programs such as welfare and social security.[13]

[10] John H. Mollenkopf, *The Contested City* (Princeton: Princeton University Press, 1983), 28.

[11] Juan Ramon Garcia, *Operation Wetback: The Mass Deportation of Mexican Undocumented Workers in 1954* (Westport, Conn.: Greenwood Press, 1980), 23–36; Teresa L. Amott and Julie A. Matthaei, *Race, Gender, and Work: A Multicultural Economic History of Women in the United States* (Boston: South End Press, 1991), 79–80, 274–79.

[12] See Kenneth T. Jackson, *Crabgrass Frontier: The Suburbanization of the United States* (New York: Oxford University Press, 1985), 190–245, for a discussion of these discriminatory policies.

[13] Marty Jezer, *The Dark Ages: Life in the United States 1945–1960* (Boston: South End Press, 1982), 119–22; Douglas F. Dowd, *The Twisted Dream: Capitalist Development in the United States Since 1776* (Cambridge, Mass.: Winthrop, 1974), 65–75, 105–7.

Along with greater government intervention in the economy, consumer spending fueled the postwar boom. After fifteen years of economic crisis and war, Americans in 1945, encouraged on by consumption ideologies promoted by the mass media, were ready to spend. Between 1945 and 1950, for instance, manufacturers sold 21.4 million automobiles and more than 20 million refrigerators.[14] Suburban growth and demands for housing, appliances, automobiles, and shopping malls encouraged this explosive consumption.[15]

As part of a national corporation with its own direct political and economic interests, and as an institution with responsibilities to its investors and advertisers, *Life* supported government and business efforts to maintain a stable economy and political consensus. Far from being subtle, the magazine repeatedly stated in both editorials and economic news coverage that it was Americans' patriotic responsibility to consume in order to maintain high demand and the economic prosperity. Toward that end, *Life* often cajoled its readers to be civic-minded by spending more money. In a May 1947 article, "U.S. Tackles the Price Problem," *Life* linked domestic ideals to the state by making the family accountable for economic prosperity.[16] The article ends with a two-page spread on Ted and Jeanne Hemeke and their three children. The headline specifically associates consumption with civic responsibility: "Family Status Must Improve: It should buy more for itself to better the living of others." The editors use a popular photo essay formula of a before-and-after narrative: the Hemekes appear first in their present home, an old frame house, then visiting a new suburban home. The text explains the latter as the vision of the future, "what life should be like in the U.S. by 1960."

In the foreground of the first picture, Ted Hemeke stands with his back to the camera holding a child's hand, having just returned from work. The photographer's perspective encourages the viewer to identify with Hemeke's vision by literally putting us in his shoes. Following his gaze, we look past the foreground figures toward the house, observing the weeds and lack of grass on the lawn as well as the other poorly maintained house next door. In the background, Jeanne Hemeke stands in the doorway holding one child while another child sits on a barrel next to her. The other picture on this page shows Jeanne Hemeke using a large shovel to scoop coal into a "dirty coal furnace next to the stove" while her baby daughter sits on the floor nearby. This shot emphasizes the antiquated facilities of the old house as well as the woman's hard work.

[14] Susan M. Hartmann, *The Home Front and Beyond: American Women in the 1940s* (Boston: Twayne, 1982), 8.

[15] Jezer, *Dark Ages*, 120.

[16] "U.S. Tackles The Price Problem," *Life*, 5 May 1947, 27–33.

On the facing page, two photographs parallel the ones on the previous page in composition, size, and layout. The first picture again shows the Hemekes in front of a house. This time, however, the wife stands in the doorway of a modern ranch-style house. The visual narrative suggests that once again he is arriving home from work by repeating the action of Ted Hemeke walking into the scene from the street. Repeating the composition encourages a reading of economic progress from the old house to the new one even though the text explains that the Hemekes are visiting a model home.

The second photograph of the alternative vision shows Jeanne Hemeke again in the kitchen, but this time the kitchen is modern with gingham curtains and shiny new appliances. She stands at a counter with her hands on an electric beater, as if she were baking while behind her a kettle gleams on a gas stove. The baby no longer sits on the floor dangerously close to the furnace but plays with a toy in a high chair that has a bottle of milk on the tray. Visually, if not in actuality, Jeanne Hemeke and her family have attained these middle-class accoutrements. The realistic *mise en scene* (for this is a staged performance by two different photographers) reinforces the reading that this woman is cooking in her own home. Placing the woman in a modern kitchen with new appliances, a composition frequently used in advertisements, objectifies her as an ideal consumer, while positioning her only in the private space of the home reinforces conventional gender roles. Her husband, however, occupies space in the outside public world, signified by the sidewalk and narrative journey from work. Visually and textually, *Life* presents a vision of America that characterizes people like the Hemekes through gender ideals and material possessions.

Life locates the consumer ideal in the physical space of the suburbs, an isolated space in which no one else appears on the sidewalks. This vision of the nation integrates ideals of social progress with ideologies of consumption and the private realm of domesticity. Moreover, the article claims that families have civic responsibilities based on their roles as consumers. Thus, *Life* creates a portrait of the nation that legitimizes the social order by connecting moral authority to familial consumption. As other authors in this volume show, obligations and loyalties are crucial to definitions of patriotism. In the postwar years, *Life* relied on domestic ideals, as they aligned with class, race, and consumer imperatives, to foster patriotic commitments. Stories about people like the Hemekes denied class and racial inequalities when they pointed to consumption as evidence of upward mobility. Instead, the homogenous domesticity that pervades photo essays like this one offered a portrait of a national community of families.

Life's postwar pictorial record borrowed from the rhetoric of wartime emergency by linking the family to moral obligations and patriotic behavior.[17] This strategy is most evident in news coverage of class conflict where *Life* repositioned workers' actions as threats to democracy, not critiques of capitalist inequalities. One of the greatest fears at the conclusion of World War II was that the country would return to the desperate conditions of the 1930s. This fear seemed warranted when, along with rising inflation and unemployment, conflicts between labor and management escalated in the immediate postwar years. Unions and corporations attempted to rationalize labor relations in ways that often ignored or hurt workers' interests. Workers, in turn, registered their anger and frustration in wildcat strikes that insisted on not just wage increases but control over the work place.[18] Although *Life* was an avowedly conservative journal, the editors accepted the trend toward union involvement in corporate management and even praised successful contract negotiations. But it would not tolerate disruptions in the economy. *Life* represented labor strikes through photographs of empty warehouses and idled factories, which surely must have resonated with middle-class readers' pictorial remembrances of the Depression. Rather than looking at the faces of workers, pictures of empty warehouses illustrated how work stoppages affected the middle class. Moreover, *Life*'s news coverage of labor conflicts often deflected the politics of class struggle by focusing on the middle-class family as the location for the successful resolution of social discord.

The 3 June 1946 feature news story, "The Great Train Strike," angrily denounces a nationwide work stoppage by railroad workers because it asked too much of Americans.[19] According to *Life*, although Americans accept that "workingmen [*sic*] had a constitutional right to organize, negotiate and, if necessary, strike, to improve their working conditions," when strikes threaten the quality of life, the "United States" loses its temper. The text establishes social boundaries here by distinguishing Americans who are patient and the United States that loses its temper from the workers who test this patience. Such rhetorical moves exemplify how *Life* addressed its readers as an imagined community facing

[17] See Robert Westbrook, "'I Want a Girl, Just Like the Girl That Married Harry James': American Women and the Problem of Political Obligation in World War II," *American Quarterly* 42, no. 4 (December 1990): 587–614; and "In the Mirror of the Enemy: Japanese Political Culture and the Peculiarities of American Patriotism in World War II," chap. 9 in this volume.

[18] George Lipsitz, *Class and Culture in Cold War America: "A Rainbow at Midnight"* (South Hadley, Mass.: Bergin & Garvey, 1982).

[19] "The Great Train Strike: Railroad Shutdown Brings Wrath of People Down on All U.S. Labor," *Life*, 3 June 3 1946, 27–33.

external problems. Along with textual distinctions, *Life* visualizes class differences by depicting an America inconvenienced. The only photograph of labor shows two white male workers sitting on the steps of a train "waiting for the deadline." Their inactivity, along with pictures of empty train yards and factories, identifies those responsible for the breakdown of economic life resulting from this transportation crisis. The workers turn their heads to the left (narratively looking for a signal) so that they look at the facing page. One photograph on the opposite page depicts two stranded women travelers seated amid their luggage while their three children sprawl on the floor in front of them. In the space of the layout, the workers look at what they are inconveniencing: middle-class families dislocated by labor's idleness.

A letter written by a woman from Connecticut forms the centerpiece of the story. Instead of placing it in the letters section, *Life* prominently displays it in the photo essay, printed in large typewritten letters offset by a thick gray border. Betty Knowles Hunt, identified as a housewife and mother, condemns strikers for paralyzing the country and "killing our prestige abroad." She also criticizes the government for jeopardizing democracy by placing the public welfare in the hands of pressure groups. Who, she asks, "will save Democracy for America and the World?" This letter invokes not only democracy but also domesticity to legitimize the hierarchical inequalities of capitalism.

> Much of my time and energy has been spent in trying to teach my three little minorities that their private interests will often conflict, but that they must learn to sacrifice in the larger interest of our family as a whole. For what am I preparing them? Is it of any value to teach them Democracy at home, while our government in Washington fails to teach its minorities to sacrifice and work together for the common American good?[20]

Hunt establishes an us/them relationship by comparing "our family" and "our government" with working-class "minorities." Moreover, she trivializes political efforts of the working class by equating her children and striking workers as minorities. Hunt patronizingly represents labor activists as children to be taught by their parent, the government.[21] Patriotic demands of loyalty and responsibility use the narrowed self-interests of one social class against another in constructing a vision of a unified nation.

Hunt defines democracy as a matter of working together for the common good—economic prosperity—just as children must put aside their

[20] "Great Train Strike," 32.

[21] *Life* also uses this strategy on the first page of the essay when the writer quotes a dentist from Des Moines who said, "Labor is like a kid who gets too much money from his parents."

"private interests" for the sake of the family. In addition, Hunt represents workers' demands for self-determination as private interests of lesser value than the needs of (dominant) America. The letter legitimizes capitalist structures by displacing political critiques of the system in favor of family concerns. Indeed, the text presents class struggle as a threat not merely to a generalized social welfare but more specifically to the home.

Framing the train strike as a family crisis conforms to *Life*'s larger discursive attempt to align middle-class domesticity with the political economy. One consequence of *Life*'s reliance on family pictures was the surveillance of private life through a discourse that repeatedly emphasized a singular domestic ideal and silenced differences. This is especially apparent in stories that explicitly linked domesticity to anticommunist rhetoric. *Life* helped sustain Cold War tensions by repeatedly contrasting the dangers and oppression of the communist state with the opportunities and freedoms of capitalist America, as embodied in its vision of suburban domesticity. For example, a 1957 photo essay on refugees in flight from Hungary after the December 1956 uprising follows them from a nighttime escape in a snow storm to their arrival in the United States.[22] The narrative then features one refugee family, the Csillags, as they settle into an American home.

The photo essay connects the Csillag family to the nation-state through the figure of Vice President Richard Nixon, pictured visiting a New Jersey refugee center. The writer states that they have the opportunity "to be what Vice President Nixon called 'the kind of people who make good Americans.'" The photographs define the Csillags as good Americans and in turn envision "America," through pictures of them in their new home filled with consumer products. In depicting "good Americans," the photo essay encodes patriarchal values central to some of the most prevalent hegemonic narratives in American culture. The top half of one two-page spread shows Mrs. Csillag shopping, using a washing machine, and watching television with the children. The text emphasizes the novelty of these tasks for the Hungarians, but visual images of a woman performing gender-specific tasks define the Americanized home. Other photographs of the mother shopping and the father at work similarly visualize stereotypical gender roles.

Pictures of the Csillags' as they settle in the United States combine domesticity and consumption to represent what the American nation offers these refugees. This circumscribed vision ignores alternative national traditions such as cultural diversity or political and religious freedom. Instead, the Csillags join an imagined community of families that

[22] "They Pour In . . . And Family Shows Refugees Can Fit In," *Life*, 7 January 1957, 20–27.

defines social conventions in terms of gender divisions and political action in terms of consumer habits.

Life represented the middle class as the norm of American society and showed working-class people as different, outside that norm. News stories about labor conflicts accomplished this distinction by identifying the working class as a group while leaving the middle class unidentified except as "Americans." The story about the Csillags may appear to contradict this claim because they were clearly not middle class. The final photograph, for example, shows Mr. Csillag at work in a bakery. Nonetheless, the depiction of assimilated immigrants denies class structure and economic barriers. The writer quotes a wealthy uncle on the accessibility of the American Dream through men's hard work: "I told him he has the same chance I had if he'll apply himself and work like everyone else in this country." The reference to "everyone else" reproduces common myths about equality and democracy. It ignores the difficulties of language as well as race, gender, and sexual differences while encouraging a reading of the photograph as a visual reflection of this work ethic. Realistic strategies present a seamless narrative in which the Hungarians appear as a "classless" family just like other American families. This narrative of assimilation submerges ethnicity as the Csillags become the "kind of people who make good Americans" through the products they consume. Perhaps more than any other national story, this narrative of the successful immigrant enjoying the riches of capitalism embodies the American dream.

PUBLIC AND PRIVATE PATRIOTISM

Scholars of the postwar period identify radical changes in family life as a crucial development within American society. In explaining the baby boom, they frequently argue that the cohort of adults who grew up during the Depression and World War II compensated for earlier deprivations by turning to the pleasures of domesticity.[23] Elaine Tyler May demonstrates, however, that prosperity is only a partial explanation for the baby boom because postwar America cannot simply be read as a period of affluence and complacency. She observes that in the face of Cold War anxieties and fears, many Americans turned to the private space of their families for stability and security.[24] The powerful reach and scope of the media reinforced this process through recurrent depictions of the nuclear

[23] For a recent articulation of this position, see John Patrick Diggins, *The Proud Decades: America in War and Peace, 1941–1960* (New York: W. W. Norton, 1988), 181.

[24] Elaine Tyler May, *Homeward Bound: American Families in the Cold War Era* (New York: Basic Books, 1988).

family as a safe and ideal haven. Photo essays like the one on the Hungarian refugees turned to family pictures to mediate global conflicts; political and domestic interests merge in such a way as to challenge assumptions about cultural divisions between public and private spheres.

One of the most significant contributions of modern feminism has been to argue that personal relations are political because hierarchies of power pervade men's and women's personal lives. In this regard, the family has central importance as a site reproducing power relations. Another way to rethink the relationships between the public and private is to consider how the state has become increasingly involved in family life in the twentieth century.[25] Since the Depression, social welfare legislation has supported public intervention into the private sphere through bureaucratic regulations of American families.[26] Intervention, however, has taken different forms related to class and racial divisions in society. Housing subsidies for middle-class white families encouraged their migration to the newly built suburbs. Meanwhile, extensive welfare regulations have meant greater state intrusions into the lives of poor families; at the same time they have been denied the federal housing loans offered white suburbanites.

Just as state intrusions deny a truly private space, consolidation of national authority rests on aligning public spheres and gender, class, and race ideals. If women have traditionally been identified with family and home, then men's performances in the public spheres of education, business, politics, and sports typically form the basis for constructing masculine ideals such as aggressiveness and independence. During the Cold War, patriotic imagery likewise depended on ideals of white, male heroism to legitimize national authority. *Life*'s coverage of the Sputnik crisis exemplifies how news practices envisioned this public sphere. In 1957, the launch of the space satellite Sputnik set off a wave of anticommunist fears about Soviet technological superiority. *Life* devoted more than one-third of its 18 November 1957 issue to this topic without including a single picture of white women or people of color. The coverage shows the public world of science and warfare as comprised of white male scientists and politicians who have the capabilities to explain technology. Here the distinct separation of spheres proclaims this public world of white men as the patriotic one capable of protecting the nation against this visible threat.

---

[25] There is now extensive literature on this subject; see, Linda J. Nicholson, *Gender and History: The Limits of Social Theory in the Age of the Family* (New York: Columbia University Press, 1986); and Susan Moller Okin, *Justice, Gender, and the Family* (New York: Basic Books, 1989), esp. chap. 6.

[26] See Mintz and Kellogg, *Domestic Revolutions*, for a discussion of these historical developments.

In other coverage of the Cold War in *Life* magazine, however, the presence of the family indicates a reliance on both public and private spheres to define social worlds and political objectives. Focus on middle-class families may seem out of place in news reporting of these contentious global events until we realize that in the ideological battleground of Cold War politics, family pictures offered patriotic symbols of America. In the process, these domestic portraits contradictorily reified and undermined divisions between spheres as the magazine turned to family pictures to mediate political conflicts and tensions.

The most fearsome and potentially dangerous events of the postwar period coalesced around the ongoing struggles of the Cold War.[27] Anticommunist rhetoric pervaded *Life* as it pervaded other mass media. Notably, photo essays on Cold War politics frequently contained seemingly trivial or unrelated pictures of wives and children in private spaces. These images not only contrasted with men's public worlds to equate politics with masculinity, but they also offered visual evidence of American military and political objectives. A February 1954 news story on Secretary of State John Foster Dulles attending a foreign ministers' conference in West Berlin juxtaposes the formal posed portraits of male diplomats with the private world of Mrs. Dulles.[28] The large central photograph in this two-page spread displays the public world of diplomacy. Delegates from Great Britain, the United States, France, and the Soviet Union stare somberly at the camera during the opening session of the conference. Another photograph shows Dulles on his way home from the meeting in the back seat of a car reading with the aid of a special light. Signifying a transitional space between home and work, this photograph demonstrates men's ability to move between public and private spaces. In contrast, Mrs. Dulles appears only in the last picture waiting for her husband's arrival. She stands silhouetted, looking out a window that frames and thus contains her within the home. This last photograph tells the reader nothing about the foreign ministers' meeting, but it delineates the boundaries between public and private spheres by putting the woman "in her place."

Photo essays appear credible because they purport to depict realistically the events on which they are reporting. The picture of Mrs. Dulles appearing in the window of her apartment, for example, seems

[27] For recent discussions of Cold War historiography and current reassessments, see Thomas J. McCormick, *America's Half Century* (Baltimore: Johns Hopkins University Press, 1989); and Charles S. Maier, ed., *The Cold War in Europe* (New York: Markus Wiener, 1991).

[28] "Cars, Clocks and the Four-Power 'Klatsch': Foreign ministers dispose of some routine talk and get down to the business of hard diplomacy," *Life*, 8 February 1954, 32–33.

unstaged. The photograph's placement in the context of a Cold War news story, however, reinforces an ideal of the private sphere by identifying Mrs. Dulles exclusively as a wife in the physical space of her home while keeping vigil for her husband. In visualizing public and private spheres, this photo essay enacts a narrative ideal of America in which Dulles, the Cold Warrior who has just done battle with the Soviets (elaborated on in the text), returns home to his wife. In the context of other postwar images that equated domesticity with national identity, the juxtaposition of Cold War rhetoric with the photograph of Mrs. Dulles suggests that the secretary of state fights the communists in order to preserve the home. Similarly, at the 1959 opening of the American National Exhibition in Moscow, Nixon engaged in a verbal battle with Nikita Khrushchev. In this exchange, now referred to as the "kitchen debates," the vice president pointed to suburban homes filled with appliances and cared for by full-time housewives supported by their breadwinner husbands as evidence of the superiority of American democracy over Soviet communism.[29]

To infer, therefore, that news stories simply define public and private spheres limits our understanding of the role of the family in American political culture. As the Dulles photo essay demonstrates, public and private spaces interact to construct powerful ideological messages about patriotism and national identity. Similarly, *Life* published reports on the Korean War that depict military men fighting or planning strategy while pictures of wives, mothers, and girlfriends show them waiting at home. "Marines Come Home from the Front," from March 1951, opens with two photographs dividing the top half of the page.[30] One half features a photograph of a combat soldier running through a field under fire. The other half shows the same soldier arriving back in San Francisco. These pictures of the returning male hero contrast with photographs of women standing in groups looking out anxiously into unspecified distances. At the end of the story, a six-photograph sequence depicts a woman waiting for her fiancé's arrival. Each photograph shows a different emotion as the woman first expresses nervousness, then frustration, then recognition, and finally excitement. The photographs detach the woman from the specific context so that her gaze, like that of Mrs. Dulles, remains undirected. The culminating image of the sequence, in which the woman buries her head into her fiancé's chest, obscures her face, denying her subjectivity and turning her into a spectacle of desire for the returning male hero. This story reenacts the drama of heterosexual romance in

[29] For an excellent analysis of the gender and consumption ideologies in the kitchen debates, see May, *Homeward Bound*, 16–20.

[30] "Marines Come Home From the Front," *Life*, 19 March 1951, 35–39.

which women's identities are determined by men's actions. Moreover, the absence of any pictures of people of color or female military personnel in most photo essays of the Korean War promotes a nationalist rhetoric that relies on the division of spheres to present white men as protectors of their families and the nation. Male heroism, based on dominant gender and race conventions, connects moral obligations signified by domestic ideals of protection with the patriotic objectives of war.

Photographs of women and families that visualize a distinctive domestic world often depoliticize war by focusing on the concerns and obligations of the private sphere. In an April 1953 news story on the war, for instance, *Life* turns to the family to represent the political dilemma of prisoners of war in Korea, a problem defying diplomatic resolutions.[31] Instead of text discussing the experiences of the prisoners or diplomatic efforts to get them released, photographs tell the story of one prisoner's wife, Dot Beale, and her three-year-old son, Billy. The photo essay depends on visual conventions of both the gaze and organization of space to signify domesticity. The photographic layout depicts Beale's daily activities including pictures of her watching her son Billy saying his prayers, standing next to the new car she bought, and reading a newspaper while Billy gets a haircut. The final photograph on this page shows Beale with her head bowed in tears as she sits on the floor next to a trunk full of her husband's papers and memorabilia. Unlike other pictures of women's undirected stares, here the photographer, Robert Kelley, shows the reader the objects of her attention. Yet, Beale's gaze remains framed by male authority, for she reacts to her husband through his possessions which "act as memory traces of authority-in-absence."[32] Showing her desire through this memory trace secures heterosexual relations even though no man is present. Moreover, the pictures of Beale all depict a world of domestic spaces and activities, thus limiting her role in this political story about prisoners of war exclusively to the care of her child and house. This story foregrounds domesticity to explain American involvement in the Korean War; in this instance, the husband has gone to war to protect the family.

The layout contrasts the domestic space that contains Beale with masculine culture through pictures of men in public spaces. One photograph depicts Beale's three-year-old son watching a drill exercise by Navy cadets at The Citadel. Kelley positions the camera so that it looks down

[31] "The Communist Peace Dove . . . and the Wife of a Prisoner of War," *Life*, 13 April 1953, 27–31.

[32] Mary Ann Doane, *Desire to Desire: The Woman's Film of the 1940s* (Bloomington: Indiana University Press, 1987), 80, uses this phrase in her analysis of World War II films such as *Since You Went Away* (1944) in which photographs function as memory aids of absent husbands' male authority when they are away at war.

two rows of ramrod straight cadets to the background where Billy stands looking at them. Like the boys playing with toy missiles in the Atlas satellite article, this scene of Billy observing the rituals of his male elders visualizes the process of acquiring gender identity through learning proper masculine codes of behavior. Interestingly, the male gaze is made concrete here by the spatial conditions, for the photo essay removes the boy from domestic spaces and places him in the world of the military.

This family not only establishes the gender roles central to domestic ideology but also displaces politics by turning war into a personal crisis. In contrast to photo essays on battles, which visualize the need for a strong military, the Beale story diverts attention from politics to the private realm, thereby validating the war by never questioning its purpose. *Life*'s focus on the private interests of the family relies on commonsense concerns rarely analyzed for their ideological content. In this way, the family legitimizes government actions by framing political issues as background to the central, familiar drama of domesticity.

"The Kind of People Who Make Good Americans"

Life's visual attention to domesticity promoted a particular set of values integral to postwar national culture. In so doing, it tied this family form to the patriotic ideal of a unified and powerful nation. When *Life* turned to representative families to signify America, they were always white families, as in the photographs of the Hungarian Csillags. Other kinds of families appear in the magazine as representatives of social issues or political problems, but never as representatives of "America." *Life*'s representations of Latinos, Native Americans, and other social groups, typically depict them as poor, illiterate, and outside the norms of the nuclear family. In an August 1947 article on Puerto Rican immigration, for instance, the final photograph features a family in New York. Unlike the Oleksiaks comfortably seated in their living room, however, this picture visualizes the immigrants' status as outsiders by showing an unnamed extended family living in poor cramped conditions.[33] The magazine did report on civil rights activities, usually from a sympathetic perspective based on a liberal rhetoric of equal rights. News coverage included features on African-American families; they legitimize African-American claims through symbols familiar to its readers. Yet this exclusive representation of African Americans in articles on civil rights or urban problems precludes their inclusion in the imagined community of the nation. Certainly, *Life* was not the first to connect an ideal of America to a con-

---

[33] "Puerto Rican Migrants Jam New York," *Life*, 25 August 1947, 25–29.

cept of whiteness. In a society in which racial divisions determine privilege and oppression, all Americans are marked by race; to be white is to belong to a social category as much as any other ethnic and racial groups. Throughout the nineteenth and twentieth centuries, coalitions of otherwise antagonistic interests have formed around whiteness as a unifying symbol against people of color.[34] Yet, whiteness is neither a unified nor stable category but one whose meanings change historically. The magazine's postwar narrative of "America" depended on pictures of white families that visually connected racial privilege to national identity.

The absence of gays and lesbians further reveals how news discourses naturalized the white, middle-class family as the social norm. Homosexuality was beyond the representational limits of the magazine for most of the period. Postwar persecution of homosexuality and the homophobic currents in anticommunist rhetoric are well documented.[35] Interestingly, in *Life*, the denial of sexual difference, rather than an attempt to condemn it, was most prominent.[36] Along with this denial, homophobic rhetoric permeated the magazine, as did the heterosexual imperative that shaped its representation of social life. The general invisibility of different social and racial groups clearly shaped the news discourse to produce an extremely limited portrait of "the kind of people who make good Americans." This is crucial because, through the denial or invisibility of hierarchical relations of difference, patriotic rhetoric depended on representations that make this particular family form appear natural and transhistorical.

Life's narrative about consensus America did not merely reflect the trends of the baby-boom or middle-class affluence; instead, *Life* actively constructed meanings for its readers. This has significance for a postwar American society that was more heterogeneous than is typically imagined by stereotypes of postwar suburbanites. A mixed group including

[34] David Roediger, *The Wages of Whiteness: Race and the Making of the American Working Class* (London: Verso, 1991), and Alexander Saxton, *The Rise and Fall of the White Republic: Class Politics and Mass Culture in Nineteenth-Century America* (London: Verso, 1990), offer two excellent studies of coalition building around whiteness in the nineteenth century.

[35] For discussions of the repressive measures taken against gays and lesbians during the Cold War, see, e.g., Lillian Faderman, *Odd Girls and Twilight Lovers: A History of Lesbian Life in Twentieth-Century America* (New York: Penguin, 1991), chap. 6; May, *Homeward Bound*, chap. 4; and John d'Emilio and Estelle B. Freedman, *Intimate Matters: A History of Sexuality in America* (New York: Harper & Row, 1988), 292–93.

[36] See Lee Edelman, "Tearooms and Sympathy, or, The Epistemology of the Water Closet," in *Nationalisms and Sexualities*, ed. Andrew Parker, Mary Russo, Doris Sommer, and Patricia Yaeger (New York: Routledge, 1992), 263–84, for an excellent discussion of Cold War attacks on homosexuality and the role of the media in promoting virulent homophobia. He examines *Life*'s first photo essay on gays and lesbians, "Homosexuality in America," which appeared on 26 June 1964, 66–80.

returning GIs, second-generation immigrants and working-class people moved into suburban developments.[37] While the majority of *Life*'s readers were middle-class professionals, its audience included a broad spectrum of readers who cannot be reduced simplistically to singular identities. Letters to the editor indicate a degree of diversity among the magazine's readership. For instance, a woman responding to a news article on a strike at a Detroit GM plant in 1946 identified with the striker by explaining that her husband was also on strike and therefore they could no longer afford her subscription.[38] Many in this heterogenous group may have felt insecure about their place in the American Dream. Even 1950s television demonstrated more social diversity than just middle-class family comedies, especially in early shows like *The Goldbergs*, *The Honeymooners*, and *Amos n' Andy*. What united these shows, however, was a capitalist ethos that typically resolved problems of work, family, and politics through consumption.[39] Similarly, *Life*'s news reports worked to convince its readers just then moving into the suburbs that they too belonged to "America," an upwardly mobile and consumer-oriented America.

Readers saw in *Life* an optimistic vision of American society that, they were told, reflected their lives as homeowners. *Life*'s photo essays encouraged viewers to make connections between a single-family form and national interests through identification with signs of domesticity.[40] Stories about individual families urged them to relate emotionally to the people in the news.[41] Readers frequently sent in pictures or stories that resembled the ones published in the magazine; this interaction fostered a climate that invited people to recognize the similarities. Seamless narratives present the working-class Hemekes, or even the Hungarian Csillags, as families just like other Americans. In this way, the photo essay hails the reader into the signifying spaces of national identity, a space severely circumscribed by the patriarchal and racist ideals of domesticity. Underlying the clear anti-communist message in the Csillag story, for instance, is a didacticism common to *Life* in both photographs and texts that demonstrate "good

[37] Jezer, *Dark Ages*, 192–93.

[38] "Letters to the Editor," *Life*, 11 February 1946, 4.

[39] George Lipsitz, "The Meaning of Memory: Family, Class and Ethnicity in Early Network Television," in *Time Passages: Collective Memory and American Popular Culture* (Minneapolis: University of Minnesota Press, 1990), 39–75.

[40] This reading of how photographs secure identification derives from Judith Williamson's study, *Decoding Advertisements: Ideology and Meaning in Advertisements* (London: Marion Boyars, 1978), 44–45. She argues that advertisements work by combining unrelated signifiers, like a product and an actress, an association that leaves the reader making the meaningful connections between the two. Thus, the advertisement draws the reader into the space of the signified so that the reader identifies with the message.

[41] Fiske, *Television Culture*, 169.

Americans." These immigrants are clearly not middle class. Rather, through a narrative about characters who embody the American success myth, the story about the Csillags depicts the aspirations of Americans. Readers are urged to identify with the emotional efforts and achievements of an imagined community of like-minded families that displaced class and ethnic differences. In part, *Life* was so effective in this regard because realistic photographs encourage a reading of images as transparent mirrors of social reality.

For *Life* magazine, the task of constructing a unified nation out of a diverse polity depended upon news presentations that advanced the twin ideologies of consumerism and domesticity, not just as goals of the nation-state but as the fulfillment of the democratic aspirations of the people in the nation. The family was a primary site through which *Life* hailed its audience as part of that unified nation. Nationality often coalesces around ethnic or racial identities. In the United States, however, nationalistic rhetoric relies on more abstract concepts of liberty, democracy, and citizenship. Family ideals and obligations mediate these abstract concepts and offer a source of identification because family is a site of emotional attachment and personal commitments. Representations of the nuclear family work so well because they blur commercialism with the seemingly voluntary ties of intimacy and affection. *Life*'s representations of postwar society combined pictures of domesticity with American political rhetoric of democracy to construct an imagined community of middle-class families as the American nation.

Chapter 11

DILEMMAS OF BESET NATIONHOOD: PATRIOTISM, THE FAMILY, AND ECONOMIC CHANGE IN THE 1970S AND 1980S

GEORGE LIPSITZ

D
URING THE 1990S, debates over immigration policies, the North American Free Trade Agreement, and the role of U.S. troops in overseas conflicts have once again raised anxieties about national identity in the United States. The 1991 Gulf War seemed to solidify a strong sense of collective national identity, but in its immediate aftermath the continuing globalization of the economy under the control of transnational corporations and the concomitant decline of the nation-state as a source of solutions for social and economic problems combined to raise new questions about the meaning of national identity.

Exploring the dynamics of nationalistic rhetoric and patriotic display during an era of economic and political internationalization can help us understand the interplay of political, psychological, and economic elements that have determined the contours of contemporary public discourse about nationalism, citizenship, and personal identity. Close study of the patriotic revival of the post–Vietnam era especially reveals organic links between discussions of the American defeat during the Vietnam War, deindustrialization, changes in gender roles, and the rise of an emphasis on acquisition, consumption, and display characteristic of the increasingly inegalitarian economy of the postindustrial era. Perhaps most important, close analysis of the interconnections among these events and practices enables us to see how "American patriotism" has functioned paradoxically as part of the project of transnational corporations to extend their power beyond the control of politics as expressed within the contours of any one nation-state.

In his brilliant analysis of the 1915 D. W. Griffith film, *The Birth of a Nation*, Michael Rogin demonstrates the persuasive power of scenarios depicting "the family in jeopardy" for the construction of nationalistic myths. By representing slave emancipation and the radical reforms of the Reconstruction Era as threats to the integrity and purity of the white family, Griffith's film fashioned a new narrative of national unity and obligation based upon connections between patriotism and patriarchal protection.[1]

The kind of patriotism articulated by neoconservative politics in the United States since the 1970s has successfully updated the formula advanced by Griffith in 1915. This patriotism was perhaps best exemplified during ceremonies in 1984 commemorating the fortieth anniversary of the World War II Normandy invasion when President Ronald Reagan read a letter written to him by the daughter of a veteran who had participated in the 1944 battle. A serious illness had made it impossible for the veteran to attend the anniversary ceremonies himself, but his daughter had promised that she would travel to Normandy in his place and attend the ceremonies, visit monuments, and place flowers on the graves of his friends who had been killed in combat. "I'll never forget," she promised him. "Dad, I'll always be proud." Her father died shortly before the anniversary, but she kept her word and sat in the audience at Omaha Beach as Reagan read her letter to a crowd of veterans and their families. In an image broadcast on network newscasts (and featured repeatedly in an advertisement for the president's reelection campaign that year), tears filled her eyes as the president read her words; his voice quivered with emotion.[2]

Media analyst Kathleen Hall Jamieson identifies the imagery encapsulated in that scene as emblematic of the key themes of the Reagan presidency. In a short, sentimental, and extremely cinematic moment, the president depicted military service as a matter of personal pride and private obligation.[3] The drama of a father's military service and a daughter's admiring gratitude reconciled genders and generations, even beyond the grave, through a narrative of patriarchal protection and filial obligation. It offered a kind of immortality to the family by connecting it to the ceremonies of the nation-state, and it served the state by locating and legitimating its demands for service and sacrifice within the private realm of family affections. In Reagan's rhetoric, the political purposes ostensibly served by the Normandy invasion—defeating fascism, defending democracy, and furthering freedom of speech, freedom of worship, freedom from fear, and freedom from hunger—are eclipsed by his enthusiasm for a story celebrating personal feelings and family ties.

Reagan's appeals to private interests as motivation and justification for patriotic political obligation had enormous appeal for viewers and

---

[1] Michael Rogin, *Ronald Reagan, The Movie: and Other Stories in Political Demonology* (Berkeley: University of California Press, 1987).

[2] Kathleen Hall Jamieson, *Eloquence in an Electronic Age* (New York: Oxford University Press, 1988), 162.

[3] Ibid., 163.

voters in the 1980s, but they also drew upon a long history that is outlined, in part, by many contributors to this volume. For example, Cecilia O'Leary delineates the ways in which public appeals to patriotism and nationalism in the late nineteenth century rewrote the history of the Civil War by focusing on battlefield heroism of soldiers on both sides to build national unity at the expense of recognizing the war as a crucial part of the struggle for black freedom. Andrew Neather shows how those who conceived of the state primarily as an instrument of national unity and power depicted the state in masculinist terms, in part, as a way of as suppressing egalitarian ideals. Finally, the essays by Kimberly Jensen, David Glassberg and J. Michael Moore, Robert Westbrook, and Lawrence Samuel underscore the importance of war to modern definitions of patriotism.

From the popularity during the Korean War of Lefty Frizzell's song, "Mom and Dad's Waltz," with its improbable rhyme "I'd do the chores and fight in wars for my momma and papa," to the government distribution of pin-up photos of Betty Grable to soldiers during World War II, to Senator Albert Beveridge's description of U.S. annexation of the Philippines in the 1890s as an "opportunity for all the glorious young manhood of the republic—the most virile, ambitious, impatient, militant manhood the world has ever seen," patriotism has often been constructed as a matter of fulfilling one's proper role as a family member and gendered subject.[4]

In his interesting and important work, Robert Westbrook argues that the appeal to private interests as motivation for public obligations stems from a fundamental contradiction within democratic liberalism as it has emerged in Western capitalist societies. Drawing upon the scholarship of liberal political theorist Michael Walzer, Westbrook explains that liberal states must present themselves as the defenders of private lives, liberty, and happiness. But precisely because they are set up to safeguard the individual, these states have no legitimate way to ask citizens to sacrifice themselves for the government. Lacking the ability to simply command allegiance as absolutist states do and unable to draw on the desire to defend an active public sphere that might emerge within a broad-based participatory democracy, in Westbrook's view liberal capitalist states

---

[4] Lefty Frizzell, "Mom and Dad's Waltz," Columbia Records 20837, appears in *Billboard* on 18 August 1951 and stays on the charts for twenty-nine weeks. Joel Whitburn, *Top Country Hits, 1944–1988* (Menominee, Wis.: Record Research, 1989), 107. Robert Westbrook, "'I Want A Girl Just Like the Girl That Married Harry James': American Women and the Problem of Political Obligation in World War II," *American Quarterly* 42 (1990): 587–614. Amy Kaplan, "Romancing the Empire: The Embodiment of American Masculinity in the Popular Historical Novel of the 1890s," *American Literary History* 2 (Fall 1990): 659.

must cultivate and appropriate private loyalties and attachments if they are to mobilize their citizens for war.[5]

Westbrook's analysis helps us understand some of the deep-seated emotional appeal and political capital tapped by Ronald Reagan's remarks at the Normandy commemoration. Like so much recent scholarly work, it helps us see the connection between the nation and the imagination.[6] Westbrook captures one aspect of the relationship between citizens and the liberal state quite cogently and convincingly: the state may borrow legitimacy and command obligation by insinuating itself into family and gender roles. But the state also creates those very family and gender roles in a myriad of ways. The state licenses marriages and legislates permissible sexual practices, regulates labor, commerce, and communication, and also allocates welfare benefits, housing subsidies, and tax deductions to favor some forms of family life over others. Just as the state uses gender roles and family obligations to compel behavior that serves its interests, powerful private interests also use the state to create, define, and defend gender roles and family forms consistent with their own goals.

In his speech at Omaha Beach, Ronald Reagan not only used the family to serve a certain definition of the state, but he also put the power of the state behind specific definitions of acceptable gender and family roles that have enormous ramifications for distributing power, wealth, and life chances among citizens. While clearly colonizing private hopes and fears in the service of the state, Reagan's framing of the Normandy observance also mobilized the affective power of the state to address anxieties in the 1980s about private life, gender roles, jobs, community, and consumption patterns during the president's first term in office.

Reagan's celebration of a daughter's fulfillment of her father's last wish relied on clearly defined gender roles that situate women as dutiful, grateful, and proud. By taking her father's place at the ceremony, the letter writer wins the approval of the president whose tears and quivering voice add another layer of paternal approval for her actions. The ceremony affirmed the enduring continuity of male heroism, female spectatorship, and national glory as the answer to anxieties about change, death, and decay. In the context of national politics in 1984, the Normandy observance celebrated gender roles and family forms consistent with Reagan's policies as president. It addressed anxieties about combat raised by Reagan's acceleration of the Cold War and by the deaths of U.S. service personnel in Lebanon and Grenada. It projected a sense of

[5] Robert Westbrook, "Private Interests and Public Obligations in World War II," in *The Power of Culture: Critical Essays in American History*, ed. Richard Wightman Fox and T. J. Jackson Lears (Chicago: University of Chicago Press, 1993), 195–222.

[6] Benedict Anderson, *Imagined Communities* (New York: Verso, 1983).

national purpose and continuity in an age of community disintegration engendered by deindustrialization, economic restructuring, and the evisceration of the welfare state. It offered spectacle without real sacrifice, a chance for audiences to recommit themselves to the nation without moving beyond personal emotions and private concerns. By fashioning a public spectacle out of private grief, it combined the excitement of action with the security of spectatorship. In a country increasingly committed to consumption and sensual gratification, it presented the nation-state as a source of spectacle, producing the most spectacular shows of all. As J. A. Hobson noted a century ago, "jingoism is merely the lust of the spectator."[7]

Ronald Reagan's success in establishing himself as both president of the United States and as what some critics have jokingly called "the most popular television character of all time," depended in no small measure upon this ability to project an aura of reverent patriotism and confident nationalism. Elected to the presidency in the wake of the Iranian hostage crisis and the U.S. national hockey team's victory over the Soviet Union's team in the 1980 Olympics, Reagan cultivated support for his policies and programs by making himself synonymous with beloved national symbols. By skillfully using mass spectacles like the ceremonies marking the Normandy invasion, the opening of the 1984 Olympics, and the centennial of the Statue of Liberty in 1986, the president guided his constituency into a passionate appreciation for displays of national power and pride.

Reagan's skills as a performer and politician notwithstanding, he was more the interpreter than the author of the "new patriotism." Revived nationalistic fervor and public displays of patriotic symbols predated his presidency, and they have permeated popular culture and politics even after his departure from office. Popular support for the Gulf War and for the invasion of Panama, the tumultuous parades provided for soldiers returning home from Operation Desert Storm (and retroactively for veterans of Vietnam and Korea as well), and the continuous production of films, television programs, and popular songs with nationalistic, militaristic, and heroic themes signal broad support for nationalistic public patriotic celebration and display.

For all of its apparent intensity and fervor, the "new patriotism" often seems strangely defensive, embattled, and insecure. Even after the collapse of the Soviet Union and the end of the Cold War, a desperate quality permeated the discourse and display of loyalty to the nation's symbols. Only in the rarest of cases did the "new patriotism" address the aspects of national identity that genuinely make the United States differ-

[7] Quoted in Kaplan, "Romancing the Empire," 677.

ent from other nations—the expressive freedoms of speech, press, assembly, and worship guaranteed by the Bill of Rights, the rule of law and system of checks and balances authorized in the Constitution, or the history of rectifying past mistakes exemplified by the abolitionist and civil rights movements. To the contrary, the covert activities carried on by Oliver North in the Reagan White House, press self-censorship about U.S. military actions in Grenada, Panama, and the Persian Gulf, and popular support for a constitutional amendment to prohibit flag burning, all indicate that (to borrow a phrase from singer and activist Michelle Shocked) many Americans are more upset by people who would "wrap themselves in the Constitution to trash the flag" than they are by those who would "wrap themselves in the flag in order to trash the Constitution." Long ago, Samuel Johnson called patriotism the "last refuge of a scoundrel," but scoundrels evidently had more patience in those days; in recent years refuge in patriotism has been the first resort of scoundrels of all sorts.

In place of a love for the historical rights and responsibilities of the nation, instead of creating community through inclusive and democratic measures, the "new patriotism" has emphasized public spectacles of power and private celebrations of success. It does not treat war as a regrettable last resort when all other means have failed, but rather as an important, frequent, and seemingly casual instrument of policy offering opportunities to display national purpose and resolve.

In several instances, spectacle has seemed to serve as an end in itself, all out of proportion to the events it purports to commemorate. For example, after the thirty-six-hour war in Grenada in 1983, 6,000 elite U.S. troops were awarded 8,700 combat medals for defeating the local police and a Cuban army construction crew. President Reagan announced that "our days of weakness are over. Our military forces are back on their feet and standing tall."[8]

When a group of antiwar Vietnam veterans picketed an appearance by actor Sylvester Stallone in Boston in 1985 because they thought his film *Rambo, First Blood: Part II* simplified issues and exploited the war for profit, a group of teenagers waiting to get Stallone's autograph jeered the veterans and pelted them with stones. The teenagers screamed that Stallone was the "real veteran," compared to the demonstrators.[9] Stallone actually spent the Vietnam War as a security guard in a girl's school in Switzerland, but like Pat Buchanan, Newt Gingrich, Dick Cheney,

[8] Francis X. Clines, "Military of U.S. 'Standing Tall,' Reagan Asserts," *New York Times*, 13 December 1983, 1.

[9] Kevin Bowen, "'Strange Hells': Hollywood in Search of America's Lost War," in *From Hanoi to Hollywood: The Vietnam War in American Film*, ed. Linda Dittmar and Gene Michaud (New Brunswick, N.J.: Rutgers University Press, 1991), 229.

David Stockman, and Rush Limbaugh—all of whom conveniently avoided military service themselves—Stallone established credentials as a "patriot" in the 1980s by retroactively embracing the Vietnam War and ridiculing those who had opposed it.

In direct contrast to previous periods of patriotic enthusiasm like World War II—when Americans justified military action by stressing mass mobilization in defense of common interests by armed forces firmly under civilian control—the revived patriotism of the last twenty-five years has often been focused on the actions of small groups of elite warriors.[10] In popular paramilitary magazines like *Soldier of Fortune*, in motion pictures ranging from *Red Dawn* to *Rambo* to *Missing in Action*, and in the actual covert operations directed from the White House by Oliver North and John Poindexter during the Reagan administration, elite warriors defying legal and political constraints to wage their own personal and political battles have presented themselves as the true patriots.[11]

Proponents of the "new patriotism" often cite their efforts as an attempt to address the unresolved legacy of the Vietnam War. In their view, antiwar protest during that conflict undermined the welfare of U.S. troops in the field, contributed to the U.S. defeat, and ushered in an era of military and political weakness in the 1970s. Moreover, they claim that Vietnam-era opposition to the war, the military, and the government in general, ushered in a broad series of cultural changes with devastating consequences for U.S. society. As William Adams notes, "in the iconography of Reaganism, Vietnam was the protean symbol of all that had gone wrong in American life. Much more than an isolated event or disaster of foreign policy, the war was, and still remains, the great metaphor in the neo-conservative lexicon for the 1960s, and thus for the rebellion, disorder, anti-Americanism, and flabbiness that era loosed among us."[12]

Thus, the new patriotism not only seeks to address the issues of war and peace, unity and division, loyalty and dissent left over from Vietnam, but it also contains a broader cultural project. While purporting to "put Vietnam behind us," it actually tries to go back to Vietnam, to retroactively fight the war all over again, but this time to not only win the war but also undo the cultural changes it is thought to have generated. Just as former National Endowment for the Humanities Director Lynne Cheney called for the replacement of social science textbooks stressing "vacuous concepts" like "the interdependence among people"

---

[10] James William Gibson, "The Return of Rambo: War and Culture in the Post-Vietnam Era," in *America at Century's End*, ed. Alan Wolfe (Berkeley: University of California Press, 1991), 389.

[11] Ibid., 390.

[12] William Adams, "Screen Wars: The Battle for Vietnam," *Dissent* 37 (Winter 1990); 65.

with textbooks filled with "the magic of myths, fables, and tales of heros," the new patriotic spectacles avoid examining the complex causes and consequences of U.S. involvement in Vietnam and instead celebrate the redeeming virtues of violent acts and heroic stories.[13]

These attempts at "putting Vietnam behind us" actually began in the 1970s, almost as soon as the war ended. In 1976, less than a year after the communist victory in Southeast Asia, President Ford sent an armed force to rescue thirty-eight U.S. merchant sailors aboard the cargo ship *Mayaguez*. The ship and crew had been seized by the Cambodian navy in the confusion of the Khmer Rouge's ascendence to power in that country, and the Cambodian government had actually released the *Mayaguez* crew before the U.S. attack began. Forty-one U.S. Marines died (and forty-nine were wounded) in an effort to free thirty-eight Americans who had already been let go. But Senator Barry Goldwater, among many others, hailed the raid as a boost to America's self-image. "It was wonderful," the senator argued, "it shows we've still got balls in this country."[14]

Later, Ronald Reagan boasted that the invasion of Grenada in 1983 and the bombing of Libya in 1985 proved that America "was back and standing tall," while George Bush contended that the U.S. invasion of Panama demonstrated the same point. In the mid to late 1980s, many cities including Chicago and New York held massive parades honoring Vietnam veterans—a decade after the conclusion of that war. On the eve of the Gulf War, Bush contrasted the forthcoming campaign with the Vietnam War where, he claimed, American forces fought with "one hand tied behind their backs," and at the war's conclusion he proudly announced that "we've licked the Vietnam syndrome."[15]

When massive public parades welcomed home the veterans of Operation Desert Storm from the Persian Gulf, "new patriots" spared no opportunity to draw parallels to previous wars. In an opinion piece in the

[13] See Lynne Cheney, "Report," in *On Campus* 7, no. 3 (November 1987), 2, as well as Lynne Cheney, "Report to the President, the Congress and the American People," *Chronicle of Higher Education,* 21 September 1988, A18–A19.

[14] It was reported that the *Mayaguez* carried only paper supplies for U.S. troops, but as a container ship its cargo could have included much more sensitive material for surveillance or combat, which may account for the vigorous government reaction to its capture. See Marilyn Young, *The Vietnam Wars, 1945–1990* (New York: Harper Collins, 1991), 301. See also Thomas J. McCormick, *America's Half Century: United States Foreign Policy in the Cold War* (Baltimore: Johns Hopkins University Press, 1989), 178–79.

[15] Anonymous, "A Force Reborn," *U.S. News and World Report,* 18 March 1991, 30. Harry G. Summers, Jr., "Putting Vietnam Syndrome to Rest success of Persian Gulf War Aftermath of War," *Los Angeles Times,* 2 March 1991, A6; E. J. Dionne, Jr., "Kicking the 'Vietnam Syndrome'" Americans Embrace Military Values, *Washington Post,* 4 March 1991, A1; Kevin P. Phillips, "The Vietnam Syndrome: Why is Bush hurting if there is no war?" *Los Angeles Times,* 25 November 1990, M1.

Los Angeles Times, a Vietnam-era veteran confessed his jealousy of the Desert Storm vets and their rousing homecoming receptions.[16] Korean War veterans from New York staged a parade on their own behalf two months after the end of the Persian Gulf War, contrasting the immediate gratitude shown to Desert Storm veterans with their own perceived neglect. "My personal feeling was, God, they got it fast," explained the executive director of the New York Korean Veterans Memorial Commission; he added, "Some guy came over to me and said is that the memorial for Desert Storm? I said, 'Do me a favor, walk the other way. We've waited 40 years. Desert Storm can wait a couple of months.'"[17]

Yet, no matter how many times they have been declared dead, the memories of Vietnam—and their enduring impact on U.S. society—have not gone away. In national collective memory, the Vietnam experience looms large, as it should. The deaths of more than fifty thousand Americans and more than two million Vietnamese, Laotians, and Cambodians, demand our attention, grief, and sorrow. In a guerilla war with no fixed fronts, savage punishing warfare took the lives of soldiers and civilians alike. U.S. forces detonated more explosives over Southeast Asia during those years than had been exploded by all nations in the entire previous history of aerial warfare. The devastation wrought by bombs, toxic poisons, napalm, fragmentation grenades, and bullets continues into succeeding generations in all nations affected by the conflict. Small wonder then, that an overwhelming majority of respondents to public opinion polls for more than twenty years have continued to affirm that they view U.S. participation in the war to have been fundamentally wrong, not just a tactical error.[18]

But the realities of mass destruction and death in Vietnam are not the realities addressed by the "new patriotism." There has been no serious confrontation with the real reasons for the U.S. defeat in Vietnam—the unpopularity and corruption of the South Vietnamese government, the claim on Vietnamese nationalism staked by the communists through their years of resistance against the French, the Japanese, and the United States, the pervasive support for the other side among the Vietnamese people that turned the conflict into an antipersonnel war, and our own government's systematic misrepresentation of the true nature of the conflict to the American people.[19] Despite all the subsequent celebrations of

---

[16] Robert McKelvey, "Watching Victory Parades, I confess some envy: Vietnam Vets Weren't Feted by Parades," *Los Angeles Times*, 16 June 1991, M1.

[17] James S. Barron, "A Korean War Parade, Decades Late," *New York Times*, 26 June 1991, B3.

[18] Young, *The Vietnam Wars*, 314.

[19] George C. Herring, *America's Longest War* (New York: Wiley, 1979), George Mc. Kain, *Intervention* (New York: Knopf, 1986), and Stanley Karnow, *Vietnam: A History*

uncritical militarism, unwavering nationalism, and unquestioning obedience to the state, the still-open wounds of Vietnam have not been
salved. But perhaps this is not a failure at all; perhaps evocations of Vietnam have not really been designed to address that conflict and its legacy,
as much as they have been intended to encourage Americans to view *all*
subsequent problems in U.S. society through the exclusive lens of the
Vietnam War.

This strategy not only prevents us from learning the lessons of Vietnam, but, even more seriously, it also prevents us from coming to grips
with quite real current crises—the devastating consequences of deindustrialization and economic restructuring, the demise of whole communities and their institutions, and the social and moral bankruptcy of a
market economy that promotes materialism, greed, and selfishness, that
makes every effort to assure the freedom and mobility of capital while
relegating human beings to ever more limited life chances and
opportunities.

Evocations of powerlessness, humiliation, and social disintegration
that the "new patriotism" ascribes to Vietnam in reality perfectly describe what has been happening within U.S. society ever since the war.
Since 1973, a combination of deindustrialization, economic restructuring, neoconservative politics, austerity economics, and the transformation of a market *economy* into a privatized market *society* where every
personal relation is permeated by commodity relations have brought revolutionary changes to American society. Stagnation of real wages,
automation-generated unemployment, the evisceration of the welfare
state, threats to intergenerational upward mobility, privatization of public resources, and polarization by class, race, and gender have all radically
altered the nature of individual and collective life in this country. At the
same time, the constant aggrandizement of property rights over human
rights has promoted an oppressive and unremitting greed, materialism,
and needy narcissism focused on acquiring consumer goods, personal
pleasure, and on immediate gratification.

These changes have created a society that deprives people of meaningful
participation in the decisions that most affect their lives. Our society no
longer offers enough jobs at respectable wages; it discourages work while
encouraging speculation, gambling, and profiteering. Entertainment
spectacles nurture voyeurism, sadism, and sensationalism, while stoking
envy, avarice, and resentment. Advertising messages colonize the most
intimate areas of desire and imagination for the purposes of capital accu-

---

(New York: Viking, 1983), present different perspectives on the war, but their cumulative
evidence reveals the untenable nature of any hypothesis blaming internal division in the
United States for the outcome of the war.

mulation, while the power of concentrated wealth pits communities against each other in an ever more desperate competition for declining resources and services. As capital becomes more and more mobile—rapidly circling the globe in search of profitable returns on investments—people become less and less mobile and less and less able to control the ordinary dimensions of their own lives.

In such a society, patriotic spectacles serve an important function. In the midst of agonizing changes, the imagined power and majesty of the nation-state compensates for the loss of individual and collective power. As we control our own lives less and less, we look increasingly to images outside ourselves for signs of the power and worth that we have lost. Both patriotism and patriarchy fill the voids in our own experience; to ease the anxieties of powerlessness, humiliation, and social disintegration, they offer us identification with the power of the state and larger-than-life heroes or at least authority figures as compensation for the power we have lost over our own lives.

Systematic disinvestment in American cities and manufacturing establishments has forced millions of people to suffer declines in earning and purchasing power, to lose control over the nature, purpose, and pace of their work, wreaking havoc in their lives as citizens and family members. Plant shutdowns have disrupted once-stable communities, truncated the possibility of intergenerational upward mobility, and made speculation, gambling, and fraud more valuable than work. Investments in plant and equipment by U.S. corporations declined from an average of 4 percent of the gross national product between 1966 and 1970 to 3.1 percent from 1971–1975 and 2.9 percent from 1976 to 1980.[20] Unemployment averaged more than 7 percent in the United States between 1975 and 1979, after having been 5.4 percent between 1970 and 1974 and only 3.8 percent between 1965 and 1969. Real median family income doubled between 1947 and 1973, but it fell 6 percent between 1973 and 1980.[21]

Despite massive spending on armaments and radical reductions in the tax obligations of corporations and wealthy individuals, capital continues its exodus to more profitable sites of exploitation in other parts of the globe. In the United States thirty-eight million people lost their jobs in the 1970s as a result of computer-generated automation, plant shutdowns, and cutbacks in municipal and state spending.[22]

At the same time, the emerging postindustrial economy generated new sales and service jobs with much lower wages, benefits, and oppor-

[20] Thomas Ferguson and Joel Rogers, *Right Turn: The Decline of the Democrats and the Future of American Politics* (New York: Hill and Wang, 1986), 79.

[21] Ibid., 79, 80.

[22] Katherine S. Newman, "Uncertain Seas: Cultural Turmoil and the Domestic Economy," in *America at Century's End*, ed. Wolfe, 116.

tunities for advancement than the jobs they replaced. Between 1979 and 1984 more than one-fifth of the newly created full-time jobs paid less than $7,000 per year (in 1984 dollars). For the entire decade, the lowest paying industries accounted for nearly 85 percent of new jobs. By 1987, 40 percent of the work force had no pension plans, and 20 percent of employees had no health insurance. Between 1979 and 1986 the real income of the wealthiest 1 percent of the population increased by 20 percent, while the real income of the poorest 40 percent of the population fell by more than 10 percent. Real discretionary income for the average worker by the early 1980s had fallen 18 percent since 1973. At the same time, housing costs doubled, and the costs of basic necessities increased by 100 percent.[23] Changes in tax codes in the 1980s further penalized working people by making them pay more in payroll taxes; but investment and property income became more valuable than wage income.[24]

By presenting national division during the Vietnam War as the root of the diminished sense of self and community experienced by many Americans during the past twenty years, the new patriotism deflects attention and anger away from capital, away from the disastrous consequences of neoconservative economics and politics. But it also makes a decidedly class-based appeal to resentments rooted in the ways that the working class unfairly shouldered the burdens of the war in Vietnam. The ground war in Vietnam was a working-class war: out of a potential pool of 27 million people eligible to serve in the military, only 2.5 million went to Vietnam, according to a recent study by Christian Appy. Of those who served, 80 percent came from poor or working-class backgrounds.[25] As one veteran complained, "Where were the sons of all the big shots who supported the war? Not in my platoon. Our guy's people were workers. . . . If the war was so important, why didn't our leaders put everyone's son in there, why only us?"[26]

The sons of the important people backing the war, like the sons of most of the important and unimportant people actively opposing it, did not serve in combat because of their class privileges. When protest demonstrations at home and insubordination, desertions, and low morale at the front made it politically dangerous to continue the war, President Nixon and other leaders chose to buy time for a "decent interval" allow-

[23] Ibid., 116, 117, 121. William H. Chafe, *The Unfinished Journey: America Since World War II* (New York: Oxford University Press, 1986), 449.

[24] See Michael I. Luger, "Federal Tax Incentives as Industrial and Urban Policy," in *Sunbelt/Snowbelt: Urban Development and Regional Restructuring*, ed. Larry Sawers and William K. Tabb (New York: Oxford University Press, 1984), 201–34.

[25] Christian G. Appy, *Working Class War: American Combat Soldiers and Vietnam* (Chapel Hill: University of North Carolina Press, 1993), 6.

[26] Ibid., 11.

ing them to withdraw "gracefully" by trying to turn resentment against the war into resentment against antiwar demonstrators. Richard Nixon realized that the public could be persuaded to hate antiwar demonstrators, especially college students, even more than they hated the war. Military leaders picked up on Nixon's cue, telling soldiers that antiwar demonstrators hated them, blamed them for the war, and actively aided and abetted the enemy. Of course, much of the antiwar movement made it easy for their enemies by all too often displaying elitist and anti–working-class attitudes and by failing to make meaningful alliances with the working-class public that opposed the war (according to public opinion polls) in even greater numbers than did college students.[27]

The new patriots are certainly correct when they charge that the American people have neglected the needs of returning Vietnam veterans, but they reveal more about their own agendas than about neglect of veterans when they cite the absence of homecoming parades as proof of this maltreatment. The miserable state of Veterans Administration's hospitals, the scarcity of education and job-training opportunities for veterans, and corporate/government refusals to acknowledge or address the consequences to veterans of defoliants like Agent Orange have all demonstrated far more neglect of Vietnam-era veterans than has the absence of parades. Ironically the dishonorable treatment afforded Vietnam veterans has been in no small measure a direct consequence of the neoconservative attack on the welfare state that provided extensive social services for previous generations of veterans. Thus, by directing veteran resentment toward antiwar protestors, neoconservatives hide from the consequences of their own policies, from what they have done to social welfare programs, to the social wage in the United States, and to the ability of government to respond to the needs of its citizens.

In addition, the neoconservative new patriots have been extremely selective about which veterans should be given attention. When antiwar veterans attempted to tell their story at the 1971 Winter Soldier hearings or when they flung their medals onto the steps outside the halls of Congress to protest the continuation of the war that same year, few individuals and groups angry about the lack of parades did anything to attend to

[27] There were, of course, important exceptions to this pattern. Antiwar activists supported coffee houses, draft counseling centers, and antiwar newspapers at dozens of military bases. Many local peace coalitions united trade unionists, intellectuals, suburban liberals, students, and poor people, and especially after 1970 the antiwar counterculture had a substantial working-class presence. But almost nowhere did any of this produce a class-based critique of why the war was fought and who had to fight it. Of course, the antiwar movement emerged as an ad hoc coalition based on college campuses with few other institutional resources. McCarthyism's destruction of the Old Left and the timidity of social democrats left the work of radicalism to politically inexperienced children of the middle class.

the concerns of these veterans. The dangers faced and overcome in Vietnam by Chicano, Black, Native American, and Asian American soldiers have not persuaded Anglo Americans to root out racism from the body politic and recognize the ways in which "American" unity is threatened by the differential distribution of power, wealth, and life chances across racial lines. Most important, by ignoring the ways in which social class determined who went to Vietnam, the new patriots evade the degree to which their station in life has been diminished because they were workers.

The mostly working-class veterans of the Vietnam War returned to a country in the throes of deindustrialization. They participated in the wave of wildcat strikes resisting speed-up and automation in U.S. factories during the 1960s and 1970s. They played prominent roles in the United Mine Workers strikes and demonstrations protesting "black lung" and in the Amalgamated Clothing Workers campaigns against "brown lung" and other industrially caused health hazards. They have been visible among the ranks of the unemployed and the homeless. But their status as workers victimized by neoconservative politics and economics in the 1970s and 1980s is far less useful to the interests of the new patriots than their roles as marchers in parades and as symbols of unrewarded male heroism.

The "official story" disseminated by new patriots and the news media about Vietnam veterans has obscured the connection between deindustrialization and the national welfare since the 1970s, but many representations of Vietnam veterans in popular culture have brought this repressed reality to the surface. Billy Joel's 1982 popular song "Allentown" and Bruce Springsteen's 1984 hit "Born in the U.S.A." both connect the factory shutdowns of the post-1973 period to the unresolved anger of Vietnam veterans at broken promises and frustrated hopes.[28] Joel's "Goodnight Saigon" has become the basis for the climactic moment at his live concert performances as audience members wave lighted matches and cigarette lighters as they sing the son's anthemic verse "We said we would all go down together." Similarly, Bobbie Ann Mason's novel *In Country* presents a Kentucky town filled with fast-food restaurants and advertising images but lacking meaningful jobs for its disillusioned Vietnam veterans.[29] Unfortunately, even these progressive representations focus solely on U.S. veterans, obscuring completely the people of South-

---

[28] Billy Joel, "Allentown," Columbia Records 03413, entered *Billboard* charts on 27 November 1982, reached as high as number 17 and remained on the charts for twenty-two weeks. See Whitburn, *Top Pop Singles*, 266. Bruce Springsteen, "Born in the U.S.A.," Columbia Records 04680, entered *Billboard* charts 10 November 1984, reached number 9 and remained on the charts seventeen weeks. Whitburn, *Top Pop Singles*, 475.

[29] Bobbie Ann Mason, *In Country* (New York: Perennial Library, 1985).

east Asia and the war's dire consequences for them. These popular culture representations presume that the psychic damage done to some Americans by the experience of defeat in Southeast Asia outweighs the brutal nightmare visited upon Vietnam, Cambodia, and Laos by the war itself. Yet, despite their callousness toward the real victims of the Vietnam War, these representations nonetheless call attention to an important unspoken dimension of the war—its class character.

Hollywood films about the Vietnam War have repeatedly drawn on the class character of the war for dramatic tension and narrative coherence. In contrast to films about previous wars where the experience of combat often leveled social distinctions and built powerful alliances among dissimilar soldiers, Vietnam War films seethe with what one critic found to be "a steady drone of class resentment."[30] Perhaps expressions of class resentment only "drone" for those who feel they are being resented. For working-class audiences in the 1970s and 1980s, no less than for working-class soldiers in the 1960s and 1970s, expressions of class anger might be long overdue. In these films, draftees and enlisted men hate their officers, soldiers hate college students, and corruption almost always percolates down from the top.[31] For example, the Ukrainian-American workers portrayed in *The Deer Hunter* fail in their efforts to protect themselves from surprises either in the dying social world of their hometown in the industrial steel-making city of Clairton, Pennsylvania, or in the equally unpredictable and rapidly disintegrating social world they enter in Vietnam.[32] The combat soldiers in *Hamburger Hill* constantly compare themselves to college students who have escaped military service, while Rambo reserves his greatest rage for the automated technology in his own supervisor's operations headquarters. Lone wolf commandos in the *Rambo* films, *Missing in Action*, and other action/ adventure stories assume underdog status by reversing roles from the war itself: this time the Americans fight as guerrillas with primitive weapons against foes with vastly superior arms and technology.[33]

Thus, in spectacles on screen and off, the new patriotism attempts to channel working-class solidarity into identification with the nation-state and the military. Opposing the government and its policies is seen as opposing working-class soldiers in the field. But the class solidarity pro-

---

[30] Adams, "Screen Wars," 71.

[31] Ibid., 71–72.

[32] Frank Burke, "Reading Michael Cimino's *The Deer Hunter*: Interpretation as Melting Pot," *Film and Literature Quarterly* 20, no. 3 (1992): 252–53.

[33] Adams, "Screen Wars," 72. Gaylan Studlar and David Dresser, "Never Having to Say You're Sorry: Rambo's Rewriting of the Vietnam War," in *From Hanoi to Hollywood*, ed. Dittmar and Michaud, 111, 108. Stephen Prince, *Vision of Empire: Political Imagery in Contemporary American Film* (New York: Praeger, 1992), 66, 69.

claimed in political and entertainment narratives rarely includes both genders. If there is a crisis for the working class in the Vietnam of the new patriotism, it is a distinctly gendered crisis for working class men only. They often become surrogates for all men, as representations of Vietnam in politics and entertainment alike use the war as a site for demonstrating and analyzing a perceived crisis of masculinity centered on an alleged erosion of male prestige and power.

In a compelling and quite brilliant analysis, Lynda Boose notes the narcissistic and homoerotic qualities of contemporary warrior films. Rather than citizen soldiers, the characters played by Sylvester Stallone and Chuck Norris more closely resemble World Wrestling Federation performers playing out a little boy's fantasy of bodily power and domination over other men. *Iron Eagle*, *Top Gun*, and *An Officer and a Gentleman* all revolve around anxious sons and absent fathers.[34] For Boose, these representations reflect an arrested development, "a generation stuck in its own boyhood" attempting to recover the father.[35] She notes that in *The Deer Hunter* there are no fathers, only brothers. In that film and many others like it, the idealized nuclear family dies in Vietnam, providing audiences with an opportunity to mourn the loss of patriarchal power and privilege produced by not only defeat in Vietnam but also deindustrialization at home with its decline in real wages for white male breadwinners and the attendant irreversible entry of women into the wage-earning work force. But rather than presenting either the war or deindustrialization as political issues, these films and the national political narrative they support present public issues as completely personal. In Boose's apt summary: "the political is overwhelmed by the personal and adulthood by regressive desire."[36] Yet, in our society, regressive desire and a preoccupation with the personal are intensely political phenomena: they nurture a combination of desire and fear necessary to our subordination as submissive citizens and craving consumers. The binary oppositions between males and females reinforced by the Vietnam War narrative of the new patriotism serve broader ends as nodes in a network of repression and control.

As Boose, Susan Jeffords, Philip Slater, and others have argued, the glorification of the military in our society has served as a key strategy for forces interested in airing anxieties about feminist and gay/lesbian challenges to traditional gender roles.[37] During the 1980s the core of Ronald

[34] Lynda Boose, "Techno-Muscularity and the 'Boy Eternal': From the Quagmire to the Gulf," *The Cultures of United States Imperialism*, ed. Amy Kaplan and Donald Pease (Durham: Duke University Press, 1994), 588–89, 602.

[35] Ibid., 24.

[36] Ibid., 600.

[37] Susan Jeffords, *The Remasculinization of America: Gender and the Vietnam War* (Bloom-

Reagan's supporters from the extreme Right viewed patriotism as intimately connected to restorating heterosexual male authority. Religious writer Edward Louis Cole complained that in America "John Wayne has given way to Alan Alda, strength to softness. America once had men," he asserts, but now it has "pussyfooting pipsqueaks."[38] Similarly, Reverend Tim LaHaye argued that "it has never been so difficult to be a man" because so many women are working outside the home for pay. In Reverend LaHaye's opinion, women who worked outside the home gained "a feeling of independence and self-sufficiency which God did not intend a married woman to have."[39] Yet the solutions offered by the New Christian Right, like the solutions offered by paramilitary culture or consumer society, do not prescribe adult interactions between men and women to determine mutually acceptable gender definitions. Rather, they offer men juvenile fantasies of omnipotence through the unleashing of childish desire for control over others.

War films and other narratives of military life provide ideal sites for representating and validating of aggressive and regressive male behavior. Psychoanalyst Chaim Shatan observes that basic training can strip recruits of their identities and discourage their participation in broader communities on or off base. All power is vested in the drill instructors and training leaders. In Shatan's view, "the dissolution of identity is not community, though it can relieve loneliness. Its success is due to the recruit's ability to regress to an earlier stage of development, in which he is again an unseparated appendage of the domain ruled over by the Giant and Giantess, the DI's of the nursery."[40] Rather than teaching independence and responsibility, the social relations and subjectivities glorified by the new patriotism actually fuse the needy narcissism of consumer desire with the nascent authoritarianism of the warfare state.

Shatan's formulation helps us distinguish between what our culture often describes as an oedipalized journey into adulthood characterized by deferred gratification and independence from others and what we might call a preoedipal desire to derive sustenance from pleasurable emotional and sensual connection to others. The glorification of masculine authority and conflation of patriotism with patriarchy in the military might make us think of combat films as exemplars of what our culture often

---

ington: Indiana University Press, 1989); Philip Slater, *A Dream Deferred: America's Discontent and the Search for a New Democratic Ideal* (Boston: Beacon, 1991).

[38] Quoted in Michael Lienesch, *Redeeming America: Piety & Politics in the New Christian Right* (Chapel Hill: University of North Carolina, 1993), 60.

[39] Quoted in ibid., 54, 58.

[40] Chaim F. Shatan, "'Happiness is A Warm Gun,' Militarized Mourning and Ceremonial Vengeance: Toward a Psychological Theory of Combat and Manhood in America," *Vietnam Generation 1*, no. 3–4 (Summer–Fall 1989): 147.

calls an oedipalized identity—of a coming into adulthood through sacrifices that make individuals distinct from others and responsible for their actions. If this were true, they would help teach discipline, restraint, and responsibility. But the identities encouraged in the military by identification with the group, denials of difference, unquestioning obedience to cruel authorities, and bonding through hatred, anger, and violence really better conform to what our culture calls preoedipal traits—dissolution of the self into a more powerful entity, unleashing normally repressed behaviors and emotions, and fueling hatred for the subjectivities and desires of other people. Rather than teaching responsibility, the new patriotism stages sadomasochistic spectacles that use revenge motifs to justify unleashing the most primitive and unrestrained brutality by imitating the enemies we claim to fear. But then, to manage the anxieties generated by this regression, the new patriots have to affirm all that much more intensely in the abstract their fidelity to leaders, causes, and entities outside themselves.

The volatile dynamics of militaristic spectacles have a self-perpetuating character. Oedipal and preoedipal identities mutually constitute one another. Regression to primitive desires generates an anxious longing for identification with powerful patriarchal authority; systematic submission to superior authority gives rise to anxious feelings of loneliness and isolation, which in turn fuels the desire for even more connection to powerful authorities. In *The Origins of Totalitarianism*, Hannah Arendt argues that people in putatively democratic societies become ready for totalitarianism when loneliness becomes a routine feature of everyday existence. The combined effects of deindustrialization, economic restructuring, and the oppressive materialism of a market society where things have more value than people all feed a sense of isolation and loneliness. Privatization prevents people from active engagement in civic society, from participating in processes that might lead to a healthy sense of self. Militarism becomes one of the few spaces in such a society where a shared sense of purpose, connection to others, and unselfish motivation have a legitimate place.

The denial of the political in combat films and fiction no less than in public patriotic rhetoric connects the new patriotism to the needy narcissism of consumer desire as the unifying national narrative. The ascendancy of greed and materialism in U.S. society during the 1980s has been widely acknowledged, but the distinctive form this assumed in an age of deindustrialization has attracted less attention and analysis. Changes in investment policies and tax codes during the Reagan years accelerated trends favoring consumption over production, leveraged buyouts over productive investments, short-term profits over long term investment, and love of gain over collective obligations and responsibilities. People at the highest income levels embraced behaviors previously associated with the poor; the wealthy seek short-term sensations and pleasures rather than pursue disciplined long-range investments, programs, or policies. At the macro-social level, these policies have produced paralyzing levels of public and private debt, squandered the social capital and industrial infrastructure of the nation, and generated long-term costs to individuals and their environments while imposing burdens on future generations. On the micro-social level, they have encouraged the very attitudes displayed most often in adolescent warrior fantasies—regressive desire, narcissistic grandiosity, and anxieties about identity that lead to craving for sensations, distractions, and displays of power offering compensation for the diminished sense of self and connection to others engendered by deindustrialization's pernicious effects.

In his role as a performer in commercials for the General Electric company in the 1950s no less than as president of the United States, Ronald Reagan communicated the language of consumer desire with extraordinary skill. He offered more for less, promising that tax cuts would not reduce government revenues because they would stimulate massive economic growth. He claimed that ending government regulation would free the private sector to find market-based solutions to social problems. He told Americans that they could have it all, as in his 1986 State of the Union Speech when he announced, "In this land of dreams fulfilled where greater dreams may be imagined, nothing is impossible, no victory is beyond our reach, no glory will ever be too great. So now, it's up to us, all of us, to prepare America for that day when our work will pale before the greatness of America's champions in the 21st century."[41] When this philosophy led the government to accumulate a larger national debt during Reagan's terms in office than had been incurred by all previous presidents combined, when it produced massive unemployment, homelessness, and health hazards, and when it created the preconditions for massive fraud in the savings and loan industry leading to enormous debts that executives from deregulated industries then passed on to consumers, Reagan continued to insist that his policies were working. In their own way they were, not in the sense of solving problems and making the nation stronger, but rather they were working to transform the political system into a branch of the entertainment industry, into an entity seeking scapegoats for social problems rather than solutions to them.

Of course, the severe economic decline experienced by most people in the United States during the 1980s should not be attributed solely to Reagan; it predated and postdated his terms in office. The stagnation of real wages owed much to long-term imbalances in the U.S. economy

---

[41] Jamieson, *Eloquence*, 161.

between the needs of capital and the needs of the majority of the population. But the political culture that Reagan nurtured in the wake of this devastation perfectly complemented the escape from responsibility promoted by a consumer commodity society fixated on instant gratification. Reagan basked in the glow of the "glory" he attained by invading Grenada, bombing Libya, and by identifying himself with the overwhelming U.S. "victory" at the 1984 Olympics (gained largely because the Soviet Union and other Warsaw Pact nations did not participate). By timing the Libya bombing for maximum exposure on network prime time, he set the stage for the voyeurism of the Gulf War, where "news reports" often appeared indistinguishable from video games or commercials by weapons manufacturers. In return for all the broken promises and devastated lives of his era, Reagan left the nation with a better developed taste for spectatorship of the kind described long ago by J. A. Hobson— gloating "over the perils, pains, and slaughter of fellowmen [sic] whom he does not know, but whose destruction he desires in a blind and artificially stimulated passion of hatred and revenge."[42]

The new patriotism arises from deeply felt contradictions in U.S. society. It arbitrates anxieties about changes in gender roles, jobs, communities, and collective identity brought on by deindustrialization and economic restructuring. Narratives of national honor take on increased importance as the practices of transnational corporations make the nation-state increasingly powerless to advance the interests of its citizens. Private anxieties about isolation, loneliness, and mortality fuel public spectacles of patriotic identification by promising purposeful and unselfish connection to collective and enduring institutions. The new patriotism serves vital purposes for neoconservative economics and politics; it provides psychic reparations for the damage done to individuals and groups by the operation of market principles while at the same time promoting narcissistic desires for pleasure and power that set the stage for ever more majestic public spectacles and demonstrations of military might.

While providing logical responses to the unbearable diminution of collective and individual power in an age of deindustrialization, the new patriotism is more an evasion of collective problems and responsibilities than a solution to them. It interferes with serious public discussion of the world we have lost and the one we are building through deindustrialization and economic restructuring. It promotes male violence and female subordination, builds authoritarian identification with outside authorities at the expense of personal integrity and responsibility, and stokes the flames of grandiose desires that can only be sated by domination over others.

Perhaps most ominously, the new patriotism builds possessive identi-

---

[42] Kaplan, "Romancing the Empire," 679.

fication with warfare and violence as solutions to personal and political problems. Although aggression is often portrayed as "natural" in our culture, the elaborate nature of patriotic ceremonies and rituals may indicate precisely the opposite—that aggression needs to be nurtured and cultivated. It is not easy for humans to kill other humans; one study of the World War II Normandy invasion showed that even among specially trained combat troops, large numbers of the soldiers failed to fire their weapons once the battle started. Nightmares, guilt, and other signs of postcombat stress have plagued veterans of all wars, not just Vietnam. The attention devoted to ceremonial commemoration of past wars may be not so much evidence about how easy it is for people to go to war, but rather how much persuasion, rationalization, and diversion are required to make warfare acceptable. Unfortunately, elaborate public appeals to honor the memory of slain soldiers from the past only create the preconditions for new generations of corpses whose sacrifices will have to be justified and repeated by succeeding generations. Shatan explains that "ceremonial vengeance" perpetuates rather than resolves the legacy of past wars because it requires repression of the genuine agonies caused by combat. In his eloquent formulation, "unshed tears shed blood." Grief and mourning become transformed into scapegoating and fantasies of revenge. Unresolved grief and guilt leads us to inflict our wounds on others; reincarnating yesterday's dead as today's warriors "promises collective rebirth to all who have died for the Corps," but at the price of creating more martyrs whose deaths must be avenged in the future.[43]

Ceremonial celebrations of militarism perpetuate dangerous illusions about warfare. They hide the ambiguous outcome of every conflict, the limited utility of force in resolving real conflicts of interest and ideology, and the ways in which the resolution of every war contains the seeds of the next one. But even beyond any practical shortcomings of war as a way of resolving conflicts lies its atrocious immorality. Our nation is not the first, and it will not be the last, to believe that participating in the systematic destruction of the lives of other humans will not fundamentally compromise our morality and our humanity. But the weight of the historical record is inescapable. Author and Vietnam War veteran Tim O'Brien counsels that moral lessons cannot be learned from warfare. He tells us that a war story "does not instruct, nor encourage virtue, nor suggest models of proper human behavior." O'Brien asks us to cease believing in the morality of war; he advises us that any time we feel uplifted or righteous after reading a war story that we have been made the victim of "a very old and terrible lie."[44]

---

[43] Shatan, "Happiness," 140–41.
[44] Quoted in Young, *The Vietnam Wars*, 329.

Of course, this is not to say that nothing of value is ever salvaged from war. Certainly many people who have actually seen combat become ferociously opposed to war precisely because they have seen the waste and destructiveness of warfare first hand. In addition, as George Mariscal points out in his important work on progress, for communities of color in the United States, the Vietnam War (like previous conflicts) sharpened contradictions and accelerated demands for civil rights from soldiers who saw themselves asked to fight and possibly die overseas for freedoms that they did not enjoy at home.[45] At the level of soldiers in the field, lessons about mutuality and interdependence often work to break down prejudice and parochialism. For these individuals and those they influence, warfare holds meanings that counteract the stories of heroism and glory that dominate combat narratives.

The myth that attributes U.S. social and economic decline to division over the Vietnam War lets transnational capital off the hook. It prevents us from addressing the actual causes and awful consequences of economic stagnation and social disintegration. As diversion and distraction, as escape and evasion, war works—at least for a little while. But it sows the seeds of its own disillusionment by pretending that we can win back on the battlefield the sense of shared social purpose that we are destroying everyday through deindustrialization, economic restructuring, and neoconservative politics.

[45] George Mariscal, "'Our Kids Don't Have Blue Eyes, but They Go Overseas to Die': Chicanos in Vietnam" (paper read at the "America and Vietnam: From War to Peace" conference, University of Notre Dame, South Bend, Indiana, 4 December 1993).

Chapter 12

EXALTING "U.S.NESS": PATRIOTIC RITUALS OF THE DAUGHTERS OF THE AMERICAN REVOLUTION

BARBARA TRUESDELL

IN MONTHLY chapter meetings across the country, the women of the Daughters of the American Revolution (DAR) gather in living rooms, church basements, or restaurants to socialize, conduct the business of their organization, and reaffirm their patriotism through the practice of devotional rituals. Through their rituals, the DAR dramatizes the conservative vision of the nation they celebrate and the nature of the patriotism they practice. In this chapter I analyze these rituals and their performance: their emphasis on the glory and power of the nation-state; their iconization of military men and traditional women; and their philosophy of service, sacrifice, and negotiation of personal ambition within the confines of duty to larger loyalties.

When I asked Jan, a member of the DAR, to define patriotism, she considered a long moment before replying, "Patriotism . . . is like faith."[1] Jan's brief definition has important implications for revealing the experience of American patriotism expressed in the DAR's rituals. If we begin with Jan's premise that patriotism is like faith, then patriotism's manifestations and functions—including its institutional homes such as the DAR—may be illuminated by drawing upon an interpretive model that recognizes the religious quality of civic devotion and action. From its inception, the DAR has utilized the aura of legitimacy and authority derived from metaphorically invoking a religious model for civic loyalty.

Jean-Jacques Rousseau coined the term "civil religion" to denote a nonsectarian, state-supported religion that could consecrate the social life and political institutions of a nation-state.[2] In this concept, he recognized religion's capacity to forge a collective identity and direct the values and

[1] Interview with Jan B. [pseud.], interview by author, tape recording, Bloomington, Ind., 11 April 1991.

[2] Jean-Jacques Rousseau, *The Social Contract and Discourses*, trans. G.D.H. Cole (London: Dent & Sons, 1913).

actions of its adherents. Rousseau's vision carries within it two elements that have since remained consistent in all the definitions of civil religion: an affective dimension evokes emotional attachment to integrate individuals into a feeling community; and a rhetorical dimension directs the individual and the community into action in the service of the state. In the paradigm of civil religion, we find both the emotional dimension of patriotism as "love of country" and patriotism's role as a charter for social action.

Clifford Geertz writes: "Culture patterns—religious, philosophical, aesthetic, scientific, ideological—are 'programs'; they provide a template or blueprint for the organization of social and psychological processes, much as genetic systems provide a template for the organization of organic processes."[3] Civil religion is a potent symbolic model that offers the DAR a venue for exploring and legitimating the collective power of the nation-state, a paradigm to meaningfully interpret social forms and institutions in civil society. In this study, the paradigm places the symbolic action of the DAR's rituals into a coherent system to examine the DAR's relationship to the dominant culture, the organization's appeal for its female members, and the negotiation of power the DAR mediates between individual members and the nation-state.

Symbols of civil religious belief and ritual are drawn from American culture and history. The resources for this civil religious dimension are formed over time and passed on by formal and informal means: ideological and ritual elements like the idea of America as "the land of opportunity" or repeating the pledge of allegiance; icons like Washington, Lincoln, and a throng of regional and local heroes; objects like the flag; texts such as the U.S. Constitution; music such as "The Star-Spangled Banner"; places like Valley Forge and Arlington Cemetery; and holidays commemorating ideas or events representative of America's self-image, such as Thanksgiving or Memorial Day.[4] The DAR's paradigm of civil religion also utilizes the family as a symbolic resource, especially the idea of lineage, with its implications of connection, continuity, and inherited obligation.

Civil religion provides a metaphorical transference of sacred themes and strategies to the civil sphere, evoking a sense of mission larger than individual lives, deeper than the present moment's trials, calling upon loyalty and communal effort to realize a vision of a shared, better future, justifying that vision by invoking the lessons of the past. What that vision is, how it is to be achieved, and how people might live together as a

---

[3] Clifford Geertz, *The Interpretation of Cultures* (New York: Basic Books, 1973), 216.

[4] Claude-Jean Bertrand, "The American Ideology: A Triangular Model," *Studies in Popular Culture* 8, no. 2 (1985): 71–76.

community in the meantime are some questions that different incarnations of civil religion address as groups use it to compete for primacy in defining America.[5]

The multivocality of symbol systems like the DAR's civil religion allows disparate groups and dissenting beliefs to exist within a single institutional entity by maintaining membership without necessarily adopting every article of dogma and tradition endorsed by the group's leaders or the group's official stance. The latitude for dissent in concert with the assent of membership keeps a group both inclusive by compelling it to find ways to minimize differences and vital by providing a "safe" sounding board for the discussion of alternate ideas without recourse to "outsiders" and their possibly hostile influences. This process allows members who disagree with any of the organization's ideological stands to put aside their reservations and participate in the shared practice and feeling of its rituals.

Within this symbolic cultural matrix, civil religion connects hegemonic ends and more intimate realms of experience through vernacular images and ideas to "a compelling natural or supernatural force that voices authority and provides the populace with the illusion that the right forces are in control."[6] Alliance with hegemonic power bestows reflected power on the women who serve it and lends transcendent meanings to the members' everyday lives and to their vision of their roles in American society.

In the DAR, we find a grass-roots expression of both official culture advancing its concerns and vernacular culture utilizing official culture's prestige to enhance its own power. Ethnographic data collected at the DAR's Centennial Continental Congress, which I attended as a participant-observer in April 1991, are the primary resource for this study. To fully understand the rituals, the context in which they are practiced must also be understood, for all the elements of the congress are carefully orchestrated to repeat the same themes of patriotism, service, and power in many different forms. In the DAR's national celebration of itself and its ideals, we see the organization connect individuals' private

[5] Conrad Cherry's article, "American Sacred Ceremonies," in *American Mosaic: Social Patterns of Religion in the United States*, ed. Phillip E. Hammond and Benton Johnson (New York: Random House, 1970), 303–16, observes that "sects" of civil religion exist along regional, ideological, socioeconomic, and ethnic lines and provide the potential for each group to put their own interpretation on any civil religious performance's meaning. John Markoff and Daniel Regan, "The Rise and Fall of Civil Religion: Comparative Perspectives," *Sociological Analysis* 42, no. 4 (1982): 333–52, in their crosscultural study of civil religions, find alongside civil religion's ability to legitimate and support the state the potential for counterclaims to the state's legitimacy.

[6] Beverly Stoeltje, "Making the Frontier Myth: Folklore Process in a Modern Nation," *Western Folklore* 46 (October 1987): 240.

lives and the power of the nation-state by means of rituals practiced year after year by members. The organization perpetuates itself by identification with both spheres, reflecting the prestige of the public and the intimacy of the private. The Daughters' rituals delineate the parameters of that mediation by activating emotion and rhetoric in the service of hegemonic power.

The National Society of the Daughters of the American Revolution was officially founded on 11 October 1890, the date chosen because it was the date Columbus first sighted America, "and because that discovery was made possible by the generosity of Queen Isabella."[7] The choice of this date and the rationale behind it were the first of many decisions by the DAR to ally the organization as closely as possible with the history of the nation, to imbue every act of the DAR with civil religious significance, and to recognize the acts of women in the nation's life. Founded in an era of rising immigration and industrialization, the DAR was one expression of the widespread nativist anxiety over the ferment for change in the democracy called for by new groups and new ideas, an organization meant to reaffirm the primacy of place and voice held by the descendents of pre-revolutionary immigrants to these shores. Founded as a reaction to the Sons of the American Revolution, which excludes women, the DAR also became a venue for negotiating women's place in the country's history and future.

Today the DAR is the largest hereditary patriotic organization in the United States. It has more than two hundred thousand members and more than three thousand chapters, including units in Australia, the United Kingdom, France, Mexico, and Canada. The great majority of its members are older than fifty years of age, and the membership is almost exclusively middle to upper-middle class. Most are well-educated women; some, but not all, are passionate genealogists or history buffs. Predominantly conservative in their political leanings, they do represent a broad range of the conservative spectrum. Most junior members I have met—women aged eighteen to thirty-five—became involved in the DAR through their mothers or grandmothers or aunts; many older members were also brought in by their female elders, creating a sense of continuity and connection through membership.

The DAR complex of three buildings in Washington, D.C., comprises the largest public buildings in the world owned and operated by women.

---

[7] National Society Daughters of the American Revolution, *Early History, Daughters of the American Revolution* (Washington, D.C.: Board of Management, NSDAR, 1908). Cited in Ann Arnold Hunter, *A Century of Service: The Story of the DAR* (Washington, D.C.: NSDAR, 1991), 8.

At this headquarters, the organization maintains an extensive genealogical library, runs a museum of early American artifacts, and publishes a monthly magazine that discusses historic sites, current issues, and genealogy. The DAR's three objectives—preserving history, supporting education, and promoting patriotism—were chosen by the founding members for their perceived influence on the nation's direction and self-image. Membership in the DAR is open to women eighteen or older who have documented proof of their lineal descent from a soldier or a person (male or female) who rendered service (a "patriot") to the American side in the Revolutionary War.

Lineage welds the members together as kindred, both symbolically and literally. One form of socializing that two or more Daughters might indulge in is comparing notes to find bloodlines or other hereditary societies in common. Lineage confers upon its inheritor a sense of self-esteem through a special relationship to the country's past and by extension to the country's future. Sherry Ortner and Harriet Whitehead note that women's rank in the world of men emphasizes and depends upon relationships; women are seen as sisters, wives, and daughters, whereas men's rank is generally defined by prestige in the public domain.[8] The Daughters carry dependent, relational rank into the public domain to celebrate blood connections to their personal and national past.

Idioms denoting the nation are often drawn from images of kinship and home; this invests the nation with the quality of a natural connection.[9] The Daughters link obligations and duties levied upon them by their ancestry with their duties to the DAR, the nation, and God. This sense of lineage-imposed obligations of honor and service—is expressed in the DAR's opening ritual, performed at every meeting of the organization from the small local chapter to the national congress:

> REGENT: To perpetuate the memory and the spirit of the men and women who achieved American independence; to promote the development of an enlightened public opinion; and to foster patriotic citizenship;—these are the objects of our Society, Daughters of the American Revolution.
>
> CHAPLAIN: Guard that which is committed to thy trust. [1 Timothy 6:20]
>
> RESPONSE: Yea, I have a goodly heritage. [Psalm 16:6]
>
> CHAPLAIN: Thou shalt remember all the way which the Lord thy God led thee. [Deuteronomy 8:2]
>
> RESPONSE: Blessed is the nation whose God is the Lord. [Psalm 33:12]

[8] Sherry B. Ortner and Harriet Whitehead, "Introduction: Accounting for Sexual Meanings," in *Sexual Meanings: The Cultural Construction of Gender and Sexuality*, ed. Sherry B. Ortner and Harriet Whitehead (Cambridge: Cambridge University Press, 1981), 19.

[9] Benedict Anderson, *Imagined Communities: Reflections on the Origin and Spread of Nationalism*, rev. and ext. ed. (New York: Verso, 1991).

CHAPLAIN: Our Heavenly Father, we pray for Thy guidance. May Thy abiding presence be realized in the daily life of our country. We thank Thee for all those yesterdays and pray for an awareness of the lessons of history that have become our heritage. May all who are a part of this great Society accept Thy blessings with humility, setting their goals with the high standards of perfect love in Thee. Grant us growth, strength and loyalty in faith, with binding ties of friendship. Amen.[10]

The opening ritual explicates each Daughter's relationship to the United States as an inherited guardianship of the national community's past, present, and future—a guardianship she shares with God, thereby simultaneously participating in a religious and nationalistic exercise in loyalty. Connecting religious legitimation of power to national legitimation of power, the Daughters draw these two realms together in an image of the nation as divinely inspired. The god of the DAR's civil religion is broad enough to embrace the religious affiliations of most members, generally invoked in tandem with the nation-state, the society, or both. Through this ritual, DAR membership implies involvement in national and transcendent concerns, even at the intimate level of friendships and personal faith.

The DAR centers its civil religion in the intimate, private sphere traditionally assigned to women in America, but the organization expands that sphere to embrace the public and the national by allying "country" to the other two loci of faith and service in the DAR's motto, "God" and "home." This perspective on private influence exerted on the public suggests the era in which the DAR arose, when the cult of domesticity ascribed a moral influence to women's lives that extended into the world at large through its action upon the men and children who entered and left that private sphere while women remained within it. The DAR acknowledges this influence as well as direct influence by women upon the country, and this dyad is suggested in the multivocality of their central symbols, the emblem and motto.

The DAR emblem is a platinum distaff overlaid by a gold spinning wheel enameled with blue; the spokes of the wheel are tipped with thirteen stars, and "Daughters of the American Revolution" is printed in white around the rim. The spinning wheel was chosen as representative of female industry; the stars stand for the thirteen original colonies.

The DAR's motto is "God, Home, and Country."[11] The allegiances to

[10] National Society Daughters of the American Revolution, *Ritual*, centennial ed. (Washington, D.C.: NSDAR, 1991), 6–7.

[11] Marie H. Yochim, "A Century of Service to the Nation," *Daughters of the American Revolution Magazine* [special centennial issue] 124, no. 7 (August/September/October 1990): 458.

God, home, and country are not hierarchical or autonomously compartmentalized for the Daughters; they are seen as interdependent. This holism permits the most traditional members to identify their private lives as serving the public sphere, while those leading career-centered lifestyles can see connections between their lives in the public and private spheres. Effort is made to integrate career women and nontraditional choices in a variety of ways, such as offering notable DAR members and female heroes, especially of the revolutionary era, as icons to be admired and emulated. However, as with the spinning wheel, these icons are presented so as not to slight or diminish the traditional contingent and traditional pursuits. As with most traditional groups, change is incorporated as much as possible into the existing symbolic and institutional structures of the organization.

One further loyalty is implicit in the motto—loyalty to the DAR as an organization. The conflation of service to the DAR as an institutional structure and service to both the wider and more intimate spheres is part of the wirewalk that every member, and the organization itself, must negotiate. Although loyalties to God, home, and country are seen as equivalent, gradations of fealty exist in the organizational structure itself, with power heavily concentrated at the national level. The average member's ability to influence the organization's policy is severely limited because of this hierarchy, and entrance into the upper echelons of rank is a slow process of networking and organizational service. The concentration of power in the hands of high-ranking Daughters mutes dissent and enhances their prestige as symbols of the organization and liaisons to the power of the nation-state.

Through the DAR, a member may feel herself a part of the nation-state, with all its attendant glory; she may feel herself a part of the organization itself, with its power structures, history, and drama; and she may feel through these two alliances the exaltation of her selfhood and the bonds of her private life, as well as the instrumentality of her existence as a citizen of the United States. The affirmation of this three-tiered legitimacy and loyalty to that legitimacy are the ultimate purposes of the DAR; they shape its mission and its civil religion, especially as that civil religion manifests itself in DAR ritual.

The playing out of allegiances, power, and esteem is clearly foregrounded at the DAR Continental Congress. This six-day marathon of business, social events, and rituals always falls the week of 19 April, the anniversary of the Battle of Lexington, the start of the Revolutionary War—another example of the DAR consciously invoking connection with America's "mythic" origin. Social events—breakfasts, teas, banquets, and receptions—are held at the Mayflower Hotel. Processions, concerts, business meetings, and serious ritual or celebrative gatherings are held in the auditorium of Constitution Hall or the rooms of Memorial Continental Hall, which also houses the library. Connecting the two buildings is the Administration Building, which houses the museum.

For the duration of the congress, the basement of Constitution Hall becomes a bazaar selling crafts with colonial, historical, or patriotic themes. Red, white, and blue bunting, eagles, and American flags dominate every table in this room; even some vendors wear aprons decorated like flags. Objects with DAR initials or insignia are also for sale. The foyer of Constitution Hall holds tables for DAR committees such as the Columbus Quincentennial and the Juniors' Bazaar, and for the prestigious vendors at Congress, most notably J. E. Caldwell & Company, the official vendor of all DAR pins, and Blackstone Florist, Inc., which sells orchid corsages.

In addition to the DAR insignia pin, members wear pins engraved with the names of revolutionary ancestors discovered by the member's genealogical research and confirmed by the DAR. There are also pins to denote offices held, support for particular committees, or commemorative events attended (such as the DAR centennial or the anniversary of the Battle of Yorktown). The pins are worn on a blue-and-white ribbon (or ribbons, depending on the number of pins) over the left breast. State regents and national officers are additionally set apart by blue and white sashes, the width and pattern of which indicate their status.

On Sunday, the day before the official opening of congress, the activities of the pilgrimage and the memorial service are under the jurisdiction of the chaplain general.[12] At the 1991 Centennial Congress, a cold, drizzly morning found a half dozen tour buses and the "Yochim Mobile," President General Marie Yochim's minibus, lined up outside the Mayflower Hotel and loaded with box lunches. The purpose of the pilgrimage was to place wreaths at three sites: the Tomb of the Unknowns in Arlington, the tomb of George and Martha Washington at Mount Vernon, and the Vietnam Veterans' Memorial (the Wall).

At Arlington, the buses had special leave to drive up to the amphitheater adjoining the shrine. At the steps overlooking the Tomb, the guard silently kept his paces. The women took pictures, jockeyed for a good view, and grumbled about open umbrellas blocking their line of sight. The sergeant came out with the relief guard and asked the audience to remain standing and silent during the changing of the guard. The Daughters quietly observed the ritual, which elevates the utilitarian to the level of drama—each movement of checking the relief guard's accoutrements stylized and precise. It set the mood of the space apart from the everyday,

---

[12] Descriptions of the 1991 DAR Congress are drawn from my field notes of that event, recorded 14–19 April 1991.

heightened and solemn. There was no sound from the Daughters but the clicking of their cameras. Following the guards' ritual, a procession came down the steps from the amphitheater: Ms. Yochim and her inner circle (other national officers and the president general's pages) appeared with a wreath—greenery with red, white, and blue ribbons—escorted by two soldiers, one of whom carried a bugle. One woman murmured to her friend: "Oh, dear, they're going to play taps—it always makes me cry."

Ms. Yochim and her entourage were conducted to the very edge of the sacred space. The rope was opened. One of the guards accepted the wreath and placed it over the center grave. Taps was played. The soldiers saluted; the women stood in respectful silence or quiet tears. The president general's photographer took pictures. The wreath was carried away to one side by a soldier; the rope was closed. The guard took up his paces again as Ms. Yochim and the inner circle exited with their military escort.

Soon everyone was back on the buses and off to Mount Vernon. Some chose to remain on the bus because the path to the tomb was muddy gravel, but most walked down the hill, past the house to the graveyard. The mood of the ceremony here was very different than at the Tomb of the Unknowns, more cursory and less solemn in its tribute, although the Daughters were equally respectful in their silence during the brief ceremony itself. The women maneuvered for a good view on the rain slick brickwork around the open iron gates of the brick tomb. Police kept guard here for the occasion. The wreaths for George and Martha had blue and white ribbons, the colors of both the DAR and Washington's army. When the wreaths were in place, Ms. Yochim said a prayer, recalling the Washingtons' lives, hardships, and service to the country, asking that their example be remembered as an inspiration for those committed to serving God, home, and country. When the photo opportunity was over, everyone trudged back up the hill.

With the mood of the first two stops so different, I was looking forward to the service at the Wall, but the buses arrived to find the wreath had been quickly placed, and the inner circle had already retreated back into the Yochim Mobile. The ground between the buses and the Wall was deemed too muddy and treacherous for the women to traverse. Those who wanted to were invited to get out and take pictures, but no one on my bus did so. The mood further soured when the women learned that the buses would take them to the DAR complex for the memorial service, not back to the Mayflower Hotel where the pilgrimage had started. At this point, a number of women left the bus rather than be taken where they did not want to go. Many who stayed on grumbled about the cost and the unfairness of it all.

The memorial service was held on the stage in Constitution Hall. A total of 4,517 members had died that year, including a member of the National Board of Management, twelve past national officers, and fifteen past state regents. At the far left of the stage (from the audience's point of view) was the American flag, to the far right was the DAR flag, at center stage, immediately to the right of the podium, was the Christian flag. To the right of the Christian flag stood a three-foot cross of wire mesh covered with greenery.

Opening music was followed by a responsive scripture reading and a prayer. The national officers assembled on stage wearing their sashes and pins. The chaplain general recited the total death count from each state; the members from that state stood up, and a page placed a white carnation in the mesh cross to represent that state. An officer of equal rank recited the names of deceased state and national officers, and carnations in the cross represented each of these women. Audience members from individual officers' states rose again for the placement of the late member's flower. Classical music with religious themes provided interludes between the recitations for the members and state and national officers. After the Lord's Prayer and the benediction, the audience remained in place until the dais cleared. Pages—junior members of the DAR serving at the Congress—carried the completed cross outside. The inner circle and photographers followed. They placed the wreath before the DAR Founders statue, a woman with arms outspread in welcome or benediction. When I asked one of the attendees later in the day what she thought of the service, she said, "It's good they remember those who passed. That's what the DAR is all about."

Rituals represent a group's structure, values, and beliefs essential to any religion for shaping the belief system and the social order within which the religion functions. Rituals metaphorically connect different domains of experience into superordinate categories, creating a sense of transcendent wholeness uniting diverse elements.[13] These metaphoric relationships offer participants an opportunity to transcend the rational to the level of inspiration and give ritual the sense that it knits the disparate spheres of society into an ultimate, meaningful whole by linking the past with the present, the novel with the traditional, the ideal with the actual. Rituals, in particular celebratory rituals like those above, are also metonymic, affirming and reinforcing in succinct symbolic forms "a version of the social order that is meant to be believed, or at least acknowledged and adhered to" by ritual participants.[14]

[13] James W. Fernandez, "The Argument of Images and the Experience of Returning to the Whole," in *The Anthropology of Experience*. ed. Victor W. Turner and Edward M. Bruner (Urbana: University of Illinois Press, 1986), 176–77.

[14] Frank E. Manning, "Cosmos and Chaos: Celebration in the Modern World," in *The Celebration of Society: Perspectives on Contemporary Cultural Performance*, ed. Frank E. Manning (Bowling Green, Ky.: Bowling Green University Press, 1983), 27.

In the pilgrimage rituals above, the Daughters perform a communion with American history, a tribute that attaches their present with "those who passed." The participants enter a sacred space and leave behind wreaths, a tangible symbol of themselves. In honoring both George and Martha Washington, the Daughters acknowledge America's primary icon of the revolutionary era, that mythic period of origin with which they identify through their ancestry and their citizenship. They also honor Martha's traditional role as helpmate and the strength required to perform that role despite the hardships of that era, identifying with her through their own life roles.

All the sites where the DAR leaves wreaths are associated with military campaigns, and the military is a continuing symbolic resource for the Daughters. The military evokes complex layers of meaning associated with wars: ideas like sacrifice, hardship, and struggle for the birth or continuity of the nation-state. Hierarchical, traditional, powerful, and patriotic, the military and martial imagery in many ways are echoed by the DAR's structure and aspirations. The military also evokes more intimate connections with war that the participants bring to the ritual from their life experiences. One woman at the Tomb of the Unknowns said that Arlington brought home to her "the terrible waste of life" in war. Such emotional associations deepen the significance of the ritual for participants and begin the entire Congress on a note of reverence for the individual sacrifices that made the nation's survival possible.

After the pilgrimage is the memorial service, a ritual of commemoration for the DAR's own dead. The juxtaposition of these two events implies, if not consciously intends, metaphorical connection. Service to the country in the military becomes service to the country in the DAR. The wreath becomes a flowered cross, with each flower symbolically weighted as representative of the dead, the DAR's hierarchy acknowledged one last time during the service before all the dead become equal in honor in the indistinguishable white carnations. The cross is placed before the Founders' statue, the visible memorial to the women who are "mothers" of the organization, as Washington is seen as the "father" of the country. As with the pilgrimage, participants' personal memories of the dead blend into the larger symbolic universe of those who died in service to the nation; both represent an ideal to be met by those who survive.

Service to the nation and the DAR along its three foci is the rhetorical exercise of patriotism's affective dimension expressed in the memorial rituals. The DAR identifies itself as a service organization, not a political organization. Patriotic sentiment's translation into patriotic action— whether in favor of or in opposition to the organization's ideology— cannot be publicly exercised by DAR members *as* members. Only the president general may speak on behalf of the DAR as a whole, and she avoids overtly political pronouncements. Daughters who take political action are enjoined not to identify themselves as DAR members lest the organization be identified as political, even when that action is taken on behalf of a stand espoused in the DAR's conservatively aligned annual resolutions.

This rhetorical sleight-of-hand serves a number of purposes. It helps preserve the DAR's tax-exempt status; without it the organization could never afford to keep its buildings in Washington. It allows members who disagree with the political stands espoused by the DAR to distance themselves from them, because the organization ostensibly supports the political independence of its members. It shifts the focus of the DAR's activities from political to cultural arenas, a move that encourages members to use their energies to influence civil society and the intimate spheres of life that are more "traditional" areas for the exercise of women's power. It sanctions those who take political action—especially action that coincides with the DAR's ideological slant—with a ready-made connection to motives perceived as nonpolitical because such action can always be tied back into the DAR's worldview and primary allegiances to family or religious faith or the nation, attaining the status of defending "natural law" rather than taking a public political stand.

The performance of these complex messages in a form that discourages dissent and encourages allegiance is clearly seen in the Congress' National Defense Evening. The National Defense Committee is one of the most powerful committees in the DAR, both internally in its money and influence and externally in the visibility of its conservative politics in the resolutions the committee supports for consideration each year by the DAR Congress. The committee's stated mission is to ensure "an informed and active electorate." Along with the publication of the *National Defender*, a conservative digest of issues of the day, the committee presents "good citizenship" medals to schoolchildren and ROTC medals to outstanding cadets. Presided over by Phyllis Schlafly as chairman for at least three DAR administrations, the National Defense Evening is the most martial and controversial of the congress' annual events, a continuing source of delight or irritation—according to individual political leanings—for individual members.

The 1991 National Defense Evening began with a repetition of the pageantry of the opening night ritual: the procession of flags and national officers. The procession gathered in the foyer of the auditorium, separated from the milling membership by white-clad pages holding velvet ropes. Many women wore evening clothes, as did all the high-ranking officers. As the Hall filled, the U.S. Air Force Ceremonial Brass gave a concert. Over the stage hung a Patriot missile, courtesy of the Raytheon Corporation.

At the conclusion of the concert, the band struck up the processional march. Everyone stood as pages in white entered single file up the center aisle of the single file carrying the American flag and DAR flag. Many women placed their hands over their hearts as the American flag passed. More pages bearing the state flags entered in pairs behind the first two. The pairs parted at the base of the stage to climb the steps at opposite ends. They crossed the length of the stage, passing each other to stop behind their flagstands, holding the flags at attention.

More pages entered to line the center aisle, facing each other across it as the national officers paraded to their places on the stage. After a dramatic pause, during which the lights went down, the president general entered, attended by her eight personal pages. A spotlight followed her up the aisle. When she reached the center of the auditorium, the big American flag suspended from the roof of the auditorium unfurled above her with a great sweep, raising an enormous cheer from the crowd. When she reached the podium, the opening ritual was recited, followed by the pledge of allegiance, the American's creed, and two verses of the national anthem. The president general then ordered the colors posted, and the pages retired to their chairs at the back of the stage.

The pageantry of this ritual, particularly the moment when the flag is released, is an image that members often refer to when speaking of the Congress. One member described it as "the most exciting thing I've ever seen in my life, and I've been around the world." Another told me she "can't catch her breath for a minute" from the lump in her throat as the flag drops. As in the memorial service, this ritual displays the DAR's hierarchical structure and its effort to represent a nonhierarchical, all-inclusive community. The flags of the nation, the organization, and the Christian faith, followed by all the states of the union, represent members' stewardship of the nation and its perceived ideological underpinnings. The procession of national officers in their sashes, pins, and formal gowns, flanked by pages in white, repeats the entrance of the flags, creating a connection with the flags' symbolic power while displaying the status and authority of the DAR. The pages underscore the senior members' prestige by their attendant service, and their comparative youth implies a second hierarchy of fealty by the younger generation to their female elders. These symbolic valences are underscored by the attendance of eight pages on the president general, who represents the organization as a whole, and whose presence triggers the release of the flag, a powerful national symbol fluttering over her as if bestowing a blessing on the faithful she represents, a magical moment uniting the nation, the organization, and the individual members in symbolic action.

After the invocation ritual, Phyllis Schlafly introduced the evening's guests; then she added: "To illustrate the National Defense Evening is a time for patriots, we have a real Patriot missile on the platform tonight. This is the same Patriot missile that had such a dramatic success in zapping the Iraqi missile called the SCUD. . . . As you know, in our Centennial year DAR has always been an organization that honors Patriots. We like this patriot and all SCUDs can now leave the hall."[15] Her comment provoked a cheer from the audience; she linked the metonymic missile's power with that of the organization by setting up a dichotomy of patriot/nonpatriot in Patriot/SCUD and calling up the martial imagery that DAR members recognize and respond to in other contexts. She argued that the Gulf War proved the DAR was right in supporting SDI and a strong military and that war should be run by the military, not politicians. These comments met a mixed reaction; applause mingled with grumbles and whispers of disagreement. With such powerful unifying imagery leading off the evening, however, it is understandable that one prominent member's preprocessional complaint—"We'll have to listen to Phyllis Schlafly's crap again tonight!"—while it might reflect the sentiments of many individual members, would be muted when weighed against the symbolic consensus of the opening procession.

The presentation of the evening's awards followed the keynote speech by Chief Justice Warren Burger. The "Dr. Anita Newcomb McGee Army Nurse Award" was presented to Lieutenant Colonel Kathryn Brand Scheidt. Then Ms. Etling, chair of the Veteran-Patients Committee, presented the Outstanding Veteran-Patient, Judge Jeptha Charles Tanksley of Georgia. He had lost both legs and his left eye in World War II. He wept as he accepted the award, and I noticed a number of the audience in tears as well. The Outstanding Youth Volunteer was Elizabeth Selby of Denver, Colorado; in her acceptance speech she praised her mother for teaching her "the right values." The Outstanding DAR volunteer for veteran patients was a teacher from Iowa, a forty-two-year volunteer in a VA hospital. She thanked her great-great-grandfather who fought in the Revolutionary War; her great-grandfather who fought in the War of 1812; her brother who was in World War I; her nephew who was in Korea; her students, some of whom were in the Gulf; and her patients, five of whom were named on the Vietnam War Memorial. She also thanked "all of those veterans who have made freedom possible, the ones that I and perhaps some of you have taken for granted because someone has done it for us." She lastly thanked God for giving her "the strength to have served 4,926 hours as a volunteer."[16]

As with the opening procession, movement from the national to the

[15] National Society Daughters of the American Revolution, *One Hundredth Continental Congress Annual Proceedings* (Washington, D.C.: NSDAR, 1991), 168.
[16] NSDAR, *Congress Annual Proceedings*, 178.

organizational implies a correlation of purpose and importance in these two levels of service to the nation-state. From the army nurse and wounded veteran judge, we move to volunteers who serve veterans— one a young woman, one an elderly DAR member. Both women volunteers, interestingly, mentioned familial connections in their acceptance speeches, tapping into the Daughters' deep attachment to lineage with its emotional resonances and attendant obligations. The political causes that made veterans of men and women in the service of the nation-state are not addressed save in uncritical celebration because the complexities of national policy are overshadowed by the ideals of communal duty and individual sacrifice represented and foregrounded by the award winners. Whatever an individual member's political leanings or complaints with the DAR as an organization, she finds it difficult to recall them in the emotional, communal atmosphere conjured by the National Defense Evening.

The rituals practiced by the Daughters of the American Revolution as a civil religious expression of devotion explore the relationship of the individual to the nation-state, the means of nation building, and the goals of that process. Individuals make up a nation by their involvement with its traditions and institutions. The nation is an idea, an "imagined community," as Benedict Anderson described it. Upon its "reality" are built constructs of meaning that answer the same kind of elemental questions put to religion about purpose in life and continuity beyond death.[17] By participating in the rituals, the individual enters the life of the nation, serves a larger entity as a small but important part of the whole, and extends her life's importance beyond the scope of a single physical lifetime.

A vision of the nation is invoked, constructed, and lived in the moment, in the lives of individual citizens, and, even more important, in the groups of citizens practicing its invocation together. The means of that invocation are symbolic; the process is folkloric—the expressive intertwining of tradition and creativity in performance to share information, emotion, and the delight of dramatic invention. The goals of the process of nation building in the DAR are instilling patriotism—allegiance to this invisible construct's visible political arm, the state—and directing patriotic enthusiasm to action that supports and sustains the nation-state's power.

The force of this influence is directed toward its effect upon other facets of civil society. Patriotism, like its kindred emotions love and faith, connects the individual to something larger than herself: a coherent vi-

---

[17] Anderson, *Imagined Communities*, 15, 18.

sion of the world, a belief system, and a sense of one's place in the world. From that vision springs action. Faith without good works is dead, and the Daughters apply this aphorism to their patriotic attachment to the United States. They exalt the nation-state through symbols of its power and partake of its exaltation through their blood connection to its beginnings.

The exaltation of the nation is inextricably bound up in the exaltation of the other symbolic levels in the DAR: the celebration of the organization and the celebration of women. Unquestionably, DAR symbology has deep roots in patriarchy at every level, as its fascination with all things military demonstrates, but I also see in the DAR an ongoing manipulation of the patriarchally based structures and roles to assert female power, value, and community. The Daughters do not struggle for separation from the hegemony; they are part of it; they accept, even celebrate, it. At the same time, they find in the organization domains of experience and prestige that traditional white middle-class culture once permitted only to men. Added to the power of a community of women for women among the Daughters, and the power of the nation-state, is the power of patriarchy transposed to the feminine in such forms as the DAR hierarchy and the DAR's support of members' endeavors at all levels of the culture, although the scope of these endeavors is generally focused in civil rather than political society.

While honoring women's traditional roles, the DAR also provides a venue for exercising power on larger issues. Members can find ways to critique male hegemony while associating with the dominant culture by using its models of hierarchy and power for the glorification of women's power. To speak only of the marginalizing and countering of the patriarchy is to remove these women from the complex context in which they live and strive.[18] Identity is negotiated contextually among different spheres of loyalty, and the DAR's rituals are important means of negotiation. One prominent member told me that another member had suggested dispensing with the DAR's ritual aspects to attract new members:

> [She] said, "Well, the young women just don't want to spend their time on all of these rituals and things like this." And that's when I drew the line. I said, "Look, that's what we're all about, and if they don't want to say the Pledge of Allegiance and the American's Creed and so forth at their meetings, then perhaps they belong in a social sorority, Tri Kappa or something like it, where

[18] Elizabeth Fox-Genovese, "Between Individualism and Fragmentation: American Studies and the New Literary Studies of Race and Gender," *American Quarterly* 42, no. 1 (March 1990): 22.

they do other things, because," I said, "that's what we are all about." I mean, you can't ditch the things that you stand for.[19]

Loyalty to the things they stand for is dramatically expressed in the rituals of the Daughters of the American Revolution. This organizational venue allows the Daughters to practice their conservative form of patriotism as a vernacular civil religion, and their perception of themselves as the faithful is affirmed for them in the symbolic continuity of their lineages, their organization, and their vision of the nation's power and prestige.

[19] Interview with Hanna R. [pseud.], interview by author, tape recording, Huntingburg, Ind., 17 November 1990.

Chapter 13

MORAL PATRIOTISM AND COLLECTIVE MEMORY IN WHITING, INDIANA, 1920–1992

JOHN BODNAR

JOE SOTAK and Douglas MacArthur expressed dissimilar views of patriotism. Sotak was an average American who spent his life working at the Standard Oil refinery in Whiting, Indiana and discharging his duty to his family, union, and nation. MacArthur was a famous general and war hero who exhibited a high degree of devotion to his country and its defense. At age seventy-seven Sotak worried about the fate of the nation. "Once we leave this country it is going to hell," he warned. He located the problem in the values of the generation that followed him whom he thought were "living for today and the hell with tomorrow." To him the future viability of the nation depended upon the need to strike a balance between egoism and altruism. Two years before his death in 1964 at age eighty-four, MacArthur told cadets at West Point that as soldiers they ought to devote themselves to the ideals of "duty, honor, and country." Although they lived in the same nation, MacArthur's version of patriotism was narrower than Sotak's for it did not explicitly acknowledge the need to restrain self-seeking. Rather, he told a younger generation of soldiers to let civilians worry about politics and morality.[1]

The brand of patriotism advanced by Joe Sotak was tied more closely to the moral questions of selfishness and generosity than the version expressed by MacArthur because it was ultimately based more in the historic experience of a particular set of relationships than it was in dogmatic creeds that venerated idolatry to the state. As such Sotak and his fellow citizens in Whiting held a complex view of patriotism that mediated both

I would like to thank Gary Gerstle and Jeffrey Gould for reading earlier versions of this paper.

[1] Joseph Sotak interview by John Bodnar, 6 November 1991 (Indiana University Oral History Research Center, Bloomington). A taped and transcribed copy of all interviews cited in this paper is on file at the center. Support for this project came from the Indiana Historical Society and the Spencer Foundation. Douglas MacArthur, *Duty, Honor, and Country* (New York: McGraw Hill, 1965), 213–18.

particular and universal attitudes: experience and dogma continually contested each other in their lives and outlooks. Their conception of the
nation was never free of their moral outlook; it was never categorical.
The liberal nation that impartially mediated the competing claims of its
citizens and promised justice, the totalitarian nation that played to the lust
for power, racial domination, and order, or the welfare state that exchanged benefits for fidelity were never ideas that fully reflected their
position. They wanted justice, benefits, and power in return for their
participation in the national community, and they were capable of displaying racial bigotry. But they also were able to transcend these interests
and exhibit concern and care for others with no expectations of return.
They were loyal not only to the nation but to others who inhabited the
nation. Their patriotism and their political consciousness was not doctrinaire but a reconciliation of diverse levels of experience and conflicting
interpretations of reality that filled the life that they lived.[2]

In this chapter I argue that the patriotism of this white working-class
community in modern America is a cultural idea tied to the complex
reality of life over time and grounded in the substance and memory of
relationships and the question of authority inherent in those relations. It
acknowledges the need to honor institutional and political authorities,
but it counters that need with a dream and a demand for a society based
on justice and concern for others. This mediation approximates the definition of a truly moral society developed by scholars like Jürgen Habermas
who see the need for justice and compensation. And it embodies a more
universal call for solidarity: "a realization that each person must take responsibility for the other because as consociates all must have an interest
in the other." For Habermas and for the citizens of Whiting, a patriotic
society must also be a good society.[3]

Because the moral patriotism of Whiting attempts to serve the needs of
both citizens and powerful institutions, it is based primarily in a sense of
mutual enterprise and cooperation. No authority—individualistic, communal, despotic—dominates its ideological essence. Rather, in the fashion of twentieth-century liberalism, it opposes extremism and stands between the tenets of classical liberalism, civic republicanism, and statism.

[2] My views on patriotism have been shaped a great deal by my reading of the following
works: Raphael Samuel, "Introduction; Exciting to be English," in *Patriotism: The Making
of British National Identity*, ed. Samuel, 3 vols. (London: Routledge, 1989) 1: xviii–lxvii;
Charles Taylor, "Cross-Purposes: The Liberal-Communitarian Debate," in *Liberalism and
the Moral Life*, ed. by Nancy L. Rosenblum (Cambridge: Harvard University Press, 1989),
159–82; George P. Fletcher, *Loyalty: An Essay on the Morality of Relationships* (New York:
Oxford University Press, 1993), 3–21.

[3] Jürgen Habermas, "Justice and Solidarity: On the Discussion concerning Stage 6," in
The Moral Domain: Essays in the Ongoing Discussion Between Philosophy and the Social Sciences,
ed. Thomas E. Wren (Cambridge, Mass.: MIT Press, 1990), 224–51.

The best evidence of this point is that its adherents now feel a sense of outrage and marginalization in the 1990s. They assume that their moral position is not sufficiently considered in the workings of economic, religious, political, familial, and communal institutions; these institutions appear uncooperative. Consequently, they draw selectively and passionately upon a memory of a moral society that dominated most of their lives during the half-century after 1920. They remember their roles as patriotic citizens who collectively valued the ideals of obligation and responsibility and defined those ideals within the context of a national community. As Jonathan Reider found for Canarsie, when they defend their nation they also think they are defending their families and communities.[4]

They are also capable of attacking those who threaten to turn their ideal of obligation and loyalty into simple pursuits of self-interest or authoritarianism. Their generational identity was not formed by a single event like the Great Depression but was constructed over time through interaction with several levels of authorities at once: parental, religious, corporate, and national. The incessant call for duty and obligation, however, did not obliterate their sense of self-esteem. They managed to forge worthwhile identities that drew strength from the fulfillment of duty to others. In the context of their lives they met authorities halfway and moderated calls for unconditional allegiance with claims for contingent loyalty. When these citizens served their nation in World War II or criticized what they thought others had done to it in the 1990s, they revealed the fundamental fact that their devotion to their country always included a devotion to some people who lived in that country. They saw their place and role in a nation to be part of their place and role in a community. They could commit themselves to the nation because they had reason to believe that they had meaningful roles in the nation, their workplaces, communities, and families. They were not radical individuals or dutiful servants but participants in a massive project to sustain justice and solidarity. They now feel that the nation no longer conforms to their ideal of a community of caring and responsible individuals and is no longer capable of rewarding their fidelity; they now draw on their ability to challenge authority and articulate a moral critique of American society in the late twentieth century.

Joe Sotak is but one example of Whiting's collective memory. Expressed in the form of a narrative that offers a highly selective view of the past, the presentation of life stories from this town are essentially moral: tales about people who tried to meet their obligations to others—kin,

[4] Jonathan Rieder, *Canarsie: Jews and Italians Against Liberalism* (Cambridge: Harvard University Press, 1985), 6–7; 262–63.

employers, saints, clerics, national leaders—because they felt it was in their best interests to do so and because they cared about something other than themselves. They were motivated by self-interest, a desire for fairness, and an ideal of caring or solidarity that desired no return at all. They present themselves and their past in a moral rather than a progressive narrative of personal or group advancement because their collective memory, unlike other reconstructions of the past, serves the needs of a specific community more than the requirements of powerful institutions like the marketplace or the state. Their narrative is charged with subjective statements rather than objective analysis. Unconcerned with proper chronology, this collective account attempts to persuade listeners that the dominant values of Whiting are timeless, indispensable for maintaining a just nation. More than an exercise in nostalgia or a reactionary defense of a way of life, this story engages serious issues of power, authority, and social change in the present. It refuses to accept the argument that history is completed. The very telling of the chronicle is in itself an act of caring for others and for generations to come from people who are flawed, who have resorted to authoritarianism and bigotry to protect their interests, but who now hope to instruct the listening audience about their life histories.

Maurice Halbwachs, a French scholar, observed that collective memory is not about individual fragments of the past but about the shared experiences of a group and the things that still matter in the present. Because it is collective, it is about relationships: people to people, members to institutions, insiders to outsiders. The grounding in relationships insures that collective memory is largely about moral values—a point that scholars of social memory have been slow to recognize. Collective memory is inscribed with discussions or relations that pervade group life in the past and assessments of qualities that appear to threaten those values in the present. Despite its highly selective view of the past, its indifference toward objectivity, and its engagement with values in the present, to a remarkable extent these stories clarify what the past felt like and how the discourses of history were understood. Thus, in Whiting collective memory enshrines some values over others because those values were discussed and widely accepted in families, churches, and workplaces.[5]

[5] On collective memory see Maurice Halbwachs, *The Collective Memory*, trans. by F. J. Ditter and V. Y. Ditter (New York: Harper & Row, 1980), 43, 51; Amos Funkenstien, "Collective Memory and Historical Consciousness," *History and Memory* 1 (Fall 1989): 3–13; John Bodnar, *Remaking America: Public Memory, Commemoration, and Patriotism* (Princeton: Princeton University Press, 1992), 13–20; Pierre Nora, "Between Memory and History: Les Lieux de Memoire," *Representations*, no. 26 (Spring 1989): 7–26. Michael Kammen, *Mystic Chords of Memory: The Transformation of Tradition in American Culture*

Whiting's memory narrative, moreover, is articulated strongly and force-fully in the 1990s because, first, its narrators sense that their particular social group and the values that pervaded their relationships are now threatened with extinction. Life itself is drawing to a close for the people whose voices appear in this paper, for they were born between 1902 and 1926. Second, like Jews who now guard a memory of the Holocaust as one of a moral atrocity against reformulations that tend to mitigate the monstrosity of the event, these citizens of a working-class community near Chicago sense their values will be forgotten.[6]

In this symbolic construction of Whiting the relationship between in-dividual identity and communal need is essentially amicable. Institutional values reinforce personal ones in ways that sustain strong images of self-worth, on the one hand, and mutualism, on the other. Individual frustra-tions, selfishness, and disregard for others—spouses, authorities, racial minorities—are acknowledged but submerged in the dominant narrative of justice and solidarity. The collective memory of mutualism and obli-gation is rooted in the historical reality of key institutional relationships that were restated in ideologies that dominated the town in the several decades after World War I. Space does not permit a full exploration of these relationships and their attendant ideologies here, but I must discuss at least two issues: paternalism and corporatism. A sense of mutual obli-gation and common participation in a joint endeavor characterized the ideologies and practice of both the Standard Oil Company and the Cath-olic Church. In the corporation the ideal of paternalism flourished after 1920 and left a distinct mark on the collective account of the past. Its counterpart among Catholics was the idea of corporatism and the meta-phor of the "Mystical Body of Christ."

Paternalism, introduced to the workforce at Standard Oil in Whiting after World War I, was designed to win the loyalty of employees away from labor unions and, for that matter, from a state that had demon-strated an inclination to intervene in economic affairs during the war. This approach to labor—management relations sought to reward steady

---

(New York: Alfred Knopf, 1991), esp. 299–527 on patriotism and social memory from 1915 to 1945.

[6] See Dan Diner, "Historical Experience and Cognition: Perspectives on National So-cialism," *History and Memory* 2 (Fall 1990): 84–105. American history is taught at Whiting High School in the eleventh grade. The main text from 1985 to 1990 was Donald Ritchie, *Heritage of Freedom* (New York: Macmillan, 1985). When this text discussed immigrants who moved to industrial cities like Whiting after the 1880s it says that these newcomers came to better their lives and share in the benefits of the new industrial age. The moral voice of these newcomers and their children does not exist in this text. No mention is ever made of their demands for a just and caring society or the claims they made on authorities they met.

and dutiful workers with pensions, vacations, and options to purchase stock in the company. Officers of Standard Oil of Indiana told the residents of the town that they had turned their back on the single-minded pursuit of profits and had recognized that workers had as much of a "compelling interest" in the company as management.[7]

Paternalism became official in Whiting when Standard Oil created a Department of Industrial Relations in 1919. Employees were given an assortment of stock purchase plans, health and accident insurance, retirement programs, and social activities. Community centers with gymnasiums and pools were built in towns like Whiting, moreover, to further endorse the idea that loyalty would be rewarded. Clearly the plan and the ideal had an exploitative dimension. Most benefits went to employees who were able to remain with the company for a long period of time, something that was difficult for mobile people working at the margins of economic survival, and many employees could not afford to save part of their income in order to buy company stock. Foreign-born workers were not allowed to become representatives in the company union, and the plan did not allow nationwide collective bargaining. Thus, the company could compensate for strikes at one plant by expanding production somewhere else. Nevertheless, citizens recalled the positive aspects of fairness and care that served the purposes of collective memory in the 1990s.[8]

Paternalism in Whiting had a counterpart in Catholicism. The town's heavily eastern European immigrant population was largely Catholic and created a variety of active church communities. Although Catholic dogma and leadership could certainly be autocratic, the central ideology of Catholic corporatism in the 1920s and 1930s celebrated a vision of a cooperative community in which the clergy and the faithful played important roles. In what was considered a joint effort to realize the teachings of Christ, clerics and church members worked together to attain justice on earth and salvation in heaven. The Catholic community was referred to metaphorically as the "Mystical Body of Christ," a conception that attempted to minimize the hierarchial structure of the church and encourage the notion that each member of the body should take

[7] Ellis W. Hawley, *The Great War and the Search for a Modern Order: A History of the American People and Their Institutions, 1917–1933* (New York: St. Martin's Press, 1979), 52, 93–103, 136–39. Paul H. Giddens, *Standard Oil Company (Indiana)* (New York: Appleton-Century Crofts, 1955), 333–40; Robert W. Stewart, "Getting Acquainted Again," *Stanolind Record*, 1 (November 1919): 1–3.

[8] See Stuart D. Brandes, *American Welfare Capitalism, 1880–1946* (Chicago: University of Chicago Press, 1970), 122–25; Lizabeth Cohen, *Making a New Deal: Industrial Workers in Chicago, 1919–1939* (Cambridge: Cambridge University Press, 1990), 430; Burton H. Kline, "Employee Representation in Standard Oil," *Industrial Management* 59 (1920): 355–60; Giddens, *Standard Oil Company*, 333–40.

responsibility for the other. This ideal was popularized in the late 1940s in such organizations as the Christian Family Movement, which not only reinforced traditional forms of authority in families but also encouraged families to meet responsibilities to those in need in the larger society.[9]

Part of the reward for loyalty to the Church in Whiting was a meaningful place within the congregational community itself. At St. John's, John Kostick, the prelate, mobilized women in the 1930s to pray and raise funds to build a new church. Unable to convince male members of his parish of the feasibility of the project during hard times, Kostick turned to women and promised them communal esteem and prominence if they would take the lead in organizing dances, bake sales, and raffles. He astutely invoked the model of St. Therese, "The Little Flower," as an example of how women could make significant contributions through small, humble acts. This saint, immensely popular among second generation Catholic women in the United States before World War II, sustained the ideal of rewards for loyalty and provided these females with a way to assume public roles outside economic and political spheres where they had few opportunities. When he organized them, Kostick told the women that they could emulate the saint by performing these humble but significant acts.[10]

In the 1940s the separate spheres of loyalty and mutualism in families, workplaces, and congregations dissolved into a national effort to win both a world war and a cold war. Certainly racial and gender barriers remained impervious to much of this consolidation, but, nevertheless, wartime patriotism linked local and communal interests to national ones in ways that had not existed in the previous decades. Quotas for producing valuable oil products for the military, buying war bonds, and donating blood were now advertised in company publications as well as the benefits of the stock purchase plan. Catholic leaders who had expressed reservations about "excessive patriotism" toward the state in the 1920s and 1930s now discussed the "Christian virtue of patriotism" and the need to subjugate individual interests to those of the state. At the largest Catholic church in Whiting, the popular veneration to Saint Therese that

[9] John A. Ryan, *The Catholic Church and the Citizen* (London: Burns, Oates and Washbourne, 1988), 80–81. Concerns over excessive state loyalty are expressed in articles like "Flag Idolatry," *America* 50 (April 7, 1934): 630; Philip Gleason, "In Search of Unity: American Catholic Thought, 1920–1960," *The Catholic Historical Review* 65 (April 1979): 185–205.

[10] Karen Armstrong, *The Gospel According to Woman: Christianity's Creation of the Sex War in the West* (New York: Anchor Books, 1987), 91, 226–27. Kostick did not select St. Teresa of Avila, a sixteenth-century nun who had defied the male authorities of her time. Anna Palko interview by John Bodnar, 30 April 1992; Sophie Gresko interview by John Bodnar, 24 April 1992. "St. John's Parish News," 4 November 1934, provides an account of the fund-raising achievements of the St. Therese Club.

had encouraged second-generation Slovak-American women to play a meaningful role in their families and communities gave way in 1942 to a new project: the building of a statue to Our Lady of Victory that would redirect prayer to "our country and our boys in the armed forces."[11]

This interconnected set of loyalties between individual, family, employer, church, community, and nation was extended into the Cold War era. Catholics in Whiting and elsewhere continued their veneration of the Virgin Mary but altered their focus from "Our Lady of Victory" to "Our Lady of Fatima." Apparently the Virgin had told the faithful at Fatima in Portugal that if they prayed the rosary daily the Soviet Union—now the nation's enemy—would be converted. At this time, about 1950, the Fatima statues were carried in processions through Whiting churches. Again devotion would be rewarded.[12]

In the memory of the late 1950s and 1960s this regime of obligation and loyalty is recalled as disintegrating. Not unexpectedly the alternations began not in the public culture of the 1960s, which is certainly characterized as a period of transformation, but in the refinery that had contributed so much to the economic security of Whiting's working class. After a dramatic explosion and fire at the refinery in 1955, an event that everyone who lived in Whiting at the time remembers, the Standard Oil Company began to modernize the plant and reduce its workforce. Although the process took several years, workers saw the resulting layoffs in the early 1960s as a betrayal of their loyalty to the firm.

But betrayal comes later in the collective narrative. The beginnings render accounts of mutualism and start with depictions of life within the immigrant families that came to Whiting in the early twentieth century. Slovaks, Poles, Croatians, Hungarians, Irish, and Germans settled the town after the construction of the refinery in 1889. When the children of these newcomers tell this collective narrative, they first describe the relationships they had with their immigrant parents. Here they first learned how to restrict selfishness and how to deal with authority. In fact, this experience prepared them for either the paternalistic regime of Standard Oil or the corporate body of the Catholic church. This system of coercion and love molded their narrative of the past and facilitated their joining the nation's crusade against evil empires in the 1940s and 1950s.

Family members were expected to take responsibility for each other. In the family economy of Whiting—as in most of industrial America during the first half of the twentieth century—parents raised children, assisted them in finding employment, and often provided housing after

[11] "St. John's Parish News" (Whiting, Ind.), 16 August 1942; 1 November 1942.

[12] Palko interview; Douglas Hyde, "Fatima: Where Mary Met Marx," *Catholic Digest* 16 (June 1952): 63–67.

marriage. Housing is always recalled as a scarce commodity in Whiting because families usually bought and kept empty lots for eventual use by their progeny. In return children contributed earnings to their parents and care when they were sick or old. Residents admitted to desertions, alcoholism and arguments in households, but the dominant narrative of family life centers on obligation and unity.[13]

Memory in Whiting does not imply that reciprocity and adherence to duty are innate; rather, they need to be continually enforced by authority figures. Parents preached hard work, family responsibility, honesty, and religious devotion. The attachment that these people manifested to institutions like the Catholic church and Standard Oil was a widely shared ideal in the community in which their individual identity was forged. The defense of that ideal, however, that they now manifest is not a simple-minded expression of some form of working-class authoritarianism but an affirmation of a moral form of individualism.[14]

Life histories are grounded in stories of community as well as family. Residents describe rich networks of social life that revolved around churches. Slovaks, the largest ethnic concentration in the town, built a Slovak Dom or hall that residents remember as a center for plays, dinners, weddings, and fraternal meetings. Many describe the benefits of the Whiting Community Center, a facility donated to the town by the paternalistic Standard Oil Company. One man remembered that the center "brought the cohesion of Whiting."[15]

Community is recalled not only for its strength but also as a source of assistance. Mary Hlebasko was able to get a job rolling barrels of axle grease at the refinery at a young age because a local priest falsified her birth certificate. Several men told stories of building their own homes with the help of friends who provided their special skills. And midwives are held in high esteem in the town's collective memory for not only their role in childbirth but also their helpfulness in cleaning homes while new mothers recuperated.[16]

Justice, benevolence, and esteem were the rewards for loyalty and responsibility in Whiting's remembered past. In Whiting the creation of a good society depended on idealizations that transformed duty and obligation into virtues. Clearly these ideals were maintained by discipline and authority, but they were also engendered by a sense of participation in the

[13] Mary Hlebasko interview by Bodnar, 8 November 1990; Helen Dudzik interview by David Dabertin, 10 February 1991; John Jancosek interview by David Dabertin, 9 February 1991.

[14] Stanley Labus interview by Giovanna Del Negro, 6 April 1991.

[15] Dudzik interview. Leo Kus interview by Amy Craver, 8 March 1991, and by John Bodnar, 11 October 1991.

[16] Hlebasko interview; Kus interviews; Dudzik interview.

working-class community itself and a perception of rewards—economic security, caring families, just authorities—for loyalties rendered. And to a noticeable extent, Whiting's collective memory affirms solidarity, the assumption of responsibility without expectations of reward. Relationships were thought to be both contractual and covenantal.[17]

The covenantal aspects of collective memory are articulated strongly by females in Whiting, a suggestion that confirms arguments that female conceptions of morality are less concerned with reciprocity than male. Consider the identities presented by Sophie Gresko and Clementine Frankowski. Gresko, born in 1902, tells of a life of devotion and caregiving. Left a widow by the death of her husband from an industrial accident, she scrubbed floors at the Whiting Community Center and took in laundry to raise two children. She also received benevolence from an aunt who provided her and her children with a home in which to live. And she returned the kindness by donating her services to St. John's Catholic Church, the center of the town's Slovak-American community, for which she went door to door to raise funds. She offers accounts of how she always became angry at fellow toilers "walking slowly on the job," an indication of her loyalty to her employer. And during the 1930s she stressed how she gave meals to unemployed men who drifted into her yard from the nearby railroad tracks that connected the town to Chicago.[18]

Clementine Frankowski rendered care to not only her family but also an entire community. A remarkable woman who was valedictorian of Whiting High School in 1925, she decided to become a physician and entered medical college in Chicago. Her interest in medicine was prompted in part by the fact that she recalled her mother's suffering the death of several babies. Her memory of a mother who was "very depressed" over the death of her brother from pneumonia while he was in high school affected her tremendously. When she became a physician she decided to return to Whiting because of strong feelings of solidarity to her family and to her community.[19]

Reciprocity is also at the heart of stories of loyal workers at Standard Oil. Joseph Gresko tells a story of a worker who would inform a foreman when a light bulb went out so that work would continue rather than

---

[17] For a discussion of a covenant as a promise without expectation of reward and as an agreement, unlike contractual ties, free of coercion, see Thomas Shaffer, *On Being a Christian and a Lawyer: Law for the Innocent* (Provo: Brigham Young University Press, 1981), 89. Shaffer stresses that coercion must be muted so that individuals can retain sufficient strength to retain a conscience capable of resisting excessive authority.

[18] Lorraine Williamson interview by John Bodnar, 14 August 1991; Sophie Gresko interviews by John Bodnar, 12 March and 11 October 1991.

[19] Clementine Frankowski interview by John Bodnar, 14 August 1991.

allowing it to be interrupted—an indication of how deep attachments ran. But everyone also recalled the benefits that Standard Oil provided. Helen Dudzik said that "everybody said that if you get into Standard Oil you won't have to worry about strikes or layoffs." Some steel companies had higher wages, but strikes and unemployment were more frequent. More important, Standard Oil was prized by the local population for its pension. Employees could contribute a portion of their income to a stock purchase plan that would be matched on a 50-percent basis by the company. Countless life stories confirm the importance of this plan and the pensions employees now receive. "If you worked at Standard Oil you had a pass to any kind of marriage there was," Leo Kus adds; he meant that a woman would not hesitate to marry a Standard employee.[20]

But Standard Oil is remembered for not only rewards but also its own act of solidarity. Whiting's older generation does not tend to recall the Great Depression as a period of economic distress. Certainly there were difficulties, and stories are told of some people losing their homes or needing assistance. But the narrative of the 1930s is one of solidarity and caring. There was no brutal depression in Whiting because Standard Oil found a way to keep most employees on the payroll, at least on a part-time basis. As Kus emphasizes, "people don't forget those things."[21]

In longing for the past of their youth, the solidarity of community, and the justice of paternalism, Whiting's current residents see mainly decline in both the nation and the community. Joe Sotak's charge that the country would go "to hell" when his generation died is part of that attitude. This view is usually reinforced by stories of World War II in which men and women volunteered to do their part to help the nation. Males described their entry into the armed forces as natural, inevitable. One claims that when he heard the news of Pearl Harbor he knew he would go into the army. And women reveal pride in the production of oil products at the refinery, their support for the troops, and the fact that "people were working so hard buying bonds and everything to help our country."[22]

The demise of national society, in the eyes of these people, takes place alongside the dissolution of the local community. Sophie Gresko notes changes in her neighborhood. She claims that newcomers do not keep their properties looking as neat and clean as before. "They don't rake; they don't cut the grass; they don't do anything," she laments. Joe Sotak says that he does not even know his neighbors anymore and accuses them of not being "down to earth, good, clean people." Another native ob-

[20] Joe Gresko interview by John Bodnar, 14 May 1991; Hlebasko interview; Dudzik interview, Kus interviews.

[21] Kus interviews.

[22] Dudzik interview; Sotak interview; Jancosek interview.

serves that Whiting is "not the focus of anyone's life anymore like it used to be in the old days." She infers that people don't entertain or visit one another as they did at one time. Newcomers, largely Mexicans, are indicted for their apparent lack of civic responsibility and attachment to a community that did not welcome them.[23]

Central to the attack on changing notions of relationships is the collective critique on the rising incidence of divorce. Marital breakup, more than any other feature of modern life, represents a decline in the basic institution—the family—that sustained and mediated the meaning of authority, justice, and solidarity in this place. It also represents the substitution of idolatry—for one's self or for material goods—for mutual participation in a common enterprise. Mary Hlebasko argues that with divorce children do not know who their authority figures are and "where they stand." She attacks the values of a consumerist society by claiming that materialism has replaced discipline and caring. "Parents buy children toys but do not give them attention." She particularly directs her anger at women who work "instead of staying at home" and see "their jobs and their paychecks as more important." Leo Kus bitterly attacks the idea that a mother can work outside the house and expect to raise responsible children. Linking local and national loyalties, he predicted, "the family and the United States is going to suffer with this idea. There is no such thing as having a surrogate mother teach honesty and concepts to children that they will be able to understand and emulate." A man born in 1921 insists that he does not recall anyone from his generation in Whiting that is divorced. "I think people are too selfish and too materialistic," he charges. "They don't know how to work together. This is the key to marriage, working together."[24]

But their critique of both modern values in their community—an implicit attack upon the consolidation of power in institutions in which they could not participate—and social change is not based solely on a nostalgic defense of a world that worked. They are also angry at powerful institutions in which they played meaningful roles for abandoning and marginalizing them. The story of this bitterness begins with accounts of the most remembered event in Whiting: the great refinery fire of 1955. Everyone who was there recalled the sudden explosion and the inferno that raged for days not only because it was so sensational but because it led to formulating a policy that caused the first large layoffs in Whiting under the regime of paternalism. The destruction caused by the fire forced the company to initiate a plant modernization designed not only to improve employee safety and efficiency but also reduce the total number of those

[23] Jancosek interview; Sotak interview; Kus interview.
[24] Hlebasko interview; Kus interviews; Joe Gresko interview.

employees. This may have made some economic sense, but employees saw the layoffs, which actually began in 1960, as a rejection of the ideal of justice and solidarity that workers had agreed to support since the 1920s. In fact, the reaction to the layoffs was so severe that it led to support for an outside union—the Oil, Chemical, and Atomic Workers International —for the first time. Previously, refinery workers had voted to keep out external labor organizations such as the Congress of Industrial Organizations (CIO) and supported unions consisting only of Standard employees. There was particular concern that workers with over ten years of service were now losing jobs. As Leo Kus recalls, "The people were downhearted. . . . We were dedicated to our work."[25]

The company compounded the disruption of their relationship with these people by bringing Mexican-American workers into the refinery when they realized their reductions had gone too far. This action not only caused additional outrage over the layoffs but also led many workers to identify the newcomers with the onset of moral and communal decline. Older employees think that thefts in the plant have increased in the 1990s and argue that Mexicans are lazier than they were. Some feel all the younger workers now entering the plant, whatever their racial or ethnic background, fail to display the "loyalties of our fathers" toward the company. The patriotic generation complains that newcomers do not want to work hard and yet feel they should be paid for just showing up.[26]

The collective account of Whiting's past is a moral story that connects the past and the present. It is a tale about an agreement—a covenant and a contract—that is ultimately broken. Despite its selective, defensive, and nostalgic features, the account is also didactic and attempts to instruct others on the need for fairness in relationships. Unconcerned with objective history, the narrative is ultimately a polemic that engaged discourses in the contemporary world. Embedded in life as it was and is lived, personal identity, and reality as it is restated, patriotism in this context can never become a notion about simple devotion to a nation. The moral imperative of collective memory, often eradicated from public texts and monuments, continually reworks dogmas of submissions and the veneration of power. Moral patriotism continually contests dogmatic patriotism. The fact that these people exhibit limits to their sense of justice and solidarity opens them up to charges that they lack moral qualities themselves. Because they are not afraid to counter many of the most powerful values of American culture in the 1990s such as the celebration of individualism, however, they imply that they never fully relinquished their

[25] Kus interviews.
[26] Ibid.

sense of self—the basis of their ability to challenge power—and that they still support an ideal of a just nation for all.

Like all political language patriotism is subject to diverse meanings. As a heroic idiom patriotism has often been used to place loyalty to the state above all other loyalties, but state loyalty can also be viewed as a means to protecting objects of love and devotion like home and family or as a safeguard for the dream of a fair society. Scholars have referred to this later variant as the "secret of the patriotism of the citizens": people grant loyalty to higher authority in hopes of satisfying private and democratic aspirations.[27]

The collective memory of older Whiting residents reifies the rewards they received in return for their loyalty to others and obscures the exploitative aspects of those relations. These people tell stories from memory as a way of countering new ways of thinking in the present. Thus, they selectively rework the ideologies of their past—paternalism, Catholicism, and patriotism—and extract notions of fairness and benevolence that they believed were in them. In their minds the practice of obligation involved much more than submission. Their notion of patriotism was moral because it was directed not to the nation-state but to a community and a country that included other people and a series of institutions. Like Lincoln they thought the state could be an active agent for creating a good society. Thus, the generation that speaks here does not agree with MacArthur's call for a patriotism free of politics and morals. Authority can be served and individualism constrained in their minds, but not without some promise of reciprocity and care.

The few scholars who have thought about patriotism have noted its multi-dimensional character. They have argued that the simple veneration of the state can weaken the validity of other forms of obligation that necessarily exist in any society and foster nationalism over patriotism. Despite the ability of patriotism to be put to all sorts of political uses, they remain more hopeful about its language of obligation and responsibility than nationalism and its cant of domination and national greatness that seeks to justify mastery of subcommunities and even racial minorities within and outside a nation-state. They hope that patriotism can help to sustain an ideal of self-denial and love that, used constructively, could serve as a basis for the pursuit of the common good rather than self-interest or absolute state power.

The meaning of patriotism in Whiting is located somewhere between the tenets of modern liberalism and what Charles Taylor would call civic

---

[27] John H. Schaar, "The Case for Patriotism," *American Review*, no. 17 (May, 1973), 57–70; see Stephen K. White, *The Recent Work of Jürgen Habermas* (Cambridge: Cambridge University Press, 1988), 60–66.

republicanism. In its expression of the need to pursue the good of all, it approximated Taylor's ideal form of patriotism. But it modified the quest for virtue with claims for reciprocity in return for loyalty. Thus, its pursuit of a virtuous society was tempered by a refusal to submit to idolatry.[28]

The specific meaning of obligation and responsibility in Whiting confirmed Michael Walzer's contention that moral knowledge always implies the existence of shared values and is always acquired within a group, partially as an obligation to that group. This process inevitably starts with firsthand experience in small communities or within institutions like workplaces or churches. Obligations are not acquired simply by birth into a group, however; ultimately obligations involve "willful" decisions where individuals make choices about their obligations and the objects of their solidarity. Walzer makes the crucial point that solidarity— responsibility to others—is strongest where voluntary participation reinforces inherited membership. Familial and institutional authority certainly accounted for many values Whiting's patriotic generation manifests, but these authorities are not seen as entirely coercive or beyond the influence of "willful" individuals. Coercion existed. But people also feel that they had participated in society in a meaningful way. Modern society—with its reverence for self-interest and focus on consumption—appears beyond their control and incapable of fostering participation and unselfishness; that trend troubles them. That is why they do not like a corporation that breaks promises or a marketplace that nurtures individual interests at the expense of solidarity.[29] They are unsure that they themselves or any subsequent citizens can remain loyal to such a society. Ultimately they are not opposed to modern liberalism; they remain attached to its dream of restricting market forces. But they fear that liberalism is deteriorating and that the idea of moral patriotism can no longer survive.

[28] Michael Walzer, *Obligations: Essays on Disobedience, War and Citizenship* (Cambridge: Harvard University Press, 1970), 12–21.

[29] On the need for political narratives to address the issue of the "destiny of community" in light of the "effects" of history see Fredric Jameson, *The Political Unconscious: Narrative as a Socially Symbolic Act* (Ithaca: Cornell University Press, 1981), 70, 102. Jameson on 73, observed that radical politics has traditionally alternated between the "triumph of the collectivity" or the "liberation of the soul." The Whiting narrative appears to exist somewhere in the middle of these extremes. On the tendency of modern American liberalism to stand between the radical poles of socialism and competitive capitalism see Richard Pells, *Radical Visions and American Dreams: Culture and Social Thought in the Depression Years* (New York: Harper and Row, 1973), 79–81.

Chapter 14

"TALKING LORDS WHO DARE NOT FACE THE FOE": CIVILIAN RULE AND THE MILITARY NOTION OF PATRIOTISM IN THE CLINTON PRESIDENCY

Robin Wagner-Pacifici

WILLIAM JEFFERSON CLINTON has never served in the military. After all of the awkward and anarchic interactions between President Clinton and members of the United States military during the first year of his administration, the above is surely an understatement. But it is the fact with which this essay must begin. Clinton is a thoroughly *civilian* president. At this particular point in American history, that is a remarkable status. That it is remarkable (in the sense that it is put into high relief) is, on the face of it, perplexing. Don't we assume civilian rule in a democracy such as ours? There are no inherent philosophical or procedural grounds for insisting that all presidents must have served in the military. This is true even though, as Samuel Huntington points out, Gouveneur Morris insisted on the eligibility of senators and representatives for military office. Morris stated: "Exclude the officers of the army & navy—and you form a band having a different interest from & opposed to the civil power: you stimulate them to despise & reproach those 'talking Lords who dare not face the foe.'"[1]

But surely, even given such concerns, there is nothing to question in the straightforward election by the populace of a candidate of a major political party. And yet, it cannot be just a coincidence that it is the first president not to serve in the military since Franklin Roosevelt (FDR having served as secretary of the navy in World War I) who is jeered at a war memorial, indifferently received on an aircraft carrier, and made the butt of humor by an air force general. For me, these moments of authoritative

---

I wish to thank John Bodnar and Charles Moskos for reading and commenting on previous drafts of this chapter.

[1] Morris quoted in Samuel Huntington, *The Soldier and the State* (Cambridge: Harvard University Press, 1957), 166.

slippage are interesting for what they can tell us about contemporary notions of patriotism and authoritative national voice. The overriding question then is only partially about whether Clinton is or is not considered sufficiently patriotic by the military. Beyond that it asks whether twentieth-century patriotism is undergoing a difficult transformation, a possibility suggested and given substance by John Bodnar's paradigm of "contested notions" of patriotism in the introduction to this volume. Are we witnessing, in the discomfort of the military with Clinton's rule and the public confusion about his authority, a provisional transformation of the very concept of patriotism?

Of course, the case of Clinton and the military involves more than the fact of his nonservice. It includes the *modality* of his nonservice (moving toward and retreating from the ROTC and into and out of the draft—thanks to his high lottery number), his open opposition to the war in Vietnam while a student, his taking on the military's opposition to the service of gay individuals, and his overseeing of base closures and other cost reductions in this post–Cold War period. One might say that this presidency is, in fact, overdetermined in its assertion of civilian rule over the military. And that is precisely what makes this a moment of such rich analytical importance. Some conjunction of forces, including those listed above, is creating a moment of great, if not yet crystallized or self-conscious, realignment. Confusion about or resistance to this realignment takes strange forms in institutions like the military that do not have vocabularies capable of articulating confusion, ambivalence, or resistance easily. I specify some forms of resistance and confusion that may appear trivial or accidental but that, on the contrary, tap into very deep political and existential shifts. They all take place in public arenas of ritual contact between the commander-in-chief and the military where authority and patriotic gestures are the mediums of exchange. These moments of interaction are at the heart of this chapter.

Who Is an American?

I'll begin with a strange and revealing contretemps between *MacNeil-Lehrer* commentator Mark Shields and former Secretary of Education William Bennett. Their discussion took place on the *MacNeil-Lehrer* program covering the 1992 Republican National Convention in Houston. It was the first night of the convention and the colloquy focused on a comment made by Republican National Chairman Rich Bond, to the effect that they (the Republicans) were America and the Democrats were not America. Mark Shields—*both* a liberal and a marine corps veteran—reacted immediately and vigorously to this:

I think it is the most jarring note of this convention. . . . I mean it has the rancid stench of McCarthyism about it, if in fact Rich Bond, the Republican National Chairman, one of George Bush's oldest and most loyal lieutenants is going to open this convention with this kind of stuff and that kind of garbage that signals what kind of a campaign lies ahead. . . . George Bush was there when the Berlin Wall collapsed and for that reason he does reap some political benefit from it, but to suggest that one party fought the Cold War and won the Cold War is not simply a misreading of history, it is error, it is wrong, and it's unpatriotic in the truest sense of America.

Bennett responds with a qualification that *some* Democrats, Truman and Kennedy for example, fought the Cold War with commitment. But, he adds:

In recent years in the last twelve years it was primarily Republican and conservative leadership. . . . And it was people in the Democratic Congress, it was people in the Democratic Senate who would oppose and did oppose Ronald Reagan . . . who made fun of him when he talked about the evil empire, who argued for a unilateral disarmament.

These comments push Shields over the edge, and he comes back with an extremely interesting final sally. His is the trump card of the Vietnam Veterans Memorial:

I don't know anybody in the Democratic party in a position of authority or responsibility who's ever argued for disarmament and if Bill Bennett wants to go down to the Vietnam Memorial with me and go through the names with me and see which ones of those kids came from Democratic families and Democratic neighborhoods, I'll be happy to do it.[2]

This argument caught my ear because I had rarely heard so many things brought together so overtly in the business of defining "America." The question of who was really American, really patriotic, immediately elicited references to war (hot and cold), military service, partisan politics, and Vietnam. The military discourse is so pervasive here that even Mark Shields, defender of the Democrats, refers nonironically to Rich Bond as Bush's "lieutenant." Politicians and soldiers become interchangeable. Or, even better, the soldiers' political alignments give legitimacy to the politicians in these parties. I find it particularly telling that the Vietnam War and its memorial is chosen as the arbiter of legitimacy. First, it was such a contested and ultimately unforgiving war. Second, it was the war in which Bill Clinton could have fought but did not. So even in the process of defending him, albeit obliquely, Mark Shields prob-

[2] Transcript of PBS/NBC Joint Republican National Convention Coverage, 17 August 1992, 19–20.

lematizes the candidacy of Clinton. How and why does the notion of patriotism devolve into military participation? And how and why do patriotism, militarism, and partisanship become indissolubly linked?

Historian Richard Kohn specifies that during the McNamara years, years of "a new form of civilian control [of the military] through new bureaucratic procedures and structures," the recent conjoint processes of militarizing politics and politicizing the military began. The former went into high gear during the Vietnam era: "The two major political parties divided pro- and anti-military: the Democrats anti-military spending, anti-intelligence, anti-weapons procurement, and largely anti-intervention; the Republicans simply opposite. Jimmy Carter's openly contemptuous anti-military administration only exacerbated the trend." Kohn attributes the latter, the process of politicization of the military, to "Vietnam division which angered the military [and] officer corps began to attract few people for careers except those from the most traditional or conservative parts of society; then the all volunteer policy even further diminished whatever ideological diversity existed in the officer corps earlier. The result has been an increasingly politicized military: traditional in values, Republican, conservative, and increasingly conscious of itself as a separate entity in American society."[3]

These trends and other related civilian/military dynamic-altering trends identified by such scholars as Charles Moskos and Russell Weigley lead us back to some fundamental questions about the stability and essential nature of civilian rule.[4] In his classic book, *The Soldier and the State*, Samuel Huntington painstakingly analyzed the variations upon civilian/military rule relationships in the history of the United States. Huntington identifies several factors in the Constitution and ideological formations of the United States that have complicated and sometimes hindered this development of what he terms "objective" civilian control, that form of control in which a professionalized military has a distinct, nonpolitical role. One is the very constitutional separation of powers of which we are often so proud. Huntington states: "The separation of powers is a perpetual invitation, if not an irresistible force, drawing military leaders into political conflicts. Consequently it has been a major hindrance to the development of military professionalism and civilian control in the United States."[5] Here Huntington not only refers to the separation of power between the Congress and the president, but he also

[3] Richard H. Kohn, "The Erosion of Civilian Control of the Military in the United States" (speech delivered to the Washington area region of the Inter-University Seminar on the Armed Forces and Society, Fort Lesley J. McNair, 30 September 1993), 4–6.

[4] Cf. an interview with Charles Moskos in the *Chicago Tribune*, 20 April 1993, 19, and Russell Weigley, "The American Military and the Principle of Civilian Control from McClellan to Powell," *Journal of Military History* 57 (October, 1993): 27–58.

[5] Huntington, *Soldier and the State*, 177.

invokes the constitutional confusion over the chain-of-command from president to cabinet secretary to military chief.

In terms of ideological deterrents, Huntington identifies the complicated nature of the relationship of liberalism to the problem of war. He writes: "Liberalism tends to assume the existence of that very national security which the military man considers to be continually threatened. . . . Liberalism has many pacifist tendencies, but the liberal will normally support a war waged to further liberal ideals."[6]

Robert Westbrook further develops this exploration of the fraught relationship of liberalism and war by focusing on the question of the obligation of individuals to risk their lives in war. Elaborating on Michael Walzer's writings, Westbrook writes: "A man who risks his life for the [liberal] state accepts the insecurity which it was the only end of his political obedience to avoid: war is the failure of politics. Hence there can be no political obligation either to die or to fight."[7] Westbrook concludes that the liberal state has fallen back, successfully if illogically, on the link between private obligations (to family, friends, etc.) and wartime participation in an attempt to make an end run around the paradox of liberalism.

Ideological and constitutional constraints upon the development of, on the one hand, what Huntington calls objective civilian control and, on the other hand, what Westbrook defines as communal-based obligations to fight wars are exacerbated in historical moments of domestic and/or international political realignment, military-related technological advancement, or economic shifts. The Clinton presidency represents and inherits the legacy of all these changes. And with the inherited chairman of the Joint Chiefs, General Colin Powell, at the helm Clinton's presidency confronted an extremely diffident military.[8] Taking all the developments outlined above: the constitutional paradoxes regarding civilian and military rule, the ideological blind spot of liberalism toward war, the contemporary moves toward downsizing the military during the post–Cold War era, the residual ambivalences associated with the Vietnam War,[9] the politicization of the military and the militarization of the polity,

---

[6] Ibid., 90.

[7] Robert Westbrook, "Fighting for the American Family: Private Interests and Political Obligation in WWII," in *The Power of Culture: Critical Essays in American History*, ed. Richard W. Fox and T. J. Jackson Lears (Chicago: University of Chicago Press, 1993), 195–222.

[8] Cf. Kohn, "Erosion of Civilian Control," and Weigley, "American Military," for the particular posture of Powell toward Clinton as commander-in-chief. This chapter cannot fully develop the implications of Colin Powell's very recent emergence as a possible presidential candidate. But such a candidacy may be viewed as a logical response to the fully civilian presidency of Clinton.

[9] Cf. Robin Wagner-Pacifici and Barry Schwartz, "The Vietnam Veterans Memorial: Commemorating a Difficult Past," *American Journal of Sociology* 97, no. 2 (September 1991): 376–420.

the election of the first Democratic president in twelve years, and the election of the first president in nearly fifty years who (very self-consciously) did not serve in the military, I want to claim that we are in a period of realignment—of not only foreign and domestic policy goals, but perhaps of the very nature of the relationship between civilian and military authority. Whether this realignment occurs depends, it seems to me, on whether the military finally accepts the Clinton presidency *as is*, or whether the Clinton presidency will change sufficiently to be accepted by the military as *it* is. Ultimately, I believe that the very notion of American patriotism ("who is America," as Rich Bond, Bill Bennett, and Mark Shields put it), is tied up in these interregnum transformations. Let me now turn to the specific moments in this interregnum that epitomize, in their key terms and ritual gestures, the diffidence and ambiguity about authority and patriotism that has plagued the Clinton presidency.

THREE (AND A HALF) MOMENTS

Let me proceed chronologically. The first of the moments occurred during the January 1993 inauguration of Clinton and involved a CBS interview with an air force colonel responsible for coordinating the military part of the inaugural parade. The second moment took place on the decks of the *USS Theodore Roosevelt*, a nuclear aircraft carrier, during a visit of President Clinton in March 1993. The third moment encompassed Clinton's Memorial Day appearance at the Vietnam Veterans Memorial in May of that year. And finally, the third and a half moment occurred during Bobby Ray Inman's speech in December at the White House accepting Clinton's nomination for secretary of defense after Les Aspin's resignation. Each moment took place in a space of ritual or commemoration. Furthermore, two of the moments occurred during a time of ritual transformation or remembrance.

THE CRYING COLONEL

On 20 January 1993, Dan Rather hosted a CBS *48 Hours* segment titled, nostalgically, "Here Comes Mr. Clinton." The television program focused exclusively on the preparations for and unrolling of the inauguration, with many Clinton friends and Bush administration workers interviewed. For the purposes of this essay, the interview with Air Force Colonel Victor Tambone, chief of staff at the "op center" (operation center for the coordination of the military part of the inaugural parade), stands out as remarkable. Correspondent Wyatt Andrews begins his interview of Tambone by comparing him to "Norman Schwarzkopf in his bunker." Tambone is first heard saying that this operation is important because "we're also sending a signal to the rest of the world. We're sending a signal that this is the United States of America. This is the leader of the free world and when we do things we do it right and we do it right the first time." Some shots are then shown of the parade itself and Andrews's voice-over says: "In many countries the change of government means the military is taking over. In our country, the military is running the parade." Tambone picks up on this theme continuous with a most striking acknowledgment or admission:

> TAMBONE: We are changing command of the military. We are doing it without anybody forcing us to do it. The American people have voted. The American people have said we want to make this change. And we are going to do it. The civilians are those folks over us. We will never, ever forget that.
>
> ANDREWS: I sense when you said that—a lot of pride. It's an emotional day for you?
>
> TAMBONE: (long pause, eyes watering) Yeah, it is. The greatest day the military will ever see. It always is, every inauguration.[10]

This moment is redolent with the very themes under examination here. It both asks and answers the question: what is the relationship between the military and the civilian president? And, in repetitively asking and answering that question, it also asks the unaskable question: what is the relationship between the military and *this* civilian president?

Wyatt Andrews begins by simultaneously aggrandizing and domesticating Tambone's enterprise; it is worthy of comparison with Norman Schwarzkopf, undisputed military hero of the Gulf War. Yet, in contrast with other militaries in other countries who may be actually taking over their governments, this military is (merely?) running the parade. Of course it is good that our military is not taking over the government, but the viewer is left to ask why this differentiation needs to be asserted.

For his part, Tambone equates the efficient management of the parade with leadership of the free world: "We do it right the first time." This is not entirely of a piece with a military discourse of operations and targets and hits. A slight shift in discursive grounds has introduced a language of management and efficient production. In fact, it is hard to imagine producing an inauguration and then throwing it away and producing it again as you might a defective product.

But the final interchange between Tambone and Andrews strikes me as most remarkable. In this exchange, Tambone opens the Pandora's box

[10] CBS, *48 Hours*, "Here Comes Mr. Clinton," 20 January 1993.

of civilian rule in a democracy. He refers to the fact that nobody is "forcing" the military to change its command—nobody, that is, but the civilians who voted to make a change. The viewer is left to wonder if the
decision to make this change is automatic (as it must be in a democracy)
or if it is, even for a moment, *considered* (in which case the democracy is
imperceptibly destabilized). This reflexive reminding of civilian control
is startling both because it usually goes unsaid and because it makes Tambone cry. Why are Andrews and Tambone so persistent in reminding us
of the military's status in this moment of delicate transition?

Is it simply the case that, as Alexis de Tocqueville said, "Elections
. . . may be conducted with such simplicity and rapidity that the seat of
power will never be left vacant; but notwithstanding these precautions, a
break necessarily occurs in the minds of the people"?[11] Does this break
constitute some kind of built-in point of potential crisis, always to be
ritually warded off? Is Tambone crying because he is emotionally impressed by the idea of popular democracy once again successfully staving
off a crisis? While not questioning his loyalty to this idea, it is thought-
provoking to find someone in the military become emotional about the
military's subordination to an extramilitary force. And why is *this* day's
event, and not some armistice after a war well fought, the "greatest day
the *military* will ever see"?

Ritual transitions are clearly important, but what does this mean for
Clinton specifically? My guess is that the interview would have been
quite different if George Bush had been reelected or even if someone
without Clinton's intermittently vexed and nonexistent relationship with
the military had been elected. In such a case, there might not have been
the urgency felt here to articulate the ultimate authority of the electorate.
We must, at any rate, acknowledge some critical ambivalence in this interview that does not augur well for the administration.

AT SEA

"Ambivalence is no frame of mind for a warship. But there seemed to be
no better word for the mood that filled the hangar deck here today."[12]
Two months after taking the oath of office, President Clinton made a trip
to the USS *Theodore Roosevelt* anchored off of the Virginia coast. In the
interim, Clinton had made good on his campaign promise to raise the
issue of repealing the ban on homosexuals serving in the military. This

---

[11] Alexis de Tocqueville, *Democracy in America,* vol. 1 (New York: Vintage Books,
1945), 134–36.

[12] "Warship Gives Clinton a Not-So-Hail to the Chief," *Washington Post,* 13 March
1993, A1.

issue was quickly proving controversial, with General Colin Powell himself declaring his opposition. Clinton's visit to the USS *Theodore Roosevelt*, a ship about to leave for the Mediterranean, had the air of symbolic reparation about it. And these reparations turned precisely on the relevant question of Clinton's image. The *New York Times*, for example, was blunt in its interpretation: "For Mr. Clinton, who is fighting a perception that he does not understand military culture because he avoided the draft during the Vietnam War, it was an unaccustomed adventure on the high seas meant to convey *patriotism and martial vigor*."[13]

As it happened things turned out a bit differently from the interpolated aim. Depending on which news stories one reads, the reception on the ship from officers, pilots, and sailors alike ranged anywhere from restrained politeness to overt mockery. It is important, for my purposes, to articulate the *forms* of diffidence or disrespect toward Clinton rather than simply to record their occurrence. The main forms were jokes about masculinity, sexuality, and military bravery (or its absence) and comments about the democratic expression of support or disaffection in the act of voting. Let me first examine the jokes.

"Did you hear the one about the protester who threw a beer at the president? Not to worry. It was a draft beer and Clinton dodged it." This joke was quoted by several newspapers, including *The Washington Post*, *The Washington Times* and *The Boston Globe*. It clearly caught the attention of the media looking for a way to characterize the visit. The joke is odd and revealing. Of course, the main reference is to Clinton's avoidance of the Vietnam draft, a subject much overworked by the time of the visit. But the strangeness of the joke lies perhaps in its linking of protesters, the president, beer, and Vietnam. Who is the protester? What is the protester protesting? It's a topsy-turvy world in which the former protester (Clinton) has a beer launched at him by a contemporary (?) protester. Old-style protesters from the anti-war movement didn't, in fact, drink beer. They smoked marijuana and defied the complacent patriotism of the stereotypical macho, beer-drinking "silent majority." So everything about this joke is backward. The protester is protested; the beer drinker is now *protester* rather than asserted national *protector*. Social and historical roles have been reversed and conflated. The joke speaks to a loss of certainty about who represents authority and the establishment.

As well, what does it mean that sailors and marines are telling, hearing, and laughing at a joke in which the commander-in-chief has a beer hurled at him. That imagined act is one of such scorn and such unprin-

[13] "Unaccustomed Role for Clinton at Sea," *New York Times*, 13 March 1993, 7; emphasis added.

cipled physical aggression that its contemplation actually detracts from the joke's punchline.

The issue of homosexuals serving in the military also surfaced in a parodic form aboard the ship. *The Washington Post* reported the following scene: "While preparing a weapons display for Clinton's visit, one marine sniper donned a shredded burlap wig and began mincing around the deck. Another sniper wrapped him in an embrace. What with Clinton's visit, they said mockingly, they were thinking of declaring their love."[14] On one level, it is obvious that the policy changes contemplated by the Clinton administration might elicit strong feelings from the military. But on another level, that of decorum, respect, and obedience, it is startling to find this parody performed for the media on the ship. Clearly a kind of threat to masculinity, a core attribute of the traditional military, is associated with Clinton and his proposals. And this threat pushes against the other core attributes of duty and discipline. Psychoanalytic interpretation might call this *pas de deux* a bit of unconscious leakage. I would rather look at it as one more example of the generalized problem of boundary erosion that a too fiercely held notion of masculine military patriotism must begin to experience.

The immediate problem for Clinton is that the three hours spent on board the USS *Theodore Roosevelt* were hours during which Clinton actually had to do something. He had to look at and touch equipment and weapons. He had to wear something. He had to address the crew in words and gestures. These necessities marked strategic points of dissonance as the media watched the crew watching Clinton salute, pick up a shoulder-fired rocket launcher, wear a green naval flight jacket, and refer to the "roof" (the carrier's flight deck).[15] The very amount of time spent itself became the source of another Clinton joke, this one spoken by an executive officer of a fighter squadron: "Maybe we can call this his military service. Three hours is more than he had before."

All of this assorted noise, picked up by the sensitive microphones of an attentive media raised the unthinkable question: Did Bill Clinton have a right to be there on that ship? It is a bizarre question, but one we have seen subliminally being asked by a representative of the military on the very day of the inauguration. Proof of its (tacit) asking is provided by comments on board about the act of voting in the presidential election.

The most prominent of these references to democratic political process was that made by the captain of the ship, Stanley W. Bryant. It took the

---

[14] "Warship Gives Clinton a Not-So-Hail to the Chief," *Washington Post*, 13 March 1993, A1.

[15] Charles Moskos actually recommends in his *Chicago Tribune* interview that Clinton not take on the gestures, dress, and language of the military. He claims that they will never seem authentic and thus will always jar.

form of a preemptive strike: "I think that all of you would agree that regardless of the president's politics, we need to show support for the president of the United States and the commander-in-chief of the armed forces. *Whether you voted for him or not*, I think we all want the president and the administration to succeed."[16]

Recall Victor Tambone's flat assertion that "the American people have voted." This all seems so obvious, so much the given of our political notions of legitimacy that its repetitive assertion is perplexing. Even DeeDee Meyers, Clinton's press secretary, raised the specter of the vote in a press briefing on March 15. Meyers was answering a slightly hostile question about Clinton's visit to the USS *Theodore Roosevelt* in which the reporter characterized the visit as "less than successful." The reporter asked if Meyers thought Clinton had changed any minds about people's (meaning military people's) opinions of him. Meyers responded with: "Well, I don't know that it was intended to change people's minds. People are entitled to their own opinions and to vote as they see fit. He is the commander-in-chief. He does support the military."[17]

Why does the vote have to be brought out and brought up in ritual fashion like a totem, all strength deriving from the repetitive incantation? But does it also remain, like all ritual transformations, ultimately unconvincing and thus needing to be remembered and activated over and over again? Out there, on those rough and windy March seas, Clinton and the ballot box are brought on board together, both formally honored and practically inconvenient guests.

AGAINST THE WALL

On Memorial Day 1993, President William Jefferson Clinton paid an official and ceremonial visit to the Vietnam Veterans Memorial. In doing so, he was actually the first U.S. president to do so in the ten years since the memorial's dedication. This was, in itself, quite fitting. Barry Schwartz and I have argued elsewhere that the Vietnam Veterans Memorial marks a historical, political, and aesthetic break in America's consciousness of itself. The memorial is actually a memorial complex, containing a long, v-shaped, downward sloping, black granite wall with the names of all fallen servicemen and women carved into the stone. It also contains a realistic statue representing and titled, "Three Fighting Men." These three men, of diverse ethnicities, look exhausted and somewhat

---

[16] *Washington Post*, 13 March 1993, A1; emphasis added.

[17] The Briefing Room, Press Briefing by Dee Dee Myers from Clinton Headquarters at Campaign 1992. Provided by MIT Artificial Intelligence Lab.

lost. There is also a flag on a tall pole at some distance from the wall with an engraved message on its base. And finally, there is now an additional statue of women nurses who served in Vietnam. The various parts of the memorial complex were not all included in the original design; only the wall was. The additions came along in the process of resolving public and official debate about how exactly the Vietnam era ought to be remembered. Some wanted to draw attention to the lives lost, some to notions of heroism, and some to notions of country. In our study of the ultimate design and construction of the memorial, we noted a persistent expression of ambivalence:

> The wall embodied a controversial assertion: that individuals should be remembered and their cause ignored; the qualifications [of that] came with the flag and statue. These, in turn, were beset by their own internal tensions. The statue was conceived as a reactive assertion of pride, heroism, and masculinity, but, through the particular form that it took, it emerged as a tempering of all these things. The flag seems to be unconditionally assertive because it draws our eyes upward, but we notice in the peculiar dedication inscribed on its base a kind of backing off: "This flag affirms the principles of freedom for which [the Vietnam veterans] fought and their pride in having served under difficult circumstances." . . . By "difficult circumstances" we are to understand not the power of our enemy but the feebleness of our cause. . . . Whether we look down, across, or up, we find ambivalence about the meaning of this war and its protagonists refracted throughout."[18]

This essential ambivalence should not, however, be read as having made the memorial ineffective. The Vietnam Veterans Memorial is one the most frequently visited sites in Washington, D.C. Beyond that, it has become the site for many emotional reunions of veterans. Many visitors have also placed symbolic offerings at the wall, including military emblems, letters to and from veterans, personal articles of clothing, and flowers. It is ironic that the memorial has found its strength in spite of, or rather *in*, its ambivalence.

Meanwhile, residual concern about the relation of Clinton to the military had pushed the air force general chief-of-staff, Merrill McPeak, to write and distribute a memo to all air force commanders in late March reminding them of the need to respect and support the commander-in-chief. McPeak wrote: "It is time to remind ourselves about core values, including the principle of a chain of command that runs from the president right down to our newest airman. . . . Most of us are professional enough to realize he's the one in charge and we're better off to support

---

[18] Wagner-Pacifici and Schwartz, "Difficult Past," 399.

him and do what we can to help him rather than oppose him."[19] But this memo ran aground on the persistent hostility that took such forms as that of Air Force Major General Harold Campbell's award banquet jokes about Clinton on May 24. The jokes referred to Clinton as "draft-dodging, pot-smoking, gay-loving, and womanizing." Clinton's appearance at the Vietnam Veterans Memorial provided another opportunity for him to come to terms with such overt scorn.

Following General Colin Powell as the main speaker at the memorial, President Clinton was greeted with the following: "Shouts of 'Coward, Coward' were heard from a section behind the VIP seats. Men in combat gear hoisted signs like: 'Slick Willie: The Artful Draft Dodger.' "[20] In his turn, Clinton almost immediately responded with:

> To all of you who are shouting, I have heard you. I ask you now to hear me. I have heard you. [Applause] Some have suggested that it is wrong for me to be here with you today because I did not agree a quarter of a century ago with the decision made to send the young men and women to battle in Vietnam. Well, so much the better. Here we are, celebrating America today. Just as war is freedom's cost, disagreement is freedom's privilege, and we honor it here today. [Applause] But I ask all of you to remember the words that have been said here today. And I ask you at this monument: Can any American be out of place? And can any commander-in-chief be in any other place but here on this day? I think not. [Applause]

The British anthropologist, Mary Douglas, once defined dirt as "matter out of place." Clinton asks the very pointed and symbolic question about the appropriate "place" of any American, including most poignantly, himself. In responding to the protesters, Clinton first claims that he has "heard" them; maybe these are the protesters presciently imagined in the joke on the ship. And he asks that they hear him. Thus he appeals to an ideal of public, political dialogue, a rational discourse of the commons. Next, Clinton links war, freedom, and disagreement by claiming that they are all necessary in a democracy. Here is the old, but nevertheless still challenging, notion that soldiers fight a war so that civilians back home can continue to disagree about the grounds of the war. Finally, explicitly referring to himself as the commander-in-chief, Clinton asks the question about the symbolic relevance and rightness of his presence at the memorial. There is a certain muted lamentation in this question. Where indeed, he seems to be asking, should a president go? What is his

[19] Gannett News Service, "President Clinton: Target of Hard Feelings in the Military," 11 June 1993.

[20] "Fighting Stance Gets President Through Boos, Jeers," *Arizona Republic*, 2 June 1993.

legitimate symbolic terrain? Does it not include war memorials, battle-ships, and battlefields along with the White House, the Capitol, and more profane public spaces?

As Clinton gets into the body of the speech proper, he praises those whose names are on the wall for their commitment to freedom, for bringing honor to their communities, and for their love of country. He refers to the fact that four of those who died in Vietnam were his child-hood friends. Then, in perhaps his most positive and straightforward statement about the military in the speech, he says: "As we all resolve to keep the finest military in the world, let us remember some of the lessons that all agree on. If the day should come when our servicemen and women must again go into combat, let us all resolve they will go with the training, the equipment, the support necessary to win and, most im-portant of all, with a clear mission to win. [Applause]"[21]

In closing his speech, Clinton reveals that he has ordered that U.S. government records related to POWs and MIAs be declassified. Clearly there is an appeal to opening up this vexed period of American history both symbolically (Clinton's appearance at the memorial) and literally (declassifying documents). And then, the commander-in-chief echoes Colin Powell's echo of Lincoln: "With malice toward none and charity for all let us bind up the nation's wounds." Whose wounds are being bound up here: the veterans, the relatives of those who died, the nation's, or President Clinton's? One might see this trip to the Vietnam Veterans Memorial as a trip to heal Clinton's relationship with the military. That he does so at the least masculine or militarized of war memorials says much about how far in the direction of the world view of the military he is willing to go.

Ambivalence has its rewards. The press, in reporting the story of Clinton's visit to the Vietnam Veterans Memorial, was nearly uniform in claiming that Clinton had received a *mixed* reaction. Headlines fre-quently coupled "jeers" with "cheers" (*USA Today*, *The Washington Post*, *St. Louis Post-Dispatch*, *Los Angeles Times*, *Sacramento Bee*). Some reports claimed that this mixed reaction was due to Clinton's decision to respond to the protesters, some to the fact that the wall is deemed a sacred place where protests are viewed as obviously heretical. The argu-ment I am making here does not contradict these ideas; rather, I put more emphasis on the *fit* between Clinton and the Vietnam Veterans Memorial. Both are reflective; both are or have been ambivalent about the business of war; both have grown out of the historical moment of Vietnam.

21 Ibid.

COMFORT

On 16 December 1993, one day after Secretary of Defense Les Aspin had announced his resignation, President Clinton presented former Admiral Bobby Ray Inman as his nominee. In introducing Inman, Clinton praised him for his military experience as well as for his entrepreneurial skills. But Inman's acceptance speech took off in an entirely different direction. First, Inman felt compelled to make it known that he had not voted for Clinton; he had voted instead for Bush, his "old friend." Then, he moved beyond the issue of candidate choice to startle the listeners with a pale and opaque assessment of Clinton in Clinton's capacity as commander-in-chief. Inman stated that: "I had to reach a level of comfort that we could work together, that I would be very comfortable in your role as commander-in-chief while I was secretary of defense."[22]

Both these evaluative statements of Inman—about his ballot and about his comfort—are problematical. Presidential nominees to high office are usually pleased, proud, and somewhat deferential in their moment of (re)introduction to the public and the press. It is their bit of good fortune to have been selected. Inman, on the contrary, used the occasion to pass judgment on his nominator. But the *combination* of Inman's critical comments is key to this chapter. The fact that the issue of voting, whom one votes for, is brought together with military comfort reveals how muddy and overgrown the distinctions between civilian and military authority have become. It also demonstrates the degree to which the process of politicization of the military has proceeded; military officials naturally befriend and prefer Republicans.

To understand the blurred terrain of the legitimate voice of civilian rule in a democracy we should recall Colonel Victor Tambone's need to assert the obvious in his comment that "the American people have voted." We need also remember Captain Stanley Bryant's charge to the sailors on the USS *Theodore Roosevelt* that "We need to show support for the president of the United States and the commander-in-chief of the armed forces. Whether you voted for him or not, I think we all want the president and the administration to succeed." When the procedural forms of democracy are highlighted ritualistically in this way, they become problematized in spite of the protestations to the contrary.

That Inman should say both that he *did not* vote for Clinton for president (in his capacity as a citizen) and that he could be comfortable (although just comfortable rather than enthusiastic) with Clinton as

---

[22] *Newsday*, 17 December 1993.

commander-in-chief (in his capacity as secretary of defense) means that Inman himself is unwilling to decouple the electoral choice from the military appointment. Whatever else one might say about Bobby Ray Inman's withdrawal from the nomination process, one should certainly take pause from his brief and highly ambiguous run.

DISCUSSION

Can an American president who has not served in the military be considered a patriot in our times? What have patriotism and the presidency come to mean for the populace at large and for the military establishment? The now-famous sign above James Carville's desk in the (ironically named) "war room" of the Clinton campaign headquarters said, "It's the economy, stupid." The lesson to be learned over and over again during that campaign was that the American people wanted to hear what a candidate had to say and was willing to do about the recession, unemployment, and the deficit. The flag, America as superpower, and the traditional family were simply not uppermost in citizens' minds. Thus, little of the Clinton campaign rhetoric was devoted to the strength and/or need to strengthen the United States' armed forces.

Of course, the vicissitudes of Clinton's early and incomplete encounter with the armed forces forced itself onto the agenda of the campaign. The language of Clinton's disaffection from Vietnam was scrutinized when an old letter, written to a mentor, about his decision not to join the ROTC surfaced in the press.

Furthermore, the issue of the right of homosexuals to serve in the military became a permanent, if not of the highest priority, part of the Clinton campaign set of proposals. The selection of this issue is analytically compelling. Here is a candidate from the Democratic party (the party in disfavor with the military) who avoided service in Vietnam for all sorts of reasons, including opposition to the war, whose campaign discourse foregrounds domestic (one is tempted to say feminine) issues, and mutes international, foreign policy (one is tempted to say masculine) issues. And the one issue that focused clearly on the military in Clinton's campaign raises the delicate and threatening specter of sexuality.

Once elected, Clinton was indeed consistent in his prioritizing. The inaugural address itself was steadfastly devoted to the notion of change and renewal, largely in the domestic sphere. Only toward the end did the newly minted commander-in-chief raise what was termed "our vital interests": "When our vital interests are challenged, or the will and conscience of the international community is defied, we will act—with peaceful diplomacy whenever possible, with force when necessary. The brave Americans serving our nation today in the Persian Gulf, in Somalia, and wherever else they stand are testament to our resolve. But our greatest strength is the power of our ideas."[23] One might imagine Colonel Victor Tambone watching this on a monitor in his "op center." What indeed did he think about the place of the military in this speech? What should he have thought? The stage had clearly been set for the year's worth of strained interactions between and insubordinate reactions to President Clinton on the part of the military.

CONCLUSION

From the campaign, to the inauguration, to the battleship and the war memorial, and finally to the cabinet appointment process itself, military officials and enlisted men have chosen to express everything from grudging acceptance of Bill Clinton to outright contempt for him and his presidency. If scholars such as Richard Kohn, Charles Moskos, and Russell Weigley are correct, then this state of affairs comes out of a recent erosion of civilian control over the military in this country. In this chapter I have attempted to analyze the specific nature of that erosion, to chart the times, places, and languages of its expression. Some generalizations are possible.

There is overt grudging recognition on the part of the military that this is a democracy in which the citizens vote for president. The *overtness* itself is most telling. Many members of the military forces bring this up; they do so in the context of animosity toward the current incumbent from a posture of resentment. This is not the same thing as saying that they either do not believe it to be true or that they wish it were not true. It simply notes the posture and claims that postures are meaningful. Associated with this excessive attention paid to voting is the distinguishing between Democrats (unpatriotic, antimilitary) and Republicans (patriotic Americans, promilitary). This is the current form of the politicization of the military itself. Next, there are the jokes about Clinton (and also about Hillary). These are jokes about his military cowardice and his transgressive sexuality (womanizing and gay-loving). In fact the jokes couple military cowardice and transgressive sexuality.

The whole package comes together. A civilian elected official must have served in the military and must represent exclusively heterosexual imperatives to be deemed completely legitimate. Clinton is doomed to fail under this paradigm of legitimacy. And yet, he was jeered *and cheered*

[23] "Complete Text of Pres. Clinton's inaugural address," *The Atlanta Journal & Constitution*, 21 January 1993.

at the Vietnam Veterans Memorial, a memorial that itself has been jeered and ultimately cheered as representative of the Vietnam War. Does such an occurrence augur the possibility of change?

I would like to suggest that it does. This possibility does not derive, at least not at the moment, from any transformations internal to the military. Rather, change might come, if it does, from external events and actions. First, if it is possible to prevent a renewal of the Manichean vision of the Cold War period, where the United States has one essential enemy, the Soviet Union (all good residing with us, all evil residing with them), then it might also be possible to view the moral and political and economic interests of the United States in the complicated international context of many good and bad social and political movements and organizations. Under this perspective, the military retains its essential role, but it is clearly incompetent to judge the *political* ramifications of any given situation.

Second, if the Clinton administration (and successive administrations) can retain a focus on domestic issues, there is the possibility that "service to country" can take on a much expanded meaning. Here I am thinking about the recently passed, though funding imperiled, National Service Act. If the sense of service can be elaborated in the way the act anticipates, the notions of service, patriotism, military service, and masculinity might usefully become disentangled; each term might then be acknowledged and appreciated in its own right.

Afterword

NATIONALISM IN EUROPE

WILLIAM B. COHEN

T HE PRINCIPLE of monarchical authority in the North American colonies and much of Europe was challenged in the last three
decades of the eighteenth century; the enemies of arbitrary government declared that sovereignty was vested, not in the king, but rather
in the "nation." Since the Middle Ages, the term nation had seen its
significance expand. Deriving its meaning from Latin, the term signified
the place of birth. In medieval universities, student living quarters were
organized according to their "nations." Because some of these student
groups were identified with the support of special opinions, the term also
referred to a "community of opinion and purpose."[1] Thereafter, the term
gained a wider currency and meaning.

THE LEGACY OF THE FRENCH REVOLUTION

The construction of nationalism in France ignited and served as a paradigm for the evolution of political nationalism among its neighbors.[2]
Beginning in the mid-eighteenth century, the concept of nation was used
in France to contest authority. The noble-dominated local *parlements*
(courts registering the king's laws) opposed the right of the king to impose additional taxes on the nobility, who were resisting the king in the
name of the "nation." The term won a wider audience in the 1770s and
1780s and became increasingly democratized; pamphleteers insisted that

[1] Boyd Shafer, *Faces of Nationalism: New Realities and Old Myths* (New York: Harcourt,
Brace, Jovanovich, 1972), p. 14; Liah Greenfeld, *Nationalism: Five Roads to Modernity* (Cambridge: Harvard University Press, 1992), 4.

[2] The idea of nationalism as a construct owes a lot to Benedict R. Anderson, *Imagined
Communities: Reflections on the Origin and Spread of Nationalism* (London: Verso, 1983). A
recent scholar emphasizes that in seventeenth-century England the concept of the people
being the locus of sovereignty and hence the embodiment of the nation originated (Greenfeld, *Nationalism*, 29–87). Although such an argument might be made, one can imagine the
development of European nationalism without the English example, but not without the
French antecedent.

the common people, not the nobility, embodied the nation.[3] The French Revolution replaced royal authority with that of the nation; sovereignty was transferred from the king to the National Assembly.

Many means were used to create the sense of a national community. The Revolution wanted French spread throughout the country, for many citizens did not know the language; although the proportion was undoubtedly even higher, it was estimated that one-quarter of the population did not know French.[4] National ceremonies were held, celebrating the new Republic and nation, fused into a single identity. Marianne—the symbol of the Republic—was also the symbol of the nation. A national flag and national anthem were created and adopted.

The process of strengthening a French sense of nationhood was continuous one—the Revolution barely began the process. In the late nineteenth century, many Frenchmen still spoke no French and did not think of themselves as part of the imagined community of France.[5] It took many internal and external processes to develop such a sentiment. In the late nineteenth century, the spread of modern communications, a national school system, and military draft transformed "peasants into Frenchmen."[6]

The Revolution had proclaimed the nation as the highest object of loyalty. If in the past it had seemed proper to die for one's religious faith, now the nation was seen as a worthy object of sacrifice. The whole nation was to be mobilized to wage war; the French were able to put what for the time were remarkably large armies into the field.[7] These armies conquered Europe and reached Moscow in September 1812. French conquests led to a reactive nationalism. In Britain, an unprecedented number of men volunteered for military service—450,000 by 1804 when the island seemed to face the threat of imminent invasion.[8] Germany, which felt the sting of defeat and occupation, witnessed the development of a

[3] Robert R. Palmer, "The National Idea in France before the Revolution," *Journal of the History of Ideas* 1 (1940): 95–110.

[4] Eugen Weber, *My France: Politics, Culture, Myth* (Cambridge: Harvard University Press, 1991), 93.

[5] In the département of Finistère in Brittany, the majority of the adult population on the eve of World War I still could not understand even rudimentary French. Caroline Ford, *Creating the Nation in Provincial France: Religion and Political Identity in Brittany* (Princeton: Princeton University Press, 1993), 65.

[6] Title of book by Eugen Weber, *Peasants into Frenchmen: The Modernization of Rural France, 1870–1914* (Stanford, Calf.: Stanford University Press, 1976).

[7] Isser Woolloch, *The New Regime: Transformations of the French Civic Order, 1789–1820s* (New York: Norton, 1994), 380–426.

[8] H. T. Dickinson, "Popular Conservatism and Militant Loyalism, 1789–1815," in *Britain and the French Revolution, 1789–1815* (New York: St. Martin's Press, 1989), 117; Linda Colley, *Britons: Forging the Nation, 1707–1837* (New Haven: Yale University Press, 1992), 293.

militant nationalism; 30,000 young people volunteered to form Free Corps to fight Napoleon.

The only way to combat the revolutionary aspects of French nationalism was to mirror some values of a society that had proclaimed the principles of "Liberté, égalité et fraternité." In Britain, to fight Napoleon, the government had to mobilize the population; at least some members of the upper class recognized that reforms would have to be issued to motivate and reward the lower orders.[9] The Prussian state in the years immediately after its defeat in 1807 abolished serfdom, guilds, and other restrictive institutions; by these measures Prussia hoped to create a population that would feel a stake in society and presumably produce better soldiers.[10] Some of the main nationalist thinkers and agitators went further in their democratic aspirations; Ernest Moritz Arndt, a theologian and pamphleteer, wrote that the nation was not formed by princes, but by the *Volk*, the people. Although it was a coalition of princes and kings, leading traditional armies, who defeated Napoleon and freed German soil, a strong myth developed that the German Volk's mass uprising had actually liberated the native soil.[11]

The years from the Revolution to the fall of Napoleon in 1815 had at times witnessed expressions of egotistical nationalism, well summarized by Napoleon's own dictum, "My axiom is: France before everything."[12] More common was a cosmopolitan nationalism of the type announced by Johann Gottfried Herder, a German disciple of Rousseau. While wishing to see a German nation, Herder saw it as living in peace and tranquility in a Europe where other peoples had also achieved their nationhood. The most enthusiastic proponent of cosmopolitan nationalism in the first half of the nineteenth century was the Italian nationalist Giuseppe Mazzini. He not only formed Young Italy, a group of conspirators committed to create a free, united republican Italy, but he also launched the Young Europe movement, as the basis of his hoped-for federated Europe of free independent nations.[13]

[9] Frank O'Gorman, "Pitt and the 'Tory' Reaction to the French Revolution, 1789–1815," in *Britain and the French*, ed. Dickinson, 21–27, argues that the regime was not merely reactionary but adapted to the revolution. The Conservatives made an unprecedented appeal to the populace—quite out of tune with Conservative assumptions—which on the whole was successful; Dickinson, "Popular Conservatism," 103–25; Colley, *Forging*, 318–19.

[10] James Sheehan, *German History: 1770–1866* (New York: Oxford University Press, 1989), 291–310; Greenfeld, *Nationalism*, 373.

[11] Sheehan, *German History*, 386–87.

[12] Letter to Eugène Beauharnais, 23 August 1810, reprinted in J. Christopher Herold, *The Mind of Napoleon: A Selection from His Written and Spoken Words* (New York: Columbia University Press, 1955), 178.

[13] Denis Mack Smith, *Mazzini* (New Haven: Yale University Press, 1994), 11, 107, 154.

During much of the nineteenth century, nationalism was linked to political liberalism. The French Revolution, in opposition to royal arbitrariness and aristocratic privilege, preached the principles of the nation. German nationalists, struggling against the French, were able to imagine a German Volk without princes. Mazzini remained an ardent Republican all his life.

Most major states of Europe in the first half of the nineteenth century were multinational and authoritarian. Opposition to Austrian, Russian, and Ottoman rule often expressed itself in a discourse upholding nationalism and the principles of liberty. Greek nationalists, forming in January 1822 the Greek National Assembly, denounced "the cruel yoke of the Ottoman power" and declared the uprising "a war the object of which is to reconquer the rights of individual liberty."[14] In Hungary, in the wake of revolt against Habsburg rule, the Parliament declared in April 1849 that the country was "returning to the European family as a free and independent state."[15]

Polities that were not multinational also experienced in many cases a joining of liberal and national sentiment. If subjects of the King of Naples chafed under arbitrary rule and heavy taxes, then the alternative they imagined was a united and free Italy. In the Germanies, liberals resenting their petty authoritarian rulers, also called for a free and united nation.

CRITERIA OF NATIONHOOD

The variety of claims made to define and legitimate the nation were fully developed in the first half of the nineteenth century. The variety and arbitrary nature of these criteria reveal the subjective nature of nationalism. There were and are no objective yardsticks; if individuals or groups of individuals believe that a combination of criteria, or for that matter a single requirement, is necessary for membership in the "nation," then that is what it takes. The Germans saw language as crucial in defining the German nation. Greek nationalists in the 1810s, wanting to free Greece from Ottoman rule, reissued the classics of ancient Greek literature and "purified" the Greek language by ridding it of developments in popular speech over two millennia and reintroducing it to resemble more closely its classical antecedent. They wanted to remind their countrymen and countrywomen that they were the sons and daughters of Hellas. Language that was in eclipse could be revived for the national cause; the early

[14] Quoted in Hans Kohn, *Nationalism: Its Meaning and History* (New York: Van Nostrand, 1955), 116.

[15] Quoted in Piotr Wandycz, *The Price of Freedom: A History of East Central Europe from the Middle Ages to the Present* (New York: Routledge, 1993), 161.

nineteenth-century Serb nationalist Vuk Karajich decided that the dialect spoken in Herzegovina was the purest form of Serbo-Croatian; he transformed it into the literary language of Serbs and Croats. The leaders of these two peoples built on the idea of a common bond, especially an identical language, and established the state of Yugoslavia in 1919. When it collapsed in 1990, Serb and Croat nationalists attempted to create distinct languages. In Croatia, Serbo-Croatian versions of the international words for telephone and helicopter were replaced with Slavic words meaning "quick voice" and "air beater." Bosnian Moslems, rediscovering links with the Ottoman past, introduced Turkish words into their Serbo-Croatian.[16]

Although a common and distinct language has been used to justify nationalism, every language group has not formed its own nation or even attempted to establish one. As Ernest Gellner reminds us, there are at least eight thousand different languages in the world but less than two hundred nation-states and maybe at most eight hundred nationalisms.[17]

Appeals to history have provided an important sense of national identity. Herder saw Germans as the descendants of the noble Germanic tribes described by Tacitus. Also in Germany, Vater Jahn and his followers in the 1810s dressed in bearskin and walked around with clubs in supposed emulation of these worthy ancestors. The nineteenth century saw a flourishing of academic historical writing which furthered national sentiment. In Germany, Baron Heinrich Stein published in the 1810s the *Monumenta Germaniae historica*, the medieval sources of German history. The motto inscribed in Latin on each volume was "The sacred love of the fatherland animates us." The historian Franz Palacky attempted to create the history of the Czechs. History as a discipline was mainly devoted to study and promote a sense of a "national" history. The French *Revue historique*, one of the many new professional journals promoting the discipline of history which emerged in the nineteenth century, proclaimed in its first issue (1876) that its purpose was "to awaken in the soul of the nation consciousness of itself."[18]

Appeals to history legitimated national existence. The Greeks in fighting for their independence proclaimed themselves "descendants of the wise and noble peoples of Hellas."[19] In the Ottoman provinces that were to become Romania, nationalists claimed to be the descendants of the ancient Roman province of Dacia. Staking a special, historic descent for

---

[16] "Balkan Conflicts Are Uncoupling Serbo-Croatian," *New York Times*, 26 December 1993.

[17] Ernest Gellner, *Nations and Nationalism* (Ithaca: Cornell University Press), 44.

[18] Quoted in Boyd C. Shafer, *Faces of Nationalism* (New York: Harcourt & Brace, 1972), 203.

[19] Quoted in Kohn, *Nationalism*, 116.

his people, one Hungarian nationalist tried to prove that Adam was Magyar, while a Serb proclaimed Jesus and his disciples to have been Serbs.[20]

History could be mythologized as in the case of the Germans and their noble barbarian ancestry or created for the occasion; the Scotsman James Macpherson "discovered" two gaelic epic poems by a Scottish "Homer," Ossian. Long thought to be genuine, these epics established a Scottish claim to a noble and ancient culture and therefore presumably a right to an independent national existence.[21] As Ernest Renan was to put it, "Getting its history wrong is part of being a nation."[22]

Much of the historic claim of nationalists was that the nation had an ancient, in some cases perennial, existence. Nations had existed but then slumbered. The seal of Alexander Ypsilanti, the Greek nationalist leader in the 1820s, was the rising phoenix. The Italians spoke of their unification movement as a Risorgimento, a Resurrection. Nationalists claimed that their nations had always existed; their movements were just reawakening them.[23] And much twentieth-century writing on the history of nationalism has titles such as "Reawakening of nationalism."[24] That great mythologizer of modern French nationalism, Charles De Gaulle, was to refer to France as "eternal."[25] Such claims denied the very process De Gaulle and his nationalist predecessors throughout Europe had been engaged in—namely, the construction of imagined, supposedly immortal communities.

In some regions, religion was an important part of national identity. In England, Henry VIII upon breaking with the papacy attempted to show that the Church in England had always had an existence independent of Rome; beginning in the sixteenth century, Catholics, who at times enjoyed foreign support, were seen as traitors and Protestants as the true patriots. Protestantism continued to be a strong part of English self-identity.[26]

---

[20] Oscar Jaszi, *The Dissolution of the Habsburg Monarchy* (Chicago: University of Chicago Press, 1929), 264.

[21] Marilyn Butler, "Romanticism in England," in *Romanticism in National Context* (Cambridge: Cambridge University Press, 1988), 44–45.

[22] Quoted in Erik J. Hobsbawm, *Nations and Nationalism Since 1780: Programme, Myth, Reality* (Cambridge: Cambridge University Press, 1990), 12.

[23] Peter Alter, *Nationalism*, trans. Stuart McKinnon-Evans (London: Edward Arnold, 1989), 59.

[24] Félix Ponteil, *L'éveil des nationalités* (Paris: Presses universitaires de France, 1960); subtitles of various chapters in L. S. Stavrianos, *The Balkans since 1453* (Chicago: Holt Rhinehart, 1963); Jaszi, "National Awakening," chap. 4 in *The Dissolution*.

[25] Charles de Gaulle, Speech of 25 August 1944, *Discours et messages pendant la guerre* (Paris: Plon, 1970), 440.

[26] Colley, *Forging*, chap. 1; Greenfield, *Nationalism*, 44–66; David Cressy, "National

In the Southwestern Balkans in the nineteenth century, religion defined and divided Serb and Croat. The struggle of Belgium for independence from Protestant Holland in 1830 was largely expressed in terms of Catholic resentment against northern Protestant domination.[27] In Poland and Ireland, deprived of their independence and institutions, nationalists fervently embraced the Catholic church as a symbol of continuing resistance against foreign rule.

The physical boundaries of a nation have usually been problematic; not all nations were as clearly delineated as, for instance, the British isles. The borders of what constituted a nation were often ambiguous. German nationalists thought the nation embraced all those who spoke the mother tongue, but Germans in addition to living in what became Germany and Austria were scattered throughout much of Central Europe; thus lands that included many non-Germans would presumably be included.

The French revolutionaries appealed to natural frontiers as indicating the extent of the French nation; Lazare Carnot, the general leading France's victorious armies, explained: "The ancient and natural limits of France are the Rhine, the Alps, the Pyrenées."[28] Under Napoleon, France extended beyond the generous borders Carnot had envisaged; Holland and German lands bordering the North Sea were annexed in 1810. But, of course, now France was not only a "nation"; it had also become an empire.

Mazzini saw the borders of the Italian nation to have been drawn by "the providential hand of God"; natural borders, indicating the bounds of the nation, included the peninsula from the bottom of the boot all the way up to the Alps.[29]

From Liberal to Integral Nationalism

Sporadically from the French Revolution until 1870, states sponsored nationalism; thereafter they did so systematically. In the two decades after 1850 the states of Piedmont and Prussia respectively united Italy and Germany under their aegis. At their founding, these new nations were frail,

---

Memory in Early Modern England," in *Commemorations: The Politics of National Identity*, ed. John R. Gillis (Princeton: Princeton University Press, 1994), 61–73 .

[27] Louis Vos, "Shifting Nationalism: Belgians, Flemings and Walloons," in *The National Question in Europe in Historical Context*, ed. Milkulas Teich and Roy Porter (New York: Cambridge University Press, 1993), 131–33.

[28] Quoted in Conor Cruise O'Brien, "Nationalism and the French Revolution," *The Permanent Revolution*, ed. Geoffrey Best (Chicago: University of Chicago Press, 1989), 37.

[29] Smith, *Mazzini*, 155.

possessing little sense of unity. As Massimo d'Azeglio, the Piedmontese statesman, put it, "We have made Italy, now let us make Italians."[30] The state had to create Italians and Germans. The emergence of two large new powers in Central Europe threatened to upset the balance of power and made other European states anxious. To compete with these new powers, they resorted to nationalism as a means to mobilize their citizenry. Even if nationalism did not always create states, states were still eager to foster nationalism—except in the most hopeless multi-national states such as the Ottoman and Hapsburg empires.

Several general considerations played roles in state-sponsored nationalism: first, states legitimated themselves by appeals to nationalism; it was a way of mobilizing a large public for its purposes. Second, as several social scientists have suggested, nations are formed to provide a common cultural space in which modern man can function, or as Liah Greenfeld argues—although in a different context—nationalism provides "roads to modernity."[31] Nationalism establishes "an anonymous, impersonal society, with mutually substitutable atomized individuals, held together above all by a shared culture"; nationalism replaces a traditional, hierarchical society consisting of several micro groups.[32] Such descriptions of nationalism are not merely speculative; the historical record suggests that those groups benefiting most from the creation of a society in which the flow of goods and ideas could be freer often were among the most ardent supporters of nationalism. Businessmen and intellectuals, respectively, who desired a larger market for their goods and ideas, welcomed the emergence of the nation. As Linda Colley writes, "one of the most compelling reasons for loyalty" to Great Britain by the business class in the late eighteenth century, was "it paid."[33] In mid-nineteenth-century Italy, the single largest nationalist organization, the Italian National Society, was made up of intellectuals and businessmen who saw in a unified Italy greater economic opportunities. Much of the business community supported a united Germany in the decades before 1870 because it held out the promise of a large unified market.[34] Goods and ideas could best flow in a nation unified by roads, railroads, and a common culture.

The third reason for resorting to nationalism was to create a common glue that would preserve social peace at home. The late nineteenth cen-

[30] Quoted in Shafer, Faces, 10–11.

[31] Gellner, Nations, 56–57; part of the subtitle of Greenfeld's book, Nationalism: Five Roads to Modernity.

[32] Gellner, Nations, 57.

[33] Colley, Forging, 56 and see her chap. 2, "Profits."

[34] Raymond Grew, A Sterner Plan for Italian Unity (Princeton: Princeton University Press, 1963); Theodore S. Hamerow, The Social Foundations of German Unification, 1885–1871 (Princeton: Princeton University Press, 1972).

tury witnessed rapid industrialization, urbanization, and a long economic depression. Labor strife was common, and Socialist parties were gaining strength; by the 1890s Socialists had captured control of many city governments and became more than just a regionally based force. In Germany, the Kaiser's government launched an ambitious Weltpolitik, intended to catapult Germany into a world superpower. Building up a navy would not just challenge British sea supremacy, but also provide lucrative contracts to German industrialists and employment for the workers. It would create peace at home and silence the critics of military authoritarianism.[35]

Aggressive imperialism was also in part embarked upon to temper divisions within society. In Great Britain, empire was seen as an antidote to class tensions; Cecil Rhodes tapped into widely held convictions when he declared "the British Empire is a matter of bread and butter. If you wish to avoid civil war then you must become an imperialist." In Italy, empire was seen as a way to provide common purpose to a peninsula plagued by regional divisions.[36]

The nationalism that developed after 1870s was more intense; liberal nationalism was supplanted by what its proponents called, "integral nationalism." This new form of nationalism was illiberal; it was no longer part of the armory of left-wing oratory; rather the political right appropriated nationalism. To advance its fortunes, the political right—in the face of mass democratic movements—resorted to demagogic appeals to nationalism.[37] This new political right, which emerged in France, Italy, and Germany in the 1880s, promoted a nationalism very different from that of the left. Rather than upholding a Europe of nations, living in harmony with each other, proponents of late nineteenth-century nationalism advocated the supremacy of their nation at the cost of their neighbors and glorified the use of force. The German historian Heinrich von Treitschke declared that Germany should "render the name of Germany both fearsome and dear to the world."[38] Italian nationalist Francesco

[35] V. R. Berghahn, *Germany and the Approach of War in 1914* (London: MacMillan Press, 1973); W. J. Mommsen, "Domestic Factors in German Foreign Policy Before 1914," *Central European History* 6 (1973): 3–43. An overall application of this thesis to the European situation is Arno Mayer, "Domestic Causes of the First World War," in *The Responsibility of Power*, ed. Leonard Krieger and Fritz Stern (New York: Doubleday, 1967), 286–300.

[36] Quoted in Henry Gollwitzer, *Europe in the Age of Imperialism: 1880–1914* (New York: Harcourt & Brace, 1969), 136; John A. Thayer, *Italy and the Great War: Politics and Culture, 1870–1915* (Madison: University of Wisconsin Press, 1964), 235–36.

[37] This process is best described for Germany in Geoff Eley, *Reshaping the German Right: Radical Nationalism and Political Change after Bismarck* (New Haven: Yale University Press, 1980); in Italy the process is described in Alexander De Grand, *The Italian Nationalist Association and the Rise of Fascism in Italy* (Lincoln: University of Nebraska Press, 1978).

[38] Quoted in Alter, *Nationalism*, 41.

Coppola, like many European intellectuals at the outset of World War I, greeted the war with enthusiasm, "War alone is the melting pot in which the national soul is repeatedly tempered."[39]

In the nineteenth century, biological thought invaded many domains of thought; nations came to be thought of as organic units. Social Darwinism, which resonated to varying degrees in different countries after the 1870s, convinced many thinkers and statesmen that their nations, following strict laws of evolution, were destined to grow, or die. Many nationalists believed their nations were locked in mortal combat for survival. Just as the century was running out, so it was believed, nations were threatened by decadence and decline.[40] By heroic action, nations supposedly could escape such a fate. The French statesman Jules Ferry preached imperialism as a way of escaping "the highway to decadence." The Italian nationalists greeted the acquisition of Libya in 1911 as ensuring "self-redemption." A year later, Wilhelm II, weighing threats to Germany's interests, considered the need to embark upon war because it was "a matter of life and death for Germany," a "struggle for existence."[41]

In this spirit, European nations competed with each other for supremacy; never before had European states armed themselves as heavily in peacetime as they did in the generation prior to 1914. Unlike the United States, protected by two immense oceans, European states in the decades after 1870 were and felt themselves to be vulnerable to foreign attack. As international crises and confrontations sharpened national grievances, nationalist organizations of various sorts mobilized public sentiment on behalf of the nation.

At home, this new nationalism shunned inclusion by becoming exclusive. Intensified nationalism in the later part of the nineteenth century led some to view minorities as not sharing in the common culture or history and hence excluded from the nation. In France the right-wing writer who would become the leader of a political movement, Charles Maurras, wrote in 1895, "Country is a certain place in the world where one has flesh-and-bones ancestors."[42] According to this view, Protestants, Jews, and descendants of foreigners were excluded from the nation. In Germany and Austria, anti-Semitic political parties flourished in the 1880s and 1890s.[43]

[39] Reprinted in Ronald S. Consulo, *Italian Nationalism from its Origins to World War II* (Malabar, Fla.: Robert E. Krieger, 1990), 223.

[40] Daniel K. Pick, *Faces of Degeneration: A European Disorder, ca. 1848–1918* (Cambridge: Cambridge University Press, 1989).

[41] Ferry quoted in Henri Brunschwig, *French Colonialism, 1871–1919*, trans. W. G. Brown (London: Pall Mall Press, 1966), 80; Thayer, *Italy*, p. 238; Wilhelm quoted in Berghahn, *Germany*, 169.

[42] Quoted in Ford, *Creating the Nation*, 23.

[43] Peter G. Pulzer, *The Rise of Political Anti-Semitism in Germany and Austria*, rev. ed. (Cambridge: Harvard University Press, 1988).

A few decades later the potent brew of Social Darwinism and integral nationalism, aggressive abroad and intolerant at home, reached its heights when Hitlerite Germany attempted to conquer Europe and create within the *Reich* a single master race.

FORCES OF MOBILIZATION

The message of nationalists occurred in print, but also in many other media that constructed a national culture by using collective symbols. In France during the Revolution symbols were expressly used to mobilize the public. In 1792, when the Republic was announced, the king's image no longer represented the state; instead, the image of a woman, who came to be known as Marianne, symbolized the new republic and the nation. In various forms of undress she represented degrees of political radicalism and militant nationalism.[44]

Other symbols also provided a powerful resonance. In Britain the building of new royal palaces and the rebuilding of the British Parliament after a fire celebrated a strong, emerging world power. In Germany, a massive monument celebrating German unity, the Niederwaldendenkmal, was erected in 1885 on the banks of the Rhine; it asserted in bronze the German claim to the Rhine. In 1913, on the occasion of the centennial of the Battle of Leipzig, the Völkerschlachtdenkmal was erected, transforming in stone the myth of a German people's war against Napoleon. Such monuments became important sites of nationalist pilgrimages and mass meetings.[45]

Through an educational system that by the second half of the nineteenth century became universal, the state inculcated love of nation in its children.[46] Likewise, war monuments became a forceful way to celebrate the nation. With rare exception, war monuments until the twentieth century memorialized important generals and military heroes. After World War I, memorials treated officers and enlisted men equally; names of the

[44] Maurice Agulhon, *Marianne into Battle: Republican Imagery and Symbolism in France, 1789–1880*, trans. Janet Lloyd (New York: Cambridge University Press, 1981); Agulhon, *Marianne au pouvoir: L'imagerie et la symbolique républicaine de 1880 à 1914* (Paris: Flammarion, 1989).

[45] A particularly strong depiction of German monuments upholding the nation is George L. Mosse, *The Nationalization of the Masses* (New York: Howard Fertig, 1975), 47–72. For France there is the overpowering set: Pierre Nora, ed., *Les lieux de la mémoire*, 7 vols. (Paris: Gallimard, 1984–1993).

[46] Jonathan Sperber, "Nation, National State and National Movement in Modern Germany" (Paper presented at "Conference on European Identities," Indiana University, 24–26 February 1994), 13; Pierre Nora, "Lavisse, Instituteur national," in *Les lieux de la mémoire I, La République*, 247–89.

dead were inscribed alphabetically or in the sequence of their death, suggesting the equality of all—the equal importance for all to make their sacrifice to the nation. Although the war monuments, so ubiquitous after World War I, had many messages, their general purpose was to mobilize and legitimate the nation in its past and future struggles.[47]

GENDERING OF THE NATION

Nationalism was strongly engendered. Paradoxically, both in France where the nation was represented by Marianne and in Britain where the female Britannia ruled, women were denied participation in the body politic as active, voting citizens. Women served as auxiliaries in the national wars; the Revolution in 1794 called on the women to "make tents and clothing and work hospitals." In England during the Napoleonic wars, women collected funds for the soldiers and knit them gloves and socks.[48] In the Crimean war, a corps of female nurses, led by Florence Nightingale, tended the wounded and dying. They served the nation in many ways, but not in the most overt form, namely as soldiers.

Soldiering was a male occupation and suffused with male-centered language. Arndt, returning from the Battle of Leipzig in 1813, wrote, "I return from a bloody battle fought among men." Nearly a hundred years later, joining the English Volunteer Force was described as a "safeguard against effeminacy." A German volunteer signing up at the outbreak of war in 1914, looked forward to the upcoming "test by fire, that we may ripen into manhood, become men."[49] Describing why his men stood fast in the face of fire from the enemy, a French officer described them as doing so in part for fear that otherwise they would be considered "sissies." Virginia Woolf, observing the slaughter on the Continent, described it as a "preposterous masculine fiction."[50]

[47] K. S. Inglis, "War Memorials: Ten Questions for Historians," *Guerres Mondiales et conflits contemporains* 42 (July 1992): 5–22; Antoine Prost, "Mémoires locales et mémoires nationales: les monuments de 1914–1918 en France," in *Guerres Mondiales et conflits contemporains* 42 (July 1992): 41–50; Thomas W. Laqueur, "Memory and Naming in the Great War," *Commemorations*, ed. Gillis, 150–67.

[48] Quoted in Strachan, "The Nation in Arms," 56; Colley, *Forging*, 260.

[49] Quoted in George Mosse, *Fallen Soldiers: Reshaping the Memory of the World Wars* (New York: Oxford University Press, 1990), 27–28, 64.

[50] Charles L. Delvert, *Histoire d'une compagnie* (Paris: Berger-Levrault, 1918), quoted in Roy E. Sandström, "Hatred and Heroism: The Combat Diary of Henri de Lecluse" (Paper delivered at the Western Society for French History, Des Moines, Iowa, October 1994); Virginia Woolf quoted in Sara Ruddick, "Notes toward a Feminist Peace Politics," in *Gendering War Talk*, ed. Miriam Cooke and Angela Woollacott (Princeton: Princeton University Press, 1993), 109.

Women were placed in the center of national concerns as a result of late-nineteenth-century demographic anxieties. France was then a nation of forty million, facing a Germany of sixty million. Various social reforms, including improving the condition of women, were introduced in France to encourage an increase in natality.[51] Such concerns were heightened and spread beyond France after the First World War killed and maimed such a sizeable proportion of the male population of fighting age. To recover national strength, several states carried out policies that would encourage natality. Women were to be used for national purpose, reduced to what Napoleon a century earlier had cynically described as "machines to make children."[52] In France, two neo-Malthusians after the war preached that women's duty was "to give birth, to give birth, again always to give birth."[53] Abortion and all birth control were outlawed.

Fascist states also encouraged large families to provide them with adequate cannon fodder. Mussolini declared, "War is to man what maternity is to woman."[54] Fascist Italy established Mother's Day in 1933. The following year, during Mother's Day, a parade was held for the most prolific mothers in each province; "fourteen, sixteen, eighteen," were yelled out, indicating the size of their broods, as each mother proudly passed by the reviewing stand.[55] Nazi Germany equally encouraged female fertility. Immediately upon Hitler's accession to power, policies were introduced to foster large families. Motherhood medals were offered: bronze to mothers of five children, silver for six, and gold for seven. A decorated mother deserved the honored salute "Heil Hitler." Claudia Koonz writes that women in Nazi Germany served only one purpose: to breed the next generation of soldiers and mothers.[56]

With rare exception, fascist and other right-wing nationalist groups did not enjoy an equal gender support; more men than women tended to be among its constituents. Such a trend continues to this day; among right-wing populist movements in Western Europe in the last six years, women never made up half their constituents, varying from a low of 38 percent in Sweden to a high of 49 percent in Italy.[57]

---

[51] Karen Offen, "Depopulation, Nationalism, and Feminism in Fin de Siècle France," *American Historical Review* 89 (June 1984): 648–76; Rachel G. Fuchs, *Poor and Pregnant in Paris* (New Brunswick: Rutgers University Press, 1992), chap. 3.

[52] Quoted in Herold, *The Mind*, 14.

[53] Quoted in James F. McMillan, *Housewife or Harlot* (New York: St. Martin's Press, 1981), 191.

[54] Quoted in Victoria De Grazia, *How Fascism Ruled Women: Italy, 1922–1945* (Berkeley: University of California Press, 1992), 281.

[55] Ibid., 71.

[56] Claudia Koonz, *Mothers in the Fatherland* (New York: St. Martin's Press, 1987), 186, 399.

[57] For support by gender of Nazism, see Thomas Childers, *The Nazi Voter: The Social*

THE DECLINE OF THE NATION

The Second World War, unleashed by the extreme nationalism of Nazi Germany, spelled the end of the European nation-state and the nationalism that had sustained it. The destruction that the war had wrought made many European leaders reassess the concept of the nation-state. In the late 1940s, West European leaders looked to some supranational organ to replace the nation-state. Dwarfed by the superpowers, European states could matter only if they joined in some larger polity. To avoid a future war, the states needed to create an intricate economic and political network that would make it henceforth impossible for any European state to wage war independently. Several major continental states had strong reasons to engage in such a venture. Italy and Germany, pariah nations as a result of their war record, saw in some European federation a way of escaping their condition; France, as the largest nation, supposedly untainted by fascism, saw itself as a natural leader of a supranational polity. Belgium, Luxemburg, and Holland, which had suffered from world wars fought on their soil by larger neighbors, also supported such a venture. These states became the center around which the most successful supranational organization was erected, the Common Market.

Economic cooperation by West European states was begun under American auspices; to qualify for Marshall Plan aid, European states had to provide a multinational, European plan; it was drawn up by what became a permanent European institution, the Organization for European Economic Cooperation (OEEC). Economic cooperation developed further. In 1951 the European Coal and Steel Community was founded; the happy experience with pooling these resources, administered by both a national and supranational authority, laid the groundwork for the decision five years later to establish the Common Market. Several European states, foremost among them Great Britain, stayed out of the customs union, but in the face of its success, Britain and a number of its economic allies, which had formed a separate European Free Trade Association, joined in 1973. By January 1995, fifteen West European states were members of what had become the European Union.

The purpose of the Common Market from its beginning was far more

---

Foundations of Fascism in Germany, 1919–1933 (Chapel Hill: University of North Carolina Press, 1983), 259–60; Jürgen W. Falter, *Hitler's Wähler* (Munich: Beck, 1991), 136–46; Herbert Tingsten, *Political Behavior: Studies in Election Statistics* (London: P. S. King, 1937), 43–49. The lower support by women of the extreme right in Austria in the 1930 election is shown in Tingsten, *Political Behavior*, 68–71. For the contemporary European situation, Hans-Georg Betz, *Radical Right-Wing Populism in Western Europe* (New York: St. Martin's Press, 1994), 142–46.

ambitious than economic; it was, as one of its founders later stated, "thought of as a stage on the way to political union." [58] Economic integration was paralleled by the establishment of a European Court of Justice and a European Parliament, elected by universal suffrage beginning in 1979. Participating in elections to the European Parliament, voters appeared to show allegiance to a supranational institution. A 1993 poll revealed that in addition to feeling a sense of national identity, the citizens of all members of the European Union, except the United Kingdom, also felt some kind of European identity. [59]

European states lost much of their national character. The economy was no longer national, but European and indeed global. Young people traveled across frontiers that were no longer policed, and to many Europeans nationalism appeared outmoded. Culturally, the nation seemed out of date as a global culture, American-fashioned and driven, engulfed Europe. By their dress and appearance one could no longer tell young Europeans apart from each other or their American counterparts; except that the former sometimes sported t-shirts from nonexistent American institutions such as "California University" or "Herverd University." More European than American homes subscribed to MTV in 1993, and in France no French movie could attract audiences of the size that went to see *Jurassic Park*. [60]

The nation-state was not only superseded by cross-national and planetary forces, but it was also challenged from within by regionalist impulses. In France, the unitary state par excellence, if Breton, Corsican, and Occitan separatism have waxed and waned, then they never fully disappeared, which suggests the possibility of a France of many "nations." In Spain, Catalan and Basque nationalism continue to thrive. In Italy, the Lombard League, a party dedicated to the separation of prosperous northern Italy from the rest of the nation, joined in the spring of 1994 a governing coalition of the state it had sworn to dismember or at least weaken substantially. In recently unified Germany, the "Ossies" and "Wessies" suspiciously eye each other; many on each side seem to regret the miraculous restoration in 1990 of a united Germany. In Great Britain, political parties are based on competing claims to nationality: one is Scottish, and another is Welsh. Major party strength is also nationally based: Labour Party's strength is in Wales and Scotland, while the Conservatives' constituency is mainly in England proper. Such re-

[58] Paul Henri Spaak, Belgian prime minister, quoted in Derek W. Urwin, *The Community of Europe: A History of European Integration since 1945* (New York: Longman, 1993), 76.

[59] European Commission, *Eurobarometer: Public Opinion in the European Union*, no. 40, December 1993.

[60] On MTV, see Daniel Tilles, "The French Disney Connection," *Mediaweek* 18 October 1993, 40.

gional and substate movements challenged the nation, undermining it from within.

The European nation-state seemed overshadowed by supranationalism when in 1991 at Maastricht, the leaders of the various member states of the European Economic Community pledged to create the European Union, unified economically and socially, having a joint foreign and defense policy and enjoying a single currency. At the time it was expected that these reforms would significantly speed up the process toward a single European political union. The difficulties in ratifying the Maastricht treaty, however, revealed still lingering national pride, an insistence on national sovereignty, and suspicion of a supranational bureaucracy that regulated too many things—including the size of bananas that could be sold within the community.

Toward the end of the twentieth century, complete European Union still appears far from accomplished; the European nation-state still exists. The competitive nationalism that in the past had set one European state against the other disappeared in Western Europe, although it reappeared in Eastern Europe after this region shook itself free in 1989–1990 from nearly fifty years of the *Pax Sovietica*.

At least in Western Europe, hostility to neighboring states has declined. But one form of integral nationalism still remains important: xenophobia. The European economy after World War II suffered from severe labor shortages, and immigration of foreign labor was encouraged. Since the 1970s, unemployment has plagued or threatened several European states; these problems and others have been blamed on the immigrant workers. In many West European countries more than half the population believes there are too many foreigners in their nation.[61] In the face of ethnic minorities that have grown in size and maintained their cultural differences and institutions, many natives expressed fears that their cultural identity was being undermined. This attitude was well reflected in the Heidelberg Manifesto, published by fifteen German university professors in 1981, which stated "every people, also the German one, has the natural right to protect its identity and singularity in its area of habitation." In France, a writer recently lamented the "decline of the representation of the nation's homogeneity."[62]

---

[61] EuroBarometer poll of 1991, cited in Christian Vandermotten and Jan Valaer, "Immigrants and the Extreme Right Vote in Europe and in Belgium," *Mass Migration in Europe*, ed. Russell King (London: Belhaven Press, 1993), 136; Betz, *Radical Right-Wing Populism*, 82.

[62] Quoted in Sabine von Dirke, "Multikulti: The German Debate on Multiculturalism" *German Studies Review*, 17 (October 1994): 519; *Quotidien de Paris*, 2 February 1993, quoted in Stanley Hoffmann, "Thoughts on the French Nation Today," *Daedalus* 122 (Summer 1993): 79, fn. 10.

Playing on fears and phobias, right-wing politicians, whose pedigrees go back to the ultra-right of the 1890s, have made a comeback in the last couple of decades. In 1994 in Austria, the Liberal party, headed by Jörg Haider, who made a regular habit of attacking foreigners and the democratic governing coalition and praised Hitler's economic policies for providing full employment, received 22 percent of the vote. In Belgium, the far right-wing bloc received 28 percent of the vote in Antwerp, a past stronghold of Socialist and Catholic parties. One of its leaders ran on a platform of establishing separate schools for Belgian and Islamic children and shipping immigrants home. On a similar platform in France, the National Front, led by Jean-Marie Le Pen, nationally reached its high point in the 1995 presidential elections, receiving 15 percent of the vote.[63] The anti-immigrant program of these extremist parties is the primary reason for the electoral support they enjoy.[64]

In many democracies the conventional parties have averted extreme right-wing success only by stealing their xenophobia. In Britain, the Nationality Act of 1981 excluded from a right to enter the United Kingdom those British subjects who did not have at least one parent who was a British citizen, thus excluding most British subjects of color. France in the mid-1970s discouraged continued immigration, and in 1992 the new, Conservative minister of interior established the goal of "zero immigration." In 1993, the German Reichstag rescinded its constitutionally mandated right to asylum for political refugees. A student of contemporary American affairs might see in these European developments the counterpart to some of the American phobias about "illegal immigration" and fears of the loss of an American identity in the face of a growing population of non-European stock.

Nationalisms, originating nearly simultaneously in the North American colonies and Western Europe, have to a large degree had parallel lives on both sides of the Atlantic; the notable exception was the fear of foreign attack animating European nationalism after 1870. The United States was usually not prone to such apprehensions until the era of the Cold War. In the past, nations flourished on the very idea of their exceptionalism; but the historic record suggests that nationalisms often have more in common with each other than their proponents have usually been willing to concede.

[63] "In Europe the Right Also Rises," *New York Times*, 14 November 1994, A8.
[64] Betz, *Radical Right-Wing Populism*, 65–106.

CONTRIBUTORS

John Bodnar is professor of history at Indiana University, Bloomington. He has published *Remaking America: Public Memory, Commemoration, and Patriotism in the Twentieth Century* (1992).

William B. Cohen is professor of history at Indiana University, Bloomington. Among his publications are *The French Encounter with Africans* (1980) and a forthcoming study of nineteenth-century French cities.

Gaines M. Foster is associate professor of history at Louisiana State University. He has written *Ghosts of the Confederacy: Defeat, the Lost Cause, and the Emergence of the New South, 1865–1913* (1987).

David Glassberg is associate professor of history and director of the public history program at the University of Massachusetts, Amherst. He is the author of many works exploring the representation of history in American culture, including *American Historical Pageantry: The Uses of Tradition in the Early Twentieth Century* (1990).

Kimberly Jensen is assistant professor of history and gender studies at Western Oregon State College. She is completing a book manuscript, "Minerva on the Field of Mars: American Women, Citizenship, and Military Service in World War I."

Cynthia M. Koch is executive director of the New Jersey Council for the Humanities. She holds a Ph.D. in American Civilization from the University of Pennsylvania. Her publications include edited volumes in architectural history and folk studies.

Wendy Kozol is the author of *Life's America: Family and Nation in Postwar Photojournalism* (1994). She is currently affiliated with the Department of History at Oberlin College.

George Lipsitz is professor of ethnic studies at the University of California, San Diego. His books include *Time Passages: Collective Memory and American Popular Culture* (1990) and *Dangerous Crossroads: Popular Music, Postmodernism and the Poetics of Place* (1994).

Stuart McConnell is associate professor of history at Pitzer College and author of *Glorious Contentment: The Grand Army of the Republic, 1865–1900* (1992). An essay on American nationalism will appear in *The Encyclopedia of the United States in the Twentieth Century*, ed. Stanley Kutler.

J. Michael Moore has organized public history projects in a number of Massachusetts communities, including "The Life and Death of Northhampton State Hospital," a traveling exhibit based on oral histories of mental health workers. He is currently industrial historian at the Worcester Historical Museum.

Andrew Neather received his Ph.D. from Duke University in 1994. He currently writes for the Publications Department of the United Auto Workers in Detroit.

Cecilia Elizabeth O'Leary received her Ph.D. in U.S. history from the University of California, Berkeley. As a Landmarks Scholar, she holds a joint appointment as an assistant professor at The American University and as a curator at the National Museum of American History.

Lawrence R. Samuel holds a Ph.D. in American Studies from the University of Minnesota.

Barbara Truesdell is research specialist/oral historian at Indiana University's Oral History Research Center in Bloomington. She is currently completing her dissertation in Folklore and American Studies on the traditions of the DAR.

Robin Wagner-Pacifici is associate professor of sociology at Swarthmore College. She is the coauthor of "The Vietnam Veterans Memorial: Commemorating a Difficult Past," *American Journal of Sociology* (1991), and the author of *Discourse and Destruction: The City of Philadelphia vs. MOVE* (1994).

Robert B. Westbrook is associate professor of history at the University of Rochester. His publications include *John Dewey and American Democracy* (1991).

INDEX